AN

UNDERGROUND

EDUCATION

ALSO BY RICHARD ZACKS

HISTORY LAID BARE:
LOVE, SEX, AND PERVERSITY FROM THE
ANCIENT ETRUSCANS TO WARREN G. HARDING

RICHARD ZACKS

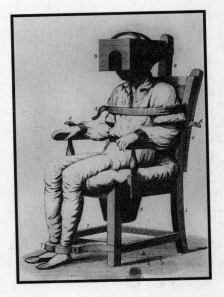

ANCHOR BOOKS
A DIVISION OF RANDOM HOUSE, INC.
New York

THE UNAUTHORIZED AND OUTRAGEOUS SUPPLEMENT
TO EVERYTHING YOU THOUGHT YOU KNEW ABOUT
ART, SEX, BUSINESS, CRIME, SCIENCE, MEDICINE,
AND OTHER FIELDS OF HUMAN KNOWLEDGE

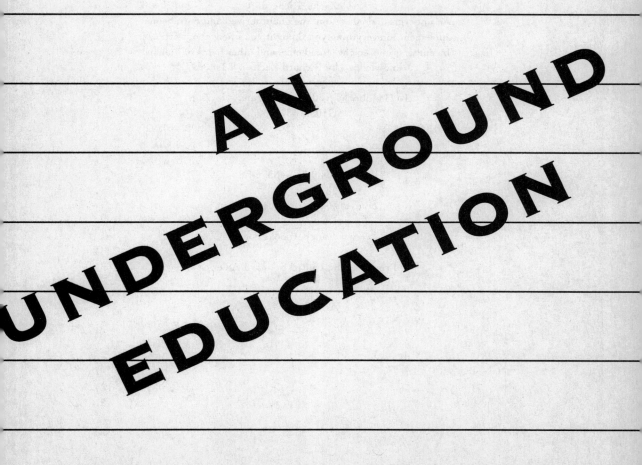

AN
UNDERGROUND
EDUCATION

FIRST ANCHOR BOOKS EDITION, MAY 1999

The Library of Congress has cataloged the hardcover edition of
this book as follows:
Zacks, Richard.
An underground education: the unauthorized and outrageous
supplement to everything you thought you knew about art, sex,
business, crime, science, medicine, and other fields of human
knowledge / by Richard Zacks. — 1st ed.
p.   cm.
1. Handbooks, vade-mecums, etc.   I. Title.
AG106.Z33   1997
031.02 — dc21   97-10892
CIP

ISBN 0-385-48376-7

Book design by Jennifer Ann Daddio

www.anchorbooks.com

Printed in the United States of America
10

For cigar-chomping, sleigh-riding Herman Zacks
(1907–96)

CONTENTS

WORLD HISTORY

AMERICAN HISTORY

INTRODUCTION

I flunked nude figure drawing in college, and that was the most liberating moment in my education. Up to my junior year at the University of Michigan, I am forced to admit that I had always tried to get A's, that I had accepted the basic agenda of academia.

But something happened that year. I started putting wise-guy captions on the bottoms of those poorly drawn nudes, as in "Caesar would have never slept here." I translated the most scatological passages in Chaucer. I went off to study Italian at the University of Perugia and wound up spending all my time in the streets, learning the language of Dante from a drunken, out-of-work Japanese tailor. To put it indelicately, I didn't have to worry about learning to roll my R's: There weren't any R's.

And I started to fashion my own education, studying French, Italian, Arabic, and Greek. I read Homer's *Odyssey* in the original and then spoofed the metrical analysis assignment given me by my professor. I read Baudelaire in French and my love life improved. And that period of postadolescent rebellion was when this book was truly hatched.

I don't know about you, but I often feel deeply unsatisfied after reading an item in an encyclopedia, any encyclopedia from Britannica to Encarta. Sure, I've been told most everything I'm *supposed* to know about the person or event. And that's just the point. There's rarely anything I'm *not* supposed to know, anything quirky or surprising.

Or take textbooks. History always follows such a logical progression of battles and treaties, of great men and women.

Remember that first snippet you read about Thomas Edison? No doubt it told you about the genius's invention of the electric light, phonograph, and motion pictures, but did it mention Edison's share in building the first electric chair or his brutal feud with George Westinghouse that almost led to a duel by electric jolts? I didn't think so.

This book aims to begin where most encyclopedias and textbooks stop, to act as a kind of unauthorized supplement. Almost every time I read about the past, I find the approach far too logical, far too orderly, far too narrow. History is messy.

Napoleon lost the battle of Waterloo. Historians can cite a hundred different reasons but they rarely include the little man's hemorrhoids flaring up, which prevented this brilliant strategist from riding out and surveying the troops. Am I saying that Napoleon's painful derriere changed the course of history. Sure, why not? Emphasizing the human side, the uncouth little truths tend to make textbook writers nervous. The past no longer flows from battle to battle, from age to age with a logic that will lull you like the ticking of a classroom clock.

Well, let's serve up the messiness, the roguish surprises, and let's also expand the agenda to include bathrooms, underwear, cannibal feasts, forgotten criminals.

Yes, this is a book gloriously into its anecdotage, ready at a moment's notice to detour to meet Pope Alexander VI's mistress or track the medieval relic quest for Jesus' foreskin. But you know what? If you follow along these two hundred or so stories, each firmly grounded in context, a surprising thing might happen to you. These disparate tales will hopefully fuse to reinvent the past for you in a way that plodding histories cannot.

You will be served up brand new takes on crime, medicine, religion, business, sex, everyday life, politics. You will see great men and women taken *off* their pedestals. The Medicine section, for instance, focuses on the often wretched state of medical care prior to the 20th century. Why don't we know more about this? It's as though some sort of professional courtesy exists; never mentioned are the blizzard of useless enemas ordered up by Renaissance doctors or all the unsterilized hands reaching into the Civil War soldier boys and *killing* them.

I have to tell you how much—despite the long hours and dead ends—I enjoyed discovering this material, expanding my own education. I was sitting in the rare book room at the New York Academy of Medicine and I stumbled on an article in a French journal from 1743 on sexual accidents. I started muttering, "You can't make this stuff up!" The scholars around me looked on in alarm.

I hope you find this material provocative. I hope it expands your view of the past; I hope it fleshes out our ancestors; I hope it amuses you.

Knowledge does not have to be serious. When Sigmund Freud was filling out his exit visa to leave Germany in 1938, he wrote on a form. "I can heartily recommend the Gestapo to anyone."

And Mark Twain, when he was being interrogated in court, suing to get his money back from some start-up company, said, "They told me I could get in on the ground floor, only there wasn't any ground floor."

Those scholars shushed me in that rare book room, but I'm pleased now to share these stories loud and clear with you.

One final note: *An Underground Education* is divided into ten major categories, i.e., chapters. (All sources, for you skeptics, are carefully listed in the back; I sought out *primary* sources wherever possible.) You can leapfrog about if you like, but I strongly recommend you read each chapter as a whole, from beginning to end. There's a method here, following natural curiosity. Bra coverage leads to breastfeeding; relics segue to cults; common knowledge precedes *un*common knowledge.

ARTS &
LITERATURE

THE ORIGINAL GRIMMER FAIRY TALES

The children are safely tucked in bed; a light breeze blows in through the window; Mom hushes them and begins to tell a sweet tale of . . . children being abandoned in the woods, lured to a witch's cottage, there to be fattened and roasted in an oven. Medium-rare.

Critics have long complained about the violent content of some of the classic "fairy tales" we read our children. However, what few of these critics realize is that we are reading *watered down* versions of the fairy tales, and that the originals were far more graphic and brutal.

Sleeping Beauty was not first awakened by a kiss; in the 1636 Italian version of the tale—the first known written version—she was raped by a man who rode off the next morning without leaving even a Dear Sleeping Beauty note. Her "morning after" came nine months later when she awoke to find herself the proud mother of twins.

Goldilocks was originally an old crone impaled by three angry bears on the steeple of St. Paul's Cathedral. A Scottish Cinderella features the desperate step-mother hacking off the heel and toes of her daughters so the slipper will fit. As for Snow White, let's just say for now there's more to that story about the queen wanting her heart.

By now you might be asking: How did anyone *ever* tell these stories to kids?

Folklorists explain that classic fairy tales grew out of an oral tradition, of adults telling children *and other adults* stories they had heard themselves. And in pre-Victorian times, in Europe, children were often not treated like, well, "children," but rather shortstop adults, a handful of years away from their own teenage wedding night. Cramped living quarters gave junior a front row seat for drunkenness, debauchery, and violence, not to mention a view of bloody-fingered Mom in the kitchen skinning and gutting dinner.

Two men—generally forgotten nowadays in the United States—deserve the lion's share of the credit for collecting and refining the oral tradition for future generations. No, not the Brothers Grimm. An Italian, Giambattista Basile wrote "Lo Cunto de li Cunte" ("The Tale of Tales"), a collection of fifty stories in Sicilian dialect published in 1636. (For some odd reason, most English-speaking scholars refer to the book as *The Pentameron*—i.e., half a Decameron.)

The other man had even more impact. Frenchman Charles Perrault's slender volume came out in 1697 containing but eight tales. Astoundingly, seven of them became classics: "Cinderella," "Little Red Riding Hood," "Blue Beard," "Puss in Boots," "Sleeping Beauty," "Diamonds and Frogs,"

(Frog-Prince) and "Hop o' My Thumb" (Tom Thumb).

So, let's turn off the night lights, children, Daddy has a few grimmer fairy tales to tell you.

SLEEPING BEAUTY (1636, ITALY)

The prophecy at her birth is bleak: she will die of a poisoned splinter of flax. Despite her father's best efforts, banning flax from the house, etc., the beautiful girl named Talia does in fact catch a flax chip under her fingernail and drops down dead.

Her grieving father, a great lord, sits her lifeless body upon a velvet throne under a canopy of lace, and he locks up the family mansion in the woods and departs, never to return.

One day, a king is hunting in the woods when his prized falcon flies off. The king, convinced that the bird has flown into a deserted house, climbs in through a window only to dis-

IL
PENTAMERONE
DEL CAVALIER
GIOVAN BATTISTA BASILE,
Overo
LO CUNTO
DE LI CUNTE
Trattenemiento de li Piccerille.
DI GIAN ALESIO ABBATTVTIS.
Novamente reſtampato, e con tutte le
zeremonie corrietto.

N NAPOLE· A la Stampa, e à ſpeſe
de Mechele Loiſe Mutio 1717.
Co lrcentia de li Superiure.

"Cinderella" and "Sleeping Beauty" both appeared as a Sicilian "Cunto" (i.e., story), long before the Brothers Grimm. Here's the title page of the 1717 edition.

cover Talia. He thinks she's only dozing in the chair, but no matter how much he yells, she doesn't answer. "Then, being inflamed by her charms," as Basile tells us, "he carried her to a bed and harvested the *'frutti d'amore'* ('fruits of love'). Then he left her there on the bed, and returned to his kingdom and forgot about the incident for a long time."

Nine months after the rape, Talia gives birth to twins, a boy and a girl, who promptly attempt to suckle at her breasts. One afternoon, missing the nipple, one of the tykes starts to suck on her fingers and pumps so hard the poisoned splinter pops out.

The teenage girl awakes to find herself alone in a mansion with two babies to feed. Luckily for her, fairies keep catering a feast on a nearby table.

The king, meanwhile, suddenly recalls the pleasant *"avventura"* with the sleeping girl and charts another hunt in those regions. When he discovers the young woman there with twins, he is delighted and reveals to her who he is and what has happened. "A great friendship and a strong bond sprang up between them, and he lingered several days in her company."

When he leaves her this time, he promises to send for her and the kids.

Night after night, back in the palace in the royal bed and at the royal table, the king keeps mumbling the name of Talia and the children, Sun and Moon.

The king's wife, i.e., the queen, whom he has conveniently forgotten to mention to Talia, becomes suspicious. She bribes one of the king's men to reveal who this

Talia is, and then she dispatches a messenger to bid Talia—at the invitation of the king—to come to the palace.

Talia scoops up the twins, and with great joy travels there. When the little fatherless family arrives, the queen orders the cook to carve the kids up and prepare them into several delicious dishes, fit for a philandering king.

At dinner, as the king enthuses over the delicately spiced meat pies, the queen mutters several times: *"Mangia, mangia; you are eating your own."* The king, tired of the repetition, barks: "Of course I'm eating my own. You didn't bring anything to this marriage."

The queen, not satisfied with her first little prank, has Talia brought to her. The queen screams at the girl, "So you're the devilish bitch who's giving me such a headache."

Talia pleads her case. "It's not my fault. Your husband raped me ("conquered my regions") while I was drugged."

The queen replies, "Light the bonfire and throw her in." The desperate girl kneels before the Nero-faced queen and begs time at least to take her clothes off. The queen, a bit baffled but coveting the gold and pearls sewn onto the girl's garments, grants the wish. "Strip yourself naked. I'd be delighted."

With each item that she removes, Talia lets out a scream. She takes off her dress, then her underskirts, then her bodice. Finally, as she takes off her last little shift, she screams the loudest. The queen's men start to drag the naked teenager toward the bonfire.

At that instant, the king arrives and demands to know what is going on and where his illegitimate kids are. The queen tells him that he has eaten them. The king begins to wail.

He orders the queen hurled into the bonfire along with his double-crossing servant. Once those two are burned to a crisp, he orders the cook to be cooked next.

But in a surprisingly windy speech, the cook reveals that he didn't kill the twins after all, but grilled up some lamb instead. The cook's wife marches in with the children.

The king is overjoyed and plants a "mill-wheel" of kisses upon each of the twins, he rewards the cook with vast wealth, and he marries Talia and they live a long, happy life together.

And so Basile concludes the story with a little moral:

"Good things happen to lucky people, even when they're sleeping."

CINDERELLA
The first Cinderella tale recorded in Europe was told by Giambattista Basile in his "Lo Cunto de li Cunte" (1636) and it was not exactly a slipper that Cinderella left behind.

The little girl's name is Zezolla, short for Lucrezuccia, and she immediately displays homicidal tendencies. She conspires with her nanny to kill her mean stepmother by luring the woman to look into an old chest, and then letting the heavy lid fall and crack her neck.

Barely out of mourning, she convinces her father to marry the nanny, but Zezolla is quickly shunted out of the soft life by her new stepmother's *six* daughters. Her chores so frequently feature cleaning the grate that she's given the nickname *Gatto Cerentola,* or "Cinder-Cat."

Cinder-Cat eventually gets hold of a magic date tree from which a fairy pops out to grant her a wish. Instead of "bippety-boppety-boo," the magic words she's to utter are:

> O my golden date tree,
> . . . Now, strip yourself naked and dress me!

Cinderella, decked in glorious clothes, attends a few royal pageants and the king falls in love. He sends a servant after her but the man fails to find her. The lovelorn royal, in a towering rage, shouts in *un*-Disneylike manner: "By the souls of my ancestors, if you don't find that girl, I'll beat you with a stick and kick you in the ass as many times as you have hairs in your beard!"

The servant, protecting his *culo,* shadows Cinder-Cat all night at the next ball and then literally hangs onto her carriage. Cinder-Cat orders the driver to whip up the horses. With a jolt, the prince's servant falls off, but so does something belonging to the girl.

The servant brings it back to the prince, who immediately showers it with kisses. What is it? A dainty silk slipper? A gold slipper? A glass slipper?

No, it's a "pianella," a kind of foot-tall stiltlike cork-soled galoshes worn *over* shoes by women in Renaissance Naples. This platform-style overshoe protected women's elegant party shoes and lifted them high enough to keep their long dresses out of mud when alighting from carriages or crossing the street.

To us, it would look like something out of disco fever with its six- to eighteen-inch-high cork heel/sole and ornate designs. (All that's missing is the goldfish.)

Picture the prince fondling this large object, while he pitches rococo woo to it: *"Ecco,* I hug and hold you, and if I can't reach the plant, I'll adore the roots. If I can't reach the carvings at the top of the column, I'll kiss the base. You used to hold a white foot, now you have caught a wounded heart; thanks to you, she who dominates my heart stood a handsbreadth and a half taller, so shall my life grow in sweetness so long as I guard and possess you."

The "handsbreath" in Italian is *palmo,* which is about nine inches, so Cinderella stood about thirteen and a half inches taller when she teetered on her pianelle as she was trying to make her fast getaway.

The prince throws a giant feast for all the ladies of the kingdom and personally tries the overshoe on each and everyone until he finds Cinder-Cat.

Before Charles Perrault came up with the glass slipper, Cinderella wore stiltlike leather *pianelle*, like this pair from Renaissance Venice.

While Basile's tale stresses the romance and shoe fetish, most of the Northern European versions climax in a bloody morality tale about jealousy.

Let's pick up Act Three in this Northern version that closely resembles Scottish and Swedish variants:

The prince leaves a trail of tar outside the ballroom and one of Ashen-puttel's slippers gets stuck. He starts roaming the kingdom trying the slipper on damsels until he finally arrives at the right house.

When asked to try the shoe on, the elder stepsister discreetly goes into a bedroom. Despite all her struggles, her big toe won't fit.

Her mother, reaching for a knife, says, "Cut off your toe, for if you are queen, you need not go on foot any longer."

The girl obeys and succeeds in squeezing her foot into the shoe. The happy prince sweeps her onto the back of his horse and the pair rides off to be married. But they are passing the grave of Cinderella's mother as two birds start singing:

Look back, look back,
There's blood upon the shoe,
The shoe's too small, and she behind
Is not the bride for you.

He looks back and sees blood dripping from the shoe. So the prince returns to the house and gives the shoe to the second stepsister. Her toes fit fine but her heel is too big. Mother gives the same advice. This time, the girl cuts off a piece of her heel, hides her pain and she too winds up altarbound on horseback with the prince.

The birds sing that same "Look Back" ditty. "The prince looked back and saw blood trickling from her shoe and that the stocking was dyed quite red."

He returns yet again and finally finds his darling Ashen-puttel, whom he marries, and the two sisters are smitten with blindness as punishment for their jealousy.

And what version is this? This is one of Grimm's fairy tales taken literally from the original German before Victorian translators edited out the blood and had the girls scrunching their toes. In fact, fairy tale editors have always felt uniquely free—for the sake of the children—to sanitize and defang the 156 folk tales that the Brothers Grimm collected from German peasants, and first published in 1812.

Cinderella is arguably the most popular fairy tale of all time, popping up in more than 700 versions over 2,500 years. The earliest version dates back to Ancient Egypt, describing a beautiful prostitute bathing in a river, an eagle snatching her sandal and carrying it off to pharoah who started a nationwide search for the owner. And, of course, when he found "Rhodopis," he married her.

GOLDILOCKS

In the first versions of the tale, the anti-heroine who breaks into the bears' house is well beyond menopause.

Goldilocks was originally a grouchy homeless old lady, and it took almost a century for her to evolve into a fair-haired little thief. (For that matter, the bears started off as three *bachelors* sharing a flat.)

Robert Southey, poet laureate of England, published a version in 1837, complete with the classic deescalating voices that give parents something to do: "'SOMEBODY HAS BEEN AT MY PORRIDGE,' said the great huge bear in his great, rough gruff voice."

As Southey tells it, the old woman breaks in, samples the porridge and the chairs, then falls asleep in a bed. When she's caught, she leaps out a window. ". . . whether she broke her neck in the fall; or ran into the wood and was lost there; or found her way out of the wood, and was taken up by the constable and sent to the House of Correction for a vagrant as she was, I cannot tell. But the Three Bears never saw anything more of her."

Brits could applaud the moral triumph over the larcenous crone. For a century or so, scholars considered this the earliest version. Then in 1951 in the Toronto Public Library, a little home-printed doggerel version dated 1831 was found. One Eleanor Mure, a thirty-two-year-old maiden aunt, created it for her nephew, Horace Broke.

Mure's tale is rather odd. First off, the "angry old woman" breaks into the bears' house because they snubbed her during a recent social call. Then in the end, when the three male bears catch the old woman, they linger in a long, slow debate over what to do with her. Finally, they figure it out:

> On the fire they throw her, but burn her
>   they couldn't;
> In the water they put her, but drown there
>   she wouldn't;
> They seize her before all the wondering
>   people,
> And chuck her aloft on St. Paul's church-
>   yard steeple;
> And if she's still there, when you earnestly
>   look,
> You will see her quite plainly—my dear
>   little Horbook!
> ("Horbook" was her nephew's nickname or
>   else the only rhyme she could figure.)

A page from the earliest (and far crueler) version of "Goldilocks," which was "The Story of the Three Bears" by Eleanor Mure, 1831. "On the fire they threw her, but burn her they couldn't."

No other known version has the future Goldilocks impaled on a church steeple. About a dozen years after Southey's very popular version, an anthology editor transformed the old crone into Silver-Hair, arguing that the fairy tale market was glutted with villainous old crones. Silver-Hair became Goldilocks in 1918. Editors had decided it was more important to scare little girls (rather than old ladies) into not entering strange houses, which brings us to the classic of the girl-scaring genre . . .

LITTLE RED RIDING HOOD

Little Red Riding Hood, in the original French version of 1697, is packed with sexual tension. As told by master Charles Perrault, it is a dark, titillating, cautionary tale about naive virginal girls being seduced by "wolves." Perrault's coda makes his point clear: "One sees here that young children — especially nice young girls with pretty faces and bodies — do very badly to listen to all sorts of people." He adds, "The most dangerous kind of wolf is the polite, gentle, agreeable wolf . . . who meets the *mademoiselles* in their homes and on the streets."

In the original, Perrault opens with an exuberant, one might say appetizing, description of how beautiful the little girl is, especially in her "petit chaperon rouge," little red bonnet. People for miles around rave about her beauty.

She meets the wolf in the woods and he tricks her into revealing where she's headed. The sly fellow races ahead, impersonating "Red"; he tricks the grandmother into letting him in. Then he devours her and crawls into the old lady's bed and awaits the main course.

Little Red Riding Hood arrives, carrying a flat pastry and *a small tub of butter*.

"Knock, knock. 'Who is there?'

"Little Red Riding Hood, who heard the deep voice of the wolf, was afraid at first, but believing that her grandmother had a cold, replied: 'It's your granddaughter, Little Red Riding Hood. I'm bringing you some pastry and a little tub of butter sent by my mother.'

"The wolf, softening his voice, told her 'Pull the peg and the latch will drop.' Little Red Riding Hood pulled the peg and the door opened. The wolf, seeing her enter, hid himself under the covers on the bed and said, 'Put the pastry and the little tub of butter on the hutch, and come into bed with me.'

"Little Red Riding Hood took off her clothes and climbed into bed, where she was astonished to discover what her grandmother was like without her clothes. She said to her, 'Grandma, what big arms you have!'

This 19th-century French "Little Red Riding Hood" stresses the original seduction angle and adds a chamber pot under the bed for verisimilitude.

" 'The better to hug you with, my girl.'

" 'Grandma, what big legs you have!'

" 'The better to run with, my child.'

" 'Grandma, what big ears you have!'

" 'The better to hear with, my child.'

" 'Grandma, what big eyes you have!'

" 'The better to see with, my little one.'

" 'Grandma, what big teeth you have!'

" 'The better to eat you with.'

"And, saying these words, this wicked wolf threw himself onto Little Red Riding Hood and ate her up."

Finis. The end. That's how the original earliest written version ends, with grandma and Red eaten up and the lecherous wolf getting off scot-free. Over. No hunter with scissors or any other rescuer, blowing the moral punch line by giving her a second chance.

Actually, one also senses a sort of sly humor in Perrault's version. Buried in the middle of that famous dialogue—considered by many the best in fairy tale history—is a wicked double entendre in the original French.

Note that line about "what big legs you have" and "the better to run with."

The French is *"Que vous avez de grandes jambes!/C'est pour mieux courir."* The word *jambe* (leg) was used in Rabelais and elsewhere for penis (i.e., "middle leg"), according to "Vocabula Amatoria"—a dictionary of French sexual slang through history—and the word *courir* (for "run") is common slang for "sexual intercourse."

A couple hundred years later, you can still hear the adults tittering in the corner.

SNOW WHITE

For once, Disney restored a gory detail left out in most American translations of Snow White. Disney has the jealous queen demanding Snow White's heart.

In the original Grimm telling, there's quite a bit more gore. The queen—who's no longer fairest in the land—orders the huntsman to bring her the heart *and* the tongue of Snow-White. Once the queen has the two organs, she eats them. (The lady, of course, doesn't realize that she is actually snacking on boar.)

At the end, when Snow White is revived and marries the prince, the evil queen attends the wedding. She is surprised when a pair of metal shoes, flaming hot from the oven, are carried out. The wicked queen is forced to put them on, and then dances herself to death. ❧

SHAKESPEARE'S SEXUAL PUNS: "SWEET BOTTOM-GRASS" AND OTHERS

In *Henry IV*, the prince's boisterous companion, Falstaff, claims that while sleeping at an inn, a valuable ring has been stolen from his pocket. The landlady, Mistress Quickly, counters: "Oh Jesu, I have heard the Prince tell him, I know not how oft, that the ring was copper!" (III, iii, 93–95)

Mistress Quickly—besides charging that the ring is worthless—is also hinting broadly that the only thing in Falstaff's pants is a copper-colored ring, i.e., his asshole.

Some study is required to plomb the depth of Shakespeare's bawdy, but to read the bard without the bawd is to fall several inches short of his full meaning.

In *Antony and Cleopatra*, a fortune-teller has told two of Cleopatra's handmaidens that their fortunes are identical, which miffs them both.

IRAS: Am I not an inch of fortune better than she?

CHARMIAN: Well, if you were but an inch of fortune better than I, where would you choose it?

IRAS: Not in my husband's nose. (I, ii, 56–59)

Shakespeare, like Chaucer, reveled in sex, celebrated it, and made many sly jokes about it. But most are couched in Elizabethan jargon. Therein lies the rub. Sexual intercourse might be as vivid as "making the beast with two backs" or as obscure as "filling a bottle with a tunne-dish," i.e., putting a funnel into a bottle.

Here, with a low bow to Eric Partridge's *Shakespeare's Bawdy* and to Frankie Rubinstein's *A Dictionary of Shakespeare's Sexual Puns and Their Significance* is a tour of a dozen-plus scenes.

LUST AND CUNNY

Shakespeare uses many euphemisms for vagina (thigh, belly, womb, etc.) but more slyly, he sometimes puns on words containing a "cun" sound, such as "encounter" and "cunning." ("Cunny" or "cunt" was common Elizabethan slang.)

Now she is in the very lists of love;
The champion mounted for the hot
encounter. *(Venus and Adonis, 595–596).*

In *The Winter's Tale*, the women are gossiping about Hermione becoming pregnant.

SECOND LADY: She is spread into a goodly bulk; good time encounter her.

Intercourse with a pregnant lady obviously

The "Chandos Portrait" of the ear-ringed Bard.

can't get her any *more* pregnant. As Roman historian Suetonius whispered about Augustus Caesar's daughter, Julia, "She took passengers only when the boat was full."

MORE VAGINA PUNS

In *All's Well That Ends Well,* the fool is asked why he wants to marry.

Fool: "Faith, madam, I have other holy reasons such as they are." (I, iii, 35–36) As in "holey."

WHEN THE WOMEN WERE BOYS

In *Pericles,* that rarely performed historical play, when the virgin Marina has defied several wealthy clients, the brothel owner decides to get tough with her. Bawd (to servant Boult): "Crack the glass of her virginity, and make the rest malleable." (IV, v, 142–144)

You can't help but hear the sound "ass" in "glass," as in the "ass" of the young male actor playing Marina.

In *Twelfth Night,* the servant Malvolio holds up a note and says of the handwriting: "By my life, this is my lady's hand. These be her very C's, her U's, and her T's; and thus she makes her great P's. It is, in contempt of question, her hand." (II, v, 95–100).

In several editions, scholars point out that there are no "great," i.e., capital letter, P's in the note. These scholars wonder why Shakespeare would be so sloppy. It is, in contempt of question, a no-brainer.

The bard was, of course, making a dirty joke. C, U, 'n' T makes P.

PENIS JOKES

Says the Fool in *Twelfth Night:*

Many a good hanging prevents a bad marriage. (I, v, 20)

Certainly, executing a loutish husband can free a wife, but a well-hung husband can, in theory, also help save a marriage.

ERECTIONS

The Bard delights in making "stand" jokes, which probably whiz by most modern audiences. A "cock stand" was a standard Elizabethan phrase for an erection. In *Two Gentlemen of Verona,* 'Speed is inquiring about one of the gentlemen and his love, Julia.

'SPEED: How stands the matter with them?

LAUNCE: Marry, thus; when it stands well with him, it stands well with her. (II, v, 20–23)

TAIL HUMOR

In this classic from *Taming of the Shrew,* Petruchio has just met his bethrothed, mule-stubborn Kate. (You can think of Richard Burton and Elizabeth Taylor, if you like.)

PETRUCHIO: Come come you wasp, y'faith you are too angrie.

KATE: If I be waspish, best beware my sting.

PETRUCHIO: My remedy then is to pluck it out.

KATE: Aye, if the fool could find where it lies.

PETRUCHIO: Who knows not where a wasp doth wear his sting? In his taile.

KATE: In his tongue?

PETRUCHIO: Whose tongue?

KATE: Yours if it talke of tales, and so farewell.

PETRUCHIO: What with my tongue in your taile.

[She slaps him.]

PETRUCHIO: Nay come again good Kate I am a gentleman. (II, i, 213–223)

Chaucer, long before Shakespeare, also enjoyed a good tail joke. At the end of the "Shipman's Tale," the wife, who was duped into sex with her husband's relative and also lost his money, apologizes to her husband, and promises to make it up to him: "I am your wife; score it upon my taille."

She's saying, "Put it on my tally," and also "Take out my debt upon my tail."

THE PRICK OF NOON AND JULIET

Lovestruck Romeo, giddy after the famous balcony scene, is back to bantering, which delights Mercutio, the ever horny, wise-guy servant.

MERCUTIO: Why is not this better now than groaning for love? Now art thou sociable, now art thou Romeo; now art thou what thou art, by art as well as nature. For this driveling love is like a great natural that runs lolling up and down to hide his bauble in a hole.

BENVOLIO: Stop there, stop there.

Mercutio insultingly compares Romeo's love for Juliet to a fool rushing around trying to shove his "bauble" (i.e., a doll's-headed stick) into a hole. This drawing from 1642 should help you picture *what's* supposed to go *where*.

Benvolio is appalled by the frankness of Mercutio's image, which probably eludes most modern audiences. What has Mercutio said? Basically, that love makes men act like a "natural" (i.e., a jester, a fool) who runs flopping up and down to hide his "bauble" (his fool's stick with a doll's head on it) in a hole. (You don't need Freud to figure out what he's referring to.)

Romeo gets a break from this crude chat when the nurse enters but, of course, Johnny-one-track Mercutio will have none of it. When the nurse asks if it's really the afternoon already, he replies:

MERCUTIO: The bawdy hand of the dial is upon the prick of noon.

NURSE: Out upon you! What a man are you!

Mercutio soon calls her a "bawd" and sings an obscure song with puns about "whores." After he finally leaves, the nurse asks Romeo what manner of rogue Mercutio is.

ROMEO: [He] will speak more in a minute than he will stand to in a month.

Romeo is saying that Mercutio is full of lewd talk and little actual sex, or, as Tennessee Williams once put it, "All hawk and no spit." Unfortunately, the same might be said of Romeo and Juliet.

SWEET BOTTOM-GRASS

Lastly, in *Venus and Adonis*, Venus tells Adonis, echoing Solomon's Song of Songs:

I'll be a park, and thou shalt be my deer.
Feed where thou wilt, on mountain or in
    dale.
    Graze on my lips; and if those hills be
    dry,
    Stray lower, where the pleasant
    fountains lie.

Within this limit is relief enough,
Sweet bottom-grass, and high delightful
    plain,
Round, rising hillocks, brakes, obscure and
    rough,
To shelter thee from tempest and from rain.
    Then be my deer, since I am such a park.
    No dogs shall rouse thee though a
    thousand bark.

Leave it to Shakespeare to make a sexual pun on an obscure agricultural term like "bottom-grass," which refers to the short thick grass in a meadow, beneath the longer sparser stalks. Sweet bottom-grass, indeed!

And why won't Adonis be rattled by the yelping dogs? No doubt, because Venus' thighs will be firmly clamped over the boy's ears. ✺

SECRET LIVES
OF THE ARTISTS

GOYA:
POISONED TO BRILLIANCE?

Francisco Goya (1746–1828) has entered that pantheon of the world's greatest artists, sharing pedestal space with the likes of Botticelli, Caravaggio, Velàsquez, if not Leonardo, and Rembrandt. But Goya's path to genius is one of the stranger and least known tales in art history.

For the first half of his life through age forty-six, Goya was a better than average court painter, a solid portrait artist with a knack for creating luminous, almost incandescent canvases. Mostly, he served up dollops of sweetness and light in portraits and pastorals. And Goya—through his brother-in-law's connections and despite a lackluster artistic career in Rome and Madrid—was now receiving ample royal commissions. Had Goya died then, art historians probably would have brushed him off in half a page, as a talented but tame artist.

Then suddenly, in the 1790s, when he was in his late 40s, Goya's work took a dramatic turn toward ferocious social satire and visions of mankind straight from hell. He transformed his nice country scenes into twisted nightmares; his use of light turned from sweet to eerie. Goya's new series of etchings, *The Caprices*, savaged the churchmen and nobles of his day, depicting some of them as fools and

sadists, literally at one point putting them on a spit and roasting them alive. The artist found evil lurking everywhere. As Arno Karlen says in his essay on Goya, "Women steal the teeth from hanged men, whores turn away their begging mothers, and shrieking witches wrestle on the wind."

Not surprisingly, the Inquisition—still rooting out heretics in Spain—thought about "roasting" Goya, especially since several of the lampooned Inquisitors were clearly recognizable. It took the intervention of his patron, the king himself,

The new, fiercer Goya—*after* his near-fatal illness—etched this vision of witches perverting little children for his *Caprices* series (1799). One crone creates a baby "bellows" to stoke the fire, while another, at her knee, fellates a toddler.

In another of Goya's *Caprices,* asses ride men. Goya's caption was "You Who Cannot."

Charles IV, who bought the plates and claimed he had commissioned the etchings, to save the artist.

Did Goya mend his ways? Certainly not. If anything, Goya upped his ferocity — and his gore level — in *The Disasters of War* in which he depicts the unspeakable human cruelty he had witnessed during the Napoleonic invasion in 1808 and subsequent civil war. All manner of mutilation — public emasculation, strangulation, amputation — fill the pages, sometimes standing above the simplest captions, such as "This I saw."

Goya still painted portraits and sometimes pastorals but a fearlessness and an anger now often pervaded his work. Jilted by the flighty Duchess of Alba, Goya depicted his former lover in the nude (from memory) in 1797, which marked only the second time a famous Spanish painter had dared paint an identifiable nude woman for public display.

What caused this sudden transformation in Goya? What catapulted him from mediocrity to brilliance?

In so many artists' careers, it is the influence of a mentor, as when Raphael studied under Perugino. In Goya's case, it was an illness, a terrible illness. In 1792, at age forty-six, Goya became deathly sick: coma, partial paralysis of the right side, impaired hearing and speech, temporary blindness, dizziness, hallucinations. Goya almost died.

Then after months recovering, his sight returned but he remained stone deaf to the grave. And several times again in his life, he became terribly sick with similar symptoms. As with some who become deaf in adult life, imprisoned in his isolation like Beethoven, he became increasingly paranoid and angry.

Early biographers and critics — taking an oblique clue from a letter from one of his friends mentioning "a lack of reflection" by Goya — pointed to syphilis. Doctors speculated as late as the 1960s that his illness at age forty-six was the third stage of syphilis. Syphilis takes many forms, and many of Goya's symptoms could fit it, but it's extremely unlikely that someone would live thirty-six more relatively stable years after the third stage of the illness.

Other doctors speculated that otosclerosis or Ménière's disease might have accounted for the vertigo, while psychiatrists have postulated schizophrenia.

Dr. William Niederland solved the puzzle, or came as close as we'll ever know without digging up Goya's bones. In the 1930s, Dr. Niederland treated city workers in Dusseldorf who scraped and repainted the city's bridges. After long exposure to *lead paint*, many exhibited the same odd list of symptoms as Goya, including temporary blindness, paralysis, and paranoia.

Dr. Niederland decided to investigate. He found that artists in Goya's day grinded and blended their own paints, and that several of the colors were quite toxic: cadmium yellow, mercury red, white lead.

Yes, his luminous landscapes evoked an eerie whiteness. Goya sometimes primed his entire canvas with white lead and very often painted with the color. Besides inhaling the lead, while grinding his paints, Goya's method of painting—fast and messy—ensured the artist would be doused in his own pigments.

Stated Théophile Gautier, in his "Wanderings in Spain": "What a strange painter, what a singular genius was Goya! . . . His method of painting was as eccentric as his talent. He scooped his color out of tubs, applied it with sponges, mops, rags, anything he could lay his hands on. He trowelled and slapped his colors on like a bricklayer, giving characteristic touches with a stroke of his thumb."

Goya suffered at least five bouts of major illness and each time he was unable to paint, which would have allowed the toxin levels of lead in his body to drop.

Goya's big career break? Lead poisoning. It's now believed that many artists prior to the development of toxin-free paints suffered from lead and mercury poisoning. Van Gogh? Lots of cadmium yellow. 🐚

ALEXANDER POPE CIRCUMCISES A PUBLISHER, 1720

Notorious for his literary feuds, the crooked-spined Alexander Pope teed off against many of the leading critics of his day, even going so far as to write an epic, *The Dunciad* to roast them in the most pub-

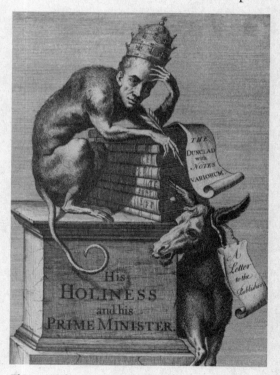

This satirical engraving from 1729 lashes Alexander Pope for his "mountain back," "distorted legs," and his pontifflike attitude.

lic cauldron. However, one feud of his is routinely forgotten.

Edmund Curll, a notorious publisher of pornography, infuriated Alexander Pope (1688–1744) by falsely attaching the famous poet's name in 1716 to a collection of poems, including one called *The Toilet*. Pope—scholarly, dwarfish, and venomous—responded by writing *A Strange But True Relation How Edmund Curll Was Circumcised*, in which Curll can only strike deals with the wealthy Jews if he converts to their religion. It's a classic deal-with-the-devil story, with a major anti-Semitic twist.

CIRCUMCISION

Whereupon [Curll] falling into company with the Jews at their club at the sign of the Cross in Cornhill, they began to tamper with him upon the most important points of the Christian faith, which he for some time zealously, and like a good Christian, obstinately defended. They promised him Paradise, and many other advantages hereafter; but he artfully insinuated that he was more inclined to listen to present gain. They took the hint, and promised him, that immediately upon his conversion to their persuasion he should become rich as a Jew.

[Curll agrees to convert, *and* to be circumcised.]

On the 17th of March, Mr. Curll (unknown to his wife) came to the tavern aforesaid. At his entrance into the room he perceived a meagre man, with a sallow countenance, a black forky beard, and long vestment. In his right hand, he held a large pair of shears, and in his left hand a red-hot searing-iron. At the sight of this Mr. Curll's heart trembled within him, and fain would he retire; but he was prevented by six Jews, who laid hands upon him, and unbuttoning his breeeches, threw him upon the table, a pale pitiful spectacle.

He now intreated them in the most moving tone of voice to dispense with that unmanly ceremony, which if they would consent to, he faithfully promised, that he would eat a quarter of paschal lamb with them the next Sunday following.

All these protestations availed him nothing; for they threatened him, that all contracts and bargains should be void unless he would submit to bear all the outward and visible signs of Judaism.

Our apostate hearing this, stretched himself upon his back, spread his legs, and waited for this operation: but when he saw the high priest take up the cleft stick, he roared most unmercifully, and swore several Christian oaths, for which the Jews rebuked him.

The savour of the effluvia that issued from him, convinced the old Levite, and all his assistants, that he needed no present purgation; wherefore, without further anointing him, he proceeded in his office: when, by an unfortunate jerk upward of the impatient victim, he lost five times as much as ever Jew did before.

They, finding that he was too much circumcised, which, by the levitical law, is worse than not being circumcised at all, refused to stand to any of their contracts:

wherefore they cast him forth from their synagogue; and he now remains a most piteous, woeful and miserable sight at the sign of the Old Testament and Dial in Fleet-street; his wife, poor woman, is at this hour lamenting over him, wringing her hands and tearing her hair; for the barbarous Jews still keep and expose at Jonathan's and Garraway's, the memorial of her loss, and her husband's indignity.

FIGHTING THE CROWDS ON WALDEN POND

Henry David Thoreau's *Walden; or Life in the Woods*, deserves its status as a great American book, but let it be known that Nature Boy went home on weekends to raid the family cookie jar.

Thoreau begins his American classic with the lines that are memorable for their simplicity, clarity, and . . . utter deception.

Thoreau, age thirty-nine, was photographed in 1856, shortly after the publication of *Walden*.

When I wrote the following pages, or rather the bulk of them, I lived alone, in the woods, a mile from any neighbor, in a house which I had built myself, on the shore of Walden Pond, in Concord, Massachusetts, and earned my living by the labor of my hands only. I lived there two years and two months. At present I am a sojourner in civilized life again.

Most Americans have an image of Thoreau as a rough-hewn, self-educated recluse, who, following the grand tradition of prophets, disappeared into the solitude to commune with nature. We picture his little shack far off in the woods, the man a voluntary Robinson Crusoe, alone with his thoughts and the bluebirds.

Nothing could be farther from the truth. Thoreau could see the well-traveled Concord-Lincoln highway across his field; he could hear the train whistles from the Fitchburg Railroad as it steamed along the track on the far side of Walden Pond.

He visited Concord Village almost every day; Thoreau's mother and sisters, who lived less than two miles away, deliv-

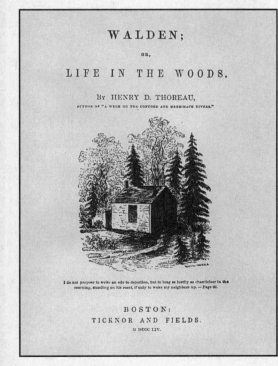

WALDEN;

OR,

LIFE IN THE WOODS.

BY HENRY D. THOREAU,
AUTHOR OF "A WEEK ON THE CONCORD AND MERRIMACK RIVERS."

I do not propose to write an ode to dejection, but to brag as lustily as chanticleer in the morning, standing on his roost, if only to wake my neighbors up. — Page 92.

BOSTON:
TICKNOR AND FIELDS.
M DCCC LIV.

The title page of the 1854 edition.

ered goodie baskets every Saturday, stocked with pies, doughnuts, and meals; Thoreau even raided the family cookie jar during his frequent visits home.

The more one reads in Thoreau's unpolished journal of his stay in the woods, the more his sojourn resembles suburban boys going to their treehouse in the backyard and pretending they're camping in the heart of the jungle.

The children of Concord visited on weekends and the cabin became a popular picnicking spot for local families. One winter, fellow writer Bronson Alcott had dinner there on Sunday nights; Ralph Waldo Emerson and Nathaniel Hawthorne were frequent visitors.

And, on August 1, 1846, the good ladies of an antislavery group held their annual celebration of the freeing of the West Indian slaves on his doorstep. The cabin once packed twenty-five visitors inside.

"It was not a lonely spot," understates Walter Harding in his excellent *The Days of Henry Thoreau.* "Hardly a day went by that Thoreau did not visit the village or was not visited at the pond." The joke making the rounds in Concord was that when Mrs. Emerson rang the dinner bell, Thoreau came rushing from the woods and was first in line with his outstretched plate.

After a year, Thoreau was giving little lectures in the Concord Lyceum on his experiment in simplified living. Word of his shack spread fast so that tourists started arriving, asking for a drink of water, hoping to catch a glimpse of the inside.

But Thoreau, a meat-eating Harvard grad, did find time away from the crowds to write about man and nature. *Walden* is a mesmerizing tale of St. Francis on a budget.

However, if you have a hankering to duplicate Thoreau's experiment in simplicity, perhaps you too should build a shack a couple of miles from the family home, just off the road, by the railroad tracks, a five minute walk from the village. And don't forget to schedule the weekend picnics. ❧

Lautrec in Drag

Toulouse-Lautrec (1864–1901), best remembered for his cabaret posters, liked to ham it up for the camera. The crippled man also liked to drink so much that toward the end of the artist's short life, he used a specially designed walking stick, concealing a flask *and* a shot glass. Here, Lautrec in 1894 has donned the hat, furs, and coat of Jane Avril, one of the most famous Moulin Rouge dancers.

FORGOTTEN FAILURE BY FUTURE GENIUSES

FLAUBERT'S AGONIZING BELLY FLOP

In September 1849, Gustave Flaubert (1821–1880) finished his 531-page opus, *The Temptation of St. Anthony,* and called his two closest literary friends—Maxime Du Camp, an irreverent journalist and Louis Bouilhet, a talented poet—to the family estate for a private reading. Flaubert was twenty-seven, this was his first major writing project, and he was very excited. (Almost a decade would pass before Flaubert would publish his novel *Madame Bovary,* which would reshape the art of fiction.)

As the friends settled into the drawing room, Flaubert's mother hovered nearby.

"The reading lasted thirty-two hours," recalled Du Camp many years later. "He read for four hours without pausing, from noon to four o'clock, from eight o'clock to midnight . . . Every so often during the silent hours while Bouilhet and I listened, we allowed ourselves to exchange a glance; the memory remains very painful. We bent an ear, hoping always that the action would heat up, and always we were disappointed . . . St. Anthony, bewildered, naive, I would venture, a bit of a nitwit, observes a parade before him of the various forms of temptation and can only figure to respond by exclaiming: 'Ah! ah! oh! oh! *mon Dieu! mon Dieu!'*

". . . We said nothing but it was easy for him to guess that our reaction was not favorable; once he interrupted himself: 'You will see! you will see!' We listened hard to the words of the Sphinx, the ghost, the Queen of Sheba, Simon the magician, Apollonius of Tyre, Origen, . . . Plato, Diana, Hercules, and even the god Crepitus. All wasted effort! We couldn't understand; we couldn't fathom where he was heading, and, in reality, he headed nowhere. Three years of labor collapsed without a trace; the oeuvre flitted away in smoke. Bouilhet and I were appalled. After each session, Madame Flaubert queried us: 'Well?' We didn't dare answer.

"After hearing the final part, Bouilhet and I had a tête-à-tête and we decided that we would be completely honest with Flaubert without holding back anything. The risk was great; but we could not let him continue this way, since at stake was a literary future in which we had absolute faith. Under the pretext of pushing Romanticism beyond the limit, he, without suspecting it, had taken it a step backwards . . . He must be halted on this path where he would lose his natural talents. This conclusion was painful for us but our friendship and our conscience demanded it.

"That same evening, after the final reading, near midnight, Flaubert banged the table and said: 'Among the three of us now, be frank and say what you think.' Bouilhet was usually shy but no one ever showed himself more firm once he decided to make his opinion known; he answered: 'We think you should throw that thing in the fire and never speak of it again.' Flaubert leaped up and uttered a cry of horror."

Flaubert's mother, who was eavesdropping, never forgave the two and accused them of being jealous of her brilliant son.

Less than a decade later, Flaubert finished *Madame Bovary.* Du Camp published it in serial form in his *Revue de Paris* (1856). So any first time writers out there who've been brutally rejected, take heart, and remember Flaubert. Once the novelist became famous, he buffed up *St. Anthony* and had it published.

Just be thankful that no one wants to read it aloud to *you.* ❧

MELVILLE'S MOBY-DICK SUNK LIKE A STONE IN THE 1850S

The novel opens with that stirring invitation, "Call me Ishmael." Instead, quite a few of the most prestigious critics chose to call the author a no-talent lunatic.

Moby-Dick—now considered one of the greatest American novels, if not the greatest—ran into a critical buzzsaw upon its debut in England in 1851, under the title, *The Whale.*

Here's what the respected British literary magazine, *The Athenaeum* (Oct. 25, 1851), had to say:

An ill compounded mixture of romance and matter of fact . . . Mr. Melville has to thank himself only if his errors and his heroics are flung aside by the general reader as so much trash belonging to the worst school of Bedlam literature—since he seems not so much unable to learn as disdainful of learning the craft of an artist.

The sea novel about Ahab was released first in England and Melville's British publisher had taken it upon himself to lop out sixty pages' worth of irreverence (such as Queequeg's "skill in obstetrics") and unwholesome biblical references. So perhaps the book—issued unexpurgated in America as *Moby-Dick,* with a new epilogue—would be better received over here?

Redburn was a stupid failure, *Mardi* was hopelessly dull, *White Jacket* was worse than either; and in fact was such a very bad book, that, until the appearance of *Moby-Dick* we had set it down as the very ultimatum of *weakness* to which the author could attain. It seems, however, that we were mistaken. In bombast, in caricature, in rhetorical artifice—generally as clumsy as ineffectual—and in low attempts at humor, each of his volumes has been an advance upon its predecessors.—*Democratic Review.*

The captain's ravings and those of Mr. Melville are such as would justify a *writ de lunatico* against all parties.—*Southern Quarterly Review.*

The *Boston Post* claimed the $1.50 cover price was far too high. "Published at twenty-five cents, it might do to buy, but at any higher price, we think it a poor speculation."

While there were a handful of favorable reviews in the United States, the book-buying public largely steered clear. Harper and Brothers (a forerunner to HarperCollins) sold only 3,797 copies in the first thirty-six years in print.

Melville's published works tanked after *Moby-Dick*, perhaps reaching a commercial nadir with his 571-page poem, *Clarel* (1876). He worked from 1866 to 1885 as a customs inspector in New York, died in 1891.

An obituary in the *New York Tribune* (Sept. 28, 1891) summed up Melville's career: "He won considerable fame as an author by the publication of a book in 1847 entitled *Typee* . . . This was his best work, although he has since written a number of other stories, which were published more for private than public circulation."

After World War I, Raymond Weaver helped resurrect Melville with his landmark bio, *Herman Melville: Mariner and Mystic* (1921) and his discovery of the manuscript of *Billy Budd* (1924). With Melville in the grave, *Moby-Dick* sold more than a million copies over the next three decades, with Harper and Brothers just one of the many publishers to issue the out-of-copyright book. 🐚

REVENGE AGAINST CRITICS

WHISTLER'S MOTHER OF A LAWSUIT

Leonardo da Vinci compared the opinions of critics to "wind from a fool's behind." American playwright David Mamet called two powerful New York scribes (Frank Rich and John Simon) "the syphilis and gonorrhea of the American theater." Legendary 18th-century British stage actor, David Garrick penned a vicious poem to skewer a fey theater critic.

> He deals in rancour to amuse him;
> A man, it seems — 'tis hard to say —
> A woman then? — a moment pray; —
> Unknown as yet by sex or feature,
> Suppose we try to guess the creature.

Most artists sling a few vicious words back, gnash their teeth at night and then let it go. Not so with American artist James McNeill Whistler (1834–1903) who took his tormentor to court, suing British art critic John Ruskin (1819–1900) for libel. This was celebrity versus celebrity, and the international press covered the event like a heavyweight fight. (Picture Robert De Niro versus Roger Ebert.)

Ruskin — snide, self-righteous, and arguably the most influential art critic in the world — had written of Whistler's paint-

Caricature of Whistler by Max Beerbohm.

ings at a show at the elite Grosvenour Gallery: "For Mr. Whistler's own sake, no less than for the protection of the purchaser, Sir Coutts Lindsay ought not to have admitted works into the gallery in which the ill-educated conceit of the artist so nearly approached the aspect of willful imposture. I have seen and heard much of cockney impudence before now; but never expected to hear a coxcomb ask two hundred guineas for flinging a pot of paint in the public's face". (July 2, 1877).

The courtroom was packed on November 15, 1878. Whistler was there without his mother.

To non–art history majors, Whistler is best known for *Whistler's Mother*, which conjures up images of a conservative dutiful son, an apple-pie kind of man. Not quite. Whistler was a rebellious showman who delighted in lobbing explosive "bon mots" and provocative artistic concepts into polite society. He entitled the famed painting of his dour-faced mom *Arrangement in Grey and Black No. 1,* while he called a later splash of metallic light on a black background: *Nocturne in Black and Gold: The Falling Rocket.*

Whistler, American ex-patriate in London, helped sow the seeds of increasingly nonrepresentational art. He affected lavender gloves and a pince-nez and he detested critics. The painting that so infuriated Ruskin was indeed the above-mentioned *Falling Rocket.*

The very proper attorney-general who represented Ruskin asked Whistler at the trial about how best to appreciate his art work. "You mean, Mr. Whistler, that the initiated in technical matters might have no difficulty in understanding your work. But do you think now that you could make *me* see the beauty of the picture?"

"Whistler eyed the attorney-general," according to *The World of James McNeill Whistler* by Horace Gregory. "He paused dramatically as the courtroom audience held its collective breath. 'No!' exploded Whistler. 'Do you know I fear it would be

The painting that sparked the famous lawsuit: Whistler's *The Falling Rocket.* (Before you play judge, know that this picture looks much more evocative *in color* with flashes of gold and subtle shades of sea green.)

as hopeless as for a musician to pour his notes into the ear of a deafman.' "

The courtroom erupted in laughter.

But the trial was not all fun and games. It led to one of the most famous lines ever uttered about putting a price tag on a work of art.

"Now, Mr. Whistler," asked the attorney-general. "Can you tell me how long it took you to knock off that nocturne? [i.e., a type of painting]"

"I beg your pardon."

"Oh! I am afraid I am using a term that applies rather to my own work. I should have said: "How long did you take to paint that picture?"

"Oh, no! permit me, I am too greatly flattered that you apply to a work of mine any term that you are in the habit of using with reference to your own work. Let us say then how long I did take to—"knock off," I think that is it—to knock off that nocturne; well, as well as I remember, about a day."

"Only a day?"

"Well, I won't be quite positive; I may have still put a few more touches to it the next day if the painting were not dry. I had better say then, that I was two days at work on it."

"Oh, two days! The labour of two days, then, is that for which you ask two hundred guineas! [about five times the yearly salary of a factory worker]"

"No I ask it for the knowledge of a lifetime."

The jury agreed, sort of. Whistler won his libel suit but was awarded only one farthing (i.e., a quarter of a cent) in damages.

The lawyers got paid and in fact, Whistler's legal fees tipped the struggling artist over into bankruptcy. He lost his house and his furniture and moved to Venice, and backtracked from his provocative style to sell a series of conventional etchings.

Ruskin, for his part—already a bit unhinged—was so outraged by the verdict that he resigned from Oxford University, and became an angry recluse.

So, as usual, in this battle between artist and critic, neither side was the winner. And to this day, critics are divided over whether Whistler sowed the seeds for "modern" art or whether he was a no-talent poseur. ☙

TRUMAN TRIES TO BOMB A MUSIC CRITIC

Give-'em-hell Harry Truman (1884–1972) once aimed both barrels of rage at an arts critic for the *Washington Post*, who had penned a savage review of Truman's daughter Margaret's singing debut. President Truman wrote the following note and mailed it himself.

I have just read your lousy review buried in the back pages. You sound like a frustrated old man who never made a success, an eight-ulcer man on a four-ulcer job and all four ulcers working. I never met you but if I do, you'll need a new nose and a supporter below. ☙

SUPPRESSED ILLICIT WORKS

MARK TWAIN DEFENDS SMALL PENISES

The American drawing room audience that made Mark Twain a rich man also gagged him at times. Publicly, Twain made a career out of battling his urge to smoke, drink, carouse, and curse; and the great humorist carefully kept his published works clean enough to suit the church-going crowd. (The word "nigger" was no problem for that audience.)

But, privately, Twain loved to tell off-color stories—as well as smoke, drink, carouse, and curse—and three of his blue after-dinner speeches have survived: *1601, Some Remarks on the Science of Onanism,* and *The Mammoth Cod Club.*

1601 has made its way into semipolite anthologies; it's an extended fart joke about breaking wind in the presence of Queen Elizabeth, a kind of one-note joke. The *Science of Onanism,* on the other hand, a riff on masturbation, ranks among Twain's funniest short works. The legend of American lit puts masturbation opinions in the mouths of famous charac-

Mark Twain carrying a big stick in 1909, a year before his death.

ters in history. Julius Caesar says, "Sometimes I prefer it to sodomy." Robinson Crusoe: "I cannot describe what I owe to this gentle art." Queen Elizabeth: "It is the bulwark of virginity."

Twain later advises, "If you *must* gamble away your lives sexually, don't play a Lone Hand too much." Read the whole thing; excerpts don't do it justice. It's been published a few times. You can find it in my book, *History Laid Bare* (HarperCollins, 1994) or *The Outrageous Mark Twain* (Doubleday, 1987).

The third of Twain's surviving off-color works is less known and more controversial. In fact, it was almost lost forever, except for the scholarship of Gershon Legman (*Ora-genitalism, The Limerick*) who found it in an unpublished anthology—Henry Cary's *Treasury of Erotic and Facetious Memorabilia*—where it was wrongly attributed to forgotten Civil War–era humorist, Petroleum V. Nasby.

Legman proved it was Twain's because of the little poem that opens it and then snooped around to re-create the circumstances during which Twain wrote it.

Twain, whose success stemmed from *Tom Sawyer* back in 1876, had made some horrendous investments that sent him into bankruptcy. By 1900, Twain's humor—as can be seen in *Letters from the Earth*—had taken on more of an edge.

According to Legman, in 1902, millionaire Henry H. Rogers, who had helped Twain climb out of debt, invited the humorist to sail with him on his yacht along with a bunch of high rollers, well-fed men past midlife out for a voyage of drinking, smoking, gambling, and fishing. The gentlemen, fond of codfishing, had dubbed themselves *The Mammoth Cods*.

Twain, unfortunately, missed the New York departure date because of some lingering houseguests; he sent his regrets, along with this letter which he said might serve as an after-dinner speech.

Dear — — —,

Yours, inviting me to join the excursion of the "Mammoth Cods" on the 29th inst., is at hand. Of course, I thank you, for I know you only desire my good; but whether it will be for my good to always accept your invitations is a question. I have been led from the sweet simplicity of my ordinary life into questionable paths too often by accepting your invitations, not to make me pause and consider when I receive one. I do not understand the meaning of the title of your organization made up of gentlemen whom mistaken nature has endowed with private organs of a size superior to common mortals. The word "cod" is frequently used in ancient literature to signify penis, and I take it that you use it in that sense. In a little poem that I wrote for the instruction of children, I used the word in the same way. I give you a copy of it. I wrote it to show the youth of the country that animals do better by instinct than man does by reason, unless it is properly guided. I intended it for Sunday Schools and when sung by hundreds of sweet, guileless children, it produces a very pretty effect.

I.
I thank Thee for the Bull, O God!
   Whene'er a steak I eat.
The working of his Mammoth Cod
   Is what gives us our meat!

II.
And for the ram a word of praise!
   He with his Mammoth Cod
Foundation for our mutton lays
   With every vigorous prod.

III.
And then the Boar, who, at his work,
   His hind hoofs fixed in sod,
Contented, packs the Embryo Pork,
   All with his Mammoth Cod!

IV.
Of beasts, man is the only one
   Created by our God,
Who purposely, and for mere fun,
   Plays with his Mammoth Cod!

I object to your Society for several reasons:

1st. I fail to see any special merit in penises of more than the usual size. What more can they achieve than the smaller ones? I have read history very carefully, and I nowhere find it of record that the sires of Washington, Bonaparte, Franklin, Julius Caesar, or any of the other worthies whose names illuminate history, were especially developed; and as it is not a matter of history, it is fair to assume that they carried regular sizes. In this, as in everything else, quality is more to be considered than quantity. It is the searching, not the splitting weapon that is of use.

2nd. It is unfair for a set of men who are thus developed to arrogate to themselves, superiority. It is something they are not responsible for, except, indeed, they increase its size by means that no man should be proud of. In my green and salad days a lady whom I wickedly tried to overcome for months, finally yielded. In just eight days I had a penis, or as you term it, a "Cod" of a size that would have entitled me to admission to your Order, were you all as well hung as jackasses. Was I to put on airs because injection of Nitrate of Silver swelled that organ? Heaven forbid! On the contrary I wore a sack-cloth and ashes, as soon as I could get it out of its sling, and was ashamed.

3rd. It is unscriptural. We are as we were made. Can any of you by taking thought add one cubit to his stature? [Matthew, vi. 27.] I have, at times, by taking thought added inches to this organ; but it was not a permanency, and should not therefore be counted.

4th. Largeness of organ is proof positive that it has been cultivated. The blacksmith gets an enormous arm by constantly exercising that limb, and I suppose a man by constantly using his private member will increase the size of it. Membership in your Society is a confession of immorality.

5th. I never go where I am looked upon as an inferior. Having devoted myself all my life to pious study and meditation; having formed my delights, not in the fleeting and unsatisfactory pleasures of sexuality and debauchery, but in the calm pursuits of religion and other learning, I really don't know whether I have such a thing as a "Cod" about me. I know there is a conduit about my person which is useful in conveying the waste moisture of the system, and is therefore, I suppose, necessary, but that is the only use I have ever put it to, except the natural one of procreation. I may be excused for this, for it would be a shame to have this kind of man I am die out with myself. I would not inflict such an injury upon the world. As for what men of the world call pleasure, I have heard, accidentally, many names for it, but I know nothing about it and care less. My recollection of it is, that while it was, perhaps, pleasant, it was so brief and transitory it was not worth my while to repeat; still there may be pleasure in it for those who are not wrapped up in mental pursuits, and who make a study of it. As a philosopher I would investigate it had I not more important matters in hand.

Dear — — —, I trust these reasons are sufficient for my not joining the expedition; still, as wicked as you are, and as much as you are given to the vain and transitory pleasures of this life, I trust you will have a good time. You cannot sin much on the water and if you play I know you will lose your money and thus lessen your means of sinning when you get ashore. Go with the gay revellers and have what you call a "good time." While you are thus engaged think of me, busy in my translation of the New Testament, and varying the monotony of the labor with the preparation of my hymns for Children, — a sample of which I have sent you.

May the Lord (?) Bless you,

Faithfully,

— — —

•

Dear — — —,

I enclose a letter which will perhaps answer your purpose. It is not very witty nor very wise, but, if read when the audience is half drunk, may answer. Write and tell me if I take the boat Thursday night, do I get in Boston in time to join the expedition? I am going to be there if possible, but I don't want to leave here until Thursday night, and I want to go by the boat. Write me all about it and where shall I come? Shall I have to rush straight to the boat, or will I have time to come to the Store and go with you like a Christian. Let me know about this at once. I am anxious to come, and shall if it be possible. May the Lord (?) Bless you, and keep you, and watch over you. You are too wicked to die, and too good to live. I *do* want to go on that excursion; I want to play poker once again before I die, and to breathe the salt air out of the mouth of a champagne bottle and be wicked. I have been good too long.

Truly,

— — —

Twain also did a spoof of the Rubaiyat—"a loaf of bread, a jug of wine, a book of verse," etc.—on the subject of impotency.

A WEAVER'S BEAM

A Weaver's Beam—the Handle of a Hoe,
A Bowsprit once—now thing of dough:
  A sorry Change, lamented oft with
  Tears
At Midnight by the Master of the Show.
Behold—the Penis mightier than the
  Sword,
That leapt from Sheath at any heating
  Word
    So long ago—now peaceful lies, and
    calm,

And dreams unmoved of ancient Conquests
  scored.

World class pun in line five!! Mark Twain was sanitized by his daughters and his early biographers and editors; America's greatest humorist certainly knew how to play blue. Luckily, a few fragments have survived. ❧

THE AROUSING LETTERS HOME OF JAMES JOYCE

Irish novelist James Joyce *(Ulysses)* took his "blackguard schoolgirl" Nora Barnacle, a chambermaid, as his common-law wife in 1904, and was traveling in 1909 when the pair exchanged a series of remarkable letters. In those pre-telephone-in-the-bedroom days, these were communications by which to masturbate. Joyce specifically suggested ripe topics to his wife, and, in effect, let her listen in as his reminiscences of their sex acts helped him to orgasm.

He revels in inhaling her aromas; he remembers plowing her from behind as each of his thrusts propeled her tongue forward from her lips; he begs her to tell him about her other

James Joyce and common-law wife, Nora Barnacle, in Paris in 1924.

lovers; he dictates the exact type of frilly underwear to buy and then hopes that it will someday bear a dark stain; he can't wait to surprise her in the middle of the night, her drawers open, his tongue exploring until . . .

But why am I paraphrasing James Joyce? Because it is against the law to reprint these letters at this time. Why? Because the heirs to the great Irish novelist have expressly forbidden it.

In an ironic act, the executors of the estate of an author who pioneered the frank use of language (*Ulysses, Finnegans Wake*) and battled against censorship have opted to *censor* their own ancestor's letters.

Dear Mr. Zacks:
I regret to say that under no circumstances will the James Joyce Estate give permission for you to include the letter of 2nd December 1909 from James Joyce to Nora . . . The Estate will not permit the use of any of the 1909 letters to Nora. I am sorry to disappoint you.

Well, I am sorry to disappoint the Joyce heirs, but it's my duty to tell readers that there is a way for them to get a hold of these letters. They were published during this century and can be found in good libraries in an out-of-print edition, *Selected Letters of James Joyce*, edited by Richard Ellman (Viking, 1975). Turn to pages 180 to 192. Photocopy them for your private home use. Show them to your friends for their private home use.

These letters are brilliant erotica. They are vivid, lusty, articulate, guilty, soaked in sin, full of smells and tastes, a bit brown, a bit frilly. While *Ulysses* might be difficult for some readers, these letters are direct and supremely erotic—ten thousand times sexier than the rococo predictability of John Cleland's *Fanny Hill* or the grinning swordsmanship of Henry Miller. Go now!

I hereby claim "Fair Use" and will provide one single sentence from a Joyce-to-Nora letter. (Write me in Sing Sing, dear reader; I did it for you.)

My love for you allows me to pray to the spirit of eternal beauty and tenderness mirrored in your eyes or to fling you down under me on that soft belly of yours and fuck you up behind, like a hog riding a sow, glorying in the very stink and sweat that rises from your arse, glorying in the open shame of your upturned dress and white girlish drawers and in the confusion of your flushed cheeks and tangled hair.

Nora's letters have not survived; Jim's have. Go read 'em. ✷

HIGH ART: SNORTING AND SWIGGING THE MUSE

Coleridge on Opium, Baudelaire on Hashish . . .

In this era of "Just Say No," it is much more fashionable to speak of an artist's accomplishment *in spite of* his or her addiction to narcotics. That, in my humble opinion, is crap, an example of fuzzy-headed thinking by very sober critics.

Drug use by talented artists is a deal with the devil. In exchange for moments of heightened perception, they run the risk that addiction will set in and destroy their lives. (Just sign here, baby; sure, you'll OD at twenty three but you'll go platinum first.)

Can anyone imagine Coleridge writing *Kubla Khan* or *The Rime of the Ancient Mariner* without opium? Or Poe penning *Ulalume* without whiskey or laudanum? or Baudelaire *Les Fleurs du Mal* without some hashish?

Doctors speak of a so-called "honeymoon period" in a person's path to addiction when the user is enjoying the narcotic's ability to open up recesses of the mind without suffering the downside of craving an increasingly debilitating dose.

Thomas Edison worked nights, needed little sleep, drinking plentiful gulps of Vin Mariani, a cocaine-laced wine. Robert Louis Stevenson apparently went on a six-day cocaine binge when, feeeble from tuberculosis, he suddenly rushed out the entire story of Dr. Jekyll and Mr. Hyde. (Don't forget the good doctor is turned maniac by a new drug, a "powder.") Commented Mrs. Stevenson: "That an invalid in my husband's condition of health should have been able to perform the manual labor alone of putting sixty thousand words on paper in six days seems incredible."

Robert Louis Stevenson (1850–1894), sickly from childhood on, used cocaine for medicinal purposes. The side effects were often quite artistic, such as when he created *Dr. Jekyll and Mr. Hyde.*

Quite a cocaine curiosity flowered during the late Victorian era. Explains Sherlock Holmes in *The Sign of the Four,* as to why he takes cocaine: "My mind rebels at stagnation. Give me problems, give me work, give me the most abstruse cryptogram or the most intricate analysis and I am in my proper atmosphere. I can dispense with artificial stimulants. But I abhor the dull routine of existence."

Composer Hector Berlioz tried to win over a lover, Harriet Smithson, by gulping down an overdose of laudanum. During his subsequent binge, he composed *Symphonie Fantastique.*

French poet Charles Baudelaire and his cronies formed "Le Club des Hashashchins," meeting frequently at Hôtel Lauzun to test the effects of opium and hashish on creative writing. They experimented with drug trances. Baudelaire's

"Les Fleurs de Mal" surely benefited from his *inhaling*.

> Une ile parasseuse où la nature donne
> Des arbres singuliers et des fruits
> savoreux
> Des hommes dont le corps est mince et
> vigoreux,
> Des femmes dont l'oeil par sa franchise
> étonne.

("A lazy island where nature creates singular trees and savory fruits, where the men's bodies are lithe and vigorous and the women's eyes startle you with their frankness.")

But perhaps the poster child of pre-20th century druggies—at least on the literary side—is the British poet Samuel Taylor Coleridge. The standard theme in the criticism of Coleridge for two centuries has been that the poet would have been so much more prolific and would have created so many more brilliant works had he not been seriously addicted for twenty-five years of his life. Perhaps a more valid comment would be to state that without opium Coleridge would have never written *Kubla Khan* or *Ancient Mariner*. But both of these "what if" queries can never be answered without a time machine and a truant officer to keep S.T.C.'s pudgy hands away from the vial. We will never know.

Around 1800, laudanum—an alcoholic tincture of opium, which is in turn derived from the dried juice of poppy seeds—was as easily available as aspirin is today. Doctors and pharmacists doled it out for ail-ments ranging from stomachache to typhoid. (Many workers robotically toiling in manufactories of England's industrial revolution commenced their day with a dram of laudanum; Britain imported 22,000 pounds of opium in 1830.)

COLERIDGE

In 1797, Samuel Taylor Coleridge wrote one of the greatest poems in the English language, *The Rime of the Ancient Mariner*. Take a taste of the scene where our anti-hero is cursed for killing the albatross.

> . . . Day after day, day after day,
> We stuck, nor breath nor motion,
> As idle as a painted ship
> Upon a painted ocean
>
> Water, water, everywhere
> And all the boards did shrink;
> Water, water, everywhere,
> Nor any drop to drink.
>
> The very deep did rot: O Christ!
> That ever this should be!
> Yea, slimy things did crawl with legs
> Upon a slimy sea.
>
> About, about, in reel and rout
> The death-fires danced at night;
> The water, like a witch's oils,
> Burnt green, and blue and white.

As for *Kubla Khan*, Coleridge states in his introduction to the poem that it came to him during a drug-induced dream after reading a history book.

In Xanadu did Kubla Khan
A stately pleasure-dome decree:
Where Alph the sacred river, ran
Down to a sunless sea.

Remember those lines. Enjoy those lines. I think we should celebrate—lift a glass, fire up a pipe, *inhale*—that opium helped Coleridge create these astounding works of art. It is true the drug later tortured him. "You bid me rouse myself," he once retorted to a well-meaning minister. "Go, bid a man paralytic in both arms rub them briskly together & that will cure him."

He spent the last years of his life under voluntary house arrest at the home of a doctor friend who doled him out a daily trifle of laudanum. While some scholars point with pride to his flurry of witty talk and his religious philosophizing during that period, Coleridge never burst forth in song on a par with his early drug-bingeing days.

An unmeasured amount of the world's greatest writing has been drug- or alcohol-enhanced. This in no way demeans the poems or the stories. If a writer smokes cigarettes while writing, is this an unfair advantage over writers who don't smoke? Piffle. 🌀

FRAUD: OLD MASTER ON TRIAL

The Dutch take their Old Masters very seriously, and when World War II ended, the government set out to track down and recover every single work of art hijacked by the Nazis. A collaborator convicted of trafficking could face the gallows.

In a salt mine near Salzburg, Austria, the Allies unearthed some masterpieces squirreled away by that culture-lover, Field Marshal Hermann Goering. Amid the loot was a never-before-seen Vermeer, *Christ and the Adulteress*.

Who sold this Dutch national treasure to the Nazis?

The trail led back through a German banker, through a Dutch art dealer to a second-rate Dutch artist named Han van Meegeren, who had once scratched out a living doing tourist portraits on the French Riviera.

Van Meegeren steadfastly denied trafficking in the painting. Finally, after six weeks of harsh interrogation in jail, deprived of his regular morphine fix, the fifty-five-year-old van Meegeren confessed . . . to painting the picture himself.

He was laughed at; he became the butt of bar jokes. Van Meegeren claimed that he had *not* collaborated with the Third Reich, but rather he had duped it, conning Field Marshal Goering into exchanging 173 paintings for this one fake Vermeer.

The veteran judges viewed the man's words as a ruse to slip off with a two-year sentence for forgery. The art world—atwitter with stolen Nazi art rumors—was also highly amused, with one critic calling him "a muddy-minded fantast with a grudge against museums." But the critics became a tad nervous when van Meegeren claimed he had forged six other Vermeers, including one that was hanging in a place of honor in Rotterdam's prestigious Boymans Museum; another hung in Edinburgh's National Gallery. And these works had received glowing praises from art critics and experts worldwide. In 1938, for instance, Dr. Abraham Bredius, Holland's leading art critic and director of the Royal Museum, had commented on one of the Vermeers: "Neither the beautiful signature nor the *pointille* on the bread which Christ is blessing, is

necessary to convince us that we have here a—I am inclined to say *the*—masterpiece of Johannes Vermeer of Delft."

So was it a ruse by van Meegeren or was the con man telling the truth? The judges decided to ask the cantankerous fifty-five-year-old artist, going cold turkey from his morphine addiction, to paint a copy of Vermeer's *Christ at Emmaus*. Van Meegeren told them any talented art student could paint a copy; no, he would paint a fresh Vermeer, to the specifications of Holland's leading art critics. The court agreed. As one newspaper headline drummed it: HE PAINTS FOR HIS LIFE.

Van Meegeren was returned to his studio, given a small daily dose of morphine, and under the eyes of two armed guards and several leery art critics, he began.

"He called for his brushes, paints and

Accused Nazi collaborator, Han Van Meegeren (*right*), paints a Vermeer in 1945 to try to save himself from the gallows.

canvas," reported a press release from the Netherlands government. "Working with the consummate skill of a master, a painting in the very spirit of the famous 17th-century artist slowly began to materialize. There can be no doubt that this mad genius did paint the seven pictures attributed to Vermeer."

Han van Meegeren is probably the greatest art forger of all time, and also a fine painter in his own right. He tracked down lapus lazuli to grind for blues; he bought worthless seventeenth-century canvases and painted over the bottom layer to achieve the proper filligree of surface "crackle"; he washed India ink in the cracks; he baked them for two hours at a precise temperature; he used a yellow varnish, and above all, he studied Vermeer.

From 1937 to his arrest in 1945, van Meegeren lived the high life, accumulating at one point dozens of houses and several night clubs. At his trial, he was asked why he did it. He answered simply, "Because no one noticed my work."

Van Meegeren, as a young artist, had won prizes and sold out two prestigious shows. Then the critics turned on him, and called him a "second-rater." They savaged his work, and especially damned him for his traditional style and for his ignoring the latest trends.

Deeply wounded, he fled Holland and eked out a living on the French Riviera doing tourist portraits, and he spent four long years experimenting to perfect his forgery techniques. He was consumed with a desire to defy those critics who had scorned him. His original plan—so he said—was to sell one work, then reveal the fraud and claim his rightful place as a master.

The money, the women, the drugs all seduced him—maybe even the deliciousness of the fraud. (He once complained to the curator at the Rotterdam museum that he thought their famed Vermeer might be a fake.) Van Meegeren earned at least $2.8 million from selling his own work under famous names.

Han van Meegeren was acquitted of collaborating with the Nazis, but convicted of fraud and sentenced in November 1947 to one year in jail. The Dutch public embraced this man who had humbled the arrogant critics; one opinion poll ranked him the second most popular man in Holland.

Ill, and with a pardon from Queen Wilhelmina in the works, van Meegeren died of a heart attack on December 30th before serving any jail time. After his death, works by him shot up in value.

Van Meegeren should be remembered by the words he uttered after repeatedly denying that he had ever sold any Vermeers to the Nazis. He shouted at his interrogators: "Fools, I painted it myself."

FLAGRANT MISQUOTES FROM "GO WEST, YOUNG MAN" TO "SPARE THE ROD"

Mark Twain said a trainload of witty things in his life, but several of his most famous sayings never passed by that great mustache. For instance: "Giving up smoking is easy, I've done it hundreds of times." Caroline Hansberger scoured Twain for *Mark Twain at Your Fingertips* (1948) and never found it.

It is startling to discover how many time-honored quotations were never uttered by that particular person associated with them or were first said by somebody else. Here—with a major nod to *They Never Said It*, by Paul Boller Jr. and John George (Oxford, 1989), and Tom Burnam's *Dictionary of Misinformation*—are a handful of the spicier choices.

MARK TWAIN

"There are three kinds of lies: lies, damn lies, and statistics."

Twain quoted the line in his autobiography and he honorably credited it to Benjamin Disraeli.

"Everybody talks about the weather but nobody does anything about it."

An editorial appeared in the *Hartford Courant* on August 24, 1897, with the line: "A well-known American writer once said that while everyone talked about the weather, nobody seemed to do anything about it." The editorial writer, Charles Dudley Warner, had collaborated with Twain on *The Gilded Age*, and *might* have been thinking of Twain, but Twain himself gave the credit to Warner.

As *They Never Said It* points out, Twain's weather line was a bit different: "If you don't like the weather in New England now, just wait a few minutes."

MARIE-ANTOINETTE

Maybe if the line had been translated "Let them eat brioche," it wouldn't have become so famous. Marie-Antoinette (1755–1793) when informed of a bread shortage among the peasants, has been quoted in every schoolbook from here to Zimbabwe as saying: "Let them eat cake." (The actual French is *"Qu'ils mangent de la brioche."*)

Apparently, she never said it: Jean-Jacques Rousseau in his *Confessions* (1781), recalled an incident that happened in Grenoble in 1740, more than a decade *before* Marie Antoinette was born. Wrote Rousseau:

"At length, I recalled the thoughtless remark of a great princess, who, when she was told that the peasants had no bread, replied: 'Let them eat cake.' "

It's very likely that propagandists hung the remark on Marie Antoinette to speed her path to the guillotine.

KING LOUIS XIV

"L'etat c'est moi." or "I am the State."

It would have been in character for the Sun King but no contemporary jotted it down after hearing it directly from the king's lips. According to the *Dictionary of Misinformation,* the man who spread the pithy phrase (and perhaps piped it as well) was Voltaire.

SIR ISAAC NEWTON

"If I have seen further, it is by standing on the shoulders of giants."

Pundits use this quote as the ultimate expression of humility in genius, but what they miss (and almost everyone else does too) is that Newton wrote that line to a *very very short man,* a hunchbacked fellow scientist with whom he was having a bitter feud.

Newton (1642–1727) was furious that Robert Hooke (1635–1703) was staking claim to many key discoveries in optics and calculus. (Hooke did in fact build the first reflecting telescope.)

Biographer John Aubrey, who was a personal friend of Robert Hooke, described him as "but of middling stature, something crooked, pale faced . . . head is large; his eye full and popping."

Newton wrote a long letter to Hooke on February 5, 1675, defending himself from charges of intellectual piracy, praising Hooke for trifles, and then Newton built to the famous "standing on the shoulders of giants" line. (Newton, by the way, adapted it from a line about *pygmies* in a then-famous book called *Anatomy of Melancholy.*)

You might translate Newton's sentiments: "While I admit to building on the work of my scientific predecessors, I certainly didn't learn anything from a dwarf like you."

HORACE GREELEY

"Go west, young man, go west."

Cited by politicians and real estate brokers, by teachers and term paper writers, this line ranks as one of the best known quotes from American history. The teeny rub is that Horace Greeley never said it.

The line was written by a now forgotten and never very famous Indiana journalist, named John L. Soule in the *Terre Haute Express* in 1851. Greeley grew so exasperated denying that he had said the remark that he reprinted Soule's original article but the general public apparently wasn't paying attention that day.

GEORGE WASHINGTON

"I cannot tell a lie."

Maybe George couldn't, but Washington's biographer, Anglican minister "Parson" Weems, certainly could.

Weems made up that story about chopping down the cherry tree, including the punch line. Conveniently, Weems's saintly bio of the first president appeared just after Washington's death in 1799.

ETHAN ALLEN

"In the name of the great Jehovah and the Continental Congress!"

That's what patriot Ethan Allen supposedly said when a British officer asked him by whose authority he was demanding the surrender of Fort Ticonderoga. Ethan Allen's men remember it a bit differently. They recall that the British commanding officer was sleeping and didn't exactly race outside. One man heard Allen say, "Come out here, you damned old Rat"; another heard, "Come out here, you sons of British whores, or I'll smoke you out." Ethan Allen's nobler words were suddenly remembered four years after the deed by Allen and no one else.

In fact, war stories seem to bring out the quote machine. As *The Dictionary of Misinformation* points out: At Waterloo, after the tide had clearly turned against the French, the English sent a message to the commander of Napoleon's famed Imperial Guard to surrender. History books record the man's answer was, "The Guard dies but never surrenders." What he really said was: *"Merde"* (which is French for "shit").

NAPOLEON

"England is a nation of shopkeepers."

The corkscrew-forelocked conqueror said it, but he was compacting a long quote from economist Adam Smith (1723–1790). "To found a great empire for the sole purpose of raising up a people of customers, may at first sight appear a project, fit only for a nation of shopkeepers. It is, however, a project altogether unfit for a nation of shopkeepers; but extremely fit for a nation that is governed by shopkeepers."

Right, Adam. Napoleon's line in French, by the bye, has quite a ring: *"L'Angleterre est une nation de boutiquiers."*

SHERLOCK HOLMES

"Elementary, my dear Watson."

Credit Basil Rathbone and Hollywood screenwriters for popularizing a phrase that author Sir A. Conan Doyle never once put on the lips of his deductive detective.

W. C. FIELDS

"On the whole, I'd rather be in Philadelphia."

It's not on his tomb, which bares the simple knee-slapper: "W. C. Fields 1880–1946." The line first appeared in a *Vanity Fair* cartoon in the 1920s and was later hooked to Fields.

THE BIBLE

The Devil *can* quote scriptures but apparently, many well-intentioned do-gooders *cannot,* at least accurately.

"God *helps* him who helps himself."

That might be true, but it's not in the Bible. One scholar traces it back to Greek storyteller Aesop, whose fable about Hercules featured: "Do not pray to me for help until you have done your best to help yourself; otherwise, your prayer will be in vain."

"Spare the rod and spoil the child."

While the Book of Proverbs clearly endorses this black-and-blue approach to child care, the exact phrase was written by English satirical poet Samuel Butler (1612–1680) in *Hudibras* (1664). Samuel Butler also wrote *Dildoides*, a long poem about a shipment of French dildos that were confiscated and destroyed by British customs. ("Some were of wax, where ev'ry vein,/And smallest fibre were made plain," etc.).

"There's safety in numbers."

Somebody red-penciled this one and completely changed the meaning. The actual line in Proverbs is: "Where no counsel is, the people fall, but in the multitude of counselors *there* is safety." So not safety in a mob but in a multitude of leaders. ❧

DIRTY MONEY: TRACING FAMOUS AMERICAN FORTUNES

Look in the tomb of many, if not most, of the "old money" families in America, the so-called American bluebloods, the Whitneys, the Vanderbilts, the Astors, and you're bound to find a crook moldering away somewhere.

Once a fortune's made, the next generation conveniently forgets the sins of the father. We're not talking about sharp, opportunistic, ruthless business practices (traits often praised), we're talking about lawbreaking, whether it be via bribes, stock schemes, or bookmaking.

With far too many famous names to choose from, a handful will have to suffice.

AMBASSADOR ANNENBERG AT THE COURT OF THE LUCKY FILLY

In the 1980s at *TV Guide*, Walter Annenberg (1908–   ) was addressed by editors as the "Ambassador," a holdover from his stint as "Ambassador to the Court of St. James," appointed by his close Republican pal, Ronald Reagan. Annenberg built up the largest circulation magazine in the world, *TV Guide*, which he sold with other properties to Rupert Murdoch for $2.8 billion in 1988; he once donated $365 million to endow various institutions, including the Annenberg School of Communications at the University of Pennsylvania.

However, the roots of the family fortune and the family expertise in delivering complicated information clearly and quickly across the country date back to Moe Annenberg delivering odds to bookies.

Walter's father, Moses Annenberg (1878–1942), owned the *Daily Racing Form*, but big profits came from delivering racing odds and results by telegraph to mob-controlled bookies nationwide through the 1930s, according to the *Encyclopedia of World Crime* (J. Robert Nash, ed.) and to *Secret File*, by Hank Messick.

Bookies in the 1930s who needed the latest odds at the tracks couldn't wait for the morning newspapers and, being outside the law, couldn't exactly subscribe to the Associated Press. They needed their own wire service. A complicated interwoven skein of Annenberg wire companies built a near-monopoly nationwide, even going so far as publishing and printing the giant wall posters used in that precomputer era to post odds in bookie parlors and pool halls.

Annenberg worked with Chicago gangsters, the likes of Al Capone. "Moe Annenberg was for the bookies of America what Arnold Rothstein was for rum-runners and narcotics peddlers—the man who put the racket on a businesslike basis," states mob expert Hank Messick.

Like Capone, he wasn't convicted of racketeering but rather of tax evasion. The government investigators were lost in the maze of Annenberg's vast empire of publications (including the *Philadelphia Inquirer)* and wire services when they got a break. A shipment of files marked PRIVATE RECORDS arrived from Annenberg's Long Island home and was handed to Special Agent Nels Tessem instead of going to Annenberg's lawyer, then preparing his defense. This "little mistake" allowed the government to force Annenberg to agree to pay $8 million in back taxes and he was later sentenced to a three-year prison term.

Annenberg apparently got out of the bookie's wire service business at that point. James Ragen, who next ran the business, had a little quarrel with Chicago gangsters over divvying the profits. He was gunned down in 1946.

Walter Annenberg's fortune was estimated by *Forbes* in 1995 at $3.7 billion. ❧

ASTOR: DRUNKEN INDIANS AND ANIMAL SKINS

The Astor Library in New York City is certainly among the most prestigious cultural landmarks in the United States.

John Jacob Astor (1763–1848), born in Germany, emigrated at age twenty to America, where he took a job in New York City beating and fluffing furs for two dollars a week. Soon after, Astor opened his own shop and parlayed it into a giant empire called American Fur Company. How?

"The trader's ancient trick of getting the Indians drunk and swindling them of their furs and land was carried on by Astor on an unprecedented scale," states Gustavus Myers in *History of the Great American Fortunes* (1907).

Although territorial law at the time severely restricted the sale of whiskey to Indians, Astor's men flouted it. "The traders that occupy the largest and most important space in the Indian country are the agents and engagees of the American Fur Trade Company," observed government rep, Andrew Hughes on October 31, 1831. "They entertain, as I know to be the fact, no sort of respect for our citizens, agents, officers of the government, or its laws or general policy."

Astor's men not only got the Indians drunk to hustle them out of their pelts, they profited off the booze, selling it at hugely inflated prices, as high as fifty dollars a gallon back when an unskilled laborer earned ten dollars a month.

Reports poured in from government agents in the western territories about the machinations of Astor's men. "He who has the most whiskey carries off the most furs," wrote Colonel J. Snelling in August 1825 from Detroit. Astor—a tightfisted micromanager—personally oversaw the shipping of great quantities of liquor to New Orleans and then up the Mississippi to his main trading posts. The outpost in Detroit, for one, received a shipment of 3,300 gallons of whiskey and 2,500 gallons of wine in one year. Snelling noted seeing "the road strewed with the bodies of men, women and children in the last stages of brutal intoxication."

Military officers pointed out that the liquor invariably led to skirmishes and brawls with the Indians.

The vast fortune Astor made in furs was then reinvested, primarily in New York City real estate. Thanks to inside information from banks and juicy land grants from corrupt city officials—and, of course, shrewd predatory foreclosing instincts, Astor became the largest single landlord in Manhattan. His fortune at his death in 1848 was pegged at $20 million, probably ten times greater than the *next* richest man in New York. ❧

THE ART OF THE WHITNEYS

New Yorkers talk about going to "the Whitney," when making a pilgrimage to that renowned modern art museum. Patients receive state of the art treatment in Payne Whitney wing of New York Hospital.

And it's good the family is giving something back, because a big chunk of the roots of the Whitney family fortune came directly from looting a turn-of-the-century New York public transit project, graft on a genuinely monumental scale.

Ironically, William C. Whitney (1841–1904) made his big public splash while helping bust the corrupt practices of the Tweed Ring. Whitney, a lawyer trained at both Harvard and Yale, after serving as Secretary of the Navy, returned to New York City, and along with partners, combined several street railways into the Metropolitan Street Railway Company in the 1890s.

They raised $261 million in capital from publicly sold stock and bonds. Richard Armory, a former executive with Metropolitan, accused the company top brass of siphoning off the then mind-boggling sum of $90 million. Armory charged: "Their crimes comprise conspiracy, intimidation, bribery, corrupt court practices, subornation of perjury, false reporting, the payment of unearned dividends year after year, the persistent thefts of stockholders' money, carried on over a long period by a System constituting the basest kind of robbery . . . and finally, as a result the wreck and ruin of a great corporation." The company completely collapsed in 1907.

Various long investigations—some apparently quite half-hearted—wound down to the prime partners' paying less than a million dollars in penalties. Perhaps more significantly, though, the principles never sued Armory or its other accusers such as Ambassador Joseph Choate for libel, although these men publicly launched charges in court and in print. "I do not hesitate to say that the greatest enormity committed in New York was the floatation and inflation of the Metropolitan Street Railway Company," accused Choate.

Over time, however, William C. Whitney's image was polished to an aristocratic philanthropic glow. When his son, Harry Payne Whitney, died in 1930, the *New York Times* wrote of the man's father, William: "He amassed an immense fortune by amalgamating a score or more of surface railways, had remarkable success in everything he undertook. He was a statesman of more than national prominence; one of the shrewdest of the country's politicians in the better sense of the word; a constructive financier of the utmost astuteness . . ."

CIVIL WAR: SELLING OUT THE UNION

On April 12, 1861, when General Beauregard fired that first shot on Fort Sumter, Northern states suddenly found themselves at war and desperately in need of men and supplies in a hurry.

Lincoln called for 75,000 volunteers, then 200,000 more in July. Blood would be shed to try to save the Union and stop slavery.

Some of the businessmen who would one day be among the most famous names in American enterprise—J. P. Morgan, Cornelius Vanderbilt, Du Pont, Armour, Studebaker—stepped forward to sell supplies to the government in this time of great patriotic need, and *many of them cheated the government blind.* They profiteered with fervor. "The most important of the nineteenth-century American capitalists acquired their first great fortunes during the war," according to *The War Profiteers* by Richard Kaufman.

Stated *Harper's Monthly* in July 1864: "For sugar, [the government] often got sand; for coffee, rye; for leather, something no better than brown paper; for sound horses and mules, spavined beasts and dying donkeys."

About 350,000 Union soldiers died in the war, and it's estimated that more than half died from disease. Some of these men wore shoes with no soles, were wrapped in transparently thin blankets, slept in disintegrating tents, and fired weapons that blew up in their hands—often due to the greed of the likes of America's great capitalists.

JOHN PIERPONT MORGAN

J. P. Morgan (1837–1913) financed an arms sale in which the U.S. Army bought back thousands of rifles that its *own* in-

Ruthless financier, J. P. Morgan (1837–1913), was photographed by Edward Steichen around the turn of the century. "Meeting his black eyes," later commented Steichen, "was like confronting the headlights of an express train bearing down on you."

spectors had already condemned as use-less. Morgan, then twenty-three years old and starting out in business, bankrolled a scheme whereby one Arthur Eastman bought 5,000 dangerous obsolete carbines for $3.50 each from the U.S. Army arsenal at Governor's Island, New York, in May 1861. (In tests, these guns blew thumbs off.)

Eastman had a partner named Simon Stevens who contacted General John Frémont, commander out west, and offered him 5,000 "new" guns at $22 each. The fiasco at Bull Run in July had put the North in a military panic. Frémont wired to ship them immediately. It was August.

Morgan was the silent partner behind it all; he paid for the guns with his own check. After 2,500 were shipped, the whole thing exploded. Did Morgan back down in embarrassment, caught defrauding the country? No. He sued for full payment, and eventually his side won. The Court of Claims ruled a contract was a contract. In a time of war, they had sold *dangerous* $3.50 guns for $22 each from one branch of the U.S. Army to another.

Since the need for guns was so great, some of the worst price gouging and dumping occurred in this product category.

Colt charged the government $25 for a revolver that normally retailed for $14.50, and received an order for 31,000 of them, according to Fred Shannon in *The Organization and Administration of the Union Army.* Remington, nonplussed, offered an equivalent handgun for $15 each but was only able to secure a contract for 5,000 guns.

CORNELIUS VANDERBILT

Patriotic "Commodore" Vanderbilt trafficked in ships. Already a wealthy man from his steamship line, Vanderbilt cashed in during the war by having *his* agent take 5 to 10 percent kickbacks on vastly overpriced shipping contracts that he personally awarded. Scallywags lined up to unload their half-wrecked tubs on the government for troop transport.

Vanderbilt bought the decrepit *Niagara* for $10,000, according to government testimony. Indignant soldiers gouged out a piece of thoroughly rotted timber from one of the vessel's beams and sent it as evidence to Congress.

Congressional testimony showed that Vanderbilt repeatedly overpaid for leasing ships. The "Commodore" paid $900 a day when he chartered the steamer *Eastern Queen* for troop transport, while the government in a prior use of the boat had paid $500 a day. Testified Ambrose Snow, a reputable shipping merchant: "When we got to Commodore Vanderbilt we were referred to Mr. Southard; when we went to Mr. Southard, we were told we would have to pay him a commission of five per cent."

Vanderbilt wasn't arrested for inflating prices and taking kickbacks. When Congress passed a resolution stating that contractors handling ship leasing were "guilty of negligence," Vanderbilt's name was removed at the last minute.

"Many a millionaire," states Civil War historian Shannon, "who later sought so frantically to achieve respectability through alliance with foreign nobility might well have inscribed 'Shoddy' as the legend on his costly coat of arms."

Shannon estimates that entrepreneurs made the then ungodly sum of half a billion dollars in wartime profits, trafficking with the government. We will never know whether adequate and timely supplies would have ended the war earlier.

"How anybody but fiends," shrieked the *New York Tribune* in May 1861, "can for lucre, willfully palm off upon the government sleazy and rotten blankets and rusty weapons and putrid pork . . . passes comprehension." ✺

DRAFT DODGING FOR PROFIT

One of the oddest ways in which wily businessmen profited during the Civil War was by acting as a "substitute broker." The draft law allowed that anyone could hire a substitute to fill their place in the Union army; wealthy men paid poor men as much as $2,000 to serve in their stead, at a time when a laborer's yearly wage was $300.

Enter a new class of speculator-middleman. Substitute brokers would pay men a "bounty" up front to sign a contract to agree to serve in the army and then sell that commitment for a fat profit to anyone wishing to avoid service. Congress, hoping to end the practice and to raise some money for the war effort, passed a law allowing any man to pay $300 *directly* to the government to avoid the draft. (Of the first draft of 292,441 names, 52,288 paid the money to skip out.)

Ironically, substitute brokers still raked in profits. Because of the new buy-out option, local governments now had an even harder time finding enough men to fill their federal enlistment quotas and so they still had to turn to the brokers. "Men in all parts of the United States have been compelled to see their sons bought and sold in this way," complained Rep. James A. Garfield (R-Ohio), who would later become president. The Union army suffered the extremely high tally of 268,000 desertions during the war, as quite a few poor men cashed in by collecting enlistment "bounties" several times under several names. Adam Worth, one of the most notorious criminals of the 19th century, got his first bankroll this way. ✺

CHILD LABOR: RAMPANT IN THE UNITED STATES BEFORE WORLD WAR II

The reasons proudly cited for America's current financial success are often a strong work ethic, great salesmanship, and independent entrepreneurialism. Another is routinely left out.

Photographer Lewis Hines traveled around, chronicling child labor all across the United States. In 1910, Hines took this shot and noted: "Rosy, an eight-year-old oyster shucker, works steady all day *from 3 A.M. to 5 P.M.* in Dunbar Cannery [in Louisiana]." He added: "The baby will shuck as soon as she can handle the knife."

Prior to 1940, the United States had a long tradition of keeping labor costs down by using child labor, especially in puritanical New England. While abolitionists thundered against slavery, twelve-year-old children were working ten-hour shifts in the mills of Massachusetts. And after the Civil War, the slave labor force in the South was predominantly replaced by a child labor force. "Just as the shadow of Negro slavery had hung over the fields of the Old South," states one historian, "so the shadow of child slavery hung over the cotton mills of the New South."

The search for cheap labor has pushed some American companies in the 1980s and 1990s to employ underage labor overseas, but what is rarely noted is that America has a century-and-a-half tradition of employing children, starting with America's first cotton-spinning factory in 1790 in Rhode Island. It was only in 1938 that Franklin Roosevelt signed the first comprehensive child labor law in the United States.

How did child labor start in America, and why was it widely tolerated (and often praised) for three quarters of this country's history?

We have to travel back to the Elizabethan Poor Laws over in England. The Poor Law of 1601, for instance, authorized the involuntary "binding out" of needy children—and praised the practice as a way to banish idleness and to reduce the burden on the state.

Imagine, if employers today could go to foster homes, pick out dozens of kids, and work them for no wages with no work rules, while receiving a sum from the government to pay for the kids' upkeep?

"This allegedly benevolent gesture," states Walter Trattner in *Crusade for the Children*, "usually served the interest not of the child but of the master, who looked upon his charge as a cheap source of labor and compelled him [or her] to work long, arduous hours, often at menial tasks only to cast him loose at the end of his tenure into a strange competitive world without money or a trade."

The first colonists brought these attitudes over with them. Documents have survived of settlers in Virginia in the early 1600s acknowledging receipt of a boatload of 100 children ("save such as died on the way") who would be put to work, and requesting another hundred to be sent the following spring. A letter from 1627 mentions "there are many ships going to Virginia and with them fourteen or fifteen hundred children." Another surviving missive requests that the City of London send over "one hundred friendless boys and girls."

As blatantly exploitive and self-serving as those actions may seem today, back then this was considered *charity*, especially in devout New England.

"Satan finds some mischief still for idle hands to do," warned the ministers. "It is well for a man that he bear the yoke in his youth."

While apologists claim that these youngsters, these apprentices would learn a trade, that wasn't always the case. One colonial statute states the children must "gladly obey" the master's "lawful commands" for "the person who takes a child off the town shall have him to be his servant until he comes of age."

In Massachusetts and Connecticut, the authorities sometimes forcibly removed children from poor families and relocated them. An early Poor Law in Connecticut stated that "any poor children who live idly or are exposed to want or distress" are to be bound out (i.e., "apprenticed"), the males till age twenty-one, the females till age eighteen or marriage.

With the founding of the United States, little changed for junior. Samuel Slater's cotton-spinning factory in the 1790s was depicted as an efficient labor model for the entire country, and Slater (1768–1835), regarded as the "founder of the American cotton industry," employed children seven to twelve years old. He openly preferred young quick hands to work for him.

As the industrial age took hold, employers realized with glee that children (receiving lower wages) could handle the machinery as well as adults. Throughout, employers justified themselves, praising work "as a cure for juvenile delinquency and female promiscuity."

"An editorial in the *Manufacturers' and Farmers' Journal* in 1820 predicted that the certainty of finding employment for all their healthy children seven years of age and older would lead parents to choose New England rather than the newer Western states as a place of residence. By that year, according to the *Digest of Manu-*

factures, children comprised 43 per cent of the labor force in the textile mills of Massachusetts, 47 per cent in Connecticut and 55 per cent in Rhode Island."

Corporal punishment was standard, everything from a poke to wake a sleeping kid to the "whipping rooms" of the cotton mills. One overseer recalled seeing whips in Rhode Island that were "strips of leather 14 inches long and four inches wide and three-eighths of an inch thick, sometimes with tacks inserted." A Senate investigation of 1837, for instance, found whipping widespread in Pennsylvania factories.

In fairness to the United States, child labor exploitation here paled compared to England. (Charles Dickens satirized conditions there in his description of "Coketown" in *Hard Times*.) Testimony at a hearing in England (1842) about children employed in coal mines to drag coal through eighteen-inch-high shafts: "Chained, belted, harnessed like dogs in a go-cart, black, saturated with sweat, and more than half naked—crawling upon their hands and feet, dragging their heavy loads behind them, [the children] present an appearance indescribably disgusting and unnatural."

A visiting slave owner observed a British cotton mill. "I have always thought myself disgraced by being the owner of black slaves, but we never . . . thought it was possible for any human being to be so cruel as to require a child of nine years old to work twelve and a half hours a day; and that you acknowledge is your regular practice."

This 1920s Robert Minor cartoon shows a businessman who knows how to keep his labor costs down.

Grotesque conditions inspired Sarah Cleghorn's four-line poem:

> The golf links lie so near the mill
> That almost every day
> The laboring children can look out
> And see the men at play.

Outrage mounted in Britain as it did in the United States, where New England led the way with the first sprinkling of laws defending children. Ironically those laws detailing what's forbidden, reveal much more about the prevailing practices. In 1842, Connecticut limited the work day to *twelve* hours for children under *fourteen*. In 1848, Pennsylvania ruled that children under *twelve* were forbidden to work in cotton, woolen, or silk mills. In 1866, Massachusetts passed a similar law, but set the minimum age at *ten* years old.

All the while before the Civil War in the South, young black slave children worked hard while young white children rarely did. Ironically, after the war that condition was often reversed.

One bulwark of the Southern revival after the war was the cotton mill, and almost all mill workers were white. One turn-of-the-century overseer, no doubt exaggerating, testified that "Negro children attend school while white children work in the mill." The South, very resentful of federal interference, fought hard against child labor laws. Three federal laws were overturned by Southern courts on their way to the Supreme Court.

But, again in fairness, child labor was widespread across the country; cotton mill owners were simply less apologetic. A strong force fighting child labor in the U.S. were the labor unions, who recognized the competition: Children working earned less and took jobs away from grown-ups.

In 1896 in New York, a fourteen-year-old named Fannie Harris testified she worked sixty hours a week in a garment sweatshop. She was illiterate, and her mother lived off her wages.

The National Child Labor Committee lobbied hard to spotlight what it called "Our National Disgrace"; for its poster child in 1906, the committee showed an eight-year-old girl who worked the twelve-hour night shift in a Georgia cotton mill.

In 1938, Franklin Delano Roosevelt signed the Fair Labor Standards Act, which set sixteen as the minimum employee age during school hours for companies who ship their products across state lines. The age limit of eighteen was set for dangerous occupations, while children under fourteen could work after school hours outside of mining and manufacturing.

Nowadays relatively few children work full-time in the United States, except perhaps some children of Central American migrant farmworkers or some kids helping their parents in big city sweatshops. Nowadays, American companies seeking the cheapest labor (which often is child labor) find it in places like India, China, and Singapore.

The Anti-Slavery Association, based in Melbourne, Australia, estimates (circa 1995) that between 104 million and 146 million children work worldwide, making everything from car parts to brass candlesticks. Documentary filmmaker Peter Lee-Wright personally witnessed child labor in India, Bangladesh, Malaysia, Brazil, Thailand, Portugal, Turkey, Philippines, and Mexico.

Lee-Wright, for instance, posing as an export-import man, observed eight-year-old Mustafa working in the 113° heat of a brass factory in Moradabad, India, churning out candlesticks. This was the boy's second year working full-time in the factory; he has never been to school.

CHIM-CHIM-CHIMNEY: ROASTED ENGLISH BOYS

In Disney's *Mary Poppins*, Dick Van Dyke leads a delighted troop of chimney sweeps (including little Jane and Michael) through a joyous, exuberant rooftop dance. Not exactly . . . the reality of that occupation in Victorian England was far from joyous.

Boy chimney sweeps—often sold by their parents to master sweeps (perhaps not all like Dick Van Dyke)—started as young as age five and were washed up by age sixteen. Small boys were better suited to climb inside narrow soot-filled chimneys where they had to learn to perch themselves as they scrubbed the walls.

A Nottingham master sweep testified in 1864: "No one knows the cruelty a boy must undergo in learning. The flesh must be hardened. This must be done by rubbing it, chiefly on the elbows and knees, with the strongest brine close by a hot fire. You must stand over them with a cane, or coax them by a promise of a halfpenny if they stand a few more rubs. At first they will come back from their work streaming with blood, and the knees looking as if the caps had been pulled off. Then they must be rubbed with brine again."

One eight-year-old forced into the chimney over a just extinguished brewery stove became stuck and was roasted to death in 1813. Laws were passed but none had any real impact till the Chimney Sweepers Act of 1875.

Chim-chim-chimney, chim-chim-chimney, chim-chim-chirree. ✺

BITTER BUSINESS FEUDS

EDISON VS. WESTINGHOUSE OVER THE FIRST ELECTRIC CHAIR

In one of the more bizarre marketing feuds in business history, Thomas Edison helped develop the electric chair to sabotage the business of an archrival. He secretly pushed New York State to use that *other* company's generator, hoping that it would make that *other* company's electrical products seem very dangerous. While some experts suggested this new lethal process be called "electrocide" or "dynamort," Edison pushed for "the prisoner was Westinghoused."

Edison (1847–1931)—a genius with more than one thousand patents—is justly enshrined for his role in inventing the electric light, the phonograph, and motion pictures, but his share in creating the electric chair is routinely overlooked by textbooks and encyclopedias.

In the 1880s, electric lighting came to the cities of America for the first time, and Edison, Westinghouse, and several other companies engaged in a fierce battle to wire the streets, build the power plants, and sell the power and bulbs. At stake were millions in profits and these future technocrats were literally carving up the country.

Edison had the unquestioned head

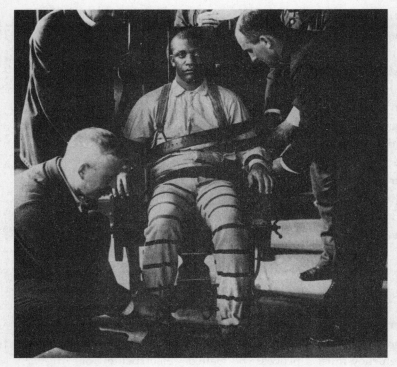

An unidentified prisoner is strapped into the electric chair at Sing Sing prison in New York State, c. 1910.

safer and could eventually be made more cost-efficient. "Just as certain as death," Edison wrote to one of his top execs, "Westinghouse will kill a customer within six months after he puts in a system of any size."

The feud between the two had mushroomed beyond mere business. George Westinghouse had parlayed his invention of a railroad air brake into a burgeoning techno empire. But it wasn't until Westinghouse started competing directly with Edison by marketing a railroad steam engine that the Wizard of Menlo Park took notice. "Tell Westinghouse to stick to air brakes," Edison commented acidly. "He knows about them. He don't know anything about engines." Westinghouse, a year older than Edison, was furious.

Edison grew even more irate when Westinghouse's very aggressive salesmen started combing the country to sell AC electric light systems; Edison told a colleague that the "man has gone crazy" and "is flying a kite that will land him in the mud."

While electricity was clearly the hot new energy source, the safety issue kept looming larger as dozens of well-publicized accidental shock deaths had occurred, mostly to workmen. And alert representatives of the law had taken notice of

start, wiring a square mile of downtown New York financial district in 1882, but by the end of the decade, his dominance was faltering.

Edison used low-power direct current (DC) while his rivals—especially that upstart George Westinghouse (1846–1914) —were using high-power alternating current (AC) that could travel farther from the generator over less copper wire. By 1889, AC was starting to crush DC. Edison's own employees begged for permission to use AC, but Edison, quite stubborn when it came to abandoning his *own* invention, adamantly refused.

He firmly—and apparently sincerely— believed that his low-power system was

the dark power. As far back as 1878, the Ohio State Penitentiary had experimented with disciplining prisoners by sitting them naked in three inches of water and giving them a jolt.

In 1887, the New York State Legislature—searching for a more humane means of execution than hanging—appointed a three-member study panel including one Dr. A. P. Southwick, who wrote to Edison for advice. At first, Edison refused to help, stating he would lobby against capital punishment.

Then—coincidentally as Westinghouse's business prospered—Edison suggested that alternating current in a dose of 1,000 volts would do the trick. The legislature committee chairman, Elbridge T. Gerry, called Edison an "oracle" and credited him with swaying the committee.

The New York State Legislature passed the law, but didn't specify AC or DC, or which company's machine to use. (Americans were nervous enough about bringing electricity into the home; no company wanted their generators to be used to kill people.)

Enter Harold P. Brown, a self-taught electrical consultant, who wrote a letter to the *New York Evening Post*, pushing AC as much more lethal. When Brown found himself flooded with vicious criticism by Westinghouse execs, he sought out Edison for permission to use Edison's state-of-the-art laboratory in Orange, New Jersey, for research. Edison not only agreed but provided his chief electrician, A. E. Kennelly, to work closely with Brown.

The two of them decided to stage a demonstration of the comparative lethalness of AC and DC at Columbia University before an invitation-only audience of leading doctors, scientists, and city officials. Brown led out a seventy-six-pound mixed breed Newfoundland dog. Reported the *New York World:*

> Three hundred volts of *direct current* made the dog jump and emit a bark as though struck with an old shoe; 400 volts made it bark three times and jerk up its feet; 500 made him howl with pain and struggle to get free, coming so near succeeding as to scare several spectators out of the room; 700 volts caused him to struggle out of his halter, and 1,000 volts to turn over as though dying, but he rallied when released.
>
> The *alternating current* was then applied and the dog gave a series of pitiful moans, underwent a number of convulsions and died.

The Society for the Prevention of Cruelty to Animals (SPCA) then jumped in and stopped the proceedings. "The only place where alternating current ought to be used," Brown told the *New York Times*, "is the dog pound, the slaughter house and the State prison."

Harold Brown—working with the Medico-Legal Society of New York—became the lead engineering expert working for State of New York. (Brown in the course of his research killed more than fifty stray

Thomas Edison sits in a nonelectric chair at his failing iron ore plant in New Jersey in 1895.

dogs and cats at the Edison lab in Orange.) His critics claimed, though, that his July demonstration of killing a seventy-six-pound dog proved nothing about a heavier human being.

On December 5, 1888, with Edison present, Brown and Kennelly made another demonstration before New York State officials and newspapermen. At the Edison lab in Orange, Brown, using AC current, electrocuted a 124-pound and a 145-pound calf and, to settle the weight issue, zapped and killed a horse weighing 1,230 pounds using 700 volts of alternating current. Commented the *New York Times:* "The experiments prove the alternating current to be the most deadly force known to science, and less than half the pressure [voltage] used in this city for electrical lighting by this system is sufficient to cause instant death. After January 1, the alternating current will undoubtedly drive the hangman out of business in this State."

Westinghouse fired off a letter to the *Times* in rebuttal. "It is generally understood that Harold P. Brown is conducting these experiments in the interest and pay of the Edison Electric Light Company."

Brown shot back. "Allow me to deny that I am now or ever have been in the employ of Mr. Edison or any of the Edison companies."

This whole marketing feud over the first electrocution might have ended there except someone broke into Brown's office and stole the consultant's letters. Was it a private eye hired by Westinghouse? As good a guess as any. They wound up in the *New York Sun* under the headline: FOR SHAME, BROWN! QUEER WORK FOR A STATE'S EXPERT/PAID BY ONE ELECTRIC COMPANY TO INJURE ANOTHER.

The forty-seven letters spell out the whole sleazy covert operation, involving both Edison and another hidden company. Executives at Edison were then in secret merger negotiations with another powerful electric company, Thomson-Houston of Boston. (The two companies would later merge to form General Electric.) Here are some highlights (or lowlights) of the scheme:

- Edison employees were paying Brown to publish anti-AC pamphlets and telling him where to send them. "My dear Mr. Brown, Here is a list of legislators and officers of the State of Missouri . . ."

- Edison execs told him in what newspapers to write "expert" editorials.

- Edison himself sent a letter of recommendation for Brown to Scranton officials. "I take much pleasure in enclosing a testimonial signed by myself."

- Advice was relayed from Thomas Edison on how to silence critics who claim that human flesh will burn during an "electrocide," making it a "cruel and unusual punishment." Edison suggested that Brown experiment on a corpse immersed in salt water.

- Brown requests $5,000 from Edison.

- Brown receives $1,000 from Thomson-Houston and the promise of $500 more and the offer to buy Westinghouse

generators at far below market cost, which Brown could resell for a profit to the State of New York.

On March 29, 1889, William Kemmler killed his girlfriend, Tillie Ziegler, with a hatchet while in a drunken rage. He was sentenced to die, pegged to become the first prisoner ever executed by electricity.

Kemmler's lawyer appealed, arguing that this experimental method amounted to "cruel and unusual punishment."

A macabre atmosphere pervaded the judicial hearings. Westinghouse expert, T. Carpenter Smith had testified earlier that he had received three shocks of AC of 1,000 volts and not been hurt. Edison then offered to pay Smith $100 to come to the Edison lab and take 100 volts of alternating current. A bystander tossed in another $100, but Smith declined.

The inventor was partially deaf and Kemmler's lawyer had to shout questions at Edison.

"How much of a current do you think it would take to burn a man?" Kemmler's lawyer asked.

"Well," the witness replied meditatively, "if you applied a current of several thousand horse power to a fellow you'd probably burn him up."

"Have a nice little bonfire with him, would you?"

Outraged *New York Times*, August 7, 1890, coverage of the first "electrical execution" in the United States. (Note the outrage wasn't over capital punishment per se but just over the newfangled means of doing the job.)

"Oh, no, just carbonize him," said Edison.

Despite ongoing appeals, Brown was so confident of victory that he desperately (and secretly) wanted to secure a Westinghouse generator for use in the first execution. This would be the *ultimate* bad publicity for Westinghouse. Thomson-Houston execs found a used equipment dealer to front for them in buying three units. Brown still worried about Westinghouse bribing prison officials. "They will cripple [the machine] if the liberal use of money will do it."

Brown wrote out elaborate coded instructions for delivering the "W. plant," completely wrapped in rubber sheets, with a tiny label, traceable to him, not Thomson-Houston, and above all it should be guarded at all times. "These precautions may seem absurd to you, but I can assure you that there is a desperate attempt to have the use of the Westinghouse dynamo [i.e., generator] for this purpose a failure, and if anything happens to that machine, another make of dynamo will have to be used to meet the emergency."

Kemmler's appeal ultimately failed at the U.S. Supreme Court. On August 6, 1890, the first execution would take place. Here's the *New York Times* front page account, beginning as Kemmler enters the death chamber, crowded with twenty-two hand-picked observers.

After he had crossed the threshold, there was for an instant the deadest silence. It was broken by Warden Durston.

"Gentlemen," he said, "this is William Kemmler." And Kemmler bowed.

"Gentlemen," he said, "I wish you all good luck. I believe I am going to a good place, and I am ready to go. I only want to say that a great deal has been said about me that is untrue. I am bad enough. It is cruel to make me out worse."

As he finished this little speech, he bowed again, and was about to sit down in a chair which had been placed beside the death chair. Warden Durston, seeing this, stepped forward and Kemmler, noticing his action, saw that the time had come, and instead of sitting where he had intended, turned and easily dropped into the seat. Still, he did it much as one might after a long walk fall into the arms of an easy chair. He sat with the light from the window streaming full on his face, and immediately in front of him was the semicircle of witnesses. Warden Durston stepped to the chair and at his request Kemmler arose. It was desired to see whether his clothing had been so cut away at the base of the spine as to allow of a clean contact between the electrode and the flesh. It was found that the outer garments had been cut but the lower clothing had not been so. Durston took out a pocket knife and cut two small triangular pieces out of the shirt.

Then Kemmler easily settled back into the chair again. As he did so Durston started to get the rear piece in position. A murmur of surprise passed among the witnesses when Kemmler turned calmly to the Warden and in such tones as one might speak to a barber who was shaving him, said calmly: "Now take your time and do it all right, Warden. There is no rush. I don't want to take any chance on this thing, you know."

"All right, William," answered Durston and then began to adjust the headpiece. It looked horrible with its leather bands crossing the doomed man's forehead and chin and partially concealing his features. When the job was finished, Durston stepped back. Kemmler shook his head as one might when trying on a new hat and then just as coolly as before said: "Warden just make that a little tighter. We want everything all right, you know."

The Warden did as requested, and then started to fix the straps around the body, arms and legs. There were eleven of them. As each was buckled, Kemmler would put some strain on it so as to see if it was tight enough. All appeared to suit him, and in answer to a question by the Warden, he answered: "All right." Durston then stepped to the door. The last minute had come.

Standing on the threshold he turned and said quietly: "Is all ready?" Nobody spoke. Kemmler merely lifted his eyes and for a moment turned them enough to catch a glimpse of the bright warm sunlight that was streaming through the window of the death chamber.

"Good-bye, William," said Durston, and a click was heard. The "good-bye" was a signal to the men at the lever. The great experiment of electrical execution had been launched. New York State had thrown off forever the barbarities, the inhumanity of hanging its criminals. But had it! Words will not keep pace with what followed. Simultaneously with the click of that lever the body of the man in the chair straightened. Every muscle of it seemed to be drawn to its highest tension. It seemed as though it might have been thrown across the chamber were it not for the straps which held it. There was no movement of the eyes. The body was as rigid as though cast in bronze, save for the index finger of the right hand, which closed up so tightly that the nail penetrated the flesh on the first joint and the blood trickled out on the arm of the chair. Drs. Spitzka and Macdonald stood in front of the chair closely watching the dead or dying man. Besides them was Dr. Daniels holding a stopwatch.

After the first convulsion there was not the slightest movement of Kemmler's body. An ashen pallor had overspread his features. What physicians know as the "death spots" appeared on his skin. Five seconds passed, then ten seconds, fifteen seconds, sixteen and seventeen. It was just 6:43 o'-clock. Dr. Spitzka, shaking his head, said: "He is dead." Warden Durston pressed the signal button and at once the dynamo was stopped. The assembled witnesses who had sat as still as mutes up to this point gave breath to a sigh. The great strain was over. Then the eyes that had momentarily been turned from Kemmler's body returned to it and gazed with horror at what they saw. The men rose from their chairs impulsively and groaned at the agony they felt. "Great God! he is alive!" some one said. "Turn on the current!" said another. "See he breathes," said a third. "For God's sake kill him and have it over," said a representative of one of the press associations, and then, unable to bear the strain, he fell on the floor in a dead faint. District Attorney Quimby groaned audibly and rushed from the room.

Drs. Spitkza and Macdonald stepped forward to the chair. Warden Durston, who had started to loosen the electrode on the head, raised it slightly then hastily started to screw it back into place. Kemmler's body had become limp and settled down in the chair. His chest was raising and falling and there was a heavy breathing that was perceptible to all. Kemmler was, of course, entirely unconscious. Drs. Spitzka and Macdonald kept their wits about them. Hastily, they examined the man, not touching him, however. Turning to Warden Durston, who had just finished getting the head electrode back in place, Dr. Spitzka said: "Have the current turned on again, quick—no delay." Durston sprang to the door, and in an instant had sounded the two bells, which informed the man at the lever that the current must be turned on.

Again came that click as before, and again the body of the unconcious wretch in the chair became as rigid as one of bronze. It was awful and the witnesses were so horrified by the ghastly sight that they could not take their eyes off it. The dynamo did not seem to run smoothly. The current could be heard sharply snapping. Blood began to appear on the face of the wretch in the chair. It stood on the face like sweat.

The capillary or small blood vessels under the skin were being ruptured. But there was worse than that. An awful odor began to permeate the death chamber, and then, as though to cap the climax of this frightful sight, it was seen that the hair under and around the electrode on the head and the flesh under and around the electrode at the base of the spine was singeing. The stench was unbearable."

Kemmler was finally dead this time. The *Times* said the execution "was so terrible that words fail to convey the idea." But the paper added: "As might have been expected, such of the so-called humanitarians who witnessed Kemmler's fearful death still insist that their hobby will be a success under proper conditions."

Edison—who wasn't present but read an account in the *New York Evening Sun*—defended the lethalness of the Westinghouse AC equipment. "As I testified . . . the better way is to place the hands in jars of water in which there is a little potash to eliminate all grease from the hands, and let the current be turned on there." He contended that the head with thick skull, hair, and relatively little blood was a poor conductor.

Westinghouse, not surprisingly, was thrilled at the bungled execution and predicted there would be no more. "They could have done better with an axe," he commented from Pittsburgh.

Of Harold Brown, the *New York Times* would later note: "His interest in the new law was chiefly a financial one." (Brown, it turns out, had skimmed $4,400 buying the Westinghouse generators.)

And despite the bad press, Westinghouse's business thrived, making tens of millions, and by 1895, thanks to Niagara Falls Power Plant, AC had completely won the so-called "Battle of the Currents."

New York State, over loud objections, stayed with lethal electricity, killing more than 100 prisoners over the next fifteen years, inspiring other states to follow suit. The official New York report on Kemmler, though, recommended that for future executions an electrical generator should be custom-made instead of using equipment from any one company.

As for Thomas Edison, you *could* say he was "Westinghous'd." He stubbornly never introduced AC, and in a few years lost control of his own electrical company (when J. P. Morgan helped it become General Electric); Edison then invested all his money in a magnetic iron ore mine that failed.

G.E., on the other hand, embraced AC and profits sizzled. ✤

HEARST BATTLES PULITZER OVER A HEADLESS BODY

Pulitzer is nowadays perhaps the most respected name in American journalism thanks to the prestigious "Pulitzer Prizes for Excellence" given out annually, but back in the 1890s many of the tactics used by Joseph Pulitzer's own newspapers wouldn't have exactly won awards.

Many think tabloid coverage is modern: It's not. The *New York Post's* famous headline from the 1970s, HEADLESS BODY IN TOPLESS BAR, could have easily run back in the 1890s, *if* they had had topless bars.

On a Saturday in late June 1897, a headless, armless, legless torso floated up in the East River. Just two years earlier, William Randolph Hearst (1863–1951) had bobbed up in New York, buying the failing *Journal,* and vowing to blow past Pulitzer's *World* and other papers. (The *New York Times*—a year from Adolph Ochs—was then a twelve-page also-ran near bankruptcy.) By this point, Pulitzer (1847–1911), an eccentric Hungarian-born publisher who often controlled his empire from a yacht, had already forged his reputation by busting monopolies, championing the poor, sending Nellie Bly around the world.

Upstart Hearst took a small office in Pulitzer's *World* building and lured away the *entire* staff of Pulitzer's Sunday edition, including cartoonist Richard Outcault, who drew "The Yellow Kid," a wisecracking street urchin. Pulitzer fired back by having another artist continue the *World's* "Yellow Kid." The city's two "Yellow Kids" now dueled on billboards and in ad slogans; hence "yellow journalism." Church groups rallied against *both* papers for sensationalism.

So when the headless body floated up in 1897, Pulitzer's *New York World* and Hearst's *New York Evening Journal* fought a vicious tug-of-war over coverage of this grisly crime. Let's follow the front pages of the two papers, pitting supposed Saint Pulitzer against acknowledged rogue, Hearst. (The *New York Post* would be proud.)

Pulitzer's NY *World:*
Sunday, June 27, 1897:
BOY'S GHASTLY FIND
Part of a Man's Headless Body Floats
Down the East River
. . . The Lad Swims Out for it Thinking
It May Contain a Rich Prize . . .

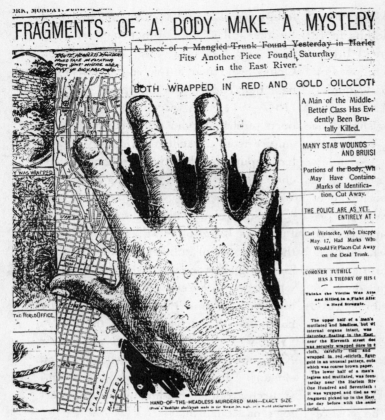

FRAGMENTS OF A BODY MAKE A MYSTERY

A Piece of a Mangled Trunk Found Yesterday in Harlem Fits Another Piece Found Saturday in the East River.

BOTH WRAPPED IN RED AND GOLD OILCLOTH

A Man of the Middle- Better Class Has Evidently Been Brutally Killed.

MANY STAB WOUNDS AND BRUISE

Portions of the Body, Wh May Have Contained Marks of Identification, Cut Away.

THE POLICE ARE AS YET ENTIRELY AT S

Carl Weinecke, Who Disappe May 17, Had Marks Who Would Fit Places Cut Away on the Dead Trunk.

CORONER TUTHILL HAS A THEORY OF HIS (

Thinks the Victim Was Atte and Killed in a Fight Afte a Hard Struggle.

HAND OF THE HEADLESS MURDERED MAN—EXACT SIZE

Joseph Pulitzer's *New York World* devoted about a quarter of its front page (June 28, 1897) to showing an "exact-size" drawing of a severed hand, based on a "flashlight photograph made in the morgue yesternight by a *World* photographer."

The finding of the upper portion of the headless trunk of a man in the East River furnishes a mystery that will not be easily solved . . .

Hearst's *New York Evening Journal:*
Monday, June 28, 1897:
$1,000 REWARD
The New York Journal *Will Pay $1,000 for Information or Clews, Theories or Suggestions Which Will Solve the Unique*

Murder Mystery of the East River.

[The paper specifies the prize can be split ten ways which transforms half the city into amateur Sherlocks.]

Pulitzer's *New York World:*
Monday, June 28, 1897:
HAND OF THE HEADLESS MURDERED MAN

New York Evening Journal:
Tuesday, June 29, 1897:
THE REAL CLEW TO THE MURDER MYSTERY

[Hearst filled *his* front page with a *colored* drawing of the wrapping paper holding the body parts.]

Fac-Simile in Colors of the Oilcloth Which Will Aid in Getting the $1,000 REWARD.

[The *Journal* also ran a cartoon, with the first panel showing a man hack-sawing a naked body.]

"If you have a friend who annoys you, butcher him and carve him neatly into sections. You need not fear any interference from our police because . . ."

[The second panel shows a beefy copper hauling off a prostitute.]

"All the brave ones are too busy arresting naughty Tenderloin ladies."

New York World: Tuesday, June 29, 1897:
WORLD MEN FIND A CLUE

Investigation yesterday by dozens of detectives, by a horde of reward-seekers and by scores of reporters, served to emphasize the ghastly butchery of the thing. That was all.

The most interesting discovery of the day was made by reporters for the *World.* It was that a wagon, in which were two men and which contained two packages, crossed to New York on a ferry from Greenpoint, L.I., on Saturday afternoon a short time before the finding of the headless shoulders in the East River.

New York Evening Journal: Wednesday, June 30, 1897:
MURDER MYSTERY SOLVED BY THE JOURNAL
MRS. NACK, MURDERESS!
She Bought the Oilcloth Found Around the Body of Her Mangled Lover, William Guldensuppe, the Turkish Bath Rubber . . . Storekeeper Found by Evening Journal *Reporters and Taken to Police Headquarters Where She Tells Her Story. Mrs. Nack Is at Once Ordered Under Arrest by the Authorities . . .*

New York World, Wednesday, June 30, 1897:

[Pulitzer refuses to surrender to Hearst.]

LIGHT ON THE MURDER MYSTERY
From College Point Comes a Plausible Identification of the Headless and Dismembered Body of the Man in the Morgue.

VICTIM THOUGHT TO BE THEODORE CYKLAM
Detective Bureau Sends Out a General Order to Search for an Insane Butcher.

Hearst's *New York Evening Journal,* Thursday, July 1, 1897:

MRS. NACK WILL BE FORMALLY CHARGED WITH MURDERING GULDENSUPPE

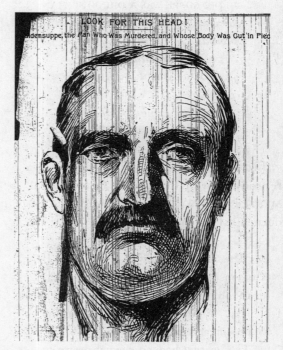

William Randolph Hearst's *New York Evening Journal* on June 30, 1897, invited readers to look for the murdered man's head.

Bruises Found on Her Body and She Shows
Signs of Breaking Down — Little Amy Miller
Slept with Her on Saturday Night. She
Feared to be Alone.

New York World,
Thursday, July 1, 1897:

[Pulitzer still refuses to surrender.]

THE MURDER MYSTERY IS A MYSTERY
STILL
The Identification of the Victim as William
Guldensuppe Seemed to Settle It, but Strange
Discrepancies Have Appeared in the Evidence.

. . . GULDENSUPPE WAS A DRINKING MAN
. . . *Doctors Say There Was No Sign Of*
Alcoholism In The Murdered Man's
Stomach.
POLICE LOSING FAITH.

New York Evening Journal,
Friday, July 2, 1897:

[To rub in its victory, the *Journal* ran a
reproduction of the *World*'s headline THE
MYSTERY IS A MYSTERY STILL and then underneath:]

. . . The [N.Y.] *World* is desperate. If
Guldensuppe is dead, the *World* feels it is
dead too . . .
The *World* tried to intimidate the
State's most important witness . . .
The *Journal* had no special desire to
obtain news which the *World* had not —
no wish to "beat" the *World* . . ."

New York World,
Friday, July 2, 1897:

[Pulitzer *still* refuses to surrender.]

THE IDENTIFICATION UPSET
. . . *The Chiropodist of the Murray Hill*
Bath Declares the Legs Not Those of
Guldensuppe.

. . . The chiropodist carefully examined
the toes.
Then, without hesitation, he said:
"This is not the man."
This statement was directly reported
to a representative of the *World* by the
Morgue attendant.
After being threatened by a second
Journal reporter the attendant refused to
talk any further . . .

New York Evening Journal,
Saturday, July 3, 1897:

[The *Journal* identifies an accomplice.]

WORLD-WIDE HUNT FOR MARTIN
THORN

. . . He is a barber by trade. He speaks
with a slight German accent.

Pulitzer's *New York World,*
Saturday, July 3, 1897:

[Pulitzer, though thoroughly beaten by
Hearst, now shifts fields and takes *credit*
for *scooping* the competition.]

The Story of How World *Reporters, Bit by Bit, Unravelled the Skein and Cleared Away the Mystery of the Crime.*

This is the plain story of how two *World* reporters yesterday, in the same surrey in which the murderers of William Guldensuppe rode last Saturday, went over the same route until the trail reached a spot in the dense thicket near Cliffside, N.J. . . . A wild briar bush, simple engine of fate, caught, as the guilty parties hurried away, a handkerchief, a woman's silk handkerchief, and held it fast until the *World* reporters found it. It will fasten the guilt of murder upon the person to whom it belonged . . .

Hearst's *New York Evening Journal,*
Wednesday, July 7, 1897:
THORN HAS CONFESSED TO THE
MURDER
Mrs. Nack, His Confederate, Lured the Bath Rubber to the Woodside House.
Thorn was in Hiding There and Shot Guldensuppe Unawares, Then Dragged Body to Bathtub.
Before he died the Murderer Seized Him and Drew a Razor Across His Throat.
Body Dismembered in the Bathtub, And the Head, Encased in Plaster of Paris, Thrown in River.

[Mrs. Nack got twenty years for helping to kill Guldensuppe, her former lover; barber Martin Thorn, Nack's latest boyfriend, was executed in the electric chair at Sing Sing on August 1, 1898.]

Now that was yellow journalism, as both sides tried to solve the crime and brag about it. In this gutter game, Hearst's upstart *Journal* completely blew out Pulitzer's giant *World*. (And Hearst's new ad campaign for the *Journal* trumpeted: "NEWS THAT *IS* NEWS — The *Journal,* as Usual, ACTS, while the Representatives of Ancient Journalism Sit Idly By and Wait for Something to Turn Up." *Journal* circulation would sky-rocket, passing the *World* and topping a million by the turn of the century. (The *New York Times* was then a paper of a mere 75,000 copies a day.)

On April 10, 1901, Hearst's *Journal* ran an anti–President McKinley editorial that stated: "If bad institutions and bad men can be got rid of only by killing, then the killing must be done." Five months later, President McKinley lay dying from an anarchist's bullet.

Lashed by criticism, Hearst added the word "American" to the name of some of his newspaper holdings. Yellow journalism seemed to ebb, with the more serious *New York Times* starting to set the tone, living up to its slogan "All the News that's Fit to Print."

However, yellow journalism laid the financial foundation for the enormously successful Hearst media empire; it also gave a black eye to the proud history of the Pulitzers. ✎

KELLOGGS BATTLE
IN BATTLE CREEK

Dr. John Harvey Kellogg (1852–1943), the cofounder of the Kelloggs empire, was obsessed with his bowels and with everyone else's. This white-suited icon of Victorian health hoped through diet, natural medication, and enemas to encourage as many as four bowel movements a day.

He manipulated his colon as few men have; he also manipulated his younger brother. When Will Keith (1860–1951) finally started to rebel in his early forties, around the turn of the century, he helped launch America's first modern breakfast cereals and the multinational Kellogg corporation, which now has revenues topping $7 billion a year.

The company's origins are a bit bizarre. Dr. John Harvey Kellogg, health guru to the celebrities of his day, ran the Seventh Day Adventist Sanitarium at Battle Creek, Michigan, a kind of Betty Ford clinic for rejuvenation.

Dr. Kellogg, so high-minded that he could at times be downright unscrupulous, was searching for an alternative to dry breakfast toast or cracker. He knew of the 1860s invention of one fanatical vegetarian hydrotherapist, Dr. James Caleb Jackson, who took twice-baked whole wheat graham dough and crumbled the results into pebble-size clusters, called "Granula."

Health guru Dr. John Harvey Kellogg (1852–1943) in his trademark white suit. His colon therapies, including corn flake enemas, were world famous.

Dr. Kellogg, the friend of presidents and robber barons, mixed wheat flour, cornmeal, and oatmeal, baked it and crumbled it. He called his creation . . . Granula.

Dr. Jackson sued, and won a judgment in 1881. Dr. Kellogg changed the product name to "Granola," and by the end of the decade was selling two tons a week.

Now, Dr. Kellogg wanted to discover an even better breakfast product; he claimed to have had a dream. When he was woken suddenly, he rushed to the kitchen, boiled some wheat, ran it through a wringer for making thin dough. "I scraped it off with a knife and baked it in the oven," he later recalled. "That was the first of the modern breakfast foods." Dr. Kellogg called these first flakes, "Granose."

Younger brother Will Keith, a bald-headed accountant who kept the "San" empire running, recalled it a bit differently. He recalled that Dr. Kellogg ordered him to come up with an alternative to that shredded wheat being made in Denver. Will, the doctor's wife, an adopted child, and several others spent days running boiled wheat through rollers and scraping off chunks and baking them. The results were like little wheat-flavored rabbit turds.

One night, the disheartened crew left a mess of boiled wheat soaking in water overnight. The following morn, when they passed the water-logged wheat through the rollers, they discovered that the moldy

When accountant Will Keith Kellogg split with his doctor brother, he was eager to change one particular brand name. This 1907 ad marks one of the last times that corn flakes bore the unappetizing name, "Sanitas."

grain formed "perfect individual flakes, crisp when baked," according to one account. The wheat flake had arrived.

The brothers started feuding more and more, especially once they developed a *corn* flake. The idealistic doctor, whose enterprises were all tied up in the nonprofit Seventh Day Adventist Sanitarium, wanted to call the cereal "Sanitas." Will Keith hated the idea, thought it sounded like a disinfectant. When the good doctor was off in Europe on a fact-finding mission, Will Keith added *sugar* to the corn flakes. Could a fraternal split be far off?

On February 19, 1906, Will Keith incorporated the Battle Creek Toasted Corn Flake Company. He marketed the cereal with the phrase on the box: "None Genuine Without This Signature, W. K. Kellogg," and the following year changed the name to "Kellogg's Toasted Corn Flakes." And most people at first probably thought they were buying the work of the famous doctor of Battle Creek, not the bald-headed accountant. Dr. Kellogg was furious.

Confusion over which Kellogg was which bubbled over into the courts in a battle that lasted for more than a decade. Newspapermen had a ball, dubbing it the "Battle of the Brans." By World War I, Will Keith controlled a growing corporate empire, while the doctor's "San" was struggling. Will claimed that his older brother was pirating the company's $2 million-a-year ad budget, especially by using near identical boxes and by marketing "Kellogg's Sterilized Bran."

He sued to force Dr. Kellogg to stop using the family name, and finally in 1921, he won total victory. Dr. Kellogg could sign his own checks and that was about it. From then until the doctor's death two decades later, the two men rarely spoke.

CHAPTER TWO: BLOOD ON KELLOGG'S CORN POPS

Will Keith Kellogg built a corporate empire, and he very much hoped to find a successor within the family. When it didn't work out with his own children, he focused on John L. Kellogg, Jr., his grandson. Will Keith adored his grandson, followed his Cub Scout career, and from as early as the age of fourteen, groomed him to take over the company. He once noted that John Jr. had "a business instinct as strong as any I have known."

Following graduation from the Ferris Institute, John Jr.—nervous, high-strung, intelligent—was made a vice president, attending board meetings and overseeing many important projects. However, after a few frustrating years at headquarters where John Jr. had trouble following through on his ideas, grandfather demoted him to cereal salesman, on the road in Wisconsin.

John Jr. eventually talked his way back to Battle Creek, where he worked in the company lab on a project to puff corn, just as Kellogg's had already puffed rice to create popular Rice Krispies.

When the research work started to show promise, John Jr. tried to sell that corn-puffing process to his grandfather, who deeply resented the young man trying to hawk something to him that was developed in a company lab on company time.

John Jr. quit in a rage, started his own company, Nu-Korn, to try to market cheese-covered corn puffs. His business faltered the following year and he then tried to sell the puffing process to archrival General Mills in 1937.

In yet another legal round for the Kelloggs, grandpa sued grandson, who was then twenty-six years old and newly married, with his wife expecting their first child. During the litigation, John Jr.—squeezed by mounting bills—committed suicide by "swallowing a shot gun," as a former company exec put it.

Whatever his motives or his guilt, Will Keith Kellogg at his death in 1951 left almost all his money to the nonprofit Kellogg Foundation, which helps children worldwide. This foundation has doled out $1.5 *billion* since 1930, and today controls 35 percent of Kellogg's $7 billion in company stock.

Soon after Will Keith's death, the company finally introduced Kellogg's Corn Pops.

SINGER SEWN UP IN COURT

American Elias Howe of Boston secured a patent for his sewing machine on September 10, 1846. As with many inventors, he promptly went broke trying to convince anyone to buy his new invention. Howe—desperate for work—sailed off to England to develop the "Iron Seamstress" for a British corsetmaker; when he returned, he discovered half a dozen companies making similar sewing machines. Most of them agreed to fork over royalties to Howe; however, I. M. Singer & Company refused.

It's true that machinist Isaac Singer vastly improved Howe's clunky device, which often jammed and required repeated repositioning of cloth, etc. but nonetheless Singer used the same lock stitch as Howe (i.e., one thread looped over a second thread) and the same eye-pointed needle patented by Howe.

In 1851, Howe came to the machine shop of Singer—a P. T. Barnum type—and demanded $2,000. Singer threatened to throw him down the stairs. The next

year, Howe demanded $25,000. "Howe is a perfect humbug," said Edward Clark, Singer's partner. "He knows he never invented anything of value."

The case wound up in court and Singer tried to prove that Howe hadn't invented the sewing machine; that one Walter Hunt—who *had* invented the safety pin—had built it a few years prior. The court—despite examining Hunt's rusty prototype—nixed the theory.

Howe won, and how. He received $15,000 up front from Singer, plus a royalty per machine. A short stitch later, Howe was receiving $4,000 a week, and headed for millionaire status. ✺

HEARD ON THE STREET AND LEFT ON THE TABLE

During harsh financial battles between titans at the turn of the century, financier J. P. Morgan decided the quickest way to head off any moves by steel magnate Andrew Carnegie was simply to buy him out. Morgan personally approached Carnegie in 1901 and brusquely asked him what he'd take for his entire enterprise. Carnegie suggested the then preposterous sum of $300 million (*$200 million* more than he had recently agreed to sell it to his own partner, Henry Frick). Morgan instantly agreed.

At first it looked like Carnegie had snookered Morgan; Carnegie—who had a *touch* of genuine religion—traveled around the country building libraries and schools, preaching it a sin to die wealthy. However, over time it became clear that, thanks to the opportunities to manipulate stock offerings of the monopoly, U.S. Steel, Morgan had gotten the far better deal.

The *Wall Street Journal* of August 3, 1909, reported: "Many months later Carnegie and Morgan were on the same Atlantic liner bound for recreation in foreign lands. Coming down late to their morning coffee, there was a few minutes for reminiscence between them.

" 'Do you know, Mr Morgan,' said Carnegie. 'I have been thinking it over, and I find I made a mistake. I should have asked you another hundred million for those Carnegie properties.'

" 'If you had, I should have paid it,' responded Morgan in his frank unfeeling truthfulness.

And Carnegie, so the story goes, was so soured in his soul that he could take no more toast and marmalade." ✺

UP AND DOWN ON BROADWAY

"In 1913 when New York performers tried to organize the Actor's Equity Association," reports Peter Hay in his *Book of Business Anecdotes*, "they found a formidable opponent in George M. Cohan, the greatest star and producer on Broadway. The original Yankee Doodle Dandy threatened to shut out the union from his productions, and, to make his opposition perfectly clear, he purchased in the New York papers large ads with the following notice: 'I'd sooner lose every dollar I have and make my living as an elevator operator than do business with Actor's Equity.'

"The union took his bluff seriously because the next day they hung out a sign: 'Wanted—elevator operator. George M. Cohan preferred.'" 🌀

BUSINESS ETHICS: AN OXYMORON?

PIRACY AS ECONOMIC TERRORISM

While the popular image of buccaneers is wooden-legged, eye-patched rascals, the ultimate antiauthority free agents roving the seas, plundering ships, raping women, brawling, the reality is much worse. They did all that *and* worked for the government.

At least some of them did. Of course, we can't generalize 4,000 years of piratical history, but a pattern does emerge. Prior to the Declaration of Paris of 1856, it was standard operating procedure for Western nations either to commission privateers directly or to wink at the actions of freelance pirates, so long as those thieves were preying on the commerce of *other* nations. Piracy was often state-supported economic terrorism. Crackdowns on piracy usually meant crackdowns on freelancers.

Henry Morgan (1635–1688), a Welsh exile, was commissioned by the British royal governor of Jamaica to fight the Spaniards in 1667. Ruthless Morgan attacked ships of many nations, sacked and pillaged seacoast towns, including Panama City. His men turned entire cities into drunken orgies, torturing citizens to reveal the hiding places for their gold. All this rape and violence was done with the look-the-other-way approval of the British government.

The Caribbean of this period was a hotbed of piracy. Some of the predatory ruckus can be traced back to the papal ruling granting the Spanish and Portuguese *exclusive* trading rights in the New World. The Spanish demanded that foreign vessels seek a license from them to operate in those North American waters, such as the Caribbean. Not surprisingly, other nations balked and a privateering war ensued against Spain and Portugal.

"For the first hundred years or more after the establishing of colonies in the New World," writes Edgar Maclay in *The History of American Privateers*, "the distinction between privateers, slavers, pirates, and even government cruisers was vague, and at times obliterated altogether. It was a period in which, on the high seas, might was right; and when their home governments were at war with each other—and sometimes when at peace—the colonial seaman seized whatever he could."

In the colonies, Charleston, South Carolina, was the preferred port for pirates, and local authorities conveniently winked so long as the pirates spent Spanish gold and silver there. Charleston juries were notoriously lenient toward accused pirates. In fact, it's whispered that the fortunes of

several leading Charleston families can be traced to plunder from Spanish ships.

"Buccaneers like Morgan, Captain Avery, William Dampier and Edward Teach, the famous 'Blackbeard,'" writes Christopher Hibbert in *The Roots of Evil,* "all received official and quasi-official support in return for a share in their profits and all of them traded openly with the American colonists."

Morgan, it seems, though, overstepped his commission, raiding Panama City in 1671, seven months *after* England and Spain had signed the Treaty of Madrid. That was the first time Spain recognized British colonies in the Caribbean, and now both countries agreed to crack down on pirates.

Morgan was hauled back to England to answer for his actions. Nonetheless, this is how entrenched privateering was back then and perhaps how much England hated Spain. Despite his ruthless behavior toward the ships and peoples of several nations, Captain Morgan was knighted in 1674 by King Charles II and appointed Lieutenant Governor of Jamaica. He lived out the rest of his life in drunken luxury on his 6,000-acre estate, eventually growing too obese to walk. ✺

CAPTAIN KIDD WAS FRAMED, 1701

Captain Kidd was no Joan of Arc, but he was no "Captain Kidd," either.

William Kidd (1645–1701) was a plain-speaking, high-tempered Scotsman, who had served bravely for Britain in the French wars in the West Indies and made his fortune as captain and ship owner trading goods in the colonies. In 1696, the fifty-one-year-old Kidd was a prosperous New York businessman, comfortably settled with his wife and family. That year, his friend Robert Livingstone—from one of the more powerful British families in the colonies—connived with the newly appointed governor of New England, Richard, Lord of Bellamont, the king's cousin, for the creation of a syndicate to receive an unusual privateering commission.

In times of war, wealthy investors routinely funded a privateering vessel to attack the enemy's merchant ships and divvy the plunder. This was an English naval tradition dating back to Sir Francis Drake.

But what was extraordinary about Kidd's commission was that it also entitled him to attack pirate ships of all nationalities and keep their booty—few or no questions asked. This was an amazing financial opportunity, like offering Bill Gates the chance to attack the Colombian drug cartel and then legally keep the loot. Normally, the British navy dealt with pirates but the fierce war with France and shortage of seamen was hindering their efforts.

Kidd's royal commission—secured by Bellamont—does "give and grant full Power and Authority to Captain William Kidd, Commander of the ship Adventure Galley . . . to apprehend, seize and take into Custody the said Thomas Too, John Ireland, Tho Wake, and William Maze, and all other Pirates, Free-booters and Sea-Rovers, of what Nation whatsoever, whom he should find or meet with, upon the said Coasts or Seas of America, or in any other Seas or Parts, with their Ships and Vessels, and all such Merchandize, Money, Goods, and Wares as should be found on board of them."

The mission which began as an attempt by Britain to crack down on the four colonial pirates listed above was cunningly expanded so that Kidd would have maximum leeway to capture prizes.

In addition to Lord Bellamont and Robert Livingstone, four of the most powerful men in England secretly invested in the £6,000 it would cost to outfit the ship. The prospect of profits from this *legal* larceny were dizzying. If Kidd captured two large ships, the backers could easily receive a one hundredfold return on investment in a year. In the official contract with Kidd, four obscure merchants were listed as the investors, but they were shills. John Somers, Lord Chancellor of England, later admitted his right to receive the share of one "Samuel Newton" while the other backers were Earl of Orford, First Lord of the Admiralty and two secretaries of state, the Earl of Romney and the Duke of Shrewsbury. The king was to receive 10 percent of the booty as well, "chiefly to show that he was a partner in the undertaking," according to *The Real Captain Kidd: A Vindication,* by Sir Cornelius Dalton. Kidd and Livingstone stood to receive 7.5 percent each, while if the haul totaled more than £100,000, Kidd was to be allowed to keep the ship.

The mission got off to a bad start in March 1695; Kidd and a London merchant handpicked one hundred-plus English sailors for the *Adventure Galley,* but before they departed the coast, a British man of war press-ganged the bulk of his crew. Now, Kidd sailed to New York to get up a new crew, but his articles allowed him to offer the crew shares of only one quarter of the spoils (instead of the usual half), and there would be no regular wages; the voyage would be strictly "No purchase, no pay," or in sailor slang, "No prey, no pay."

Kidd was forced to sign the piratical scum of the New York wharf, out-of-work scallywags. Once out of the harbor, he had no luck whatsoever at finding pirate ships, and headed to the Indian Ocean. He was fired upon, but when he captured the vessel, it turned out to be a Dutch ship. His crew—led by gunner William Moore—voted to take her as a prize anyhow, but Kidd, pistols in hand, changed their mind.

Kidd then spied a merchant ship far off and he swung into action. Employing a standard battle tactic, Kidd flew French colors to trick his adversary and lured the giant *Quedagh Merchant* to come alongside. When an officer of that ship boarded, holding French papers of clear passage, Kidd hoisted the British flag and declared the ship captured. Although the *Quedagh Merchant* was clearly an Armenian ship with a crew of Moors and a handful of Christians aboard, since the officer presented French papers, this would make it a legitimate prize, given the state of war between England and France. And a rich

prize. The *Quedagh Merchant* was packed with fine cloths, silks, jewels, perhaps worth as much as £400,000.

Kidd, who had taken another ship traveling with French papers, hauled his prizes back to Ste. Marie, in Madagascar. His articles stated that he must take the captured ship(s) back to Boston (or to London, if armed British escort appeared) so that an Admiralty Court could rule on whether they were legitimate captures and could document the spoils.

In Madagascar stood the *Moca Frigate*, a former merchant ship, turned pirate by Robert Culliford. When Kidd with his mounted cannon and men hit port, the pirates abandoned ship. Kidd proposed that they capture the *Moca* as well, but instead his men swore they'd shoot him if he tried, and ninety-seven of his men mutinied over Culliford and promptly attacked Kidd.

With Kidd, the men, receiving no wages, could hope for a share of one quarter of the spoils, *if* an admiralty court ruled in their favor in Boston; with Culliford, they might split up everything, and right away. An Irishman, Darby Mullins, was later asked at trial why he turned pirate at that point. "For want, my lord," he replied.

Here's how Kidd described what happened next in later handwritten notes:

"The said Deserters, sometimes in great Numbers, came on board, the said Galley and Adventure Prize, and carried away great Guns, Powder, Shot, small Arms, Sails, Anchors, Cables, Surgeon's Chests, and what else they pleased; and threatened several times to murder the Narrator

[i.e., Kidd], as he was informed, and advised to take care of himself; which they designed in the Night to effect; but was prevented by him locking himself in his Cabin at Night, and securing himself with barricading the same with Bales of Goods; and having about Forty small Arms, besides Pistols, ready charged, kept them out. Their Wickedness was so great, after they had plundered and ransacked sufficiently, [they] went Four Miles off to one Edward Welche's House, which his the Narrator's chest was lodged, and broke it open; and took out Ten Ounces of Gold, 40 Pound of Plate, 370 Pieces of Eight, the Narrator's Journal, and a great many Papers that belonged to him, and the People of New York that fitted them out."

Kidd was left with thirteen sailors; his original ship was leaking badly (requiring eight-man shifts to bail her out) and his prize was far too big to sail with this crew. The date was early in 1699.

Kidd was two years past his contracted return date, and no doubt his powerful backers were a might antsy. And now the East India Company reported in London "they had received some information . . . that Kidd had committed several acts of piracy, particularly in seizing a Moors' ship called the *Quedagh Merchant*."

The vastly profitable East India Company had no desire to enrage the Great Mogul of India by allowing British pirates to prey upon Moorish ships, especially since the Great Mogul, a now forgotten potentate, then controlled an enormous empire and could expel the Brits with one order.

Kidd was officially declared a pirate, with all British warships to be on the lookout for him.

Captain Kidd spent six months in Madagascar trying to round up a crew; considering he was heading to Boston was no great incentive to the pirate types who bobbed up in Madagascar.

Kidd reached Anguilla in the West Indies, and found out that he and his skeleton crew were wanted for piracy. They were dumbfounded. The crew started deserting. Kidd no longer had sailors enough to sail his prize to Boston, so he traded for a smaller ship complete with crew and moved an undisclosed portion of the remaining booty aboard. (How much booty has intrigued treasure hunters ever since.)

Kidd, the alleged pirate, could have stayed in the Caribbean a very wealthy man. At least £10,000 of treaure remained and possibly as much as £40,000 or more. Kidd instead sailed north. In New York Harbor, he handed over the two French passes (which would clear him of the piracy charges) to an old friend to deliver to his backer, New England Governor Bellamont, who was then in Boston.

Bellamont—cousin to the King—sent the postmaster of Boston out to Block Island to give a message to Kidd. The note declared the governor was sympathetic to Kidd's version of the events and then concluded: "I make no manner of doubt but to obtain the King's pardon for you, and for those few men you have left who I understand have been faithful to you, and refused as well as you to dishonour the Commission you have from England . . . I assure you on my Word and Honour I will perform nicely what I have promised."

Kidd, who was joined on ship by his wife and family, responded with great relief that the governor would take up his cause; and he guessed aloud that the East India Company must have heard of acts of piracy committed by Captain Robert Culliford, using the mutinied members of Kidd's former crew. With a certain poetic understatement, Kidd claimed: "A sheet of paper will not contain what may be said of the care I took to preserve the owners' interest, and to come home to clear my own innocency."

On July 1, 1699, Kidd and his few remaining crew members sailed into Boston harbor. Governor Bellamont promptly arrested them.

England dispatched a Navy ship to ferry Kidd back to justice. The House of Commons (that brake on lordly misbehavior), sniffed a scandal and demanded that Kidd not be tried until it was back in session. Unfortunately for Kidd, that meant spending a year in "close confinement" in Newgate.

On March 6, 1701, the House of Commons began to examine Kidd's papers. Included among them, as clearly stated in the Parliament Papers, were TWO FRENCH PASSES from those ships Kidd captured.

A person with enough leisure and curiosity can read those French documents, in volume 13 of the *Journal of the House of Commons*, page 21. They begin "Nous Francois Martin, escuir, conseiller du Roy, directeur . . ." and midway through note "requirons a tous nos amiz et aliez de n'apporter aucun empechment . . ." (We, Francois Martin, Esq . . . demand that all our friends and allies in no way hinder . . .) Both ships are clearly named as the ones captured by Kidd.

Nonetheless, Kidd was ordered to stand trial in Admiralty Court, but it was specifically stated that his papers should be delivered there for his trial.

On April 16, 1701, Kidd stood before the bewigged justices and requested a delay so that his documents could be delivered to court.

KIDD: My lord, I insist upon my French passes. Pray let me have them.

COURT RECORDER (Sir Salathial Lovel): Mr. Kidd, I must tell you, if you will not plead, you must have judgment against you, as standing mute.

KIDD: If your Lordships permit those passes to be read, they will justify me. If I plead, I shall be accessory to my own death . . .

RECORDER: You are accessory to your own death, if you do not plead.

Finally Kidd consented to raise his hand to signify a not guilty plea.

The court then stunned Kidd by charging him not with piracy but with the murder of William Moore, the ship's gunner.

Testimony from paid informants painted the following picture of the crime. While the ship was anchored off the coast of Africa, after more than a year without taking a single prize, Kidd walked on the deck past Moore, who two weeks earlier had led an unsuccessful mutiny. Kidd called him a "lousy dog." Moore replied: "If I be so, you have made me one." Kidd, in a rage, swung an iron-hooped bucket, which caught Moore flush in the temple. Moore died the next day.

Kidd claimed that he never meant to kill Moore, and that threat of mutiny was still strong. Testifying for the crown were two of Kidd's crew who had mutinied, signed up with Culliford, plundered the *Quedah Merchant*, and gone out on later pirate voyages; they were offered pardons in exchange for turning crown's evidence.

After one especially absurd statement, Kidd complained: "It signifies nothing to ask any questions. These rogues will swear to anything." Then later, he asked: "Have you not been promised your life to swear away mine?"

The Judge intervened: "He is not bound to answer that question. He is very fit to be made as evidence for the Crown."

It took the jury an hour to bring in a guilty verdict.

As for the piracy charges, the judge, Lord Chief Baron shaped the trial so that it all hinged on whether or not Captain Kidd received French passes from the captured ships. The Lord Chief summed up: "And as to the French passes there is nothing of that appears by any proof; and for aught I can see, none saw them but himself, if there ever were any." Four respected British officers testified to Kidd's valor during the French war in the Caribbean and one noted that Kidd had fought off a mutiny to prevent his ship from going "a-pirating."

Kidd and four others were convicted of piracy. All four of those had turned themselves in under an amnesty offered pirates, but apparently had gone to the wrong government bureaucrat, invalidating the amnesty offer.

Each convicted seaman in his final statement wanted the court to record that he had always obeyed the orders of his captain.

When sentenced to death, Kidd told the court: "My lord, it is a very hard sentence. For my part, I am the innocentest person of them all, only I have been sworn against by perjured persons."

In prison, Kidd refused to confess to the chaplain and refused repeated requests to cast blame on the ministers that backed his mission. (Perhaps he was still hoping for a pardon.) On May 24, 1701, William Kidd was brought to Execution Dock at Wapping, following the traditional procession of the Silver Oar. The noose about his neck, Captain William Kidd kicked out unto eternity and the rope broke. Kidd would have to be rehoisted up the ladder and turned off a second time. In the little waiting period, he told the chaplain at the gallows that his greatest sorrow was leaving his wife and children in New York without getting a chance to say good-bye.

The *next day* in Parliament, Lord Chancellor Somers admitted he had had a secret share in Kidd's voyage but claimed there was nothing illegal in that. In fact, he pointed out that "owners of the said ship had lost their expenses and had not received any benefit from the grant."

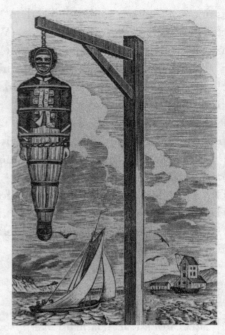

As a grisly warning to other pirates, the British Admiralty dangled Captain Kidd's dead body—encased in pine resin and bound by leather straps—for years from a specially constructed gibbet at Tilbury Point in the estuary of the Thames River.

The East India Company soon after reported to the Great Mogul that the evil pirate Captain Kidd had been hanged. Britain's inroads in India eventually led to conquering the entire subcontinent.

Robert Culliford, the pirate captain of *Moca Frigate,* applied for pardon to the *correct* bureaucrat and, with a lawyer at his side, was granted amnesty by the Court of the Admiralty.

As for Kidd, dead men tell no tales. His hard-earned estate was forfeited after his hanging, taken from his wife and children; Queen Anne used the £6,471 to found the Greenwich Hospital.

William Kidd's corpse was hung in chains off the Thames River to serve as a warning to other pirates. ✵

VANDERBILT: AMERICAN BUSINESSMAN CONQUERS NICARAGUA, 1856

Back in the early 1850s, before the transcontinental railroad was built, people marveled at the speed at which Commodore Vanderbilt's transit company could take you coast to coast: a mere *twenty-five* days.

Travelers headed south by steamer from New York to Greytown, Nicaragua, then up the San Juan River through the rain forest, across Lake Nicaragua, and finally twelve miles overland by donkey-drawn carriage over rutty roads to the Pacific, where a swift steamer carried them on to San Francisco. The price was $300, also considered a bargain compared to a forty-five-day trip through Panama for $600.

Vanderbilt made a fortune, thanks to the California gold rush and thanks to an exclusive franchise from the Nicaraguan government (for $10,000 a year and 10 percent of the profits). In 1853, Commodore Vanderbilt, a ruthless and tireless businessman who had climbed from deckhand, finally decided to take a long leisurely European vacation aboard his yacht *North Star.*

As the vessel steamed out of New York Harbor, two of his partners promptly began to cheat Vanderbilt out of his share of the profits. He had sold his stock with the stipulation that the company pay him (as founder) 20 percent of the gross, and this wily pair, both veteran shippers—Charles Morgan and C. K. Garrison—stopped the payments. Both men, having bought up shares, now effectively controlled the company.

As the *New York Herald* stated, "Trouble is anticipated upon the return of Commodore Vanderbilt."

When Vanderbilt returned, his rage was profane and boundless, but his note to his former partners was succinct:

Gentlemen:

You have endeavored to cheat me. I won't sue you.

The courts are too slow. I will ruin you.

Yours truly,
Cornelius Vanderbilt

Their feud would change the history of Nicaragua. Perhaps never in American history have two competing American business interests so boldly and baldly meddled in foreign affairs. Mercenary would fight mercenary, while the stock price hung in the balance.

Vanderbilt—hell-bent on ruining Morgan and Garrison—created a brand new steamship line, dropped his prices to the unheard-of $35 coast-to-coast steerage ticket, and was driving his rivals out of business. Morgan and Garrison reluctantly paid all back monies that Vanderbilt claimed due him, but the Commodore wasn't through with them. He also quietly bought up most of the stock of his old company, became president of the firm again, and prepared to fire Morgan and Garrison.

But these two self-made men were worthy adversaries for Vanderbilt. (Morgan had climbed from grocery clerk to president of the biggest shipping line serving New Orleans; Garrison made his first fortune in Mississippi shipping, then opened a bank in San Francisco, where he was soon elected mayor.)

Garrison and Morgan ignited that little fuse known as William Walker, an American mercenary. Walker stood 5'2", weighed about 100 pounds, and, contrary to most notions about him, was an incompetent white supremacist with severe delusions of grandeur. "Like Adolf Hitler some eighty years later, he believed in the inherent superiority of the blond blue-eyed Anglo Saxon over the dark hybrid race of Indian, Negro and Spanish heritage he found in Nicaragua," states historian Frederic Rosengarten in *Freebooters Must Die!*

Morgan and Garrison provided Walker with a company steamer, *La Virgen* to transport troops, then later gave him a $20,000 loan to set up the new government.

Walker's entire army consisted of about 100 Americans and about 150 locals, but, thanks mostly to the element of surprise and the fact Nicaragua was suffering through its thirteenth regime in eight years, this "gray-eyed man of destiny"

conquered the capital city, Granada, and installed his local ally, Patricio Rivas as president. American recruits played "Yankee Doodle" in Granada's main square.

Garrison dispatched his son on a secret mission to convince Walker to cancel Vanderbilt's franchise and confiscate company property, on the grounds that the Commodore had been cheating Nicaragua for years. The Commodore had been paying his $10,000 yearly, but as for forking over 10 percent of his profits, he claimed—in a move that would make Hollywood accountants proud—that he owed money *only* from profits from the trek across Nicaragua, not the entire New York-to-San Francisco passage, and that leg of the journey, alas, caused him deep losses.

President Rivas signed the decree on February 18, and the first steamship out alerted wily Morgan in New York, who started secretly selling off Vanderbilt company stock he still owned, and he also heavily played the stock short, i.e., betting it would fall. Vanderbilt, unaware of being canceled, started buying up shares.

Vanderbilt also allowed a boatload of 250 recruits bound for Walker's forces to sail "free" on credit to Nicaragua, thinking it wise to shore up this new American-controlled regime.

Then the news hit Wall Street on March 13: Vanderbilt's Accessory Transit franchise had been canceled in Nicaragua. The stock plummeted from 22½ to 13 within five days.

And lo and behold, the new exclusive Nicaraguan franchise had been awarded

to . . . Morgan and Garrison through a shell company.

Vanderbilt dashed off two outraged letters to U.S. Secretary of State William Marcy, complaining that millions of dollars of property owned by an American citizen had been stolen by a foreign government. The Secretary of State pointed out that Vanderbilt's company was incorporated in Nicaragua, and newspapers delighted in advising Vanderbilt to apply to the new Nicaraguan government for relief.

Vanderbilt sued Garrison and Morgan; Vanderbilt tried to bribe President Rivas; Vanderbilt pitched the neighboring countries to attack. Finally, after half a year, Vanderbilt financed a counterrevolution. Yet again, an American citizen would try to overthrow a Central American government for the sake of profit.

In November, Vanderbilt sent two mercenaries to Costa Rica with plenty of money and cases of state-of-the-art Minie rifles and ammunition. American Sylvanus Spencer—with Englishman William Webster and Costa Rican president Juan Rafael Mora—led a force of 120 men into Nicaragua and recaptured company steamers and key outposts, dooming William Walker.

Cornelius Vanderbilt confidently announced in his Christmas statement to shareholders: ". . . the Company will be rapidly restored to their rights, franchises and property upon the Isthmus of Nicaragua which have been so unjustly invaded."

On May 1, 1857, William Walker surrendered, and was deported via a U.S. warship. (Yet another Nicaraguan government would be installed.)

Wall Street gleefully drove up the price of Vanderbilt's Accessory Transit. The new company founded by Morgan and Garrison was soon wiped out. However, the Commodore wasn't done yet. When Vanderbilt eventually got his situation cleared again in Nicaragua to recommence his coast-to-coast transit company, he did nothing of the sort. He, instead, convinced the major *Panama*-based transit companies to pay him a kind of blackmail of $40,000 a month (later $56,000 a month) *not* to compete with them. The companies operating there could afford to pay him off, because they were receiving hefty subsidies from the U.S. government for carrying the coast-to-coast mail.

"The result of this system is that here comes a man . . . old Vanderbilt . . ." complained Senator Toombs of Georgia, "and he runs right at [the subsidized companies], and says: disgorge this plunder. He is the kingfish that is robbing the small plunderers that come around the capitol. He does not come here for that purpose, but he says: fork over $56,000 a month of the money to me that I may lie in port with my ships, and they do it."

And what became of William Walker? After a third failed attempt at Central American conquest, he died before a Honduran firing squad in 1860. And Morgan and Garrison, the men Vanderbilt vowed to ruin? Both lost money in Nicaragua but both survived to make large fortunes in shipping elsewhere and both at later times struck deals with and sold ships to . . . Cornelius Vanderbilt. Apparently, the war, the mercenaries, the double-crossing, it was all just business. ❧

COCAINE IN COCA-COLA AND THE CORNER DRUGSTORE

Pope Leo XIII (1878–1903) agreed to endorse this *cocaine-laced* wine, made by fellow Italian, Angelo Mariani.

This is no myth, no fairy tale, no wishful thinking. The original Coca-Cola contained cocaine, and continued to contain cocaine from its debut in 1886 until at least 1903. At first, the amount of the drug—which was then legal—was fairly potent, but gradually it declined to a mere trace before being removed entirely.

In 1886, Colonel John Pemberton, a huckster-pharmacist, brewed up his batch of Coca-Cola. "Of course, Pemberton added to this new brew the fluid extract of coca leaves," states Frederick Allen in *Secret Formula.* "Exactly how much cocaine went into this inaugural batch of Doc Pemberton's new soft drink syrup is impossible to calculate more than a century later, but even a touch of the drug, in combination with the sugar and caffeine—four times the amount in today's Coke, or about the same as a strong cup of coffee— made Pemberton's concoction quite a stimulating beverage."

Pemberton, who sold such patent medicines as Triplex Liver Pills and Globe Flower Syrup, had started out by trying to duplicate the success of a very popular European drink, a cocaine-laced wine, called Vin Mariani.

The 1800s marked a patent medicine boom and Angelo Mariani had been able to collect endorsements from grateful kings and famous creative types, including Thomas Edison and Alexander Dumas. Pope Leo XIII struck a special commemorative medal for Mariani.

But Pemberton, fearing the temperance movement and eager to cash in on the soda fountain craze, had dropped the wine and added caffeine. An early ad clearly shows the home remedy market he was still targeting.

In 1889, pharmacist Asa Griggs Candler bought the rights to Coca-Cola for $2,300, and brewed it up in an iron pot with another of his patent medicines, Botanic Blood Balm.

Coke over the next decade earned a reputation as a druggie drink. People in the South invited others to have a "dope" with them. Editorialists worried about the cocaine in Coke energizing "negroes" to violence.

Candler, a devout Baptist, reduced the coca content even further but kept just a tiny bit to retain his trademark name. In 1901, Coca-Cola sued the U.S. government, claiming it shouldn't have to pay a new stamp tax on patent medicine. The U.S. government needed to prove there was enough cocaine (i.e., medicine) in Coca-Cola to make it liable for the new tax; the company had to prove it was just a fun soft drink.

Under oath, Asa Candler admitted there was cocaine in Coca-Cola but his expert witness, Dr. George Payne, set the dose at 1/400th of a grain per ounce. "It was the merest trace," testified Dr. Payne. "A man would explode before he could drink enough to affect him." The jury accepted that Coke was mostly sugar and water, so the government lost the case and refunded $29,502 to the company.

One thing worth noting is that cocaine was *not* illegal back then. Americans could go to a drugstore and find it in any of a dozen or so cheap asthma or fatigue medicines, such as Dr. Birney's Snuff or Agnew's Powder.

Candler—getting richer and more devout—had had enough, though. He approached the nation's largest cocaine supplier, Roessler & Hasslacher Chemical, about keeping the coca extract in but removing absolutely all the cocaine. Dr. Louis Schaefer ground up the leaves, mixed them with sawdust, soaked them in bicarbonate of soda, then percolated them with toluene (coal tar solvent), and steamed it all. Cocaine the narcotic was gone from Coca-Cola in 1903.

Candler's timing was shrewd because the country, with the progressive move-

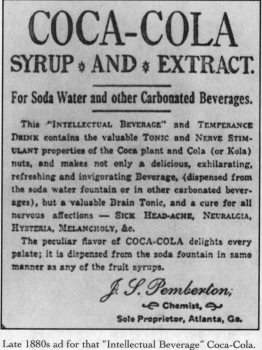

Late 1880s ad for that "Intellectual Beverage" Coca-Cola.

ment in the lead, was starting to look at outlawing certain substances. Congress passed the Pure Food and Drugs Act in 1906, which marked the first time that the U.S. government tried to regulate Americans' access to cocaine, opium and other drugs. However, the law was fairly toothless—companies could still sell medicine with cocaine in it, if it was clearly labeled and not shipped across state lines. If caught violating the above, the fine was a wrist slap, $200 maximum.

However, over the next decade, almost every state enacted some kind of anti-cocaine law, and in 1914 Congress passed a Narcotics Act, and started America down its completely failed policy of making the drug illegal, trying to cut off supply and arresting users. This policy has acted like a generous block grant to criminals world-

wide; by creating a billion-dollar illegal business, it has in effect bankrolled the planet's underworld.

In 1996, Coca-Cola had sales of $18.5 billion and ranks among the world's largest *legal* users of coca leaves. ✺

CHEAP COCAINE AT THE CORNER DRUG STORE, 1908

Around the turn of the century, Americans could buy dozens of products containing cocaine, heroin, or opium *without a prescription* at their corner drugstore or by mail order. In 1898, Bayer debuted a new cough suppressant formula, with heroin as the main active ingredient. Ads for these and other drugs routinely littered the pages of the *New York Times, Harper's, Life,* even the Sears catalogue. In 1908, the fol-

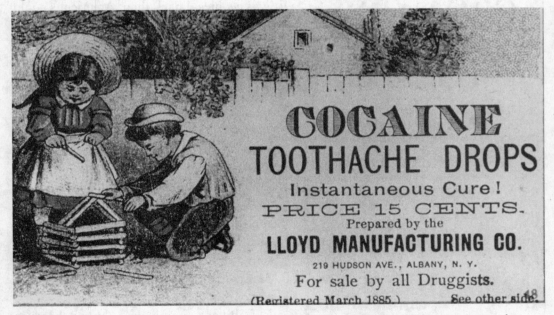

This 1885 ad reminds parents that cocaine can help their children to play happily and pain-free. Cocaine was then easily available without a prescription.

Bayer, the future aspirin giant, back in 1898 offered heroin as a cough suppressant.

lowing over-the-counter medicines containing narcotics were readily available, according to a list compiled by the U.S. Department of Agriculture.

Agnew's Powder (cocaine)

Anglo-American Catarrh Powder (cocaine)

Colwell's Egyptian Oil (opium)

Coco-Bola (cocaine)

Crossman's Specific Mixture (opium)

Dr. Drake's German Croup Remedy (opium)

Dr. James Soothing Syrup (heroin)

Dr. Moffett's Teethina; Teething Powders (opium)

Godfrey's Cordial (opium)

Gowan's Pneumonia Cure (opium)

Harrison's Opium Elixir (opium)

Jayne's Expectorant (opium)

One Day Cough Cure (cannabis indica, also morphine)

Pierce's Smart Weed (opium)

Rexal Cholera Cure (opium)

Shiloh's Cure (heroin)

Tubercine (opium)

Tucker's Asthma Cure (cocaine)

Victor Lung Syrup (opium)

Watkins Anodyne (heroin)

Wright's Instant Relief (opium)

THE BRITISH EMPIRE: SELLING OPIUM TO THE WORLD

If the sun never set on the British Empire during its heyday, then what's also true is that the drugstore never closed. What's little known and rarely mentioned is that Victorian England was regularly gulping down vast quantities of laudanum—a liquid laced with an opium derivative—and also swigging health tonics fortified with cocaine.

These products were legal and as easily available as aspirin is today. In fact, Western nations, prior to the twentieth century, rarely made any effort to regulate or outlaw drug use.

Ironically, it was the East—which we Westerners often picture in billows of narcotic smoke—that took a tougher stance on drugs. Several influential Islamic doctors warned about the dangers of hashish and opium addiction. In the 1800s, a century before the United States and Great Britain, the Chinese tried to crack down on opium use.

However, the British fought the so-called Opium War (1839–42), among other trading motives, to force China to *stop* cracking down on British smugglers selling illegal opium in China; then, after winning the war, Great Britain forced China eventually to legalize the opium trade.

POCAHONTAS LIGHTS UP AND OTHER SMOKING TALES

One of the cornerstones of early American history is the tale that Pocahontas fell in love with Captain John Smith and rescued him from certain death by placing her head next to the condemned man's on the execution block. Sorry. The incident, and the romance, almost definitely never happened, and some astute magazines were delighted to point all that out at the time of the much-ballyhooed release of the Disney cartoon version in 1995.

But what the writers of those debunking articles failed to add was that Pocahontas was also once a spokesperson for the tobacco industry, a kind of living, breathing "cigar-store" Indian in the days before cigar stores.

Pocahontas (1595–1617), an Indian princess, was kidnapped as a teenager by British settlers and held hostage so the Brits could strike a more favorable peace with her father, chief Powhatan. While in captivity, the Reverend Whitaker tutored her in English and scriptures, and tried to "civilize" her Indian ways.

(One account describes how, when she was eleven, she used to encourage the boys to do cartwheels and she would "wheel herself naked as she was all the fort over," according to William Strachey. He notes that because she was still prepubescent, she "goes unshadowed," i.e., wears nothing below the waist.)

A hostage in Jamestown Fort, Pocahontas apparently showed a great aptitude for both English and scriptures.

She was baptized Rebecca and married Englishman John Rolfe at age nineteen. He was a planter whose careful blending of tobacco strains gave the settlement in Virginia its first real economic promise for survival.

In 1616, Rolfe made a promotional trip to England to show off his English-speaking Indian wife and samples of his tobacco. She was the centerpiece.

Tobacco then was in sore need of a boost at court. King James I hated the stuff, penning that tobacco causes "a general sluggishness, which makes us wallow in all sorts of idle delights" and elsewhere called it "a custome Lothsome to the eye, hatefull to the Nose, harmefull to the braine, daungerous to the Lungs."

When Pocahontas, a dozen other Indians, and John Rolfe arrived in England, the *Indians* were invited to visit the royal court. John Rolfe, a commoner, was not. It was hoped that their presence would help raise funds for the fledgling settlement and that the king would reduce harmful taxes and import duties. The Virginia Company, which controlled the settlement, paid Pocahontas' travel and clothing expenses, the then hefty sum of £4 a week.

The American myth version of Pocahontas rescuing Captain John Smith.

Pocahontas was a big hit, especially with giddy Queen Anne, who'd been known to play leapfrog. While her fellow Indians arrived in traditional garb, Pocahontas wore a long, high-necked English dress and spoke the king's English, proof that the savages could be civilized.

The king, a rabid Indian hater who once cheered the diseases decimating the American Indians, was never won over to the cause of tobacco.

Pocahontas, however, was literally the toast of the town, exhibited and observing, even touring the Tower of London. It was at this time that John Smith for the first time ever publicly revealed his she-saved-me-from-being-crushed story, more than a decade *after* it happened. (Smith's *A True Relation of Virginia* ... [1608] makes no mention of it.) It seems likely Smith was trying to attract a little thunder for himself, and very *unlikely* that a self-promoter like John Smith would have made no mention of it for a decade. (He later wrote up the story in 1624.) There is no record of Pocahontas meeting Captain Smith during her stay in England.

Half of the dozen Indians who accompanied John Rolfe to England caught various fatal European diseases and died. Pocahontas, in her English clothes, preparing to board ship at Gravesend to return to America, died after a lingering illness in March 1617, at age twenty-two.

Pocahontas, dressed as a proper Englishwoman, sat for a portrait during her visit in 1616 to England. Note her stiff lace collar, her ostrich plume fan, and her high hat, then popular at court.

She's still buried there on the coast of England.

The political lobbying side of the mission was a failure: King James kept the export taxes high, but nonetheless thanks to consumer delight, Virginia tobacco sales doubled from 20,000 pounds of leaf exported in 1617 to 40,000 pounds the following year.

John Rolfe (1585–1622) married again, this time to an Englishwoman, and then was killed a few years later, reportedly by Indians. His legacy lives on in Joe Camel.

THE SOT-WEED FACTOR IN EARLY AMERICA

The Puritans of Massachusetts outlawed in 1634 the "taking tobacco" of two or more persons together. Connecticut followed suit.

Despite the bad press and antipuffing laws, tobacco started to catch on. For the first couple of hundred years, "taking tobacco" meant smoking a pipe or chewing plugs. (Cigars — so portable — started poking up among Civil War troops, while pre-rolled cigarettes didn't go *really* mass until almost World War I.)

The fact the deadly stuff's addictive explains most of its success, but the misinformation campaigns waged since Shakespeare's day certainly haven't hurt. William Byrd, one of the wealthiest early Americans, with almost 200,000 acres of tobacco land in Virginia, wrote: "In England, [the plague] us'd formerly to make a visit about once in twenty or thirty years; but since the universal use of Tobacco, it

Before the widespread popularity of baseball cards, many American cigarette companies included a "sporting girl" card in every pack. The idea was that while the smoker tried to collect the whole set of seventy-five, he would remain loyal to the brand. The American Tobacco Company offered this belly dancer around 1900.

has now been kept off above fifty-four years." To get the full preventive value, he recommended: "We should hang bundles of it around our beds, and in the apartments wherein we most converse."

Twentieth century ad campaigns include:

• Philip Morris: When smokers switched to Philip Morris, "every case of irritation of nose and throat — due to smoking — either cleared up completely, or definitely improved."

• Old Gold: "Not a cough in the carload."

• R. J. Reynolds: "More doctors smoke Camels."

Adolph Hitler, for one, wasn't fooled. "I am convinced that if I had been a smoker, I never would have been able to bear the cares and anxieties which have been a burden to me for so long," he wrote. "Perhaps the German people owe its salvation to that fact."

In 1966, by law, warning labels had to appear on cigarette packages: "Cigarette smoking may be hazardous to your health." Tobacco ads were banned from television in 1971. Excise taxes on tobacco increased; local antismoking laws abounded. Stiffer warning labels were mandated.

A little ditty penned by G. L. Hemminger that ran in the *Penn State Froth* in 1915 pierces the smoke and sums it up neatly:

Tobacco is a dirty weed. I like it.
It satisfies no normal need. I like it.
It makes you thin, it make you lean,
It takes the hair right off your bean.
It's the worst darn stuff I've ever seen.
I like it."

In 1995, Americans spent approximately $46 billion on 484 billion cigarettes, according to the Tobacco Institute.

SCAMS: THE ORIGINAL PONZI SCHEME

Charles Ponzi (1878–1949), an effervescent Italian immigrant, was hailed as living proof of the American dream come true. The 5'2" financier arrived at his investment headquarters in a blue stretch limousine; he puffed his cigars from a diamond-flecked holder, and he delivered on

This is how the original Charles Ponzi looked on August 2, 1920, as his investment empire *began to crash*. Imagine how he must have looked on a *good* day.

his promise to return a 50 percent profit on investments in forty-five days. Delivered, that is, to the *early* investors.

For a while, Charles Ponzi was a working-class hero, an entrepreneur who shared the J. P. Morgan secrets of high finance with the common man. One day in July 1920, as he approached the State House in Boston, an admirer screamed, "You're the greatest Italian of them all." The bantamweight millionaire demurred, "Oh, no Columbus and Marconi. Columbus discovered America; Marconi discovered the wireless."

"Sure," shouted someone else in the crowd, "but you discovered money!"

In 1919–1920, Ponzi received upward of $15 million in small investments from 40,000 Bostonians, most of them Italian-Americans. Mattresses lost their lumps as poor people who had never invested before ponied up their savings.

Ponzi claimed that he had figured out a way to cash in on the chaotic economic conditions in Europe just after World War I, by buying International Postal Union coupons from certain countries at a discount and then redeeming them in the United States for full value. Ponzi announced he had an army of agents scouring Europe to buy up all available discounted coupons, such as the penny ones in Germany that could be cashed here for a nickel.

Ponzi's Securities Exchange Company had an entrance in Pie Alley in Boston, and lines of happy investors often stretched down the stairs and out in the street. Ponzi's relatives would duly note the transaction in ledger books. His financial wizardry cast him into the national spotlight.

Ponzi bought a hundred suits, and matching shoes. His cash bankroll bulged his trousers, as apparently did his young secretary-mistress, Lucy Meli.

In the summer of 1920 it all started to crash.

The Feds announced that *all* the postal coupons cashed in this country wouldn't account for even a trifle of the profits Ponzi had claimed. (Boston financial expert C. W. Barron lampooned Ponzi's investment scheme. Ponzi shot back in an interview in the *New York World*, "Please do not think I am boasting but I have forgotten more about foreign exchange than C. W. Barron ever knew.")

Yes, the straw boater was popular that summer of 1920 as investors desperately tried to get their money out of Ponzi's Security Exchange office in Pie Alley in Boston.

But the evidence was mounting. A public relations man temporarily in Ponzi's employ named William McMasters told the *Boston Globe,* "The man is a complete financial idiot, he can hardly add." And then McMasters himself added, "There is money stuffed into every conceivable place in his offices. He sits around with his feet on his desk smoking expensive cigars in a diamond holder and talking complete gibberish about postal coupons."

Perhaps more to the point, McMasters claimed that Ponzi had never issued or received a foreign financial draft.

On August 9, a bank commissioner declared Ponzi's account overdrawn. On August 11, it was revealed that Ponzi had served prison time in Canada for forgery and time in Atlanta for smuggling aliens.

Blue-collar investors swarmed Pie Alley trying to pry their hard-earned money loose. Friday, August 13, Ponzi was locked up.

With 10,500 creditors demanding $4.3 million, Ponzi was declared bankrupt. At his hearing, the aforementioned young and attractive secretary Lucy Meli was asked, "Were there any international reply coupons in your office?"

"Yes," she answered sweetly. "One or two as samples." Ponzi, seated nearby, gave a start, then burst out in a laugh.

According to a later federal audit, about $2 million wound up missing. Ponzi had, of course, used later investors' money to pay earlier investors, a classic . . . Ponzi scheme. He was sentenced to five years in federal prison at Plymouth, Massachusetts.

Upon release, Ponzi tried a few more similar dodges and duly served more prison time. After being deported to Italy in 1934 and trying there to defraud Mussolini, he wound up dying penniless in a charity ward in Brazil. ✑

CASHING IN ON RACISM: A MONOPOLY ON WHITE SHEETS

It sounds like a cruel joke, but it isn't. The Ku Klux Klan made huge profits selling white sheets. The Klan had its own sheet factory in Atlanta, called Gates City Factory, which produced hooded white robes at two dollars apiece in 1923, and these were, in turn, sold to the racist faithful for $6.50. Considering that the Klan peaked at *three million* members in 1925, there was a lot of money to be made in worsted white cotton. Many of those millions of dollars were pocketed by the Imperial Wizard and his corrupt cohorts.

In many ways, the KKK was a vast, grotesque pyramid scheme to enrich its top members. Kind of like Amway for bigots.

Red-haired former minister William J. Simmons of Atlanta revived the Klan in 1915—piggybacking on the publicity for D. W. Griffith's film *Birth of a Nation,* based on the novel *The Clansman*—and Simmons charged new members an initiation fee of ten dollars each, called a klectoken; he also sold Klan life insurance to almost half his first batch of recruits.

But it wasn't until 1920 that a couple of high-powered commission salesmen created the actual pyramid that relaunched the Klan across the nation.

In 1920, a small Atlanta public relations firm, Southern Publicity Association, which had repped clients such as the Salvation Army and Anti-Saloon League, was close to bankruptcy when it signed a deal with the KKK. The arrangement entitled the publicity firm to keep eight dollars of the ten-dollar initiation fee paid by each new Klan member it signed up.

The firm's owners—Edward Clarke and Mrs. Elizabeth Tyler—divvied up the country into "Provinces" and sent out a sales force of 1,100 "Kleagles" (also on commission) to drum up new racist members. The duo handed over a four-dollar commission per KKK member to each Kleagle, and gave $1.50 to a regional supervisor called a Grand Goblin. They kept $2.50 for themselves. The remaining two dollars went straight to the Klan's florid founder, William J. Simmons.

In the first sixteen months, Clarke and Mrs. Tyler had cleared the then hefty $212,000 in net profit, while founder Simmons received $170,000, according to business historian Charles Alexander. A muckraking campaign by the *New York World* wound up backfiring when the Congressional committee investigating the Klan in 1921 brought no charges against them. With this de facto government stamp of approval, membership soared higher than the flames of a burning cross, as did sales of hooded sheets, the Klan newspaper, even the sale of obscure titles, like Imperial Kligrapp and Klexter, Klageroo, and Kladd.

In 1922, with business booming, the Klan found itself almost bankrupt. Although it had grossed about $10.5 million in the previous two years, the looting was so excessive there was almost no money left.

A new clique—led by a chubby dentist from Texas, Hiram Walker—bullied their

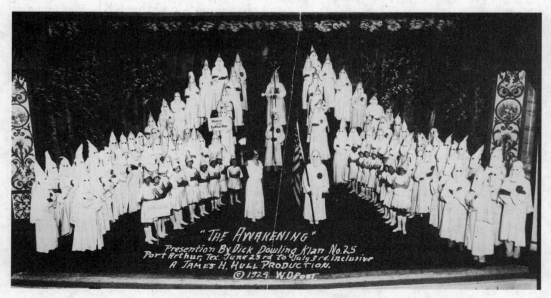

A stage performance by the *women* of the Ku Klux Klan in 1924 in Port Arthur, Texas.

way to top leadership, finally buying out Simmons for $146,500 in February 1924.

Hate was spewing a river of gold to the con men in Atlanta. The KKK levied an "Imperial Tax" on each member, to be paid by local chapters. The KKK still pushed life insurance on its members, through their own company, Empire Mutual. They held an annual Klonvocation, i.e., a racist convention; 1,000 delegates attended the 1924 affair in Kansas City.

While top officials focused more on personal enrichment, dues-paying Klansmen were still out there committing crimes and lynchings. One of their odder atrocities was charging Atlanta barber Ike Gaston with "cutting the hair of an inferior race with the same scissors used to cut the hair of white men." He was stretched between two trees and whipped with a metal-studded strap and later died from the injuries.

Although the Klan under Imperial Wizard Evans dropped the price of custom hooded sheets to five dollars, it wasn't enough to save the Klan. And, appropriately enough for a business scam, back taxes finally put the KKK out of business. In 1944, the Feds sued the KKK for $685,000 in unpaid back taxes. That year, the Klan officially disbanded. Splinter groups using the name would sporadically resurface, but never with the same national power or profitable pyramid scheme. 🌀

FINANCIAL GRAB BAG

SHYLOCK: JEWS AND MONEYLENDING

At the heart of Christian anti-Semitism — looming right beside the Jewish rabbis collaborating with the Romans to kill Jesus — stands the image of Shylock, the grotesquely hard-hearted miser wringing the last coin from starving Christian widows.

Were the Jews through European history notorious moneylenders, charging unconscionable interest?

The simple answer is "yes," for several centuries. "Among the Jews of the region between the Pyrenees and Scotland, between the Atlantic and the Elbe, usury became the main source of livelihood from about the twelfth to the fifteenth century," according to *The Economic History of the Jews*, by Salo Baron and coauthors, which was published in Jerusalem in 1975.

And by modern standards, medieval interest rates, according to that same book, were grotesquely high. The standard rate in England was generally twopence per pound a week, i.e., 43$\frac{1}{3}$ percent annually, while Frederick II of Austria capped rates at 173$\frac{1}{3}$ percent in 1244. Sanity prevailed in Italy, where interest rates varied from 15 to 25 percent, and the amount could never grow to more than the original loan.

But the Shylock question is trickier than "Did they loan?" and "Did they charge high interest?" The answer is "yes" to both questions but oftentimes they had a secret partner.

For Christians in the Middle Ages, usury was a sin. So, Jews often acted as beards for Christian kings to practice usury, a vastly profitable business. The Jew would make and collect the loans, while the king would heavily tax the Jew for the privilege; in practice, the king often collected the big profits while the Jew collected the little profits and the beatings. "Revenue from the Jews was an important part of the royal income," states Reverend James Parkes in *The Jews in the Medieval Community*. If public hatred against the Jewish lenders boiled over, the Christian king could disavow his Jews and let the mob attack, or even expel all Jews, as Edward I did in England in 1290, and King Louis IX (i.e., Saint Louis) did in France in 1253.

Another weapon to win the favor of the populace was to simply wipe out all debts to Jews. "The Christian rulers, who exploited Jews as their agents for usury—and then extorted from them a large part of their usurious gains . . . —used to proclaim moratoriums on individual, partial or total debts to Jews," according to *The Economic History of the Jews*.

But the princes and kings often fought to avoid losing profits.

This clearly happened when Pope Innocent III—trying to reward the Crusaders—issued a bull ordering Jews to forgive all interest on loans made to Crusaders. The king of France, Phillip II, refused, and in 1214 ordered all would-be Crusaders to settle up with "our men" ("*hominem nostris*") before leaving. That "our men" expression might sound odd, but Jews, having few rights, technically were often the "private property" of the king, or local lord.

Why did Jews flock to usury? Historian Reverend Parkes traces the occupation shift back to persecution of the Jews during the first Crusade in 1096 A.D.

"As long as bands of Crusaders were wandering across country, the roads were scarcely safe for Jewish merchants," writes Rev. Parkes. "Whereas previously the Jewish merchants had occasionally 'obliged' a friend with a loan, taking some object as security, now commerce began to take the second place, and the lending of money, an occupation that could be carried on at home, the first." Jews also were denied entry to most medieval guilds, which controlled various occupations.

At the same time, lending money became increasingly taboo for Christians. The Vatican repeatedly forbade usury, going so far as making it a heresy in 1311, and unleashing the dread Inquisition to enforce its ban. That left the usury field wide open to Jews, who were already heretical misfits and presumably couldn't fall any farther from grace.

Jews certainly profited from usury, but the challenge for them was to hold on to the profits. In the Middle Ages, Aaron of Lincoln was so wealthy that a special department of the exchequer had to be created to handle all his various accounts, that is, when the king of England confiscated all his property at his death.

When the Jews in 1492 were given six

months to leave Spain, they found it tough to get much value for their possessions. "They exchanged a house for an ass, and a vineyard for a small piece of cloth or linen, because they could not take out either gold or silver," wrote a contemporary chronicler. "But it is true that they secretly took out an infinite amount of gold and silver [in coin], which they swallowed and carried out in their bellies through those custom posts in which they had to be searched, and in the ports, both inland and beside the sea. The women, in particular, swallowed more; a person might swallow thirty ducats at one time."

Early on, Martin Luther (1483–1546) was somewhat sympathetic to the plight of the Jews, forced to become moneylenders and then hated for the practice. "When we forbid [the Jews] to labour and do business and have any human fellowship with us, thereby forcing them to usury, how is that supposed to do them any good?"

But twenty years later in 1543, the original Protestant lost any iota of sympathy: "Burn down their synagogues . . . force them to work and deal harshly with them, as Moses did in the wilderness, slaying three thousand lest the whole people perish . . . If this does not help, we must drive them out like mad dogs, so that we do not become partakers of their abominable blasphemy and all the other vices and thus merit God's wrath and be damned with them." ☙

A Rose Is a Rose, but a Tulip Can Bankrupt You

At its essence, buying a share of stock is making a wager that in the future other people will be willing to pay more for that same share. Ultimately, despite profit and loss sheets for the company, that share has no *absolute* intrinsic value, but is only worth what others will pay for it, generally as announced on public exchanges.

Business historians with a sense of humor (all four of them) like to point to the looniest episode in the long saga of speculative investment: tulipomania.

In the early 1600s, the normally level-headed Dutch started to prize their tulips beyond jewelry or even art. No wealthy man could throw a dinner party without showing off his rarest *Admiral Leifken* or *Semper Augustus* varieties. The tulip, more so than most flowers, is prone to mutation, especially regarding subtle shades of color, and Dutchmen started to compete with each other trying to discover and display a peacockian panoply of hues.

This passion, which spread to the middle class in that prosperous mercantile country, translated into a bidding war for rare varieties of tulip bulbs. What perhaps started as mild price inflation due to limited supply and huge demand turned into out-and-out stock trading. Tulip bulbs were listed on stock exchanges in Amsterdam, Rotterdam, Harlaem, Leyden, and later, briefly, even in Paris and London.

In 1635, a man offered twelve acres of downtown property for a single tulip bulb of the rare *Semper Augustus* species, of which only two bulbs were found in all of Holland. Another merchant was willing to pay for a *Viceroy* tulip bulb: four fat oxen, eight pigs, two casks of wine, four casks of beer, a thousand pounds of cheese, and much more. Prices kept going up.

Smart Dutch stock jobbers—who collected their commission on sales—fueled the frenzy, spreading rumors of exotic bulbs or of import ships foundering at sea.

Even carpenters, farmers, and chimney sweeps started investing with a certain sense of national pride that Holland's prize tulip could become so valuable, and foreigners played the game as well. Eventually, rich people stopped buying the flowers to show them off and instead started merely to speculate.

Finally, in 1636, some long-forgotten Dutchman got cold feet and refused to pay an agreed-upon price. Once confidence slipped, prices began to fall and fall and collapse. (The tulips were worth only what someone would pay for them.)

The Dutch government refused to step in, but an ad hoc council of buyers and sellers meeting in Amsterdam agreed that contracts for purchasing signed before the zenith of the craziness (November 1636) would be null and void while those after that date would be valued at 10 percent of face value. This bit of Solomonlike wisdom infuriated the sellers and the brokers. No court in Holland, however, would accept lawsuits regarding tulip prices, arguing that debts contracted in gambling were not debts in the eyes of the law.

Quite a few people had transferred their entire savings to a few tulip bulbs. "Substantial merchants were reduced almost to beggary," notes Charles Mackay in *Extraordinary Popular Delusions and the Madness of Crowds* (1841). "Many a representative of a noble line saw the fortunes of his house ruined beyond redemption."

Before you get too high and mighty over the folly of the Dutch, think of the international modern art market in the 1980s. Again, there is no intrinsic value to a Lichtenstein or a Klee canvas, only what people will pay for it. One day, someone took a good look at the chicken scrawls and said, Forget it. The proverbial bottom fell out. Was gambling millions of dollars on pigment splashes on canvas any saner than betting on tulip bulbs?

And, before you get too snooty over being proof against modern art speculation, think Wall Street. Think of those Initial Public Offerings for technology stocks.

A Dutch historian points out that very few tulip bulbs actually changed hands. "When *Semper Augustus* was not to be had anywhere, which happened twice, no species perhaps was oftener purchased and sold." People were betting on the future value of something.

When General Magic—a virtually untried little company spouting a lot of technodreams—went public in February 1995, brokers sold 6.3 million shares at $14 a share.

The company never turned a profit, didn't even seem to have a clear strategy or products. In January 1997, the price was $1^7/_8$. The brokerage firms taking trade commissions—just like Dutch stock jobbers in the 1600s—did quite well.

On the other hand, many investors in General Magic probably wish they had a tulip or two to show for their investment.

How to Succeed in Business: Ben Franklin

Ben Franklin, who was then postmaster, founded the weekly *Pennsylvania Gazette.* Franklin helped ensure its success by forbidding any competing papers from using the mails.

The Goodyear Name

Charles Goodyear (1800–1860) always believed that hard work and risk would pay off. He forced his family deep into debt in the 1830s while experimenting with rubber.

India rubber as it was then known was not yet widely used commercially because it had a few fatal flaws: It became sticky when hot and brittle when cold. It also lost its shape and sagged under weight.

Goodyear, an inventor with patents for safe-eye buttons and steel spring forks, used a trial-and-error method to improve the quality of rubber. He tried mixing it with everything from cream cheese to quicklime to bronze powder, all with no major improvements. One day, he had mixed a batch of the natural gum blended with sulphur, when a blob fell on the

Charles Goodyear (1800–1860)

stove, and in his haste, he forgot to wipe it off. Instead of turning into black soup, as he had expected, the concoction turned leathery. He tried to interest a couple of visiting engineers with his discovery, but since the bubbly Goodyear was always crowing about something, none of them seemed very interested. He took the newly cooked up swatch and hung it on a nail outside in the severe winter cold.

The next morning, the rubber was strong and flexible. Goodyear had accidentally discovered vulcanization, the process that transformed rubber from a novelty item to one of the most important materials in worldwide manufacturing.

The year was 1839. Despite the invention, Goodyear spiraled deeper into debt. "The certainty of success warranted extreme sacrifice," he later wrote in *Gum-Elastic and Its Varieties* (1855). When his two-year-old son died, the family couldn't afford a proper burial. For the next two decades, Goodyear tried to turn his discovery into practical and profitable use, envisioning everything from rubber stoppers for plugging cannon ball holes in ships to safety jackets for ice skaters.

He never succeeded commercially, sponging off relatives and backers to the end. Charles Goodyear died $200,000 in debt.

Frank A. Sieberling, a thirty-eight-year-old struggling entrepreneur in Akron, Ohio, founded a rubber company in 1898 and named it after Goodyear. No money ever exchanged hands for the use of the name; no patent royalties were ever paid to the Goodyear family. A statue of Charles Goodyear stands majestically in the lobby of the . . . World of Rubber museum in Akron.

CRIME & PUNISHMENT

THE NOT SO FINE ART OF EXECUTING CRIMINALS

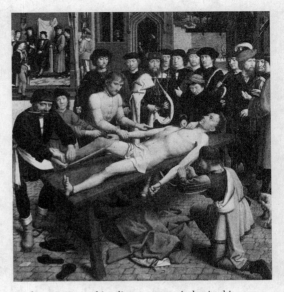

Barber-surgeons skin alive a corrupt judge in this Renaissance painting by Gerard David, commissioned to hang in the courtroom of the town hall in Brugge. How would you like to be a judge and come to work everyday and look at *that*? Notice the dog's comment in the lower right corner.

PASS THE PIE AND WATCH 'EM DIE

Executions are intended to draw spectators. If they do not draw spectators, they do not answer their purpose.

—SAMUEL JOHNSON

For almost 5,000 years of human history, public executions have been an excuse to party, from the mass stonings of biblical times to the drunken festivities at Tyburn gallows in England all the way to the wine- and blood-soaked mobs at the guillotine, that "National Razor of France."

While many liberals would like to believe that the crowds who jammed into public squares to watch their fellow humans die were mostly uneducated rabble, that's simply not true. Casanova writes of aristocrats renting expensive suites to watch the torture-execution of Damiens in 1768; Thackeray writes of "quiet fat family parties of simple honest tradesmen and their wives looking on with the greatest imaginable calmness and sipping their tea." As another observer pointed out about British attendees: The booming sales of the piemen indicate how few stomachs were turned by the events. Charles Dickens observed a hanging on November 13, 1849, and noted "fightings, faintings, whistling . . . brutal jokes" and "indecent delight when swooning women were dragged out of the crowd by police with their dresses disordered."

America was of course not exempt. Back in 1693 in Bucks County, Pennsylvania, a bargeman convicted of murder was scheduled to be hanged on July 3. The *Colonial Records of Pennsylvania* matter-of-factly state, "There were too few people there to make the affair enjoyable."

An Auto-Da-Fé, 1682

For mass public execution with the most pomp and circumstance, the Inquisitions of Spain and Portugal are difficult to top. An enormous crowd of 20,000 dressed in their finest clothes jammed the main square of Lisbon to witness the burning of twenty-one heretics on June 30, 1682, among them noblemen and Church dignitaries. (Here is an eyewitness account:)

At the place of execution, which at Lisbon is the Ribera, there are so many stakes set up as there are prisoners to be burned, with a good quantity of dry furze about them. The stakes of the *Professed*, as the Inquisitors call them, the professed, are about four yards high, and have a small board, whereon the prisoner is to be seated within a half a yard of the top . . . The *Professed* go up a ladder betwixt two Jesuits, who have attended them the whole day of execution.

When they come even with the aforesaid board, they turn to the people and the Jesuits spend near a quarter of an hour in exhorting them to be reconciled to the Church of Rome. If they refuse, the priests come down and the executioner ascends and turns the professed from off the ladder and puts them upon the seat, chains their bodies to the stake and leaves them.

Then the Jesuits go up a second time to renew their exhortations and if they find them ineffectual usually tell them at parting, that they "leave them to the Devil, who is standing at their elbow to receive their souls and carry them with him into the flames of hell-fire, as soon as they are out of their bodies."

Upon this, a great shout is then raised, and as soon as the Jesuits are off the ladder, the cry is "Let the Dogs' beards be made, Let the Dogs' beards be made!" This is done by thrusting flaming furzes against their faces with long poles. This barbarity is repeated until their faces are burnt coal black, and is accompanied with such loud acclamations of joy as are not heard even at a Bull-Feast or a farce.

Fire is then set to the furzes, which are at the bottom of the stake, but the flames seldom reach as high as the seat they sit upon . . . If the day is windy, then they do not die even after an hour and a half or two hours, and so are really roasted and not burnt to death . . . The sufferers as long as they are able to speak, cry out: *"Misericordia por Amor de Dios."* ("Mercy for the love of God.") ❧

Hanging: A Long Slow Death

Around capital punishment there lingers a fascination, urging weak and bad people towards it and imparting an interest to details connected with it, and with malefactors awaiting it or suffering it, which even good and well-disposed people cannot withstand.

— CHARLES DICKENS

Americans, from watching too many Westerns, have this image of hanging as a fairly instantaneous death. The trapdoor opens, the body falls, the neck snaps.

That's not how they did it in Europe up to the mid-1800s. Hanging was a long hu-

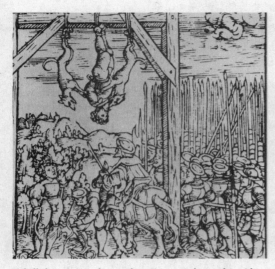

Of all the ways to die . . . the prisoner is hanged upside down between two starving dogs or wolves. Northern Europe, c. 1500.

miliating death, by slow strangulation, taking generally fifteen minutes to half an hour. Each contortion of the body—from first twitch to the often inevitable final erection—was cheered by the crowds. ❧

EUROPEAN NICETIES OF EXECUTING WOMEN

For many centuries in most of Europe through the Middle Ages and the Renaissance, it was considered "immodest" to hang women—since, given the billowy nature of skirts and lack of bifurcal underwear, their legs if not more would be visible from below the gallows.

"For as the decency due to their sex forbids the exposing and publicly mangling of their bodies, their sentence is, to be drawn to the gallows and there to be burnt alive." So stated *Blackstone Commentaries*, England's authoritative early law book.

On the European continent, this sense of modesty—in at least some Northern countries—gave rise to a different approach for performing capital punishment on females. "The burning of a woman provided a spectacle not only terrifying but terribly indecent, one that would be intolerable to the modesty of Northern Europe," writes historian Jules Michelet in *Wars of Religion* (1856). "During the execution of Joan of Arc, the first flame that flared up burned off her clothes and cruelly revealed her poor trembling nudity."

No instead, in Northern Europe as late as 1545, the authorities—out of respect for women's modesty—buried them alive. Michelet describes the process: "The uncovered coffin is lowered into the ground with three iron bars closing in the victim. Dirt is then thrown on the living person. Sometimes—out of mercy—the executioner, to limit the suffering, strangles the victim in advance."

Executing women raised other problems: pregnancy. It was obviously unjust to kill the unborn for the crimes of the mother. In virtually all Western societies, the execution would be delayed until after the woman gave birth, which no doubt gave rise to a desperate effort on the part of some condemned women to get pregnant. Says the character Filch in *The Beggar's Opera* (III, iii) who is hard at work in Newgate Prison: "Since the favourite child-getter was disabled by a mishap, I have picked up a little money by helping the ladies to a pregnancy against their being called down to sentence—but if a man cannot get an honest livelihood any easier way, I am sure 'tis what I can't undertake for another session." Poor fella.

There were no five-minute pregnancy tests back then, so most condemned women claimed to be with child, as a kind of last-ditch appeal. In fact, one of the most notorious early murder cases in American history involved just such a case. The beautiful thirty-two-year-old Bathsheeba Spooner of Brookfield, Massachusetts, was convicted of conspiring to murder her wealthy elderly husband in 1778 and sentenced to die in one of the first capital cases of the new United States. Midwives—after much argument—decided Bathsheeba was not pregnant. An autopsy later revealed a five-month-old fetus.

The modesty issue also arose during the first electrocution of a woman at Sing Sing in New York in 1899. Martha Place of Brooklyn strangled her pretty stepdaughter, then attacked her husband with an axe. *The National Police Gazette* reported that authorities took special precautions during the execution. "The warden beckoned to two women physicians to stand close, and their gowns hid the scene of the buckling of the electrode on the woman's leg near the knee. When the work was done one of the woman doctors pulled down the skirt so that the electrode and leg were covered."

In less than seven minutes, Mrs. Place was pronounced dead. "The execution had been successful in every way. The first woman to be killed under the law had been put to death humanely."

Kill convicted women? Yes, but don't embarrass them.

A British Recipe for Severed Heads, 1660

For most Americans, "London Bridge" conjures up a nursery rhyme image of a dilapidated quaint old structure with horse-drawn carts and children playing. In Shakespeare's time and after, most Englishmen probably would have thought of severed heads stuck on long spikes, displayed in the open for months.

A Quaker named Thomas Ellwood in Newgate Prison described in 1660 how the jailors and prisoners handled the severed heads of traitors. "They took them by the hair, flouting, jeering and laughing at them; and then giving them some ill names box'd them on the ears and cheeks. Which done, the hangman put them in a kettle and parboiled them with baysalt and cumin-seed; that to keep them from putrefaction, and this to keep off the Fowls from seizing on them."

Obviously this gallery of severed heads was meant to discourage anyone from committing similar crimes; so was hanging the dead body in chains or "gibbeting." We picture this practice as something out of medieval Europe, some grisly sight that Robin Hood might pass. Think again. Gibbeting occured in the American colonies. Two slaves were convicted of poisoning their master, Captain John Codman of Charlestown, Massachusetts, in 1755. After a speedy trial, the female,

Phyllis, was burned at the stake and Mark was hung at the gallows, then put up in a cage in the center of town, in Charlestown Commons. An army surgeon, Dr. Cabel Ray, passing by in 1758 noted in his diary: "His skin was but very little broken, altho he had hung there over three or four years."

When Paul Revere took his famous ride on April 18, 1775, he mentioned racing past the spot "where Mark was hung in chains." ❧

EXECUTING CHILDREN

With the juvenile crime rate soaring in the United States in the 1990s, many states started punishing young offenders as adults, locking even fourteen-year-olds in maximum security prisons. That crackdown has a long way to go before it reaches the past standards of justice in the U.S. and Great Britain.

For most of British history prior to the 20th century, the law stated that a child older than seven was liable to the death penalty, and there are numerous examples from British court records of children—even little girls—being hanged to death. In 1833 in England, a nine-year-old boy convicted of stealing twopence worth of paint from a broken store window, was sentenced to die.

However, we don't expect that kind of cruel punishment to have occurred in this country. At least not often. Wrong. Two hundred and eighty-two children (i.e., seventeen years old or younger at the time of the crime) have been executed in America, including ten females, according to Victor Streib, professor of Law at Cleveland State University. As recently as 1944, a fourteen-year-old boy was executed in South Carolina.

George Stinney, the fourteen-year-old black son of a sawmill worker, confessed to beating Betty Binnicker, eleven, and Mary Thames, eight, to death with a railroad spike. The little white girls were picking flowers and the older one apparently refused his sexual advances.

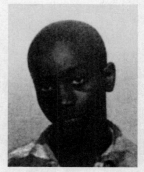

George Stinney, electrocuted in South Carolina at age fourteen in 1944, was the youngest criminal to be executed this century in the United States.

Stinney's lawyer—who was running for office—never filed an appeal. The Associated Press reported that "the guards had difficulty strapping the boy's slight form into the wooden chair built for adults" and he was so small "it was difficult to attach the electrode to the right leg." Stinney was the youngest person executed in this country during this century. In England, the youngest age at which the death penalty could be applied was raised in 1908 to sixteen. ❧

LOPPING OFF MISCONCEPTIONS ABOUT THE GUILLOTINE

Almost from its first victim on April 25, 1792, the guillotine—much like the cruci-

In this lampoon, Robespierre, high priest of the French Revolution, is shown executing the executioner, after having guillotined *all* the citizens of France. (Robespierre, himself, was guillotined on July 28, 1794, ending the Reign of Terror.)

fix for Catholics—became a fetishistic object for the French during their revolution. Men had it tattooed on their bodies; women wore dangling guillotine earrings and brooches; the design was incorporated into plates, cups, snuffboxes; children played with toy versions, decapitating mice; elegant ladies lopped off the heads of dolls and out squirted a red perfume, in which they soaked their handkerchiefs. This was no Addams Family lampoon; this was *La Famille Française*.

The guillotine itself accumulated many nicknames, such as the "Patriotic Razor," the "National Abbreviator," the "Widow." Every day criers sold the "List of winners of the Lottery of St. Guillotine."

That love affair with the window of death soon paled. First off, contrary to popular belief, more commoners than aristocrats were executed by the guillotine, with estimates ranging at four commoners to every nobleman beheaded. The paranoia and infighting among the leaders transformed the French Revolution into a foray as murderous and unjust as the Holy Inquisition.

Misconceptions surround the guillotine. First off, it was *not* a French invention; similar execution devices date back to 1200 in Italy, and the Scots had a "Scottish Maiden," a giant machine with a falling blade, lopping heads off in Edinburgh in the 1500s.

Also, it wasn't the only method of public execution during the French Revolution. At Nantes, to quash counterrevolution, the authorities resorted to mass drownings, called "noyades," killing thousands.

(Somehow I can't picture Sidney Carton in *A Tale of Two Cities* saying "'Tis a far far better thing I do . . ." then Splash.)

One of the bigger misconceptions about the guillotine concerns who actually invented the French device.

Dr. Joseph-Ignace Guillotin did *not* invent it; he was a humanitarian who proposed finding a more humane means of execution than hanging. It was a Dr. Antoine Louis who refined an Italian beheading device, and for a while, it was called a "Louison."

Dr. Guillotin later became appalled at the excesses during the Terror. "Some men are unlucky," wrote Victor Hugo. "Christopher Columbus was unable to have his discovery named after him; Guillotin was unable to prevent his device from bearing his name."

When the good doctor died in 1814, his descendants changed the family name. 🌀

IS THERE SENSATION AFTER DECAPITATION? CHARLOTTE CORDAY'S BLUSH

Charlotte Corday killed revolutionary leader Jean-Paul Marat in his bathtub, on July 13, 1793. "I knew he was perverting France," said the twenty-four-year-old impoverished aristocrat. "I killed one man in order to save one hundred thousand."

Four days later amid a blustery rainstorm, Corday—clad in the red nightshirt reserved for parricides (had she not murdered a "father" of her country?)—rode defiantly standing up in the tumbril to the packed Place de la Révolution. She fearlessly walked quickly up the steps to the guillotine and even asked the executioner to step aside so she could examine the machine. "I have a right to be curious," said the strangely calm girl, whose otherworldly manner some have compared to Joan of Arc. "I have never seen one before."

After the heavy slanted blade fell, an executioner's assistant named François le Gros picked up the severed head by the hair, and brimming with Revolutionary fervor, slapped Corday's cheek.

Several eyewitnesses saw her face flush red with anger, not just one cheek but both cheeks. Some thought they perceived disgust curl her lips.

Was her head still alive? The debate was sparked.

Charlotte Corday: her severed head sparked guillotine research.

In that basket full of bloody heads beneath the guillotine, were any of them still alert and sensate? Were any of the eyes still seeing and ears still hearing?

Sounds like a science fiction plot, or some cartoon panel of The Brain in Dick Tracy, but it wasn't. It was a topic of study for some premier doctors in France for almost 200 years.

If there was sensation after decapitation, then the guillotine wasn't the quick merciful death promised by the Revolutionary leaders. It was cruel, maybe crueler than hanging or disemboweling, to transform the victim into a disembodied head fully experiencing the agony of a horrific knife wound. Remember that the Enlightenment was an age of reason—with a turn away from religion and emotion—so the logical question was: Why couldn't the head beam on for a few more minutes of consciousness? As one French writer put it, if the severed head is conscious, then it reconfigures Descartes famed dictum to "I think but I am not."

Since these medical experiments rank with some of the more unusual ever attempted, I have created a timeline of severed head research.

SEVERED HEAD RESEARCH— THE HIGHLIGHTS

[The following is adapted from *The History of the Guillotine* by Alistair Kershaw]

❧ 1794. Dr. S. T. Sommering, a respected German anatomist, argues in a Parisian daily that "consciousness of feeling may persist, even if blood circulation in the brain is terminated, partial or weak." Dr. Sommering contends that the severed head's strongest sensation would be the "after-pain" felt in the neck.

❧ 1794. French doctors quickly rush to the defense of the Patriotic Razor. A Dr.

Sedillot counters that the German is confusing nervous spasms with sensory perceptions. He argues that if sleep ceases awareness of feeling, how can death not do the same?

Most of the debate remained very philosophical, that is, until the next century when experimentation began.

❧ 1879. At seven A.M. sharp, a murderer-rapist-necrophiliac named Prunier was guillotined and five minutes later, the head was given to Dr. E. Decaisne and his two colleagues. One doctor poised his lips over Prunier's ear and shouted "Prunier" over and over but neither the eyes nor any part of the face showed any awareness. They tried pinching him, giving him ammonia smelling salts, put a candle flame near his eyeball. All negative, that is, until the

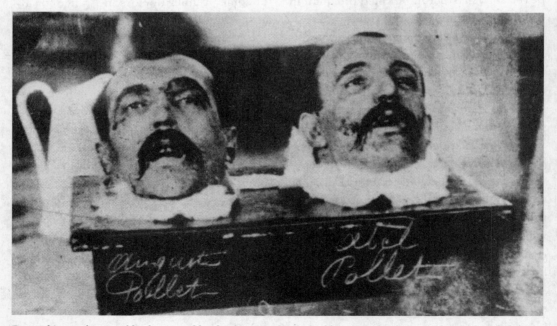

Propped in towels on a table: the severed heads of convicted armed robbers, twin brothers, Auguste and Abel Pollet, guillotined January 11, 1909.

experimenters tried jolting body parts with electricity. With Frankensteinian aplomb, they were able to make the eyelids flutter, teeth chatter. Taking the trunk, they were able to make his legs and arms move. "The [dead man's] fingers came to lock very firmly onto the hand of one of the researchers," wrote Dr. Decaisne in the *Bulletin de l'académie de medicin.* "These muscular reactions persisted an hour and a half after decapitation, that is to say, at a time when other victims have been given over to the grave-diggers."

⟐ 1880. Dr. Dassy de Lignières is given the head of the murderer three hours after decapitation. He pumps blood from a living dog into the head, and for two seconds the lips and eyelids fluttered. Concludes the doctor: "I affirm that during two seconds the brain thought."

⟐ 1905. Dr. Beaurieux is able to investigate the head *instantly* after decapitation. "Here then is what I was able to note immediately after the decapitation: the eyelids and lips of the guillotined man worked in irregularly rhythmic contractions for about five or six seconds.

"I waited for several seconds. The spasmodic movements ceased. The face relaxed, the lids half-closed on the eyeballs, leaving only the white of the conjunctiva visible, exactly as in the dying whom we have occasion to see every day. . . . It was then that I called in a strong sharp voice: "Languille!" I then saw the eyelids slowly lift up, without any spasmodic contraction—I insist advisedly

on this peculiarity—but with an even movement, quite distinct and normal, such as happens in everyday life, with people awakened or torn from their thoughts. Next, Languille's eyes very definitely fixed themselves on mine and the pupils focused themselves. I was not, then, dealing with a vague dull look without any expression that can be observed any day in dying people to whom one speaks: I was dealing with undeniably living eyes which were looking at me."

⟐ 1956. Dr. Piedelièvre and Dr. Fournier conclude "death is not instantaneous. . . . Every vital element survives decapitation. . . . (it is) a savage vivisection followed by a premature burial."

The guillotine was last used to execute a criminal in France in 1977.

Sums up Alistair Kershaw in *The History of the Guillotine:* "Most present day physiologists, secure in their merely theoretical acquaintance with the issue, display a proper reserve towards so bizarre and nightmarish a notion as that of a head, separated from its trunk, contemplating its own horrendous state. Even so, they are unwilling to affirm flatly that it is out of the question. The possibility still grimaces at us all."

A Postscript to Charlotte Corday . . . Sketch of a Dead Headless Virgin?

While Corday's severed head helped spark the bizarre research outlined above, it was another part of her anatomy that concerned the Revolutionary Tribunal. Corday had adamantly denied that she had any accomplices. It infuriated the political leaders and editors that none of Corday's co-conspirators could be identified (a kind of early "lone gunman" problem), and that a woman (!) could have pulled off this political assassination by herself.

The newspapers started reporting that Corday was four months pregnant (impugning the reputation of the would-be nun) and hinting that her lover had conceived the plan.

"To determine whether she was a 'virgina intacta' the Revolutionary Council had the body conveyed to a nearby hospital to be examined," according to *Death Comes to the Maiden* by Camille Naish. "Jacques-Louis David—the celebrated artist whose works included *The Death of Marat*—and several of his students asked to be present at this *interesting* event, and one of them even made a sketch. The drawing has since been lost but a contemporary description of it states that during the gynecological exam the head was placed back in its 'normal' position."

As a result of the ghoulish probe, the leaders grudgingly made it known that Charlotte Corday was in fact a virgin.

THE POPE BLESSES TORTURE

For more than 500 years in Europe, from the 1200s to the 1700s, including the heyday of the Renaissance, torturing accused criminals was *standard operating procedure* most everywhere except England. This was the primary means of determining guilt (or rarely innocence) in a criminal investigation, *not* eyewitnesses, *not* physical evidence, but confession. One of the prime reasons that the practice of torture survived and thrived was the stamp of approval given it early on by the enormously influential Catholic Church.

In 1252, Pope Innocent IV sanctioned torture as a way to help officials of the Holy Inquisition force heretics to confess. His papal bull ordained: "If torture is appropriate for those who break the laws of men, then it is more than fitting for those who break the laws of God." At first, priests had to farm out their iron boot work to local lay thugs, but just four years later in 1256, a second papal bull gave priests the right to absolve each other for such "irregularities."

England, to its credit throughout its history, rarely authorized legal torture. (Cynics claim British judges were more than willing to convict without the fiction of a forced confession.) And that refusal to rack and pincer infuriated the Vatican. Pope Clement V wrote to King Edward II

(1284–1327): "We hear that you forbid torture as contrary to the laws of your land; but no state can over-ride Canon Law, Our Law. Therefore, I command you at once to submit these men to torture . . . You have already imperilled your soul as a favourer of heretics." The English king in this instance caved in, and hundreds suffered.

Tortures, of course, varied from country to country, from century to century, but a few methods proved exceedingly popular. (Remember: We are not talking about punishment here, like the stocks or whipping, we are talking about methods of interrogation; the expression "giving someone the third degree" comes right from here.)

- Strappado. Perhaps the most common form of "first degree" torture throughout Europe. The hands were bound behind the back to an iron bar, the prisoner was then hoisted in the air, sometimes suspended for hours. For added persuasiveness, weights totaling as much as 250 pounds could be added to the ankles.

- Binding with cords in various ways, especially thin cords around the fingers; also binding to ladders with sharpened rungs.

- Roasting the feet, covered in lard for a longer slower burn.

- Squassation. Hoisted like the strappado, but then dropped violently, causing dislocation of the shoulder joints.

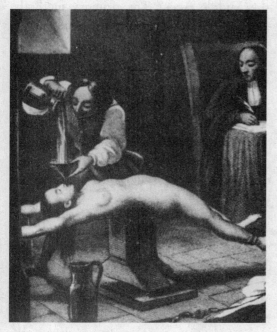

The water torture. A handkerchief is shoved down the throat, the nose is often pinched, then gallons of water are poured into the mouth via a funnel. When the suspect/victim is beyond bloated, he or she is tilted head-down to increase pressure on the heart and lungs. A very effective and popular torture since it left no marks. Note the court official ready to write down any "free and open" confession.

To cite one torture a bit *out* of the mainstream, here are the "Vigils of Spain" as described by reform-minded French jurist Augustin Nicolas in 1684. "A man's wrists and ankles are bound to four chains attached to the ceiling. He is lowered onto a pointed iron rod which is inserted in his anus. By sheer muscular effort, he must support himself for hours to avoid sitting on the pointed iron, which pierces him with insufferable pain."

Adds Nicolas with contempt: "We pretend that the human frame can resist these devilish practices, and that the confessions which our wretched victims make of everything that may be charged against them are true."

Finally in the 1700s, a voice rang out loud and angry against legal torture. Cesare Beccaria (1738–1794), a now often forgotten Italian nobleman, wrote an essay against torture and capital punishment. It was one of those rare times when one person's thoughts hit an international nerve. Top-drawer thinkers such as Voltaire and Jefferson seconded Beccaria's views, and Beccaria's *Crimes and Punishments* (1764) helped revolutionize Western jurisprudence.

The use of torture in legal proceedings was gradually phased out. The framers of the U.S. Constitution, quite aware of Beccarria, forbade "cruel and unusual punishment" (eighth amendment). The French Revolution abolished it in France in 1789, Russia cut it out in 1801; Spain abolished it in 1811. Finally, Pope Pius VII issued a bull in 1816 ending the Catholic Church's five-century endorsement of torture. ❧

INVESTIGATION: CENTURIES OF RUSHING TO JUDGMENT

DETERMINING GUILT IN THE MIDDLE AGES

We are so used to trial by jury, to witnesses testifying, to piles of evidence from fingerprints to bank security cameras. But how was guilt or innocence determined in the Middle Ages? The primary methods were oath, ordeal, and duel, "resources devised by human ingenuity and credulity when called upon to decide questions too intricate for the impatient intellect of a rude and semi-barbarous age," according to H. C. Lea. Whatever, they certainly weren't fun for the accused.

THE ORDEAL

Dunk the accused in water, especially popular in witch trials. If he or she floats to the surface, the person is guilty, since the pure body is rejecting the impure sinner. If they sink, they're innocent (and quite often dead). Another test was to carry a red-hot piece of iron. If scarring occurred, then guilty. But perhaps the most common ordeal in England was the following simple test, as described by Christopher Hibbert in *The Roots of Evil*.

"Before the ceremony began, a fire was lit in the middle of the church and a deep bowl of water and bandages were brought in by a priest. The spectators, all of whom must be fasting and have abstained from their wives during the night, then came in silently and divided themselves into two rows on either side of the church . . . When the water in the bowl was boiling the accused who for three days had eaten nothing but bread and water and salt and herbs, and had attended mass on each of the three days, approached the fire. The priest bandages his arm while the spectators prayed that God would make clear the whole truth. At the bottom of the boiling water was a stone. If he was to undergo the single ordeal, he had to plunge his hand into the water up to the wrist; if the triple ordeal had been prescribed, he had to put his arm into the bowl so that the water came up to his elbow and then pick out the stone. After three days the bandages were removed. Evidence of scalding was taken to be proof of guilt."

There was a wee bit of a double standard when it came to determining guilt for priests.

"The priests themselves, if accused, did not have to undergo these ordeals, but instead were tried by the *corsnaed*, which involved eating a piece of consecrated bread and cheese before the altar. God was prayed to send down the angel Gabriel to stop the throat of the priest if he were guilty and so prevent him swallowing the food which would be proof of his crime."

Not surprisingly, this double standard earned the clergy a certain resentment. Thanks to sharp criticism by reform-minded churchmen such as Yves of

Chartres, the ordeal was abolished by the early 1200s.

JUDICIAL DUELS

Following the Norman Conquest, the accused could challenge his accuser to a trial by battle. This quickly degenerated into the accused and accuser hiring professional fighters to joust in their stead. While nowadays we have experts for hire, back then they had thugs for hire. Quite a few muscular knights grew quite wealthy as itinerant champions. In Germany, rules have survived for when a woman wanted to fight her own battle. The gist of it is: Dig a circular pit three feet deep and the man must fight from there.

But perhaps the strangest judicial duel occurred in France during the reign of

Dog vs. Man

Charles V (1338–1380). A nobleman named Montargis was murdered. One day at court, Montargis's dog suddenly attacked a knight, Macaire, and roused everyone's suspicions about the man. The king decided there would be a "Judgment of God" and that the knight and the dog would fight on the battlefield. The enraged beast won; the knight later confessed and was executed. ❧

FEMALE CRIMINAL BODY TYPES, 1890

For the first five thousand years or so, mankind's detective work was incredibly shoddy. A criminal investigation prior to the 1800s generally meant little more than a hasty search for eyewitnesses and motives and, above all, the coercion of the accused into confessing.

That began to change in the mid- to late 1800s, as schools of forensic medicine opened up, as detectives turned to fingerprints (identified as "permanent and unique" as early as 1823), and police departments began to collect mug shots. French chemists refined blood analysis.

By the 1890s, criminologists appeared to be on the verge of a startling breakthrough: identifying criminal body types or markers.

Internationally acclaimed Italian scientist, Cesare Lombroso, claimed that by carefully examining the physical characteristics of a suspect, i.e., every nook and cranny of the body, he could help determine guilt or innocence.

Imagine the implications. Say someone was accused of rape, but the eyewitness identification was a bit shaky. What if Lombroso could inspect the man's body or skull and find definitive markers revealing the man to be a rapist? Would it be the suspect's ear? his tongue? his nose hair? No body part was off-limits to these scientific pioneers.

While this kind of analysis might seem a bit absurd today, the theories were all woven around the most respected research of the day, especially Charles Darwin's *Origin of Species*.

The body research all started when Lombroso performed an autopsy on a notorious thief named Vilella, and in a moment of blinding revelation was convinced that Vilella was a throwback to primitive man. "I seemed to see all of a sudden . . . the problem of the nature of the criminal—an atavistic being who reproduces in his person the ferocious instincts of primitive humanity and the inferior animals."

Call that Cro-Magnon character the "First Delinquent."

Lombroso published *L'Uomo Delinquente* in 1876, and his research had a vast ripple effect, sending scientists worldwide scurrying to identify criminal body types. They stripped, probed, and measured prisoners in the hopes of building up enough case histories and statistics to find patterns. The research took on the flavor of a hunt for the Holy Grail. What body part would be the key? At first they focused on heads, giving momentum to the "science" of phrenology, i.e., measurement of skull shapes to indicate behavior.

For a while, experts believed that criminals tended to have a more pronounced lower jaw, a higher incidence of pointy canine teeth, scanty beards, unusual ear shapes. This evidence was seriously doled out at trial after trial in the United States from 1875 to 1900 (see Maria Barberi later in this chapter).

It was only a matter of time before female criminals received the same scrutiny.

Prison expert Raffaele Gurrieri made the study of female criminals his lifelong specialty, and published his results in Lombroso's *Journal of Psychiatry, Penal Science and Criminal Anthropology*.

Gurrieri examined sixty prostitutes age seventeen to forty-five, arrested in the vicinity of Bologna, Italy. His body hair research revealed 23 percent had abundant hair under their arms while 16 percent had genital hair extending to their anus and 12 percent had hairs around their nipples.

As for their breasts, he found 45 percent had "voluminous breasts," while 29 percent had medium and 26 percent had small. Among those breasts, 26 percent were very firm/self-supporting while 33 percent were flabby.

His research, however, turned a bit more sinister. He decided to use the new-fangled electrical gauges in the Laboratory of Legal Medicine in Bologna to test sensitivity and pain thresholds. He extended his study group for comparison purposes. "After much difficulty," he convinced fifteen women of "good habits and social attitudes" to participate. The areas zapped included the palm, forehead, tip of nose, tip of tongue, cheek, breast, upper inner thigh, ovary, and clitoris.

	Normal women	Prostitutes
Tongue	143	137
Forehead	133	126
Clitoris	131	126
Nose	130	124

Gurrieri found that prostitutes are less sensitive than normal women.

Researchers like Lombroso and Gurrieri were searching for patterns. Needless to say, although they looked at a lot of naked bodies, they didn't find any that have held up to modern science.

And not all of these early criminal anthropologists subjected women (as well as men) to such invasive probes.

"In our research, we don't include any irregularities of sexual organs, whether it be vaginal lips, the clitoris, etc., because it is always very unwillingly that female criminals allow themselves to be examined in this regard; quite a few have categorically refused," wrote scientist Pauline Tarnowsky in her book, *Female Murderers* (1908). *Pauline*! i.e., a woman.

"Hoping to maintain cordial relationships and to avoid any coercion, we have preferred to sacrifice the bulk of our research in that direction."

After Hitler, this type of soma research, this anthropometry, has been completely discredited. ✹

UNJUSTLY FORGOTTEN CRIMINALS

Serial killer Belle Gunness, with her children Lucy, Myrtle, and Philip, in 1904.

AMERICAN FEMALE SERIAL KILLERS

When the media in the early 1990s covered Aileen Wuornos, a Florida highway prostitute accused of killing six abusive "johns," you'd have thought she was America's first female serial killer. She wasn't.

While women lag far behind men in this gruesome sport—and accounted, for instance, for only 8.6 percent of killers in solved murders in the United States in 1995—there have been a handful of documented female serial killers in this country.

FEMALE BLUEBEARD: BELLE GUNNESS

This personals ad first started appearing in Chicago area newspapers in 1906. "Comely widow desires to make the acquaintance of a gentleman equally well provided, with view of joining fortunes . . . Triflers need not apply."

Once a connection was made, the widow wrote passionate love letters. To one bachelor farmer of South Dakota, Andrew Hegelein, she closed her note: "My heart beats in wild rapture for you, My Andrew, I love you. Come prepared to stay forever."

And, of course, he did, right *under* the barn.

Belle Gunness, a portly Norwegian immigrant who owned a hog farm in rural Indiana, lured at least a dozen men to her home through the "personals."

The men arrived bearing cash and property deeds to show they weren't "triflers." She'd serve them a sumptuous feast, and top it off by playing something romantic on her baby grand piano. That night might be the guest's first time ever sleeping in a soft feather bed.

Gunness cleavered some in the back of the skull, poisoned others. Never one to waste, she fed some body parts to her pigs, and buried the rest near her barn. Over a two year stretch, she snookered lonely old men to the tune of perhaps $100,000.

The charred Gunness farm in 1908 in LaPorte, Indiana, where ten bodies were found buried, some dismembered. (The letters mark grave sites.)

Bank records indicate, for instance, that Belle deposited a $2,900 check from Andrew Hegelein. When his worried brother threatened to come search for him, a fire suddenly hit the Gunness farmhouse.

In the burning rubble the next day were found the three bodies of her children and the headless corpse of a woman, with Belle's false teeth nearby. Neighbors quickly claimed that the corpse wasn't Belle. Measurements pegged the charred remains at 5'3", with a midsize figure, while local shopkeepers, who ordered Belle's outsize garments, put her at 5'8", with measurements of 46-37-54.

Suspicions aroused, the sheriff dug up her property and found ten corpses, including her stepdaughter and Andrew Hegelein. A ranch hand, convicted of arson in that blaze, later put Belle's death toll at forty-two. Despite purported sightings of Belle for decades afterward, she was never captured. Belle Gunness even inspired a ballad:

Belle Gunness was a lady fair,
In Indiana State,
She weighed about three hundred pounds,
And that is quite some weight.

That she was stronger than a man
Her neighbors all did own;
She butchered hogs right easily,
And did it all alone.

But hogs were just a sideline,
She indulged in now and then;
Her favorite occupation
Was a-butchering of men.

To keep her cleaver busy
Belle would run an ad,
And men would come a-scurrying
With all the cash they had.

Now some say Belle killed only ten,
And some say forty-two;
It was hard to tell exactly
But there were quite a few.

The bones were dug up in her yard,
Some parts never came to light,
And Belle, herself, could not be found
To set the tally right.

And where Belle is now no one knows,
But my advice is fair:
If a widow advertises
For a man with cash, beware!
[Collected by Max Egly.] 🐚

MURDERESS MARIA BARBERI BECOMES A NATIONAL HERO

Some ways are more pleasant than others to make it into the history books. In the spring of 1896, Maria Barberi—who slit her lover's throat—was scheduled to become the first woman ever executed in the

Confessed murderess Maria Barberi in prison, midtrial, nervously twirling a piece of white tape in the *New York Evening Journal*, November 29, 1896.

electric chair. By midsummer, instead, she was a national hero for the burgeoning "New Woman" movement and had received six marriage proposals. Her crazy naked uncle came to her defense from the grave and alienists working for her lawyers discovered for her a new illness called "psychical epilepsy."

This bizarre case—one of the more unusual in the history of American justice—has almost been completely forgotten. It's time to resurrect it.

Maria Barberi, a pudgy, homely twenty-four-year-old seamstress who lived with her parents in New York's Little Italy, met a roguish bootblack named Domenico Cataldo. A few weeks later, in a short-stay hotel near his shoeshine stand, with the aid of chianti and marital promises, he seduced her. Disgraced, Maria moved in with him and waited for the wedding date. And waited, and waited.

One day when her mother begged him to marry her daughter, Cataldo demanded $200, then he changed his tune. "I can't marry her cause my friends laugh because she's got such a funny face." And the charmer added, "Only pips [i.e., fools] marry!" He claimed Maria was merely his sixth live-in girlfriend and offered to show Mama the pictures.

Maria Barberi, with his jeering friends looking on, slit Domenico's throat from ear to ear with a folding razor.

She confessed to the crime through an interpreter, and after a speedy trial before the notoriously tough Judge Goff, was sentenced to die in the electric chair. Since New York State was the first locale in the world to institute this supposedly more humane form of execution, she would be the world's first woman to receive 1,000 volts of alternating current.

Her death sentence, the death sentence of a *woman,* hit a nerve. The *New York Times* noted a "sensational craze pervading the whole country, from Cape Cod to the Golden Gate in behalf of the prisoner."

"Sob Sister" columnists—celebrating the emergence of the New Woman who could work, vote, and wear skirts above the ankle—stoked the emotions, claiming that it was outrageous that Maria should die for killing a cad. "She was not a bad girl," wrote one. "She wanted Cataldo to do what was right." Within weeks, an enormous stack of petitions bearing 60,000 signatures, including that of burlesque star Lillian Russell, thudded down on the desk of Governor Levi Morton.

Although the governor refused to intervene, the Court of Appeals granted her a new trial.

The newspapers all started recounting the case. Facts began to get jumbled. One columnist pegged the age of "the poor seduced girl" at fifteen. The *New York World* changed Cataldo's nasty line "Only pips marry!" to "Only pigs marry." By the time the *New York Times* got it, it was "Only hogs marry."

Finally, on November 17, 1896, the second trial of Maria Barberi opened. She had spent more than a year in The Tombs prison with her pet canary, Cicillo; the sob sisters made much of the killer's tender treatment of her caged bird.

In a scene-setter piece, William Randolph Hearst's *New York Journal* ran a series of drawings of Maria's hands, ears, and mouth, showing by the latest studies in criminology that she was *not* a "degenerate or habitual criminal." The newspaper did a sudden about-face when it discovered that the cornerstone of her defense was the claim that she hailed from a family of degenerates and that she suffered from "psychical epilepsy," which caused her to slice Domenico's throat during an epileptic frenzy. (This defense was a strange offshoot of "temporary insanity.")

A few days later, under the headline, AN-CESTORS ALL DRUNKEN OR MAD, the *New York Journal* recounted: "The prisoner's attorneys produced an elaborate genealogical table of Maria Barberi's pedigree, which, if it can be proved to be true, will tell, in brief form, the history of one of the most miserable families that ever existed."

Her late uncle Giovanni was cited. "He was a stupid man and used to cry a great deal," said one witness. "He used to run out of the house undressed and make a scene in the marketplace." Another uncle used to chew his wineglass; her father would get drunk and show up at town band rehearsals without his cymbals. And on and on throughout an enormous family tree.

A song in her defense was handed round to the newspapers, with this final chorus.

Madonna Mia! is still her cry;
But mark her vacant stare.
There's madness in that glaring eye,
The madness of despair.

To prove this, the defense brought "alienists" and phrenologists to the stand to inspect her and her background.

After making its case for family degeneracy, the defense now focused on Maria's newly diagnosed epilepsy. It put Dr. Alois Hrdlicka on the stand. The doctor testified emphatically that according to the science of phrenology, Barberi's skull measurements clearly revealed that she suffers from epilepsy.

The prosecutor fighting back asked the doctor, "Isn't it true that you are twenty-eight years old and recently a cigar-maker?" Judge Gildersleeve—quite sympathetic to the defendant—jumped in. "That is no disgrace or dishonor. A rail-splitter was once president of the United States."

In his cross-examination, the prosecutor handed the young doctor three diagrams of heads. "Are these abnormal heads?" he queried softly. The doctor studied them, then nodded yes.

The drawings in question turned out to be President Grover Cleveland, Cornelius Vanderbilt, and the trial judge. The defense roared an objection accusing the prosecutor of using "the old Dunlop hat-block trick."

Maria Barberi took the stand, and told of the moment when Cataldo's throat was slit. "I felt something in my head very hot and saw a flash of light," she said. "Then I don't know nothing else at all."

On December 10, 1896, after a three-week trial with more than a dozen doctors testifying, the jury deliberated for forty minutes, then returned a verdict of not guilty. "She was smiling now as if she had never done anything but smile her whole life long," reported Pulitzer's *New York World*. "Her cheeks flushed first pink, then a deep red."

"What will you do now? Will you sew again?" she was asked. "Sew? Yes, I will sew, but who will give me work? I must find work." Maria would not go home at first without her canary bird, Cicillo. At her lawyer's office, she took the first telephone call of her life and received congratulations from her blue-blooded supporters.

So ends the strange tale of Maria Barberi. As Mrs. J. Duer, president of Christian Rescue Temperance Union of South Brooklyn, had put it before the verdict: "Let Maria Barberi go free and men will not dare to treat a woman's honor lightly."

Following her release, Barberi and her canary slipped completely out of view. ❧

THE INVENTION OF THE MODERN SERIAL KILLER: BY WILLIAM RANDOLPH HEARST AND JOSEPH PULITZER

Dr. H. H. Holmes—now almost completely forgotten—confessed in the 1890s to killing twenty-seven people and was America's first nationally known serial murderer, delivered to an eager public in daily headlines. The *Philadelphia Inquirer,* in a story marketed by William Randolph Hearst, called Holmes the "greatest criminal in history." The *New York World,* owned by Joseph Pulitzer, dubbed him "the greatest murderer of modern times." During a twelve-month span, the conservative *New York Times* covered him sixty times and commented: "It is regarded as a rather uneventful day in police circles when the name of H. H. Holmes is not connected to the mysterious disappearance of one or more persons who were last seen in his company."

Holmes, a cocksure con man, for his part, ridiculed the police and the flurry of charges against him. "Next thing we hear," he told one reporter, "they will be accusing me of the Custer massacre."

The media feeding frenzy surrounding Holmes in the 1890s rivals the O.J. circus of the 1990s. We think media overkill is something new. It's not—only the technology changes. Three instant books came out on Holmes during his trial with titles such as *The Arch-Fiend*; illustrated magazines fought for photos from which to make drawings; a wax museum tried to bribe a prison guard to get a death mask.

What so terrified Americans back in the 1890s was that Dr. Holmes was handsome, charming, and well-educated, a genteelly attired man from a fine New Hampshire family, a former schoolteacher who worked his way through University of Michigan medical school. He was 5'9", with full sensual lips and large blue eyes, vulnerable, soft, almost boyishly trusting eyes. He aptly fit Hamlet's line about someone who could "smile, and smile and be a villain." A forerunner of Ted Bundy, he too would later serve as his own lawyer.

Holmes's macabre tale became one of America's first communal nightmares, thanks to the proliferation of newswire

"Multiple murderer": Dr. H. H. Holmes. This drawing appeared in newspapers across the country.

services linking papers nationwide. They doled out the story bone by bone, witness by witness, and coverage back then had even less regard for "truth" or journalistic ethics than, say, today's *National Enquirer.* Bizarre accusations against him started to mount after his capture in 1895: He supplied fresh corpses to pull off insurance scams, sold skeletons, botched abortions, built a chamber-of-horrors hotel, bilked investors in Chicago on a phony machine to convert water to natural gas. He employed a steady stream of pretty stenographers who all disappeared. And the murder toll just kept rising from one, to four, to ten, to twenty-one, to thirty-three, and then to more than a hundred.

The Holmes story helped launch the enormously successful Hearst empire and it sowed the seeds for today's checkbook journalism and sensational coverage of gruesome crimes. An agent of William Randolph Hearst allegedly paid the then huge sum of $7,500 for Holmes's detailed confession to twenty-seven murders, and the future media mogul brokered the story to papers around the country.

But what's the truth amid all the hype? How did this small-time swindler—ultimately convicted of only one murder—become the most notorious criminal of his day? In a word, the media created him, helped hang him, and then cast him off as yesterday's news.

Herman W. Mudgett (his real name) was born in Gilmanton, New Hampshire, in 1860 to well-respected parents; Dad was postmaster of the region for twenty-four years; at age twenty, Holmes married his childhood sweetheart, then worked his way through medical school in Ann Arbor, Michigan; he was especially attentive during anatomy class. This is when Holmes *says* his criminal career began. He took out a $10,000 insurance policy on a fellow student, then the two of them found a look-alike corpse, scarred the face, and contacted the company.

Suddenly flush, Holmes moved to Chicago, started running a drugstore, performing a little medicine, married a second woman, and started scamming his way to a fortune. C. E. Davis, who ran the jewelry counter in Holmes's pharmacy, told a local paper that Holmes constantly chased skirts and never paid his bills. "It was the courteous audacious rascality of the fellow that pulled him through," said Davis. When Mrs. Holmes started noticing how much time her husband spent talking to pretty young female clerks, Holmes installed a newfangled electrical bell under a loose floorboard at the top of the stairs leading from his apartment to the shop. "It was noticeable that when the bell rang he was the busiest man in [town]," recalled Davis.

However, Dr. H. H. Holmes didn't make the big time, i.e., into coverage by newspapers outside of Chicago, until November 1894, and then just a brief item speculating that he might have murdered his partner, Benjamin Pitezel (who was setting up a business for them in Philadelphia) to collect on the insurance. The story stayed hot for a week or so, then disappeared. Holmes meanwhile confessed to insurance fraud, to substituting a body for his partner's, and was awaiting a sentence of a year or two for a scam that had netted him $6,000. There was one major loose end that a plucky Philadelphia detective wouldn't let lie unsolved. The murdered man's three children were missing and were last seen traveling with Holmes.

On July 15, 1895, almost nine months after the murder, Detective Frank Geyer of the Philadelphia police force, on a mission funded by the bilked insurance company, retraced Holmes's route and found the naked bodies of two little girls in a shallow grave in a rental house in Toronto. Their mother identified her daughters, fifteen-year-old Alice, and thirteen-year-old Nellie.

As one newspaper eagerly speculated: "It is believed they were smothered in the trunk that was brought to the house with the mattress and bed. The trunk was just about large enough to hold the bodies of the two children. To get them in it, the officials say, Holmes probably played hide-and-seek with them, induced them to hide in the trunk, shut down the lid and then filled the trunk full of gas by means of a rubber tube inserted through a hole."

On August 27, Geyer found in a farmhouse in Indiana the remains of the missing little boy, Howard Pitezel, age twelve. What was left after burning in an oversize stove was teeth, bone fragments, the pelvis, a pool of congealed human grease, and some melted buttons.

Once the grisly discoveries were made, the authorities and the media (i.e., underpaid newspapermen) unleashed a ferocious foray into Holmes's past. So began the media circus, the great macabre competition to see who could deliver more death to the American public. Every detail was twisted and exploited.

It was discovered that Holmes ran a rooming house during Chicago's famed Exposition of 1893, that early World's Fair whose futuristic marvels lured hundreds of thousands of visitors to see the likes of the first Ferris wheel and elaborate electrical light displays. Newspapers claimed that Holmes's "Castle," as it was called, was a "Chamber of Horrors," a kind of precursor to the Bates Motel, equipped with trapdoors, false walls, airtight rooms with gas jets controlled from a panel in the master bedroom.

Commented *Leslie's Weekly*, the *Life* magazine of its day: "The Castle was found to be as complete a man trap, or woman trap, as ever existed in the imagination of the most lurid writer of 'sleuth' fiction. Not a room had two or even three exits, intricate passageways, trapdoors, chutes that led from the upper floor to the cellar, rooms with padded walls; a dummy vault which detectives say is useless for any purpose but to stifle a victim; secret stairways, a crematory furnace and an acid vat. In the cellar human bones were found, and fragments of bloody clothing, and in one of the upper chambers a bench

with stains of blood and marks of a sharp knife. But nothing more. The curious part of the whole horrible story is that, although the man is believed from circumstantial evidence to be a multi-murderer, no direct evidence of his guilt has yet been discovered."

(One thing is certain: Holmes *did* run a boardinghouse.)

Lack of direct evidence didn't slow most reporters. Word surfaced that a skeleton articulator had prepared three skeletons for Holmes; deliverymen started remembering numerous heavy trunks.

But the coverage didn't fully heat up until November 1895, when William Randolph Hearst personally entered the game. That month—just at the time of Holmes's trial for murder of his business partner—Hearst, a brash thirty-two-year-old West Coast rich kid, the heir to Daddy's silver mine fortune, bought the failing *Journal* in New York and staked his whole future on blowing Pulitzer and his dominant *World* and the other papers out of the water. Hearst mandated that his minions try to outsensationalize Pulitzer and the backbone of their coverage was, as one veteran put it, "Crime and Underwear."

Holmes was convicted and sentenced to die. On April 5, 1896, Pulitzer's *New York World*—with its robust half-million circulation—ran a Sunday front page picture of Dr. Holmes sitting beneath a noose writing his confession as ghouls and skeletons haunted the background. The caption read: "The most extraordinary Criminal of Modern Times says he is busy with his autobiography, describing the twenty murders which he has committed. He is sentenced to death by hanging." It was a "soft," feature piece full of hyperbole. "He tried every sort of murder, poison, suffocation by gas, strangulation with bare fingers, every sort but crude noisy murders." However, there's not a word quoted from the confession, because it didn't exist.

The next Sunday, Hearst's *Journal* delivered the confession.

It was a shocking coup in a newspaper war, and boosted Hearst's circulation by 100,000 copies.

The confession swallowed up Hearst's entire front page. "Most Appalling Record of Murder to which Any Man has ever Affixed His Signature," and right beneath was a "facsimile" of a handwritten statement signed by Holmes attesting to the authenticity of the confession. Newspapers still couldn't reproduce photographs, but there was a quarter-page-high drawing of the "arch criminal of modern history" which was identified: "From the latest photograph of the murderer. A flashlight, taken in jail for The Journal."

The confession runs 20,000 words, and includes maps and diagrams of crime scenes, even quotes from the pitiful letters of the murdered children. "We saw the ostrich at the zoo," wrote Alice, the elder daughter. "It is about a head taller than I am so you know about how high it is." The writing is a brilliant blend of fact and fiction, obviously concocted with the aid of a canny newspaperman.

On the day after the Sunday coup, Hearst followed up with "What The Alienists Say," catering to Americans' appetites for the new sciences of psychology and criminology. One U.S. government doctor wanted to wire Holmes with his "kryptograph" to measure the murderer's emotion during hanging.

More than 4,000 people requested permission to attend Holmes's execution, but only eighty were allowed into Philadelphia's Moyamensing Prison. (The *New York Times* in a pro–death penalty editorial lamented the six-month delay between sentencing and execution.)

Holmes died bravely with just a touch of swagger. Or, as Hearst's paper put it: "Holmes died as stolidly as any murderer that ever stretched hemp." When the hangman fumbled with the black hood, Holmes murmured: "It's alright. I'm in no hurry." Noted a veteran of the crime beat: "He spoke his last words without tremor or shrillness, and he did not have to be stopped. That stopping a man when he is talking to prolong his life another minute or two is the most awful thing about an ordinary execution."

However, Dr. Holmes, on the edge of eternity, did have one worry: souvenir-seeking grave robbers. So, he had himself buried in a ton of cement. His body was laid in a coffin filled with a fresh bed of cement, then he was covered over. When the pallbearers came to lift it the next day, they couldn't, and half a dozen newspapermen had to drop their notebooks and hoist the box, a fitting end for a man they had helped to create.

How many people did Dr. H. H. Holmes kill? We'll never know. The confirmed body count is four, and has been rising for a century. Media overkill isn't new. ✏

THE REAL-LIFE CRIMINAL WHO DUELED SHERLOCK HOLMES

Sir Arthur Conan Doyle patterned his great deviant mastermind, Professor Moriarty, after a real life criminal, Adam Worth, an erudite American Jew who was operating an international network of thieves from London, plotting heists as far away as Constantinople and Cape Town.

"He is the organizer of half that is evil and nearly all that is undetected in this great city," says Sherlock Holmes of Moriarty. "He is a genius, a philosopher, an abstract thinker. He has a brain of the first order. He sits motionless, like a spider in the center of its web, but that web has a thousand radiations, he knows well every quiver of each of them."

Worth—a la Moriarty—lived a life of exotic splendor, sometimes traveling from European port to port, from caper to caper, in his 110-foot steam yacht, *The Shamrock,* crewed by twenty and fitted out with an elegant casino. For a while, he operated a gentleman's club in Paris, the American Bar at 2 Rue Scribe, richly appointed with crystal chandeliers and impressive works of art. On the second floor, the wealthiest Americans abroad dropped thousands at his faro table.

If you had met Adam Worth during his heyday in London in the 1870s, you'd have encountered a Victorian gentleman dwelling on Piccadilly Circus, a few doors down from Prime Minister Gladstone.

You'd have been introduced to "Henry J. Raymond," a name he borrowed with characteristic wit from the founder of the *New York Times.* A superintendent of Scotland Yard, whom Worth delighted in baffling, called him "the Napoleon of Crime."

But it is one caper that cemented Worth's reputation in Victorian England. On May 6, 1876, Christie's of London auctioned the *Duchess of Devonshire*—an acclaimed Thomas Gainsborough portrait of the mischievous Georgiana Spencer, whose affairs with both men and women had scandalized England a century earlier. The masterpiece—for connoisseurs were dazzled by her flirtatious yet almost mocking smile, her delicate hand clasping an ironic pink rosebud—attracted £10,500, then a record for a painting sold at auction.

Crowds queued up for blocks to buy tickets to view it at the second-floor gallery of the new owner, William Agnew. American millionaire Junius Morgan

Brilliant Victorian thief: Adam Worth, who used as his lifelong alias, "Henry Jarvis Raymond," the name of the founder of the *New York Times.*

Stolen: *Duchess of Devonshire,* painted by Thomas Gainsborough, which in 1876 set a world record for a painting sold at auction.

started negotiations to buy it for his son, the financier, J. P. Morgan, but Adam Worth concocted other plans.

Worth, elegantly dressed in a Saville Row suit, strolled by Agnew's gallery that May 1876 with a newly arrived American "bankman," named Junka Phillips, described as "immensely stupid." Worth stood 5'5" tops, while Junka, a former wrestler who sometimes carried stubborn safes out of the bank, topped out at near seven feet tall.

The unlikely pair viewed the painting, and it was then that Worth decided to steal it. "A man with brains has no right to carry firearms," he once told the famed U.S. detective William Pinkerton. And the modus operandi for this audacious crime—that wound up splattered in headlines worldwide—proved maddeningly simple. At midnight on a foggy May 25, Worth and Junka went to Agnew's; he climbed atop Junka's shoulders "and raised on his arms like a circus performer," later recalled Worth. He pried open the window, entered and sliced the Duchess from out the frame.

Worth had planned to use the painting as a bargaining chip to free his bungling brother then being held without bail, but when Worth went to his brother's lawyer to explain the ploy, the barrister proudly reported that his brother had just been freed on a legal technicality. Worth now owned a white elephant, a stolen article too hot for even him to risk selling.

Despite a £1,000 reward, the brazen theft of the Duchess remained unsolved for a quarter of a century. No one caught him, not even when Junka squealed to Scotland Yard. As legend goes, the Duchess became the diminutive dapper man's frequent traveling companion—sometimes rolled up in an umbrella case, even once in an emergency down his pants leg.

Worth a few years later voyaged by steamship to Philadelphia. He duly paid customs on the goods in the *top* of the false-bottomed trunk, and later squirreled the Duchess away in a warehouse in Brooklyn, where she lay tightly rolled for years.

Adam Worth was born in 1844 to well-to-do Jewish-German parents in Cambridge, Massachusetts. Clever and well-read, he committed his first crime by collecting *several times* the $500 reward for enlisting in the Union army. A package purloined from Adam's Express delivery service landed him in Sing Sing but he quickly escaped, catching a ride on a ferry boat headed South.

His criminal résumé is far too long to recite, but a few highlights leap out.

Worth once rented a barbershop next to the Boyleston Bank in Boston, burrowed in and absconded with the then enormous sum of $400,000. When the Pinkertons started closing in, he sailed off to England to start his international network.

His confederates passed forged bank notes in Constantinople; they robbed mail trains throughout Europe. Worth was intrigued by diamond shipments sent by regular mail from South Africa. He traveled to Cape Town, befriended the local postmaster, copied the vault key and made off with $600,000 in uncut stones. He later—through a series of fronts—sold many of them to the London jeweler to whom they were originally being shipped.

Throughout, he lived like a potentate, with his toney London address, his stable of racehorses, his extensive art collection. Then it all suddenly crumbled when his lookout failed him during a simple mail train robbery in Liège, Belgium.

He served five years in a Belgian prison under the name "Edouard Grau," came out to discover his empire had been looted. His health was now failing; his gooey cough probably signaled tuberculosis. Nonetheless, he still orchestrated the daring Gare du Nord robbery in Paris in 1898 that netted him a million francs in jewels and notes.

Worth—still going by "Henry Jarvis Raymond," a family name he passed to his son—was flush again, and the Duchess still gathering dust in America.

In a "beau geste" worthy of his artistic temperament, this ailing man started negotiations to return the Duchess. Through a notorious Midwest gambler named Pat Sheedy, he contacted William Pinkerton in Chicago. "I think the Lady should return home, don't you?" he told the detective. Worth held out for more than £1,000 reward and the deal broke down, but eventually they settled on terms.

Apparently—in addition to receiving money—Worth could now return to England without facing any harassment or prosecution. (Perhaps some of his fortune is hidden there.)

On March 27, 1901, Morland Agnew, the dealer's son, opened a brown paper parcel in the Auditorium Hotel in Chicago. "He laid it carefully on the floor, opened the package and there the face of the famous painting came to light for the first time in twenty-six years," recalled William Pinkerton, who was in the room.

Agnew returned with his prize to London, and soon after sold it to J. P. Morgan for the then scrupulously *un*disclosed sum of $150,000. "If the truth came out, I might be regarded as a candidate for a lunatic asylum," Morgan sheepishly admitted later. The Duchess assumed a place of honor over Morgan's mantel, a jewel in his world-class collection. (In 1994, the Morgan estate sold the painting for $408,000, and the *Duchess of Devonshire* now hangs in Chatsworth House, the family manor of the current Duke of Devonshire.)

Commented an official Pinkerton report issued in 1903 about Adam Worth: "Of all the men the Pinkertons have known in a lifetime, this was the most remarkable criminal of them all."

Adam Worth died in London on January 7, 1902. His bumbling adversaries, the Pinkertons, claimed the criminal was penniless at his death; however, another report—probably more accurate—states that his probated will, under the borrowed name of Henry J. Raymond of the *New York Times*, bequeathed to his son the then very large sum of £23,000.

And Sir Arthur Conan Doyle bequeathed to us Professor Moriarty. 🌀

GEORGIA JUSTICE IS BLIND, DEAF, AND DUMB

FUGITIVE FROM A CHAIN GANG

In Victor Hugo's *Les Misérables* — now better known as one of the world's most attended stage plays — Jean Valjean is sentenced to fifteen years for stealing a loaf of bread. Audiences can share the drama, and at the same time be thankful this play is about French people in the late 1700s.

Robert Elliot Burns working on a chain gang in Georgia.

Sure, Europeans back then would do something like that, but not here, not in America.

Robert Elliot Burns was sentenced to six to ten years on a Georgia gang for a robbery that netted him $1.44. The year was 1922, and it was the first offense for the thirty-two-year-old veteran of World War I. (Ten years later Paul Muni would play Burns in *I Am a Fugitive from a Chain Gang*, but we're getting ahead of ourselves.)

The Roaring Twenties didn't roar for everyone. Elliot Burns, a pint-size Brooklyn accountant, returned from World War I "shell-stunned" and unemployed. One day he trudged up lower Broadway wearing a hand-scrawled sandwich sign: I FOUGHT FOR YOU IN FRANCE, AND NOW YOU HAVE NO PLACE FOR ME, NOT EVEN A JOB! Local papers bannered his photo but no one hired him.

Embittered, Burns rode the rails South. At a Salvation Army Rest Camp — barefoot and penniless — he met two men who promised him work. The job turned out to be a "job," robbing a ramshackle grocery store, owned by a Jew who supposedly carried a thousand-dollar bankroll. "When we go in, I'll throw a cabbage in his face while you two take his dough," outlined the self-appointed ringleader Flagg, a tough Aussie sailor. Burns balked, but Flagg forced him to go along.

When the grocer reached for a gun, the trio ran. They were sitting a couple miles down the railroad line divvying the take from the cash register, $5.80, when the police caught them.

Burns' court-appointed attorney advised him to plead guilty, because a conviction *after* a trial would mean a much heavier sentence. This way, he'd probably get off with thirty days. Burns took the advice and Judge Thomas of Valdosta sentenced the veteran for this his first offense to "six to ten years of hard labor, on a Georgia road gang."

The prison blacksmith welded iron collars around Burns's ankles. An eighteen-inch steel chain kept his stride to a shuffle. He slept in what looked like a barred circus wagon, the place reeking from the stink of unwashed men and a bucket full of urine and excrement. A 3 A.M. gong roused the prisoners for an equatorial workday, half-starved on undercooked cornmeal, fatback, and mucky brown water euphemistically called "coffee." When Burns didn't work fast enough, he was stretched over some rusty corrugated sheet metal and beaten with a thick leather whip studded with copper rivets. The prospect of half a decade more of all this fun convinced the Yankee to escape or die.

Burns noticed one day a giant black fellow convict with pinpoint command of a twelve-pound sledgehammer and begged him to smash his ankle "collars" into an ellipse so he could slip his heel out. It took three heavy blows on each ankle.

A few days later, Burns slipped free of his shackles, and dodged rifle fire, disappearing into the woods. The escapee with the thick New Yawk accent eventually hitchhiked and boxcarred his way to Chicago. Flat broke, living under false names, the fugitive married his landlady and graduated from street corner preaching to part-time jobs, saving every penny till two years later, when he had a nest egg to found *Greater Chicago Magazine.* By 1929, Burns's budding publishing empire occupied a fancy suite of offices on Michigan Avenue. To top it off, he was in love—unfortunately, not with his wife.

Robert Burns, escaped convict, now successful Chicago magazine publisher, in May 1929, before agreeing to return to Georgia.

He asked for a divorce. Emilia, a Mexican waitress-turned-landlady, already once divorced, refused, and made a phone call to Georgia prison officials.

Burns, the buoyant successful businessman, came to his extradition hearing before the governor of Illinois armed with eighty-six affadavits from substantial citizens—including the likes of poet-historian Carl Sandburg—vouching for his character. Nonetheless, Governor Len Small signed extradition papers. Burns's lawyers were ready to file an appeal when a Georgia prison official, Vivien Stanley, offered Burns a deal: Drop the appeal, come back to Georgia, pay the recapture costs and you'll have a pardon within ninety days. In addition, he would not be put on the chain gang but plunked down at a desk job in Atlanta. Burns agreed.

He showed up in Atlanta, wrote a check to the state of Georgia for $350, and paid his lawyer $1,250. When the checks cleared, he was promptly shackled and bused off to the Campbell County chain gang, the one he had escaped from.

"All the promises made in Chicago were forgotten," complained his brother, Vincent, a preacher. "He was just one more road convict working out his six-year sentence, plus six additional years for running away."

The state of Georgia—founded in part as a outpost for British convicts—would be damned if it was going to let Yankee do-gooders dictate what it should do with Yankee criminals.

"If we let this robber off easily, we'll have every thug and gangster from the North coming down here, overrunning our state like locusts," the assistant solicitor for Fulton County told the three-man parole board. "He has violated the laws of Georgia and he owes Georgia a debt," said the squat humorless man in black-framed glasses. "We intend to collect that debt."

They did, putting him on the meanest chain gang in Georgia, whipping him, and sweat-boxing him. Burns vowed to escape again. He had his brother send him a pack of cigarettes, and take the tobacco out of six butts and put in $150 in tightly rolled bills, and mix it into a big fruit basket full of candy, cakes, and more cigarettes.

Burns—yes-sirring every redneck whip cracker—got promoted to "trusty," i.e., prisoner overseer, which meant no shackles. One day, rubbing a couple of nickels together, he enticed a guard to go with him to a cracker country store for a couple of Coca-Colas. There, he met a farmer who let slip an off-hand remark about the raw deal Burns got. He later saw the man on the road and flashed a fifty-dollar bill at him. They eventually worked out a plan. The farmer was to hide his car in the woods down the road from the worksite, and then at 7:30 A.M., whistle like a mockingbird. Burns—who had been up all night, and at work since 5 A.M.—was crushed when the man didn't show. They met again and Burns flashed a *pair* of fifty-dollar bills and promised to mail another hundred dollars.

This time, the man showed, and sped off with Burns toward Atlanta. Burns—after accidentally walking right by a work gang—escaped to New Jersey. Living under the name of a seaman, John Pashley, he sold advertising for the *Newark Ledger,* until a Chicago acquaintance blew his cover; his next job was dynamite man at a Cateret foundry. One day he blew up a smokestack in an abandoned factory and wound up in national newsreels; he expected coppers to pounce any minute, but none materialized.

Burns, with the help of his brother, started writing articles about the hideous conditions in Georgia chain gangs for *True Detective* magazine. Irate officials in Georgia upped the reward on his head from $50 to $500. "When we do get him back," threatened one Georgia official, Vivien Stanley, "he'll be sorry he had so much to say about the way we run our prisons."

The brothers—after being turned down by almost every publishing house—finally struck a small deal to write the book, *I Am a Fugitive from a Georgia Chain Gang.* The bestseller led to a hit movie of the same title, minus the word "Georgia."

Warner Brothers even smuggled Burns out to the set in Hollywood to act as a consultant. "You don't look like a burglar at all," Daryl Zanuck told him. Added an assistant, "You might be a toothpaste salesman or a drummer for a line of women's wear." Bodyguards and aliases and studio clout kept him safe.

The world premiere was scheduled for November 11, 1932, in Atlanta. Burns sent his regrets, but he did sneak into the Newark premiere with his new girlfriend, a schoolteacher. The police—suspecting he might do just that—cordoned off the theater, and as the crowd exited, promptly arrested . . . the wrong short guy in glasses.

As the film built to a blockbuster hit, the Newark police chief, James McRell—smarting from his bungled arrest—put his best detectives on the case. One tracked Burns's preacher brother when he went to meet the fugitive. "If you think you can spit on the law and get away with it," shouted McRell as the pressboys scribbled, "you're very much mistaken." A New Jersey judge set the bail at $25,000.

The New Jersey governor would have to decide whether to sign extradition papers. A hearing was set for December 21, 1932. In the meantime, several news stories broke. Flagg, the ringleader of that penny-ante grocery store heist, told the *Seattle Post-Dispatch* that Burns had participated in several bigger earlier holdups with him. New York police unearthed an outstanding warrant for his arrest on a 1922 forgery rap. Several articles contradicted brutality and bribery charges out-

lined in his book. On the flip side, letters from the likes of Clarence Darrow were pouring in on his behalf, as were editorials.

The hearing room was packed. "They say my brother is a robber," intoned Vincent Burns, preacher and poet. "I say they are the robbers . . . I say that my brother's crime is as nothing compared to the crimes committed by their outrageous penal system."

The sympathetic crowd cheered. Photographs of stocks, sweat boxes, whips, even brutalized black prisoners were shown. Witness after witness spoke on Burns's behalf, then the attorney for Georgia stopped the tide cold. "It is a question of government by law or government by emotion." His colleague added, "The people of Georgia are proud of their great and enlightened state, and all these stories about barbarism and cruelties that you have heard here today are nothing but lies told for profit and gain."

Poker-faced governor Harry Moore listened to four hours of testimony. Suddenly, midhearing, a telegram arrived. It was from an Illinois judge who stated that a Georgia official had promised Burns a pardon if he returned voluntarily and paid his recapture costs.

Governor Moore refused to sign the extradition papers. The jubilant crowd surged around Burns, still handcuffed to the deputy.

Burns lived quietly in New Jersey, building up a nice business as a tax accountant, marrying, and raising a family.

The end? Well, not quite. Prison officials in Georgia *still* wanted to recapture

Burns and put him back on the road gang. Almost a decade later, in 1941, they applied to the new New Jersey governor, Charles Edison, for extradition but were again rebuffed. "My god, how long are they going to keep this up?" complained Burns to newsmen.

In the 1940s, the Georgia legislature voted to reform the penal system, and the new governor of Georgia, Ellis Arnall, lobbied on Burns's behalf. He met with Burns in New York and told him that he supported his cause, but that only the three-member Pardon and Parole Board could grant him a pardon. Would Burns be willing to return to Georgia?

After much soul-searching, Burns agreed. A reporter seeing the *little* man carrying a *big* suitcase off the train asked him if he was planning for a long stay. Burns didn't laugh.

The hearing dragged on and then the Georgia board spent two hours conferring privately before it finally reached a verdict, granting Burns a full pardon.

He died in 1955 at a Veterans Hospital in East Orange, New Jersey. ❧

MISCONCEPTIONS: BONNIE PARKER: SHE WAS NO FAYE DUNAWAY

Five-feet-tall Bonnie Parker (1910–1934) didn't look a bit like Faye Dunaway; she was never a hero to the poor people of Texas and Oklahoma; their penny-ante

Fun on the run: This photo of Bonnie Parker was discovered on a roll of film left behind when the Barrow gang shot its way out of Joplin, Missouri, in 1933.

robberies never netted more than $1,500; she probably never even had a great romance with Clyde Barrow, who, some reports say, was a homicidal *homosexual* who preferred men ever since his reformatory days. Here's how Ray Hamilton, a Barrow gang member, described them: "Bonnie & Clyde? they loved to kill people, see blood run. That's how they got their kicks. They were dirty people. Her breath was awful and Clyde never took a bath."

Bonnie's family, who buried the twenty-four-year-old girl's bullet-pocked corpse in Crown Hill Memorial Park Cemetery in Dallas, had a slightly different view of Bonnie. Her tombstone reads: "As the flowers are all made sweeter/by the sunshine and the dew,/So this old world is made brighter/By the lives of folks like you." 🌀

ODD CASES: BESTIALITY AND THE LAW

Colonial minister Cotton Mather recorded that on June 6, 1662, at New Haven, an "unparalleled wretch," a sixty-year-old man named Potter, was executed along with his sexual partners: a cow, two heifers, three sheep, and two sows. "His wife had seen him confound-ing himself with a bitch ten years before, and he then excused himself as well as he could but conjured her to keep it a secret." Potter stood at the gallows while the animals had their throats slit before his eyes. Biblical law (i.e., Leviticus 20:15), on which early colonial law leaned heavily, required that the beast be killed along with the human.

But you might ask—especially if you're an animal rights type: Isn't that like punishing the rape victim as well as the rapist? Wasn't it sometimes grossly unjust to kill the animal? A French court, perhaps inhaling a whiff of Voltaire's rationalism, thought the same way.

CHARACTER WITNESS FOR AN ASS

Jacques Feron, caught in the act with a she-ass at Vanvres, France, in 1750, was sentenced to die. The townspeople rallied to the defense of the donkey. According to *Criminal Prosecution of the Animals* by E. P. Evans, "the prior of the convent, who also performed the duties of parish priest, and the principle inhabitants of the commune of Vanvres signed a certificate stating that they had known the said she-ass for four years, and that she had always shown herself to be virtuous and well behaved both at home and abroad and had never given occasion of scandal to any one, and that therefore they were willing to bear witness that she is in word and deed and in all her habits of life a most honest creature." This document, given at Vanvres on September 19, 1750, and signed by "Pintuel Prieur

Cure and other attestors, was produced during the trial and exerted a decisive influence upon the judgment of the court. As a piece of exculpatory evidence it may be regarded as unique in the annals of criminal prosecutions.

". . . The animal was acquitted on the ground that she was the victim of violence and had not participated in her master's crime of her own free-will."

Now, that you're pondering these topics, you might also be wondering whether an animal might in fact be guilty of forcing a human to a lewd act. ❧

A Cautionary Tale

In 1865, a thirty-one-year-old French woman came home to their farmhouse to find her husband deathly ill. She later gave the following testimony to the police, according to French criminologist Dr. Ambroise Tardieu.

"On Sunday, June 4, coming home around 6 P.M., I found my husband in bed and vomiting; stunned, I brought him a glass of sugar water and asked him about his illness. He told me that around 5 P.M. that same afternoon, he went to relieve his bowels near our home, when he heard the bellowing of a bull in the stable. Fearing for the other animals, he ran there without taking the time to button his pants. Reaching the stable, he approached the bull, which had broken its tether, when the animal knocked him down and he found himself on his hands and knees with his ass in the air, his shirt untucked, and his legs hobbled by his fallen pants. The bull

inserted its pizzle into my husband's anus and he felt excruciating pain.

"I immediately called Dr. Pavy, and despite his frantic efforts, my husband died eight hours after the accident."

Dr. Pavy, seventy-six years old, gave the following statement to the gendarmes: "I examined the patient and discovered the anus was bleeding and leaking a slimy fluid, which I presume to be the result of the ejaculation of the animal. The patient suffered terrible pain and died at 1 A.M. on June 5. I have never witnessed a similar case, and my medical opinion is that G. had his rectum perforated by the bull."

The gendarmes decided not to execute the bull since "the day of the accident, the bull was upset by a cow that had been brought there to be mounted for breeding purposes." ❧

EVERYDAY
LIFE

THE TOILET TRAINING OF THE HUMAN RACE

Even mythic heroes do it. Hercules, drunk and staggering, is trying to urinate. This ancient *Roman* statue spoofing a *Greek* hero was found in Italy at Herculaneum near Pompeii.

"I could never be king," said the French fool to his master. "You have to crap in public and eat alone."

History too often is odorless.

It's time to dig up some vintage *merde* and try to re-create the authentic stink of the Western world prior to widespread use of the flush toilet in the very late 1800s.

To gain the king's ear during the Renaissance in France, sometimes you had to smell the king's ass, literally. On enema day, King Louis XIV would hold court for hours, surrounded by princes and ministers and it was a high honor to attend. And reaching the room was an odoriferous adventure in itself. "Around the Louvre," wrote a man requesting a public toilet concession in 1670, "in so many places in the court and surrounding areas, in the alleyways, behind the doors and almost everywhere, one sees a thousand piles of "or-dures," one sniffs a thousand unbearable stenches, caused as much by the natural needs . . . of those who live in the Louvre as by those who visit daily." Back in the Middle Ages, the first thing Chaucer's pilgrims noticed when approaching a city was the stink of human shit moldering at the base of the walls, and pilgrims heading south to the popular shrine of St. James in Santiago, Spain, stopped the night before in a town called Lavacola, whose name literally means "Wash Your Ass."

Back in ancient Greece at dinner parties where the most brilliant men—Plato, Aristotle, Socrates—would philosophize into the night, guests regularly lifted their tunic and filled a chamber pot at the table. At a banquet celebrating Anne Boleyn's coronation as Henry VIII's queen, two handmaidens crouched beneath the table during the entire meal, prepared to catch the pretty young woman's overflow—one held a chamber pot, the other a serviette.

The toilet training of the human race is rich in forgotten anecdote; it begins with the pampered ass of a Minoan queen and extends forward four thousand years to that elusive Victorian, Sir Thomas Crapper. Along the way, you'll discover that a very tangible sign of wealth and power through the ages was the right to entertain guests while seated on the "throne" and having numerous servants to immediately cart away your shit. It's time to smell the past.

A CRETAN TOILET

On the island of Crete in the Mediterranean about two thousand years before Christ, engineers designed an indoor toilet with a steady water stream to clear away the waste. If you visit the ruins at Knossos, you can see the world's oldest surviving flush toilet, which looks like a stone seat over a channel of water fed by tapered pipes. Archaeologists posit that a full bucket stood nearby to provide the flush action.

Oddly, when Minoan civilization declined, future generations remembered the story of sacrificing the virgins to the Minotaur and somehow forgot about the toilet. This lost art would not be rediscovered for 3,700 years.

Once the mysteries of indoor plumbing were lost, mankind reverted to the chamber pot for indoor pissing. Several fragments from lost plays of Sophocles and Aeschylus have drunken guests heave full chamber pots across the banquet table and court records indicate that chamber pots were a favored weapon in domestic disputes.

A true sign of wealth—beyond the size of one's chariot—was the quality of one's chamber pot. Marc Anthony preferred only gold. And Martial, that satiric poet, complains of one of his rich patrons whom he visits in the morning: "Bassus, receives me while crouched over a gold chamber pot. The jerk, he has spent more to empty his bowels than it would cost to feed me for a year."

So, apparently, Roman men and women sometimes squatted over a portable bowl, to be later emptied by the servants. For commoners, there were public toilets and, of course, the public baths. And yes, just like modern swimming pools, there was a problem with irresponsible louts peeing there. At the baths of Titus, this graffiti was found: "Whoever pees or shits here will suffer the wrath of the twelve gods, of Diana and of the great and powerful Jupiter."

In Rome, urine vases were set up in many street corners, and tanners and fullers used to drain off the contents to help in preparing leather and fabric. The Emperor Vespasian (9–79 A.D.), eager for profit, introduced a urine tax selling the liquid to those manufacturers. His son, Titus, a bit appalled, complained. Vespasian held a silver coin beneath the young man's nose and asked: "Does it smell bad? . . . Yet it comes from urine."

Taking a pee in ancient Rome was not without its dangers. Under Tiberius, peeing while wearing a ring (or holding a coin) with the Emperor's face on it was a capital offense. Reports Seneca, a drunken noble at a dinner party had his life saved when his slave slipped a large Tiberius ring off just before the man started to pee. A spy—who'd receive a reward for snitching—had already started to write up an accusation.

Public toilets from ancient Rome have survived and these show long stone slab sheets with spaced holes. Emptying the latrines and private shit buckets was not a pleasant task and an ordinance was passed forbidding the overnight shit wagons from entering Rome or its suburbs for ten hours after sunrise.

Not surprisingly, the Middle Ages brought no relief; peasants were still crapping in outhouses and backyard holes, while the big breakthrough in walled cities and castles was the concept of narrow poop chutes built up into the parapets. Imagine the aroma approaching a medieval castle.

The Tower of London, in the 1300s home to the royal family, boasted a privy room near the banquet table. You can still see it. It's a small vaulted chamber about three feet wide with a narrow window and with a short shaft set below into the stone wall which lets the matter drop down outdoors into the moat below. "Formerly defensive, moats must have become offensive," observes Lawrence Wright in *Clean and Decent: The Fascinating History of the Bathroom and Water Closet.* Actually, *merde* would only add to the defensive strength of the moat.

Apparently, though, the smell didn't deter some intruders. In 1313, Sir William de Norwico ordered a stone wall built to screen the privy outlets from view. Were Londoners watching the poop descend? Could they catch a glimpse of a royal derriere? It's not totally a joking matter. Those using the parapet holes during medieval battles had been known to get a flaming arrow up the ass.

When Henry III of England had a ground-level privy room built at Guilford Castle over a little stream designed to carry away the waste, he specified in the building order that "an iron grate be installed," presumably so that no miscreant could swim up the little canal and hold the royal testicles hostage.

In the 1200s and 1300s, despite little innovations like wall-mounted chutes, cities still stank, especially medieval Paris. A law from 1270 in Paris stated that "no person may throw 'waters' or 'ordures' from upper story windows, neither by day or night . . . or they shall pay a fine." Parisians apparently refused to obey, because a century later, a new law allowed throwing pee from an upper story window "if you shout loudly three times: *'gare à l'eau!'* (i.e., 'look out for pee/water')."

Not only did Parisians relieve themselves in doorways and alleyways all over town, but they did so in the palace itself.

French royalty lived in the Louvre back

then. In 1364, a man named Thomas DuBuisson "was paid to paint many vermillion crosses in the Louvre . . . in the gardens and other areas of the Court, to prevent those who would use those areas as their retreat for pissing." So, in addition to a fine, the red crosses would make it a sacrilege to pee there.

Again, the headstrong locals defied the law and the problem persisted through the French Revolution.

Leonardo da Vinci, no less, was so appalled by the stench in French castles that when he drew up plans for the castle at Amboise for his patron King Francis I, he designed a flushing toilet. Da Vinci's plan called for flushing channels inside the walls and ventilating shafts reaching to the roof, but like the helicopter and submarine, he was a couple hundred years ahead of his time. The design was never executed.

Besides Leonardo, another inventive sort attempted to jerk mankind forward (or back to Crete). Sir John Harrington, who happened to be the godson of Queen Elizabeth I, built a working model for the queen in 1596, complete with a water tank above, and a faucetlike handle for flushing the refuse.

Harrington, a courtier from (where else but) Bath, made a costly error. He wrote a pun-filled tribute to himself and his design of the queen's new toilet, called *The Metamorphosis of Ajax* ("jakes" being slang for chamber pot). She banished him and after hearing too many jokes about the royal seat, she had it removed as well. Harrington's unit also had one major design flaw: the stench.

"Gardy-Loo!" Look out below. Note the chamber pot being emptied from the second floor over the barber-dentist's office in this William Hogarth (1697–1764) drawing.

Elizabeth complained that the smell of excrement wafted up through the pipes. Amazingly, it took two hundred years—including the entire lifetime of Sir Isaac Newton—to solve the problem. (Hint: think curved pipe.)

During that time, with no flush toilets, Great Britain like the rest of Europe was splattered with filth. Here's a glowing portrait by historian G. M. Trevelyan of Edinburgh in the early 1700s.

Far overhead the windows opened, five, six, or ten storeys in the air and the close stools of Edinburgh discharge the collected filth of the last twenty-four hours into the street. It was good manners for those above to cry "gardy-loo!" *(Gardez l'eau)* before throwing. The returning roysterer cried back "haud yer han" and ran with humped shoulders, lucky if his vast and expensive full-bottomed wig was not put out of action by a cataract of filth. The *ordure* thus sent down lay in the broad High Street and in the deep, well-like closes and wynds round it making the night air horrible, until early in the morning it was perfunctorily cleared away by the City guard. Only on a Sabbath morn it might not be touched, but lay there all day long, filling Scotland's capital with the savour of a mistaken piety.

During this period, the *"chaise percée"* was popular, a kind of portable padded chair with a hole above and a compartment for a removable basin below. Some of the world's leading furnituremakers expended great creativity in designing *"chaise percées"* that hid their real function, and instead resembled a chest of drawers,

Find the toilet. Premier furniture-makers competed in the 1600s in trying to hide a *chaise-percée* (or portable potty) inside another piece of often elegant furniture. Here is one hidden inside what appears to be a stack of books resting on a footstool.

a desk, or even a pile of books, entitled *Voyage aux Pays Bas* ("Trip to the Low Countries"—there was a war against Holland at the time). The most costly woods, jewels, and fabrics were used.

Emptying the basin was not fun, especially not during the enema craze of the late Renaissance. (For that story, see page 181 in "Medicine".)

Over time, the pomp and circumstance surrounding a person's bowel movements could signal true power. French kings starting with Francis I (ruled 1515–1547) appointed *"porte-chaise-d'affaires,"* basically royal porta-potty attendants. This much-sought after position included a stipend, the right to carry a sword in the Louvre and most importantly access to the king. Catherine de Medici, the wily queen mother, pioneered the practice for royal women to have potty attendants, and when her husband died, as a show of respect, she switched the color of her padded velvet seat to black. Following *la mode*, French nobles, both male and female, started holding "court" on their elegant porta-potties, which no doubt bred some resentment from their underlings. "Today we hold the basin beneath a lord's ass," commented a royal surgeon in the late 1600s, "so that tomorrow, when he's out of favor, we can dump its contents on his head." Could the French Revolution be too far off?

Finally, however, the odorless future dawned. In 1775, one Brit named Alexander Cummings, an unsung hero, twisted the refuse pipe underneath the toilet into a U shape so that a small amount of standing water would always keep the stink from rising. Cummings deserves credit for designing the first modern flush toilet.

And if any readers had thought the honor belonged to a Victorian named Sir Thomas Crapper, they've been hoaxed. Wallace Rayburn in 1969 wrote a straight-faced satire called *Flushed with Pride: The Story of Thomas Crapper.* The book's wickedly well done, down to quoting obscure royal charters, with antique spellings.

So there you have it. A Cretan queen in 1900 B.C. parked her lovely derriere indoors on a stone seat and knew her offering would be swept away by running water. Now, 3,800 years later, that luxury would reach most everyone and in some way reduce the gulf between rich and poor. ❧

FATAL VATICAN GRAFFITI, 1570

Future saint, Pope Pius V (1504–1572) had an elaborate new lavatory installed at the Vatican. At the time, even the slightest building project rated a formal dedication and Latin inscription. So, with mock solemnity, one Nicolo Franco scrawled the following bit of graffiti on the walls there: *"Papa Pius Quintus, ventres miseratus onustos/Hocce cacatorum nobile fecit opus."* Which translates: "Pope Pius V, filled with compassion for our full bellies, has erected this noble monument of caca seats."

According to scholar Gustave Witkowski, Nicolo Franco was hanged for his blasphemy. ❧

THE TIP OF PETER THE GREAT, 1717

Peter the Great, czar of Russia, was visiting Paris on May 19, 1717, according to chronicler Jean Buvat. "The day after the Easter holidays, the czar passed by Hotel des Invalides, where it's said, he had to relieve himself. Sitting in a small room on a 'pierced chair,' he asked the valet who brought him there for some toilet paper. The man had none to give him, so this prince made use of a 100-franc note instead, and then offered it to the valet, who declined to receive it. He excused himself, saying the concierge had absolutely forbidden him to receive any tips. The Czar, after prodding him to accept it several times, finally cast it full of shit to the ground.

"The concierge, when he heard about it told the valet to go fetch the bill. 'When you wash it off, it will buy just as many drinks.' "

Peter the Great (1672–1725), czar of Russia, once left a memorable tip.

AIMING AT BEN FRANKLIN

Ben Franklin, the American ambassador to France, became a huge celebrity in Europe for his scientific inventions, his clever phrases, his irreverent attitude. He stood as a kind of symbol of the American common man (tenth child of a candlemaker) triumphing over British tyranny.

The French started making all kinds of Franklin souvenirs from commemorative medallions to clocks.

One day, King Louis XVI attended an exhibition at Versailles of beautiful porcelain pieces made by the royal craftsmen at Sèvres. As he wandered the aisles, he noticed a commemorative plate, which bore the portrait of cult hero Franklin over the Latin inscription: *"Eripuit coelo fulmen, sceptrumque tyrannis."* ("He ripped lightning from the sky, and the sceptre from tyrants.")

The king, seething, said nothing at the time, but, according to Marie-Antoinette's lady-in-waiting, Madam Campan, he commissioned the porcelain makers at Sèvres to make him a chamber pot with Ben Franklin's picture inside on the bottom, along with the antiroyal slogan.

Years later in 1793, after splashing unknown gallons of urine across Franklin's face, King Louis stopped being a tyrant, as his head dropped into the basket beside the guillotine. 🐝

THE EVOLUTION OF UNDERWEAR

Peter the Great, visiting Paris in 1717, was riding down a crowded street when a woman slipped and fell in front of his horse. The czar, intently watching the pretty Parisienne scissor and squirm out of danger, observed with some delight: "The gates of Paradise are open."

What's interesting is not that *that* particular French woman didn't wear any underwear, but that almost no French women at the time wore any underwear that would have blocked the czar's view. Or any English women. Or any German women. Or any American women.

It amazes us (or at least me) to learn that women for the first five thousand years of Western civilization wore nothing between their legs beyond their natural chinchilla. "Until the late 18th century, [women's] underwear consisted only of smocks or shifts, stays [i.e., corsets] and the highly important petticoats of all kinds," harrumphs *The History of Underclothes* by Willet and Cunnington. But nothing *between* the legs.

It seems fairly mind-boggling to consider millions of women for thousands of years with no garment snugly covering their Delta. Sure, they generally wore very long dresses, but why not any close-fitting underwear?

Yeast infections and crab lice, among other reasons, argue authors Janet and Peter Phillips in their masterful article,

In this lampoon about the first manned balloon flight in Paris in 1783, "amateur scientists" are caught aiming their telescopes at . . . the women climbing over the wall. This print clearly shows what French women wore back then *underneath* their dresses.

History From Below: Women's Underwear and the Rise of Women's Sports. "Pre–20th century women had to do without knickers and the like because of the perpetual threat of thrush [i.e., yeast infection]," state the British authors. "Since the vagina is naturally warm and moist, any covering increasing the temperature will put out a welcome mat to thrush," they contend, pointing out that yesteryear's lower standards of personal hygiene, due to lack of indoor running water would have greatly promoted thrush and lice.

Near Eastern women who did bathe more frequently than their European sisters did wear trousers or "harem pants," sometimes under skirts. And it's speculated that during the Renaissance, these garments were imported into Europe and gradually adapted into drawers, i.e., loose-fitting under-trousers, with ribbons to "draw" them tight at the waist and the legs. But these imported strange items (considered masculine and somehow perverse) never caught on with working-class women, who could still squat and pee in an alleyway.

In fact, almost the only French women in the 1700s who wore drawers did so by law. A ballerina in 1727 got her skirt caught on a piece of stage scenery. Her exposure led to the passage of a police regulation in Paris that "no actress or dancer should appear on stage without drawers."

Finally, mid-1800s fashion began to change.

Forgotten early woman's libber Mrs. Elizabeth Smith Miller crusaded for women to stop having to wear floor-length dresses. Instead, she promoted loose ankle-length trousers to be worn below their *knee*-length skirts. A rival crusader, Amelia Jenks Bloomer (1818–1894), started wearing the outfit while on a lecture tour in 1850, and promptly got egged and ridiculed and had her name semi-immortalized.

Two unlikely events sped the draping of women's privates worldwide: the Brazilian rubber seed theft of 1876 and the bicycle craze of the 1890s.

British botanist Sir Henry Wickham convinced Brazilian authorities to let him have tens of thousands of rubber tree seeds for the Royal Gardens at Kew in England; Wickham promptly shipped seedlings out to Ceylon and Malaya and efficient British plantations promptly broke the Brazilian stranglehold on rubber and vastly improved the product, speeding the development of cheap elastic. By 1900, drawers no longer needed cumbersome drawstrings that might dangle into privies or come undone during tennis matches.

The second event ending the many millennia of pleasurable updrafts for women was the cycling boom, ignited by John

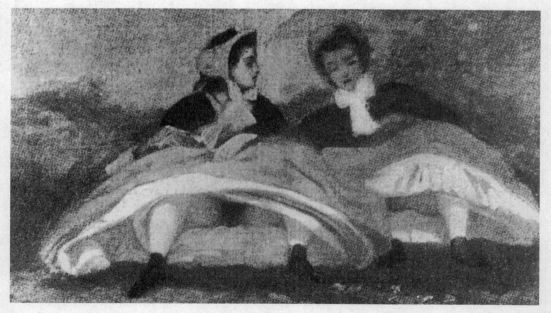

Famed painter Gustave Courbet (1819–1877) captured the continuing gap in women's underwear, that lasted well into the 19th century. (Plenty of petticoats, etc., but nothing directly guarding the shrine.)

Dunlop's invention of the pneumatic tire. Bicycles couldn't be ridden side-saddle; long skirts were dangerous. "When biking became fashionable, the studentesses of Paris adopted it," states an article in the *New York Journal*, Nov. 15, 1896. "As a matter of course, they adopted bloomers also." The *New York Sun* noted Parisian women wearing bloomers in public even when they were not biking. "They are simply mad over this free-and-easy costume," enthused a young American woman just returned from Paris.

The trend just kept gathering momentum, leading from the airy cotton drawers of the turn of the century to today's nylon "nothings."

It's worth noting that female fashion through the ages — before the 19th-century women's movement — provided little protection against unwanted advances by husbands, lovers, or for that matter, rapists. Is it a coincidence that as women took more control over their lives, they were able to introduce another line of sexual defense?

Maybe men kept vetoing the change until they lost their veto. ❧

HISTORY'S QUEST: AVOIDING BIG BREASTS

Large breasts — in the genre of Elle MacPherson, Sophia Loren, beloved Marilyn Monroe — have very, very rarely been venerated throughout the history of Western civilization. Americans refuse to believe it, but it's true: This 20th century (mostly American) obsession for over-

Roman women did not want large breasts; here, in this 3rd-century mosaic found in Sicily, a couple of young women exercise while wearing tight breast bands. Yes, this is the world's first recorded bikini.

sized mammaries on a thin frame is a complete aberration. The women who grace the covers of *Playboy* — with their birdlike shoulders and 3-D cleavage — would have been considered almost freaks in most of Europe and the United States through the mid-1800s. They'd have been viewed as too skinny, with a man's derriere, and their large breasts would have been deemed maternal, not sexual, and more suited for peasant wet nurses.

Martial, the Roman poet, wrote of the perfect breast as not overflowing one hand. And the Romans — so efficient in public works — left nothing to chance. The women of ancient Rome wore a "fascia," a light but firm undergarment to support and *suppress* the bosom. "This device opposed the growth of the breasts," wrote Dr. Augustin Cabanes, a 19th-century medical historian, "just as tight shoes of the Chinese women reduced the size of their feet."

The ancient Greeks—during the so-called Golden Age of Aristotle and Aeschylus—had a temple dedicated to Aphrodite Kallipygeia, Aphrodite of the Beautiful Derriere. One Greek dramatist penning cosmetic advice to a prostitute recommends suppressing her large breasts while supplementing her hips via padding. "Like ourselves, the Greeks detested bulky breasts," stated another French medical historian in 1895, "the signs of beauty were elevation, smallness and regularity of contour."

Renaissance corsets so brutally squashed breasts that quite a few medical texts for women from that period discussed how to cure nipples inverted by a lifetime of corset-wearing.

Unlike today's Wonderbra, the prevailing challenge was always to minimize, not maximize, to understate, not poke somebody's eye out. "The formulas for reducing and firming up the breasts are countless," notes Dr. Cabanes elsewhere and cites by example a French handbook from the Renaissance. The *Bastiment des receptes* advises: "To make small breasts remain in that state and to reduce the size of large ones, take the main viscera (heart, liver, spleen, lungs) of a hare, mince them and mix with an equal part of ordinary honey. Apply this as a poultice to the breasts and surrounding areas and renew the application when dry."

Even the most cursory glance at sculpture through the ages reveals very few figures resembling Claudia Schiffer and many more resembling Venus de Milo, who'd be considered a bit *zaftig* today. Women who would have been a goddess for Sophocles are Helen Gurley Brown's mouseburgers. ✺

HOWARD HUGHES DESIGNS A BRA

It wasn't until the 20th century that the modern bra that lifts and separates was created. In 1913, Caresse Crosby—a New York socialite right out of the pages of F. Scott Fitzgerald—had bought an expensive diaphanous gown to wear to a society ball. Caresse, a strikingly beautiful woman, was appalled that the outline of the clunky corset protruded against the silk. She and her French maid devised a homemade device out of two white cotton handkerchiefs, some baby ribbon, and a bit of string.

So many of her socialite friends requested samples that Crosby filed for a patent for the Backless Brassiere and started marketing them. When commerce proved too tedious, she sold the rights for $1,500 to Warner Brothers Corset Company of Bridgeport, Connecticut.

Many nameless couturiers contributed a bit of elastic here or a cross-your-heart there but one industrialist-filmmaker-bra designer stands out for reinforcing America's budding breast obsession: Howard Hughes.

Hughes, America's eccentric billionaire

Jane Russell in *The Outlaw* (1943). Howard Hughes tried hard to *support* his star.

who wound up hoarding his fingernails in Las Vegas, tried to construct a bra for the nineteen-year-old dental assistant Jane Russell starring in his big-budget Western, *The Outlaw* (1943). Hughes, who pored over every detail of production, was disappointed at times by the slope and sway of Miss Russell's gargantuan breasts.

Let's pick up the story in Russell's own words from her autobiography:

Howard then decided it wouldn't be any harder to design a bra than it would be to design an airplane. He tried. When I went to the dressing room with my wardrobe girl and tried it on, I found it uncomfortable and ridiculous. Obviously, he wanted today's seamless bra, which didn't exist then. It was a good idea—as usual, he was way ahead of his time—but I wasn't doing 103 takes in this subject. So I put on my own bra, covered the seams with tissue, pulled the straps over to the side, put on my blouse and started out. Emily, my wardrobe girl, was terrified. What if they found out? I assured her they'd never find out from me. Everybody behind the camera stared, and

Howard finally nodded Okay and filming proceeded.

I *never* wore his bra, and believe me, he could design planes, but a Mr. Playtex he was not.

You could argue that modern technology with light sturdy materials has enabled big breasts to become popular. Prior to the 20th century, they simply weren't very practical. ✸

THE UNDERSIDE OF BREAST-FEEDING

WET NURSES

The prophet Mohammed proclaimed, "A woman's breasts will nourish the child and delight the father."

In the dozens of centuries before pasteurized milk and bottle-feeding, breastfeeding dominated the nourishing of the infant. However, what's forgotten in the 20th century is the huge role in infant-feeding played by wet nurses and the tiny (but semi-fascinating) role played by animals.

Records of wet-nurse contracts date back to the pharaohs. Wealthier moms in ancient Greece and Rome used them. Ba-

Diane de Poitiers, King Henri II's mistress, shows off her highly praised firm *midsized* breasts, while a peasant wet nurse risks a lifetime of stretch marks and sagging by breast-feeding Poitiers's babe. (Painted by François Clouet, c. 1571.)

sically, many if not most affluent moms in Europe through the 1700s shipped newborns out to feed on strangers' breasts.

In France, which takes breasts seriously, various bureaucratic divisions dating back to the 13th century have been dedicated to placing wet nurses and scrutinizing résumés. In times of plague or syphilis, a hired pap could squirt poison. There's another reason for such careful selection of the wet nurse. Through the 1800s, it was almost universally accepted that the physical and moral traits of the wet nurse would be transmitted to the child through the breast milk. So if you hired a thief, you'd be raising a thief. One French minister in the mid-1800s went so far as to propose that prostitutes shouldn't be allowed to breast-feed their own children, lest they corrupt them with a couple of gulps of lewd character.

Given that risk of hiring the wrong breast, it seems astounding that so many women would turn to strangers to nurture their children. Sometimes the husband made the decision for the wife, and his motivation lay a few inches below his belt. Folk wisdom and medical science dating back at least to Galen (2nd century) held that breast-feeding mothers should refrain from sex for the health of both child and mother. Not surprisingly, many European and American fathers were willing to pay the extra few francs, guilders, pfennigs, or dollars for a wet nurse.

And the Catholic Church, in effect, endorsed that approach. Influential theologians accepted the no-sex rule and decided that it was best to put the child out to wet-nursing rather than tempt the father with adultery.

So, yes, convenience, health, and dad's sex life all helped sway moms to farm out junior and so did . . . vanity.

Breast-feeding inflates and deflates the breast, leaving stretch marks and sagging. Nipples can become torn and infected, leaving permanent scars.

"Breasts are the last beauty trait granted to women, and the first to be taken away," wrote Louis Mercier in his work, *In Praise of Women's Breasts*. "Very few women are as privileged as [courtesan] Ninon to preserve their breasts. And this is why women . . . entrust their babies to the mercenary breast of wet nurses."

Puppies Help Out

Dr. William Dewees (1768–1841), the Dr. Spock of his generation, recommended that pregnant women should suckle "a young but sufficiently strong puppy . . . immediately after the seventh month" to toughen and accentuate the nipples, improve secretion, and prevent inflammation.

Dr. Dewees hoped the puppy's sucking would prepare "the nipples for the future assaults of the child," according to Dr. Samuel Radbill in his article, *The Role of Animals in Infant Feeding.*

Hispanic mother seeks relief from overengorgement by giving puppies a turn while her baby gnaws his fist in this odd painting by Utrillo.

And Dr. Dewees was no quack. He wrote the first American pediatric guide, *Treatise on the Physical and Medical Treatment of Children* (1825), which was reprinted into more than a dozen editions.

For women who were a bit leery of affixing Lassie to their mammaries, but whose nipples were sunken or short, he suggested that they might use a long-stemmed tobacco pipe to draw them out, by planting the bowl on the aureole and sucking themselves.

Perhaps Dr. Dewees received some flack for setting puppies on the breasts of American women, because in the seventh edition in 1838, he noted that a nurse or another experienced person could suck just as expertly as a puppy.

Farm-Fed French Orphans

Tens of thousands of French and German children were suckled by goats, sheep, and other animals: True or false? True.

For a few hundred years in Europe, and especially in France, it was often considered best to have babies suckle at the teats of animals when neither mother nor wet nurse was available.

Essayist Michel de Montaigne wrote in 1580: "It is common . . . to see women of the village, when they cannot feed the children at their breast, call the goats to their rescue."

There's an excellent chance that some of the five children that Jean-Jacques Rousseau abandoned at state-run orphanages were suckled by animals.

France started turning to animals for

nurturing orphans when a syphilis epidemic first hit Europe in the 1500s; syphilitic babies were frequently abandoned, and it was soon believed that wet nurses working at foundling hospitals were contracting the disease. Rather than dry-feed them, it was decided that suckling directly from animals was preferred.

But which animal was best? Experts debated. Conventional wisdom held that moral traits of the wet nurse, even four-footed ones, would be transmitted to the baby through the breast milk, so this was a very important decision. It was thought that a sheep might be too docile and that a she-wolf (while fine for Romulus and Remus, founders of Rome) would hardly be a positive influence for a generation of orphans. Swine have always been social outcasts.

The decision in Europe boiled down to goats or asses. Ass milk reduced infant mortality in Paris's leading children's hospital in the 1800s, according to one study; also, "asses had a better moral reputation than goats" with children less likely to become lusty beasts.

Many important doctors repeated Hippocrates and Galen in stating that ass milk was a good general curative and potent antidote for many poisons. Galen, fearing spoilage, used to haul the ass right to the patient's bedside.

This practice of animal nurture amazingly continued at French orphanages through the early 20th century, even with the advent of *pasteur*ized milk and reliable infant formula.

"Nowadays, too," wrote Hermann Ploss around 1900, "feeding children by animal still takes place, and this occurs in Paris in the big foundling and children's hospital *(Hôpital des enfants assistés)*. Children suspected of having infectious diseases are not fed by wet nurses but are applied to asses' udders. A special pavillion has been built for this in the garden of the great institution. There are stalls attached to two sides of the actual ward where the children are, and in each of these stalls four asses are kept permanently for this purpose alone."

And animals nurturing infants wasn't limited to orphanages. A German by the name of Conrad Zwierlein—who listened at a spa to aristocratic mothers complain about breast-feeding—published a book, *The Goat as the Best and Most Agreeable Wet Nurse* (1816). It's reported that goat-suckling then enjoyed a brief vogue in Europe and the United States.

THE CORSET: CENTURIES OF HOURGLASS FANTASIES

In Margaret Mitchell's *Gone With the Wind*, Scarlett O'Hara has a few months earlier given birth to her third child. And like many mothers postpartum, she's battling to regain her former figure. She slips on her corset; her servant laces her in. Scarlett passes the tape measure around her waist. "Twenty inches! She groaned aloud. That was what having babies did to your figure! Her waist was as large as Aunt Pitty's, as large as Mammy's."

As large as Mammy's!?! (Remember that wonderful human medicine ball, Hattie McDaniel, who played Mammy?)

Mammy laces a disappointed Scarlett into her corset in this scene from *Gone With the Wind* (1939). "Twenty inches! she groaned aloud. Her waist was as large as . . . Mammy's."

Scarlett is furious (and a bit demented) over the prospect that she can't regain her girlish eighteen-and-a-half-inch waist. She vows—regardless of what it will do to her marriage to Rhett Butler—to have no more children.

If you think Scarlett was a bit fanatic compared to her fashionable sisters, think again. The Empress of Austria in 1860 had a sixteen-inch waist. The Sears Roebuck mail-order catalogue for the 1890s offered corsets starting at eighteen inches, as did U.S. lingerie giant, Warner's. The goal of all this winching was said to be a waist that a man could encircle with his hands.

Corset mania—despite the widely held impression that it was a 19th-century phenomenon—has actually tormented the female sex for thousands of years. Excavations at ancient Crete unearthed snake-priestesses whose tightly corseted waists thrust their cantaloupe breasts chinward. (If there's any justice, Cretan men used to wear *exceptionally* tight belts to achieve a similar effect.)

Western history has seesawed between two distinct periods: belly and no belly. While the ancient Greeks and Romans preferred a natural pouting belly (along with smallish breasts and an ample derriere), a body shape also highlighted in Gothic art, some European societies after the Black Death in 1348 started to venerate more of an hourglass figure.

"Who would doubt that humanity was slipping toward perdition when women appeared in public wearing artificial hair and low-necked blouses with their breasts laced so high that a candle could actually be placed upon them?" That's how chronicler Matteo Villani described the desperate pleasure-seeking survivors of the plague.

By the 1500s in France, surgeon Ambroise Paré was already blaming many body ills on excessive tightening of the corset, which featured a rigid busk in front made of whalebone, wood, ivory, or even steel. "This is body armour," he wrote.

A corseted American woman brushing her hair in 1899.

When adventurous Englishwoman Lady Mary Montagu visited the elaborate women's baths in Istanbul in 1717, she boasted to the Turkish women about a European woman's freedom to travel about the city without any veil or eunuch bodyguard. As the Moslem women clustered about her and helped her undress, they were shocked at the corset and rigid stays. "You need boast indeed of the superior liberties allowed you," commented her host, "when they locked you up in a box."

It would take the guillotine to free women from their corsets; that is to say, the French Revolution, with its high ideals, would briefly liberate women. Just as bras would be burned in the U.S. in the 1960s, so were corsets burned in Paris in the 1790s.

"It is not pleasant to see a woman cut in two, like a wasp," observed Jean-Jacques Rousseau, who helped set the Revolution's twin themes of liberty and nature. "Slenderness of waist has, like all the rest, its proportion, its just measure, beyond which it is certainly a defect. This defect would be striking on the naked body; so why should it be a beauty on the clothed one?"

Once the Bastille had been stormed, a proclamation posted all over Paris decreed: *"Vous avez la liberté des cultes et celle du costume."* i.e., "You have the freedom of worship and freedom of dress." (Two freedoms *equally* important to the French!) Citizen Armand Duval, in charge of Arts and Sciences at the Ministry of the Interior, recommended to women: "No shoes, stockings, corsets or garters. No petticoats but a simple tunic opened at the sides."

The famous historical painter Jacques-Louis David endorsed a return to flowing looseness of Ancient Greek garb. For a while, Parisian drawing rooms resembled high school costume dramas of *Medea* or *Ben-Hur.* Like so many ideals in the French Revolution, this vision of fashion freedom was startlingly fine— but here again, human nature intruded to muck things up.

Freedom fighters. Famed beauty Madame Récamier is *not* wearing a negligee; her vaguely classical outfit was supposed to be the new garb of French women, now that the Revolution had freed them from the constraints of high fashion. (Painting by François Gerard in 1802.)

"The high classical waist was not so easily achieved by ladies who led an idle life and took no exercise whatsoever," observes Pearl Binder in *Muffs and Morals.*

Just as the French restored the monarchy; they also brought back the corset, which had continued to prevail all over the rest of Europe and in the United States. In the 19th century, corsets eventually would compact millions of women to the tightest, most strangling waist measurements ever recorded.

Letters poured into English domestic magazines from women analyzing the best strategies for waist reduction. A woman wrote describing her sixteen-and-a-half-inch waist and the editor replied: "I have invariably noticed that the girls with the smallest waists are the queens of the ballrooms."

Fainting and loss of appetite soon became the traits of the well-bred Victorian woman. Some of the leading actresses of the period competed with each other over teeniness of waist and largeness of bosom. Lillian Russell boasted 42-22-38 (and dozens of other duly recorded dimensions). One popular French actress, known for her "inflexible bulwarked beauty accepted no sitting roles," recalled writer Colette.

Anna Held isn't much remembered today but she was an enormously popular turn-of-the-century actress, whose interview in a negligee once was international news. This beautiful woman with a classic hourglass shape died in 1918 at age forty-five. *Life* magazine later surmised: "Doctors said she literally squeezed herself to death."

In the United States, the feminism of the 1960s struck a death blow to the corset's descendant, the girdle (the bra was merely wounded). However, like the French Revolution, the Women's Lib movement didn't exactly mark a long-term victory for "natural pouty bellied beauty."

Cosmetic surgery is vastly on the rise, as women have their bodies reshaped via the knife, with tummy tucks, liposuction and breast implants. And exercise. And dieting. And large belts. And . . . 🌀

MISSTEPS IN MEN'S FASHION

THE SHAPELIEST LEGS THROUGHOUT HISTORY

Chaucer's Wife of Bath fell in love with her fifth husband when she saw his feet and legs "so clean and fair" as he walked after the funeral bier of her fourth husband.

Admiring a man's leg was standard back then; admiring a woman's leg in public was unheard of because a man rarely got a chance to see them in public.

Although it's hard for us 20th-century types to believe it, throughout the length of European and American history, it has been the man who has shown off his gams, not the woman. (Not the respectable

Queen Elizabeth at Blackfriars is surrounded by leggy courtiers, male, of course. Note all the women have their legs covered, all the men have theirs exposed. (Painted by Marcus Gheeraerts, around 1600.)

woman, at least; actresses, dancers, and prostitutes have always followed different fashion rules.) In ancient Greece, in ancient Rome, in the Middle Ages, during the Renaissance, men always had the much shorter robes.

It is only in the last century—as the skirt curtain has risen from the Victorian ankle—that so-called respectable women have gradually revealed calf, knee, now thigh. Shakespeare would have thought they were all hookers. ❧

JOAN OF ARC'S LEGS

Most people know that teenage heroine Joan of Arc was burned at the stake for being a witch, but actually she was convicted of another crime as well: that of dressing like a man. This was a capital offense in 1431, with the Ecclesiastical Court that tried her following the biblical injunction (Deuteronomy 22:5). "The woman shall not wear that which pertaineth unto a man, neither shall a man put on a woman's garment: for all that do so are abomination unto the Lord thy God."

What was Joan wearing that contributed to her losing her life? On the battlefield she wore armor, but in camp and in prison, as best we can tell from eyewitnesses, she donned a short gray tunic over closely fitted hose of vermilion cloth. Basically we'd call her outfit a gray jumper with red tights. That's what *men* wore back then.

(The women wore long dresses, and individual cloth stockings kept up by garters, and there was nothing at the north fork of their legs.)

To keep the men's hose from falling down in those days before elastic, the top of the tights sported pairs of eyelets, as did the doublet (a kind of low vest) through which strings could be tied. Normally, a man used as many as seven fancy little strings to keep his hose up. Joan used twenty, and all very tightly tied. Why?

Her nickname was the "Maid of Orleans," "La Pucelle," i.e., "The Virgin." Joan was *very* concerned about her honor, and felt far too vulnerable in a dress—especially surrounded by hundreds of men. In prison, Joan claimed she was afraid without the protection of the tightly laced hose she'd be raped by her five lowlife English guards.

Joan—after much brow-beating—eventually confessed to various crimes and expected mercy. As agreed, she put on a dress. Joan spent that night in her cell with her five English guards; by morning she was wearing her "tights" again, which signaled to Church officials she had reneged on the confession-and-mercy deal. Joan was now defiant and was ready for her fate.

On execution day, her captors garbed her in a long robe, tried to humiliate her with the heretic's conical cap and then they burned her. Instead of snuffing out her memory, she became a rallying cry, this cross-dresser who rescued her country from the invading English. ❧

IN COD WE TRUST

When the great William Shakespeare strode like a Colossus across the English stage, many of his fellow countrymen, especially the older ones, had pin cushion–like codpieces squinting out from the slit in their flouncy breeches.

A character in the Bard's *Much Ado About Nothing* petulantly recalls seeing a tapestry of Hercules "where his cod-piece seems as massy as his club." (Never mind there were no codpieces in ancient Greece, the speaker Borachio is drunk).

Codpieces flourished for about one hundred years from 1450 to 1550 and were still worn in the time of Shakespeare (1564–1616).

What exactly is a codpiece and where did it come from? It evolved. In the late Middle Ages, men in Europe started wearing clingy tights. The overhanging doublet or jacket also started getting shorter and shorter.

We know some people were flashing the family jewels because the Ecclesiastical Court in England found it necessary to set a fine of twenty shillings for any man, not protected by his rank, who ventured to wear a doublet "not long enough when he stands upright to cover his privities and his buttocks."

The fines and sermons apparently didn't work, so the Church ordered people to wear some kind of garment in front to cover the genitals, and ironically gave birth to the codpiece. What was supposed to be a modest cover turned into an exuberant tribute. (That's at least the theory that Pearl Binder states in her witty *Muffs and Morals*.)

Another theory holds that the cod evolved from the leather case, a kind of wallet worn by peasants in the days before pants pockets.

Men in the Middle Ages generally carried their money or valuables in little purse sacks hanging from their belt. (Hence, "cutpurse" preceded "pickpocket" as a criminal vocation.) After a few centuries of enduring cutpurses, some wise peasant decided to store his valuables in a pouch snugly secured in front of his genitals. It quickly became apparent the more stored in there, the bigger the bulge.

Victorian sex researcher Havelock Ellis concludes that upper classes—envious perhaps of the bulge—eventually adopted and refined the style, creating an elegant fashion accessory, often of silk with ribbons, gold, and jewels.

"This accessory to male attire was often indelicately prominent," understates G. B. Harrison in his introduction to the works of

The French Duke d'Alençon, minimal cod. (François Clouet, 1575)

King Henry VIII, maximum flying buttress cod. (School of Holbein, c. 1540)

William Shakespeare. "It was made in various forms such as a bow of silk, a flap tied to the hose with laces, a small padded sausage-shaped cushion ornamented with pins, or a small bag used as a pocket."

The national spirit could be revealed in codpiece fashion. The Italians favored a very large conspicuous unit with little interference from pants or jacket; the French didn't emphasize size as much as elegance, favoring gold buckles; the Germans exaggerated theirs into a giant heavily padded bow or pillow while the English chose a fair-size skyward-pointing model but tucked it into a gap in their puffy breeches. Art historians rarely boast about it but "it is possible to date and place with considerable accuracy unnamed and undated portraits of the period by studying the details of this one article of dress," states one scholar.

Not surprisingly, this item of male braggadocio sometimes annoyed men who didn't wear codpieces, such as the Turks in the 1600s. "They see nothing so strange in our garments as our codpieces, which seem to them very dishonest," stated Robert Withers, who lived in Istanbul around 1610. "If a band of Turks find any Christian man, especially a man of war, in a place where they may overcome him, they cut off his codpiece." (We can picture the turbanned Turks howling with laughter at the insignificant worm encased in the giant embroidered tallywhacker.)

Rabelais (1494–1553), the great and *earthy* French satirist, delighted in poking fun at codpieces. Here, he describes Gargantua's gargantuan model. This is the cod *ne plus ultra.*

For his codpiece was used nineteen and a half yards of white broad cloth. Shaped like a flying buttress, it was joyously fastened by two beautiful golden buckles connecting two enamelled clasps; in each of which was mounted a great emerald the size of an orange. Because . . . the emerald has a certain uplifting and nurturing power for the male member.

The out-thrusting front of his codpiece was two yards long, panelled and laced like his breeches, with blue damask puffing out as mentioned above. And, if you had seen the beautiful embroidery and exquisite goldsmith work, embellished with rich diamonds, glorious rubies, turquoises, emeralds and Persian pearls, you would have compared it to a cornucopia, a horn of plenty such as you see in antiques . . .

And like that horn of plenty, it was always gallant, succulent, droppy, sappy, pithy, lively, always flourishing, fructifying, full of juice, full of flowers, full of fruits, full of all sorts of delicacies. May God strike me if it wasn't a delight to look upon. But I will tell you more about it in the book I have written *On the Dignity of Codpieces.* In any case, suffice it to say that it was long and large, that it was also well furnished and provided within, and it in no way resembled those hypocritical codpieces of fops and dandies, which are full of nothing but wind, to the great annoyance of the female sex.

The codpiece—much criticized by the Puritans—gradually petered out. ❧

BIG SHOES TO FILL

In the Middle Ages, for a couple of centuries, there flourished the looooooooooong pointy shoe.

English nobles so enjoyed showing off the length of their shoes that they became annoyed when commoners started doing likewise. King Edward III (1312–1377) enacted a sumptuary law that "no Knight under the estate of a lord, esquire or gentleman, nor any other person, shall wear any shoes or boots having spikes or points exceeding the length of two inches, under forfeiture of forty pence."

One fashion historian without citing a source states that in England for a while the length of tip permitted beyond the shoe was twenty-four inches for a nobleman, twelve inches for a gentleman, six inches for a commoner.

When King Richard II of England (1366–1399) married Anne of Bohemia, the noblemen arriving with her sported

Pope Leo III crowning Charlemagne on Christmas Day in 800. Check out the pointy shoes worn by the king and noblemen to his right.

foot-long tips on their shoes and the fashion caught on. The shoes were called "crackowes" or "poulaines." ❧

HAIR STRATEGIES THROUGH THE AGES

PUBIC HAIR

Statues of women in ancient Greece lacked pubic hair because women in ancient Greece lacked pubic hair. That is, they shaved it or tweezed it or even sticky-plastered it off. This was Art copying Nature after a haircut.

The ancient Egyptians—both men and women—used to remove all body hair. Archaeologists have found elaborate jeweled wigs in the tombs. And those long jeweled beards on pharaohs were actually faux beards—glued on to achieve a royal air.

In the Ottoman Empire, which flourished for five hundred years and included the notorious Turkish harem, the custom was for young Moslem women to have their body hair removed during an elaborate ritual at the baths. "It is not till the very day of marriage that they are piteously stripped of the veil of nature," observed C. S. Sonnini, who traveled in Egypt (part of Ottoman Empire) in the late 1790s.

Why wait till wedding day? The Turks believed that a Turkish girl's leg hair, thigh hair, and any other wayward tufts would act as hirsute chastity belt, to make her less attractive to smooth skin–seeking Moslem men. The ceremony at the baths was quite formal: A procession of nude virgins (with body hair) surrounded the bride as she walked from married woman to married woman (no body hair) receiving expensive gifts.

Sonnini, an engineer traveling on a fact-finding mission for the government of France, made certain to explore the intricacies of the Turkish depilation process. He reports that honey mixed with turpentine was made into a paste; this plaster is applied, allowed to dry, then torn off yanking the hair with it, from the roots. "Fortunately, there is no need to return often to this rather severe process," notes Sonnini. "If a re-growth occurs, it is only a soft down, like the finest wool; and, after a few years, vegetation of this sort is absolutely destroyed."

Homosexual men in ancient Rome depilated their asses to facilitate entry, and for historians and comedic playwrights, this provided an oblique way to accuse someone of being homosexual. As for the pubes above the penis, styles varied, but a "Hitler mustache" was often popular. One man who shaved the pubic region entirely was ridiculed. "Your penis resembles a vulture's neck," scoffed the poet Martial.

After the downfall of the Roman Empire (and of bathing in general), most European women stopped shaving their pubes.

Nonetheless, for the next fifteen hundred years, European sculptors and artists generally followed the early Greek and Roman influence and rarely showed pubic hair on female statues or paintings. This is Art imitating Art imitating Nature after a haircut. 🌀

BYRON'S TANGLED KEEPSAKES

The flamboyant British poet Byron reverently kept a collection by which to remember his lovers. "Today in the offices of Byron's publisher in London are a number of envelopes in which the poet placed quantities of differently coloured very curly hair besides the names of his girlfriends," states James Bentley in *Restless Bones*. *Very* curly. 🌀

BLONDES HAVE MORE FUN?

When Clairol devised its slogan, "Blondes have more fun," it probably wasn't thinking of prostitutes in ancient Rome. Roman law required prostitutes—who were registered with the authorities—to dye their hair blond or wear a blond wig to separate themselves from honorable Roman brunettes. Blond was the hair color of Barbarians to the north and slaves of that race often wound up in the brothels.

Moralizing historians seeking clues for the fall of Rome have had a field day pointing out that wealthy Roman women started imitating hookers and dying their hair blond.

When the Emperor Claudius's wife Messalina around 45 A.D. was accused of slipping out of the palace to turn tricks at a low brothel, the satirist Juvenal wrote: "She hid her black hair beneath a blond wig and entered a brothel dank from old bedspreads."

The early Christian fathers were furious at the vanity and implied immorality of blond hair. "I see women dye their hair blond by using saffron," wrote Tertullian, who flourished around 200 A.D. "They are ashamed of their country, sorry that they were not born in Germany or Gaul!" And the Latin Father is equally aghast at wigs. "Be ashamed of . . . putting on your holy and Christian head the cast-off hair of some stranger who was perhaps unclean, perhaps guilty and destined for hell."

Or, in other words . . . "Blondes have more fun." ❦

BEARDS

While daily shaving has its risks, beards at times could be truly dangerous. Alexander the Great forbade his men to have beards; the young general thought it gave enemy soldiers too convenient a handle for lopping off heads.

And Peter the Great passed a law outlawing beards; he wanted Russkies to appear more civilized like their European counterparts. To enforce the measure, he created a beard tax, with fines as high as one hundred rubles. Peasants wanting whiskers had to pay a kopeck every time they passed through the gates of a city. Those who had paid the fine were given a copper "bearded coin" with a year stamped on it.

Nonpayment could result in a prison term and a shave. ❦

MEN'S HAIR

It seems astounding in hindsight that a nation with a long-haired George Washington on its one-dollar bill and a shoulder-length Ben Franklin on its hundred—not to mention Jesus looking out at every church—should have gotten so exercised over the hippie lengths of the 1960s.

The battle over men's hair lengths dates at least back to Saint Paul, who declared that "long hair was a shame unto a man." This set up the long-running musical of Church versus hair. Churchmen showed their piety through tonsure.

King Louis VII of France, obeying the Church, cropped himself close and his queen, Eleanor of Aquitaine, promptly left him, taking with her the vast land holdings of her dowry, which she gave to her next husband, later King of England. "She . . . thus gave the English sovereigns that strong footing in France which was for so many centuries the cause of such long and bloody wars between the nations," writes Charles MacKay in his brilliant and peppery *Extraordinary Popular Delusions and the Madness of Crowds*. So, a haircut helped lead to the Hundred Years' War?

The roots of the modern American obsession of associating short hair and good morals probably dates to our Puritan ancestors. Oliver Cromwell and his Puritans snipped their hair short in "bowl cuts" and were dubbed "Roundheads," while the royals, with their flowing locks, were called "Cavaliers." That English Civil War cost King Charles I his hair *and* his head. Plenty of prim Roundheads filled the American colonies.

Length of hair seems a monumentally silly thing to be outraged by. To his credit, Congressman "Tip" O'Neill ordered an aide in 1970 to do a detailed report on hair length through history. "We discovered that since the time of Christ, the male species has worn long hair and beards about 90 percent of the time," announced the tubby short-haired Rep from Massachusetts. "The western world turned to short hair and clean-shaven faces only after the Prussian victory over France. All the great heroes of America have worn long hair. It's nothing for Americans to get alarmed about."

For a nation split over Vietnam, it was nice to hear a politician trying to de-escalate the hair wars.

Did Saint Paul lament that Jesus didn't take a hair cut? 🌀

WIGS FOR MEN

Wigs for men seem extremely silly to most Americans, like something suited for Halloween, Howard Cosell, or for those idiotically self-important British judges.

Not surprisingly, wigs for men in modern times date back to one powerful *bald* man in the Renaissance. Louis XIII of France had male pattern baldness, which domed him by 1624 at age twenty-three. He donned a periwig. Louis XIV, who reigned from 1643 to 1715, was so dis-

pleased by his late-in-life baldness that he allowed only his barber to see him bald and required his wig to be passed every morning through the closed curtains of his four-poster bed.

In old age, Louis the Sun King wore a large white wig, which all the court members—male and female, young and old—copied. "Everyone wants to be old so as to appear wise," commented a lady-in-waiting. (For a while in the 1990s, Hollywood movie stars wore no-magnification eyeglasses to appear more intelligent. It had the same effect.)

Over in England, once the Roundhead Puritans were booted in 1660, giant periwigs became the rage. Thieves tackled

In England, in the 1760s and 1770s, certain foppish men disdained British fashion and sought to imitate what they considered the Continental style by seeking the highest, longest hair, not to mention white hands, rouged cheeks, and perhaps a beauty mark. They were dubbed "Macaronis." (Philip Danve, 1773)

teens and clipped their locks to sell to wig-makers. During the plague years, wig buyers greatly feared disease, perturbed they might be wearing hair clipped from corpses rotting in the street, according to famed diarist Samuel Pepys (1633–1703).

Wigs grew enormous, and walk-in closets were built in mansions as rooms for powdering these monstrosities. While wealthy Americans often delighted in wigs, pious Harvard College in the mid-1600s forbade "long haire, locks, foretops, curlings, crispings, partings or powdering of ye haire."

Throughout the 1700s, all British soldiers were issued a pound of flour a week to powder their wigs. Those matted, full-bottomed wigs still worn by English judges date back to the same period.

The male wig's death knell was sounded by the French Revolution. The *citoyens* lopped off wigs as well. Rousseau led the fashion charge back to nature, and the tousled—without expensive artifice—look in hair swept France. In England in 1795, a heavy tax on wig powder cooled Englishmen's ardor for high hair. Pearl Binder claims in *Muffs and Morals* that the tax was one guinea, and anyone in wig in streets was called a "Guinea-Pig." Lord Byron with his natural long hair became the new male model.

Ben Franklin wore the beaver proudly to show his (and America's) disdain for prissy wigs.

Over in America, wigs faltered. Part of it is perhaps due to a wig that didn't fit Ben Franklin, U.S. diplomat to France. He was set to be announced before the French court and he hastily tried on the wig bought especially for the occasion. It chafed. He instead showed up in his own long hair and a beaver hat (pre–Daniel Boone). Shocking attire, befitting a revolutionary. Franklin thereafter shrewdly used the image of his long natural thinning hair and his frontier beaver cap to represent the homespun, free-from-fashion values of the upstart United States of America.

THE SMELL OF HISTORY: FILTHY SAINTS

The signers of the Declaration of Independence probably stank; so did Queen Elizabeth I; so did the Renaissance popes. And, without a doubt, poor people of those eras stank. We're talking body odor from weeks of unwashed flesh, armpits that would empty a modern day elevator.

Simple daily hygiene that we take for granted and expect was actively discouraged as downright sinful for more than a thousand years. Although we've heard repeatedly the Christian piety, "Cleanliness is next to godliness," this is a *relatively recent* Christian piety.

From the fall of the Roman Empire through the Victorian era, it could be said that personal dirtiness was next to godliness.

The Romans and their conquered subjects built elaborate public baths that could rival modern-day health spas, with art galleries, libraries, gorgeous gardens. Bathers—poor or rich—stripped, selected perfume oils, perhaps exercised, then sweated in the dry heat, then entered the main domed "caldarium."

Many of the little walled-off areas featured wall jets spouting various perfumes: you might choose between sensual, flowery or invigorating scents, depending on what activity you planned for later. Nearby, masseurs stood ready to unknot muscles. Prostitutes lay ready for further relaxation.

While public baths started out as male only, soon certain hours were set aside for females, then eventually mixed bathing became the fashion. This nude mingling of the sexes outraged the early Christian Fathers.

"Women are not ashamed to strip before spectators as if exposing their person for sale," complained Clement of Alexandria. "[They] bathe with their own servants and strip naked before their slaves, and are rubbed by them." He pointed out that seeing naked flesh could lead to . . . sex.

When the barbarians overran the Roman Empire, they physically trashed the marvelous marble and tiled baths. The Christian Fathers finished the destruction of bathing for a millennia by sanctifying disdain for the body. If chastity were higher than marriage, then ignoring the body was higher than indulgent grooming.

"The cleanliness of the body was regarded as a pollution of the soul," writes William Lecky in *History of European Morals*, "and the saints who were most admired had become one mass of clotted filth."

- Saint Abraham the hermit refused for fifty years to wash his face or his feet.

- A famous virgin named Silvia, though sixty and sickly, "refused to wash any part of her body except her fingers."

- Saint Ammon never saw himself naked.

- Saint Simeon Stylites stood unwashed on giant pillars while worms gnawed at his open sores.

- Saint Euphraxia joined a convent of 130 nuns who never washed their feet and were repulsed by even the mention of the word "bath."

In the Middle Ages, the monks were not quite as fanatical about seeking personal filth; many monasteries allowed brethren *two* baths a year. The rules at the famed monastery of Cluny mandated three towels for the entire community.

These Christian ideals of course influenced lay society. "In 16th-century Italy, a land of supreme elegance and fashion superior even to France," writes Havelock Ellis, ". . . how little water found favor even with aristocratic ladies we may gather from the contemporary books on the toilet, which abound with recipes against itch and similar diseases." Worse, bad hygiene helped spread disease.

However, as doctors discovered the dangers of dirt and as engineers pioneered mass plumbing, things began to change.

Daily bathing is a 20th-century rediscovery of what the ancient Romans (and many animal species) had already mastered.

Scholars are undecided whether this medieval illustration is a nude wedding or merely a raucous party at a bordello; in any case, look at the table, there is only one knife and no forks or spoons. Tableware was still a few centuries off.

ETIQUETTE RULES FOR BREAKING WIND AND BREAD

THE FORK

William Shakespeare and Leonardo da Vinci ate their meals with their fingers; that is, unless they were having soup. They usually shared that out of a communal pot.

The fork, which we take for granted as not exactly a high-tech invention, did not come into widespread use until the 1700s. Sure, two-pronged forks were used in the kitchen, but when they finally surfaced at some Italian tables in the late Middle Ages, clergymen railed against their use. "If God had wanted us to use forks, he wouldn't have created us with hands," thundered one German priest. "It is the devil's pitchfork."

In the Middle Ages and the Renaissance, most people in Europe scooped a portion out of a communal dish, perhaps using a knife they brought with them, and then slapped the food onto an oversize piece of stale bread or a wooden plate. The wealthy might have their meal served onto a fancy plate, but they would still eat it with their fingers.

The philosopher-essayist Michel Montaigne (1533–1592) criticized himself for eating too quickly. "Sometimes, I bite my fingers in my haste."

And over in the New World, the Pilgrims frowned on anyone using Satan's pitchfork to spear their meat. Gradually, though, wealthy colonists started carrying around silver forks in little bags, which they'd trot out at inns to one-up their fellow travelers.

And there was a right way and a wrong way to dine *mano a mano*. Etiquette books in the Middle Ages and Renaissance stressed that eaters should use only three fingers of his or her right hand for picking up food, not act like boorish peasants who use the whole hand or even two hands.

Obviously hand hygiene becomes important when there are communal plates of food. Your neighbor's fingernails might attract your attention, as well as their behavior. "During the meal, do not put your fingers into your ears or touch your hair," urged Fra Bonvicino da Riva in 1290. Elizabethan table-manner experts counseled men not to explore inside their codpieces between courses.

Liquids presented unique problems as well. While spoons were common, individual bowls for each person were not through the 1700s. "If you're offered something liquid, taste it and return the spoon, but first wipe the spoon on your napkin," advised a manual from the 1500s. That advice must have often gone unheeded, because a French manual from 1672 states, "There are people so delicate that they would not wish to eat soup into which you have dipped [your spoon] after putting it into your mouth."

Cups and glasses were not that common, either, for the middle and lower classes. A tankard of ale or pitcher of wine might be passed around the table, and the mannerly among the guests would wipe his or her mouth before and after drinking.

Proper behavior has been dictated by etiquette books since the days of the Pharaohs. Here are highlights on two important topics: nose-blowing and farting.

NOSE-BLOWING

"Do not blow your nose with the same hand that you use to hold the meat." So states an anonymous 15th-century French etiquette book, *Obeying Table Manners*. Another later book advises, "If any snot falls to the ground, quickly smear it over with your shoe."

In the Middle Ages, it was considered proper to blow your nose in your fingers; a painting of the funeral of Philip the Bold shows a couple of knights doing just that.

The Renaissance, an innovative time, showed some progress in nasal waste disposal. In the 1500s, a historian tells us, while commoners blew their nose into their hand or closed one nostril and vented the other, the bourgeoisie used their sleeve and the rich began carrying a new luxury item called a handkerchief. The king of France, Henri IV (1553–1610), owned *five* handkerchiefs near the beginning of his reign. Of course, rules cropped up for handkerchief use. "Nor is it seemly," decreed Giovanni Della Casa in the 1550s, "after wiping your nose, to spread out your handkerchief and peer into it as if pearls or rubies might have fallen out of your head."

Over time, handkerchiefs became increasingly popular and ceased being a luxury item, but it wasn't until after World War I that disposable tissues appeared. Kimberly-Clark invented Cellucotton which was used as a filter in gas masks. After the war, the company marketed it as a cold-cream tissue. It took fifteen years and piles of consumer mail before they started selling it as a disposable handkerchief for nose-blowing. 🐚

To Fart or Not to Fart

Fart etiquette goes way back. A manuscript from 6th-century B.C. China forbids farting at the table. Over in India, in the 2nd-century B.C., a minister ruled that men appointed to the king's service should "not make statements that are uncultured . . . nor indulge in loud laughter when there is no joke, nor break wind."

In ancient Rome, the issue got a bit more dramatic. A rumor made the rounds that a Roman who was trying desperately not to fart at a long dinner party almost killed himself. When the Emperor Claudius (the "I" from the PBS series) heard about the incident, he planned to pass "an edict legitimizing the breaking of wind at table—either silently or noisily," according to the gossipy historian, Suetonius.

Doctors in the Middle Ages confirmed that retaining wind could damage your health, and this knowledge apparently brought some relief.

But it wasn't until the Renaissance that an influential manners book officially cracked the door to farting at table in an emergency.

"There are those who teach that a boy should retain wind by compressing the belly," observed Erasmus in his huge bestseller, *On Civility in Children* (1530). "Yet it is not pleasing, while striving to appear urbane, to contract an illness. If it is possible to withdraw, it should be done alone. But if not, in accordance with the ancient proverb, let a cough hide the sound."

The book was reprinted in dozens of editions, translations, and imitations, and was widely taught in schools. Debate on the topic ensued. One scholar considered the merits of *silent* farting, and quoted an epigram from ancient Greece. "Even though [Aethon] had to be careful not to fart explosively in the holy place, he nonetheless prayed to Zeus, *with clenched butt cheeks*. The sound of farting, especially when done on elevated [i.e., holy] ground, is horrible."

And one last bit of advice from Erasmus. "Do not move back and forth on your chair," wrote the humanist scholar. "Whoever does that gives the impression of constantly farting or trying to fart." 🐚

WHEN MEN WERE MEN AND WIVES WERE CHATTEL

Wives for Sale

In England for more than three centuries, it was legal for a man to sell his wife, much as he might sell a prize cow. The woman was often marched into the marketplace with a rope halter around her neck and auctioned to the highest bidder. The first

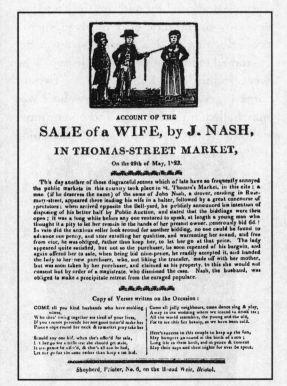

ACCOUNT OF THE
SALE of a WIFE, by J. NASH,
IN THOMAS-STREET MARKET,
On the 29th of May, 1823.

This day another of those disgraceful scenes which of late have so frequently annoyed the public markets in this country took place in St. Thomas's Market, in this city; a man (if he deserve the name) of the name of John Nash, a drover, residing in Rosemary-street, appeared three leading his wife in a halter, followed by a great concourse of spectators; when arrived opposite the Bell-yard, he publicly announced his intention of disposing of his better half by Public Auction, and stated that the biddings were then open; it was a long while before any one ventured to speak, at length a young man who thought it a pity to let her remain in the hands of her present owner, generously bid 6d.! In vain did the anxious seller look around for another bidding, no one could be found to advance one penny, and after extolling her qualities, and warranting her sound, and free from vice, he was obliged, rather than keep her, to let her go at that price. The lady appeared quite satisfied, but not so the purchaser, he soon repented of his bargain, and again offered her to sale, when being bid nine-pence, he readily accepted it, and handed the lady to her new purchaser, who, not liking the transfer, made off with her mother, but was soon taken by her purchaser, and claimed as his property, to this she would not consent but by order of a magistrate, who dismissed the case. Nash, the husband, was obliged to make a precipitate retreat from the enraged populace.

Copy of Verses written on the Occasion:

COME all you kind husbands who have scolding wives,
Who thro' living together are tired of your lives,
If you cannot persuade her nor good natur'd make her
Place a rope round her neck & to market pray take her

Should any one bid, when she's offer'd for sale,
Let her go for a trifle lest she should get stale,
If six-pence be offer'd, & that's all can be had,
Let her go for the same rather than keep a sot bad.

Come all jolly neighbours, come dance sing & play,
Away to the wedding where we intend to drink tea;
All the world assembles, the young and the old,
For to see this fair beauty, as we have been told.

Here's success to this couple to keep up the fun,
May bumpers go round at the birth of a son;
Long life to them both, and in peace & content
May their days and their nights for ever be spent.

Shepherd, Printer, No. 6, on the Broad Weir, Bristol.

A broadside, printed in Bristol, England, detailing the public sale of a wife in 1823. One man bid sixpence. The British pound was stronger then, but . . .

such sale was recorded in 1533 and scholars have unearthed at least 387 documented wife sales in England.

Wife Beating and the Rule of Thumb

Throughout most of Western history, husbands have had the legal and *moral* right to beat their wives to provide "moderate correction," according to *Untying the Knot: A Short History of Divorce* by Roderick Phillips.

The Catholic Church accepted this right of the husband as did most of the courts of Europe. The key question, though, is: What was considered "moderate correction"?

"The violence should not draw blood," stated Phillips, citing examples from many law codes, "and if a stick were used, it should be no thicker than a man's thumb."

That is actually the origin of the expression "rule of thumb." Many everyday proverbs from the Renaissance contain advice such as, "Don't expect anything good from an ass, a nut or a wife, unless you have a stick in your hand." Or, "Good or bad, the horse gets the spur; good or bad, the wife gets the stick."

The basic legal principle—expressed in canon and civil law—was that since a husband was responsible for his wife's actions, he also had the right to punish her to teach her.

The broad acceptance of wife-beating started to change with the Protestant Reformation, which frowned on the practice and made it a crime. In America, the Puritan colonies in New England outlawed wife-beating as early as 1641, but in merry olde England it wasn't until 1891 that a husband's right to "moderate correction" was officially abolished.

While wife-beating has grown in the last century to be regarded as one of the uglier and more cowardly acts in our society, it was tolerated and even endorsed for several thousand years.

FLOGGING KNOWLEDGE INTO YOUNG SCHOLARS

WINSTON CHURCHILL WAS FLOGGED

During the heyday of the British Empire, Great Britain led the world in many important categories, including the frequency with which its schoolmasters pounded upon the bloodied white bottoms of its privileged youth.

"Beating has always been common in British schools," pronounces Ian Gibson in his definitive *The English Vice*.

Gibson points out that the driving force behind corporal punishment in schools from spanking to flogging to caning was the enthusiasm of the Anglican schoolmas-ters who ran Britain's most prestigious schools, such as Eton and Harrow. In fact, there's a grand scripture-quoting tradition of birching delinquent scholars to revive their love of learning. "Foolishness is bound in the heart of a child, but the rod of correction shall drive it from him." (Proverbs 22:15)

No one was spared. Winston Churchill, who was flogged, recalled his days at St. George's. "How I hated this school! and what a life of anxiety I lived there for two years," wrote Churchill. "Flogging with the birch in accordance with the Eton fashion was a great feature in its curriculum. But I am sure no Eton boy, and certainly no Harrow boy of my day, ever received such a cruel flogging as this Headmaster was accustomed to inflict upon the little boys who were in his care and power . . . Two or three times a month the whole school was marshalled in the Library, and one or more delinquents were haled off to an adjoining

Young Winston Churchill, then Lord of the Admiralty, later complained that British naval tradition was "nothing but rum, sodomy and the *lash*."

A Renaissance scholar helps a young student to learn in this 16th-century woodcut.

apartment by the two head boys, and there flogged until they bled freely, while the rest sat quaking, listening to their screams. This form of correction was strongly reinforced by frequent religious services of a somewhat High Church character in the chapel."

While Churchill left the violence offstage in the wings (like some Greek tragedy), Virginia Woolf in her biography of artist/critic Roger Fry (1886–1934) quotes Fry describing the flogging in detail.

The ritual was very precise and solemn — every Monday morning the whole school assembled in Hall and every boy's report was read aloud.

After reading a bad report from a form master, [the headmaster] Mr. Sneyd-Kynnersley would stop and after a moment's awful silence say "Harrison minor you will come up to my study afterwards." And so afterwards the culprits were led up by the two top boys. In the middle of the room was a large box draped in black cloth and in austere tones the culprit was told to take down his trousers and kneel before the block over which I and another boy held him down. The swishing was given with the master's full strength and it took only two or three strokes for drops of blood to form everywhere and it continued for 15 or 20 strokes when the wretched boy's bottom was a mass of blood. Generally of course the boys endured it with fortitude but sometimes there were scenes of screaming, howling and struggling which made me almost sick with disgust. Nor did the horrors even stop there. There was a wild red-haired Irish boy, himself rather a cruel brute, who whether deliberately or as a result of pain or whether he had diarrhoea, let fly. The irate clergyman instead of stopping at once went on with increased fury until the whole ceiling and walls of his study were spattered with filth. I suppose he was afterwards somewhat ashamed of this for he did not call in the servants to clean up but spent hours doing it himself with the assistance of a boy who was his special favourite.

This punishment inflicted upon impressionable bottoms led to a booming sadomasochistic subculture in Victorian England, complete with flagellant brothels.

The poet Algernon Swinburne wrote a series of Whippingham Papers. Here's a taste from one of Swinburne's that appeared anonymously in *The Pearl*, Victorian erotica.

Here's the master returning,
A cigar 'tween his lips,
Hurrah! for the Master
Who smokes while he whips!
He knows how to tackle
Two pleasures at once—
The taste of the baccy,
The smart of the Dunce.

So he puffed like a demon!
And fiercely cut in,
Till you hardly could pick out
An inch of whole skin.
Then he took a new country,
And striped the white thighs,
Till the old hall re-echoed
A tempest of cries.

O! firm was his muscle!
And supple his wrist,
And he handled the Rod
With a terrible twist,
But muscles grow weary,
And arms lose their powers,
There's an end for all nice things,
For floggings—like flowers.

Shrieks Frank Fane, "I'm dying!"
Says Redgie, "You ain't,
And if you go off
In a bit of a faint,
We'll soon thrash you back
Into living again,
You've not done with swishing
Just yet, Master Fane!"

A pornographic industry sprung up around this "English Vice." A gentleman, perhaps remembering his school days, pays to be switched, nettled, and flogged.

Now the whipping is over,
And the culprit is free,
I don't think he'll sit down
This evening for tea!
And when in a fortnight
He's turned down once more,
I fancy he'll find
His bottom still sore.

Corporal punishment is still legal in privately funded schools in Great Britain and to varying degrees in twenty-seven states of the United States, while dozens of countries including Germany and France have outlawed the practice. ✸

CURSE WORDS BEFORE TODAY'S FOUR-LETTER DRUDGERY

THE BRITISH LOVE OF CURSING

Many people have an overly sanitized view of the past, as though people didn't curse as much in the old days, especially in England. Call it the Alastair Cooke effect, call it the Victorian whitewash.

Actually, throughout history, prior to Victoria, the English had a reputation in Europe for swearing.

Joan of Arc referred to the English as "Les Goddams." The peasant girl who heard voices and donned armor helped drive the English from France. She was captured by the Burgundians and sold to the English. "In prison, she was visited by the Earls of Warwick and Stafford, who held out the hope of ransom to her," recounts Ashley Montague in *The Anatomy of Swearing*. "Irritated by the specious language of the noble lords, Joan turned upon them sharply. 'I know you well,' she cried, 'you have neither the will nor the power to ransom me. You think when you have slain me, you will conquer France; but that you will never bring about. No! although there were one hundred thousand more Goddams in this land than there are now!' "

She was right, of course.

The English lost their French properties but kept their taste for swearing. Henry VIII (ruled 1491–1547), who often wrapped his lips around foul language, had a vast impact on curses, even ones that would wind up in America. At the time when Henry VIII had divorce problems and booted the Catholic Church out of England, some of the most popular British oaths were "By Saint Louis" or "By Saint George." With those Catholic saints banned, people over time started swearing "By George," instead.

Henry VIII's daughter, Queen Elizabeth I, continued the family tradition. In a rage, her preferred mutterings were reported to be "God's Death!" and "God's Teeth!"

Swearing, however, after her death, got a bit expensive. An act of Parliament in 1623 made it illegal to swear and offenders had to pay one shilling to a fund for the poor; those unable to pay sat in the stocks, while passersby politely asked them the time of day.

When Oliver Cromwell and his Puritans took over in the 1650s, they banned theater (a mere generation after Shakespeare) for its profanity. These Puritan types were the ones who filled New England.

But mere legislation is unlikely to root out something as biblical as profanity. One Captain Francis Grose around the time of the Revolutionary War compiled a *Dictionary of the Vulgar Tongue*, a fat volume demonstrating the continued creativity of British cursers. No doubt many of these slang words and phrases could be heard in the American colonies, maybe even by the Founding Fathers.

Sayings

• "He would lend his arse and shit through his ribs." Said of someone who's overly generous with his money.

• "That happened in the reign of queen Dick." i.e., never; said of any absurd story.

• "He will piss when he can't whistle." Hanged.

• "It is all honey or turd with them." Said of a rocky relationship.

Words and Short Phrases . . .

• BUTCHER'S DOG. To be like a butcher's dog, i.e., lie by the beef without touching it; a simile often applicable to married men.

• BUTTERED BUN. One lying with a woman that has just lain with another man is said to have a buttered bun.

• CLEYMES. Artificial sores, made by beggars to excite charity.

• CUNNY-THUMBED. To double one's fist, with the thumb inward, like a woman.

• CURTAIN LECTURE. A woman who scolds her husband when in bed is said to read him a curtain lecture.

• DUCK F-CK-R. The man who has the care of the poultry on board a ship of war.

• FART CATCHER. A valet or footman, from his walking behind his master or mistress.

• FIRE SHIP. A wench who has the venereal disease.

• TO FLASH THE HASH. To vomit.

• FLAYBOTTOMIST. A bum-brusher, or schoolmaster.

• LOBCOCK. A large relaxed penis; also, a dull inanimate fellow.

• MARRIAGE MUSIC. The squalling and crying of children.

• MARRIED. Persons chained or handcuffed together, in order to be conveyed to gaol.

• RABBIT CATCHER. A midwife.

• RANTALLION. One whose scrotum is so relaxed as to be longer than his penis, i.e., whose shot pouch is longer than the barrel of his piece.

• RIDING SAINT GEORGE. The woman uppermost in the amorous congress; that is, the dragon upon Saint George.

• SHORT-HEELED WENCH. A girl apt to fall on her back.

• SOT WEED. Tobacco.

The Blue Side of Linguistic Shift

King Louis IX of France (1214–1270), future Saint Louis, was pious; he decreed that those who took the Lord's name in vain, uttering oaths such as *"Sacré Dieu"* or *"Par Dieu,"* would have their tongues branded with a red-hot iron.

It is reported that the French courtiers — to

protect themselves—started to swear by the king's dog, Bleu, screaming *"Sacré Bleu"* and *"Par Bleu,"* curses which are still used today in modern France and in Pepe LePew cartoons.

This is a theory of linguistic shift; usually you can't point to a dog. (And many scholars don't.) Here's another. The word "ass" for the four-legged beast of burden was too close to the body part, "arse," so over time, people started using the word "donkey." And "cock," which was once quite common for that crowing male bird *and* the male member, over the years became replaced by "rooster."

Finally, leave it to British royalty to come up with one of the stranger shifts. In England, a princess is married to a prince; a duchess to a duke, but a countess is married to an *earl.* Geoffrey Hughes in *Swearing* (1991) points out that among English titles of nobility, the only mismatched male/female pair is Earl/Countess. "It is likely speculation," states Hughes, "that the Norman French title 'Count' was abandoned in England . . . [in favor of the Germanic Earl] precisely because of the uncomfortable phonetic proximity to 'cunt.' "

MARK TWAIN ON CURSING

His wife was always trying to reduce Twain's profane tonnage. Once, particularly exasperated, she tried to humiliate him by delivering a long string of curses. He commented, "The words are there, my dear, but the music is wanting."

PAINFULLY ODD ENTERTAINMENT

CASTRATI WERE THE SUPERSTARS OF THEIR DAY

Testicles were a major handicap for a male singer in the 1700s. In fact, it's argued by respected art historians that the first *internationally* known performing artists—who actually toured Europe and Russia and built border-crossing reputations—were the castrati, feted and paid huge sums to sing Italian opera. And most famous among them, was handsome Farinelli (1705–1782), who thrilled Paris, London, and Venice before settling as personal advisor to the king of Spain.

While soloists stole the limelight, perhaps the most acclaimed *group* singing in the world at that time was the Papal Choir of the Sistine Chapel, the private music box of the popes and cardinals, and that choir was filled with carefully chosen castrati.

The polite fallacy surrounding these clipped men with exquisite tonal range and lung power was that they had all suffered some kind of childhood accident requiring the removal of their testicles. Most castrati invented an elaborate fairy tale—perhaps involving a pig and afternoon nap—to explain their genital loss. The truth was that a black market flourished in Italy in 1700s and 1800s enticing poor parents to sell their male children into musical apprenticeship, knowing full well they would be castrated. Much like modern American doctors in the early 20th century performing back-alley abortions, so in the 1700s did Italian doctors perform clandestine illegal castrations.

With historical hindsight, the practice seems a bit barbaric, but then again there are no CDs of Farinelli or Pasqualini. "What singing!" commented 19th-century musical historian, Enrico Panzacchi, after hearing one of the last castrati perform in the Vatican chapel. "Imagine a voice . . . which leaps and leaps, lightly and spontaneously, like a lark that flies through the air and is intoxicated with its own flight; and when it seems that the voice has reached the loftiest peaks of altitude, it starts off again, leaping and leaping still with equal lightness and equal spontaneity, without the slightest sign of forcing or the faintest indication of artifice or effort."

Observed 18th-century French writer Charles De Brosses: "To enjoy the castrati one must first of all accept the unbelievable range of their voices. They are as clear and piercing as choirboys, yet infinitely more powerful. They are brilliant, loud and vibrant, an octave above the natural timbre of women, and tremendously vital."

How did the castrati come to be such musical superstars? Saint Paul expressly forbade women to sing in church *("mulier taceat in ecclesia")*, a prohibition that lasted through the 1700s in many places. So high voices were sung by boys, falsettists or castrati. The castrati were perceived to be the most talented, but they presented a theological quandary.

The Bible, in Deuteronomy, clearly states that a man "wounded in his stones" or "his privy member cut off, shall not enter the congregation of the Lord."

One story that several travelers repeated—perhaps hearing it from Sistine Chapel guides—was that the castrati had figured out a way to remain members in good standing of the congregation of the Lord *and* be allowed to sing in church. "It is accepted that a priest who is dedicated to his music may retain possession of his 'parts' in the following manner—after having them severed from his body, he will ever after carry them in his pocket."

In opera, castrati played the women's parts, and therefore they wore dresses. The finest parts in the early years of opera were written for castrati.

Leave it to memoirist Casanova to find one of the stranger stories involving a "castrata." He recounts that a very talented woman singer, frustrated by the ban forbidding females from performing on the premier stages of Italy, disguised herself as a castrato. To pass the required exam, she taped a sausage to her thigh and fooled the doddering priest.

Castrati, in effect, were the ultimate drag queens and members of *both* sexes often founded themselves attracted to them. Casanova wrote about attending a performance by a famed castrato, who also happened to be the lover of Cardinal Borghese.

In a well-made corset, [the castrato] had the waist of a nymph, and what was almost incredible, his breasts were in no way inferior, either in form or beauty, to any woman's; and it was above all by this means that the monster made such conquests . . . When he walked on stage during the 'ritornello' of the aria he was to sing, his step was majestic and at the same time voluptuous; and when he favoured the boxes with his glances, the tender and modest rolling of his black eyes brought a ravishment to the heart . . .

Rome, the holy city, which in this way forces every man to become a pederast, will not admit it, nor believe in the effects of an illusion which it does its best to arouse.

Castration was a serious crime in the eyes of the Church and the state . . . yes, these boys had had unfortunate accidents . . . yes, yes, very unfortunate accidents.

Pope Leo XIII banned castrati from singing in the papal choir in 1878. 🌀

Bullbaiting in the Time of Shakespeare

"Multitudinous seas incarnadine."

That plethora of polysyllables in the Bard's opus often intimidates American students and gives audiences the distinct impression that Elizabethans spent all their time spouting philosophy and studying grammar. Even the comedies sound that way.

What did a society that understood Shakespeare without a glossary do for an afternoon's entertainment? Go listen to a sermon? Go to an art gallery?

No, they watched a blind bear be whipped simultaneously by five strong-armed men. They watched an ape strapped to the back of a horse be nipped by dogs

trying to yank it to the ground. Those were the twists added to spice an afternoon's entertainment of bullbaiting or bearbaiting, both of which "sports" were immensely popular during Shakespeare's day.

We think of the Spanish and bulls, but actually the British enjoyed bullbaiting for more than five hundred years, according to *The Sports and Pastimes of the People of England* by Josef Strutt.

Bullbaiting was so popular that when Shakespeare was eighteen, the overcrowded stands collapsed at the Paris Garden in Southwark, killing and injuring several dozen spectators. Once Queen Elizabeth, to show off something distinctly English, treated the French ambassadors to a special performance with many dogs, bulls, bears, and horses. There were even laws in various boroughs of England forbidding butchers from selling bull beef if the animals had not been baited first.

So what exactly is bullbaiting? It is a far crueler sport than bullfighting, in which the matador runs some risk.

A fifteen-foot-long rope was tied to the base of the bull's horns and secured to an iron ring fixed to a stone or stake. The dogs then attacked the animal until they literally "worried" it to death. Any dogs that got wounded or too tired before the bull died were replaced. (We get our canine breeds bulldog and bull terrier from this so-called sport.)

Sometimes the day's jollities could be dangerous for the spectators as well. "One of the bulls tossed a dog full into a lady's lap as she sat in one of the boxes at a considerable height from the arena," noted diarist John Evelyn in August 1666.

Bearbaiting took place regularly *twice* a week near London on Wednesday and Sunday during the Bard's lifetime.

Bearbaiting followed a similar plan, with the bear tied via long rope to a post in the pit and then attacked by five mastiffs. Here's how an Englishman, who attended a show with Queen Elizabeth in 1575, describes the nuances of the activities: "It was a sport very pleasant to see the bear, with his pink eyes leering after his enemies, approach; the nimbleness and wait of the dog to take his advantage; and the force and experience of the bear again to avoid his assaults: if he were bitten in one place, how he would pinch in another to get free; that if he were taken once, then by what shift with biting, with clawing, with roaring, with tossing, and tumbling, he would work and wind himself from them; and when he was loose, to shake his ears twice or thrice with the blood and the slaver hanging about his physiognomy." Thirteen bears were attacked that afternoon.

Then to cap the day, according to another eyewitness, the ring masters often served up a treat: "the whipping of a blinded bear, which is performed by five or six men standing circularly with whips, which they exercise upon him without any mercy, as he cannot escape because of his chain; he defends himself with all his force and skill, throwing down all that come within his reach, and are not active enough to get out of it, and tearing the whips out of their hands and breaking them."

The sport of bullbaiting was banned in England in 1835. ❧

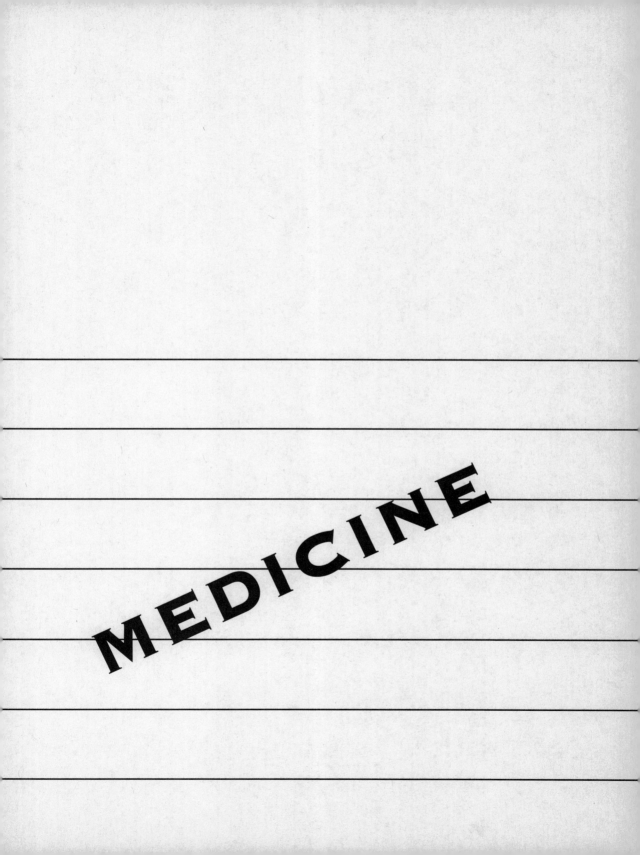

MEDICINE

MEDICAL HISTORY: A TRADITION OF INCOMPETENCE

Three medical professionals demonstrate the cure-alls of the 1600s: bloodletting, a strong laxative potion, and lastly, enemas. The kneeling man on the right is holding the syringe-style metal cylinder with plunger used for centuries to give enemas.

The day-to-day care provided by the vast majority of doctors right up through the Victorian era was as likely to have no effect, harm you, or even kill you as to cure you. Patients often healed in spite of treatments.

Dazzled by the brilliant breakthroughs of medical science in the 20th century, we forget just how abysmal medical treatments sometimes were in the past.

Astrology guided many reputable Renaissance doctors; enemas and blood-letting topped the list of treatments by American doctors at the time of the American Revolution; the completely ludicrous theory of the body's four humors (black bile, yellow bile, etc.) was the most accepted theory of health through the 1800s, when cell pathology was discovered. Many medieval doctors deemed "water-casting" (i.e., eyeballing and sometimes tasting a urine sample) as the leading guide to diagnosing illnesses.

Patients in the Middle Ages might gen-uinely have had a better chance of recovering if they prayed to (and truly believed in) the toenail of Saint Peter. A relic as placebo could easily surpass leeches on the hemorrhoidal vein in efficacy. The last century has marked a blizzard of breakthroughs (X ray, penicillin, open-heart surgery, etc.), but as recently as the Civil War, it's estimated that half of the Union's 350,000 casualties were due to complications and diseases from unsanitary treatment and half directly from the wounds. The famous poet, Lord Byron, died in 1824, from overbleeding. His doctors literally bled and purged him to death. President Garfield died in 1881, apparently because of complications from his doctors reaching unsterilized hands into his wound to try to remove an assassin's bullet.

How did medical science ever spiral downward from the relative high point of the Greeks into this pattern of often imbecile care?

A large dollop of blame must go to the medieval Church, which forbade doctors from performing surgery on live patients or from dissecting corpses to learn about anatomy. The human body was sacred; men of God shouldn't touch "shameful parts." At the time, almost all the major medical schools were located at Church-controlled universities, and thus doctors were actually clergymen.

In effect, doctors in the Middle Ages often knew as much about the insides of the body as they did about the insides of a Ford Taurus.

Or as medical historian W. J. Bishop states it a bit more elegantly: "This meant that the sciences of anatomy and physiology, which are the bedrock of all medical knowledge, could not be studied in a practical manner."

The consequence of this no-surgery-studied-at-school clause was that doctors training at universities in the Middle Ages did little more than listen to pompous theorizing about the four humors of the body. Complained iconoclast doctor John of Salisbury back in the 12th century: "[Doctors] will describe to you minutely the origin, the progress and the cure of all diseases. In a word, when I hear them harangue, I am charmed; I think them not inferior to Mercury or Aesclepius, and al-

most persuade myself that they can raise the dead. There is only one thing that makes me hesitate: their theories run directly opposite one another, as different as light to darkness."

The French playwright Molière, five centuries later, was sounding the same theme: "Doctors," states a character in *The Imaginary Invalid*, "know the majority of scholarly studies, know how to speak elegant Latin, know all the ancient Greek names for the diseases, can define them and categorize them. *But,* as for *curing* them, they know nothing at all. Listen to them speak, these best-dressed men in the world; watch them heal, these most ignorant of all men."

This is not to say there weren't medical breakthroughs prior to the 20th century. Of course there were: Hippocrates (460–377 B.C.) could set a broken leg (and write an oath forbidding doctors from seducing their patients); Fleming Andreas Vesalius (1514–1564) diagrammed correct anatomy, i.e., internal organs and veins; Frenchman Ambroise Paré (1510–1590) —using compassion and common sense—revolutionized surgical techniques and even designed a functional prosthetic arm; Englishman William Harvey (1578–1657) discovered that blood circulates, pumped by the heart.

But textbooks tend to focus on these breakthroughs by *exceptional* doctors and gloss over the pervasive failures. (Professional courtesy apparently extends even to history.) So in the interest of fair play, we will recount some of the lowlights of medical history and give "snapshots" of some genuinely odd developments.

A (Deadly) Sense of Humors

To put it bluntly, the underlying theory on which much of Western medicine was based for almost a thousand years was pure bunk. The vastly influential Salerno School of Medicine, a genuinely *medieval* academy flourishing around 1,000 A.D., borrowed from the Greeks the concept that just as the world contained four elements (fire, air, water, earth), so the body contained four corresponding humors: blood (fire), phlegm (earth), black bile (water), and yellow bile (air).

Healing a patient became the art of maintaining humoral balance. Someone coughing up phlegm, which is cold earth, would need to ingest an excess of "hot" foods, such as peppery foods or even animal blood to counterbalance the cold.

The experts at Salerno then made it a bit more complicated when they discovered that each person already had a single dominant humor which must be factored into any prescribed care. Therefore an excess of black bile would create a "melancholy" person, (i.e., gloomy and solitary) while a "sanguine" person had an excess of hot moist blood coursing through his or her veins. Obviously, a doctor would have to prescribe different treatments to restore humoral balance for each of those patients. "For several centuries, the professor of philosophy also held the chair of medicine," notes medical historian James Ricci. Basically, doctor after doctor spouted utter nonsense in analyzing arcane humors.

This theory of humors remained widely accepted until 1858, when Rudolph Virchow published *Cellular Pathology*, replacing semi-imaginary fluids with solid cells.

Medieval Medicine During the Crusades

In times of sickness, crusaders would often first pray to a saint's toenail or some other body part to get well. Relics were a prime cure-all, and each saint had his or her specialty: Saint Blaise for bones stuck in the throat; Saint Agatha to soothe sore breasts.

If that failed, they might turn to a local doctor. Listen to this eyewitness account by a 12th-century Arab doctor called in to consult with a European colleague. (Remember that Arabs, who had preserved much Greek and Roman scholarship, were far superior in medicine and science at the time.)

They took me [i.e., the Arab doctor] to see a knight who had an abscess on his leg, and a woman with consumption. I applied a poultice to the leg and the abscess opened and began to heal. I prescribed a cleansing and refreshing diet for the woman. Then there appeared a Frankish (European) doctor, who said: "This man has no idea how to cure these people!" He turned to the knight and said: "Which would you prefer, to live with one leg or to die with two?" When the knight replied that he would prefer to live with one leg, he sent for a strong man and a sharp axe. They arrived and I stood by to watch. The doctor supported the leg on a block of wood,

Medieval brain surgery to cure madness is demonstrated in this 14th-century illustration. Note the patient is standing.

and said to the man: "Strike a mighty blow and cut it cleanly!" And there, before my eyes the fellow struck the knight one blow, and then another for the first had not done the job. The marrow spurted out of the leg, and the patient died instantaneously. Then the doctor examined the woman and said: "She has a devil in her head who is in love with her. Cut her hair off!" This was done, and she went back to eating her usual Frankish food, garlic and mustard which made her illness worse. "The devil has got into her brain," pronounced the doctor. He took a razor and cut a cross on her head, and removed the brain so that the inside of her skull was laid bare. This he rubbed with salt; the woman died instantly. At this juncture, I asked whether they had any further need of me, and as they had none I came away, having learnt things about medical methods that I never knew before. (tr. E. J. Costello)

HEROIC MEDICINE

The "Western medicine" described above, as barbaric as it sounds, was not some slapdash approach concocted by one sadistic doctor. It was part of a "kill-or-cure Frankish system known in time as Heroic medicine," according to *Flowers in the Blood* by Dean Latimer and Jeff Goldberg.

"Their techniques were rooted in the notion that the way to exorcise one set of afflictions from a patient's body was to subject it to a considerably more violent set of afflictions. The heroics were entirely on the part of the patient: for even the mildest ailments, one could expect to be bled, leeched, cupped, blistered, amputated, sweated, trepanned, scourged, purged and flayed to a fare-thee-well . . . In most cases, it was useless, of course, and downright lethal in many, yet its tenets remained broadly accepted for nearly a millennium."

THE ROYAL MEDICINE CABINET, 1685, OR ATTEMPTS TO REVIVE KING CHARLES II

Charles II of England, the libertine who fathered at least thirteen illegitimate children, suffered a massive stroke while shaving in 1685. Here's the list of treatments (some Heroic), as compiled by the Royal Physician, Dr. Scarburgh:

The King was bled to the extent of one pint in his right arm; his shoulder was incised and cupped; an emetic and purgative administered, followed by an enema containing antimony, sacred bitters, rock salt, mallow leaves, violets, beet root, camomile flowers, fennel seed, linseed, cinnamon, cardamon seed, saffron, cochineal, and aloes. The King's head was shaved and blistered; a sneezing powder of hellebore root administered; a concoction of barley water, licorice and sweet almond poured down his throat, as well as white wine, absinthe, anise, and an extract of thistle leaves, mint, rue and angelica. A plaster of Burgundy pitch and pigeon dung was applied to his feet; followed by infusions of melon seeds, manna, slippery elm, black cherry water, dissolved pearls, gentian root, nutmeg, quinine, and cloves, and extracts of flowers of lime, lily-of-the-valley, peony, and lavender. When he went into convulsions, forty drops of extract of human skull were administered, followed by bezoar stone when he got worse. Then wrote Scarburgh: "Alas! after an ill-fated night his serene majesty's strength seemed exhausted to such a degree that the whole assembly of physicians lost all hope and became despondent: still, so as not to appear to fail in doing their duty in any detail, they brought into play the most active cordial." After this final ministration—consisting of pearl, julip and ammonia—was forced down his throat by his frustrated doctors, the King obligingly died.

THE FRENCH LOVE OF ENEMAS DURING THE RENAISSANCE

The way we nowadays pop aspirin for most anything that ails us, the French in the age of Rousseau, Voltaire, and Molière took enemas or had blood-lettings.

King Louis XIII, who ruled from 1610 to 1643, in one year received 212 enemas and forty-seven bleedings, according to the records of his chief physician, Charles Bouvard.

While the king no doubt purged more than most, the French en masse were dousing their insides and the job of administering enemas fell to *"apothécaires"* (pharmacists), who were cruelly dubbed *"limonadiers du postérieur"* (lemonade-makers of the ass).

When we think of enemas, most of us probably envision the modern rubber hose, some warm soapy water from the tap, complete privacy. But back in the 1600s, in the days before vulcanized rubber hoses, enemas were administered by *someone else* by means of a long-tipped, cylindrical tube of metal activated by a plunger, varying in size from dainty six-inchers resembling syringes to giant two-foot-long instruments of terror. The rich had theirs crafted of silver, and carried them on trips in velvet sacks with drawstrings.

The *"syringue,"* as it is known in French, "played a significant role . . . in the secret practices and intimate needs of our ancestors," according to Henri Havard, a respected 19th-century expert on French furniture and objects. "It reigned in the City; figured at the Court, even operated under the gaze of the Sun King and of Madame de Maintenon, without their sense of propriety being the least bit troubled, and it still continues to appear on the French stage, in the most dizzying farce that Molière has left us."

At one point in Molière's *Monsieur de Pourceaugnac*, a very funny comedy that's little-known in the U.S., an apothecary chases the hero around with a full *"syringue,"* whis-

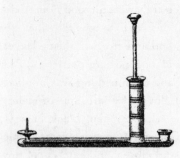

The French fascination with enemas continued through the 19th century. Found among the earliest examples of *photographic* erotica was this shot, c. 1850 by Auguste Belloc. Note the small plunger-type enema-syringe in one woman's hands and also note the larger do-it-yourself enema device lying on its side on the chair up front. The inset illustration should help explain how that device could be straddled and used, with a sort of downward "dynamite detonator" motion.

pering "gentle, gentle" and "it will do you no harm." Two giant assistants try to tackle the poor Monsieur who zealously covers his ass with his hat or in some productions by running around lugging an armchair. After he escapes, the exasperated hero, who's only pretending to be sick, makes this not-found-in-any-guidebook statement about Paris: "In this region, it rains women and enemas." The royal court—three centuries before the Jerry Lewis invasion—no doubt howled.

While Molière chose to *poke* fun, giving enemas was serious (and lucrative) business for pharmacists. A manual has survived.

The patient . . . should lean on his or her right side, bend one leg forward and expose all that is required, without shame or false modesty. For his part, the attendant . . . must not attack the area as though storming a walled city, but rather act like a wily sniper, who moves ahead, silently parting the bushes and treading down the over-growth, until he stops, locates the enemy, then he aims and fires.

Just so the [enema giver] must not "shoot" until he has found the center ring of the target. Then, reverentially placing one knee on the floor, he will guide his instru-ment in his left hand, without rushing or flailing, and with his right hand, he will push the plunger *"amoroso"* (lovingly), with control and without any jerks, *"pianissimo,"* very very slowly.

The downside of this flood of enemas was that somebody—in those days before flush toilets—had to clean up the mess. In a poem accompanying a satiric engraving, a serving-girl complains:

I've had quite enough of the stink that I
    smell;
I want to go out. Let the docs go to Hell;

They condemn Madame to the chair with
  the hole,
Forcing me yet again to clean out the bowl.

HIS DEATH WAS MORONIC, NOT BYRONIC

The name of the poet Lord Byron (1788–
1824) conjures up an image of defiance
and passion, of "titanic self-assertion"; he
was said to have died leading a troop of
Greek soldiers fighting for independence
from the boorish Ottoman Empire; he was
wounded, bloody, scornful to the end.
And it's all hokum.

"[Byron] was in Greece, yes," states
Tom Burnam's excellent *Dictionary of Misinformation,* "and he had hired some mercenaries to further the Greek cause. But
the sad even ugly truth is that following a
long walk and a horseback ride while already feverish, he was literally bled to
death by his doctors. And much against
his own better judgment. At one point, he
said, 'Drawing blood from a nervous patient is like loosening the chords of a musical instrument, the
tones of which are al-
ready defective for
want of sufficient ten-
sion.' No wonder he
referred to his doc-
tors as 'A d——d
bunch of butchers.'

"As he grew worse,
however, and steadily
weaker, he finally suc-
cumbed to the 'tearful
protestations' of one

Lord Byron, fancifully
pictured as a Greek
soldier.

of his physicians, a Dr. Bruno. Before it was
all over, the various doctors in attendance
were to remove *more than four pounds* of his
blood—and to cap it all by 'purging' him
with a devilish concoction made up of
senna, three ounces of Epsom salts and
three ounces of castor oil. The last blood
to be drawn was taken while Byron was
virtually unconscious and certainly pow-
erless; leeches were applied to his temples,
and left there all night. He was dead
within twenty-four hours." ❧

KILLING THE PRESIDENT

President James Garfield was shot at a
Washington train station on July 2, 1881,
by a dweeby, disgruntled government
worker, Charles Guiteau. Dr. D. W. Bliss
arrived quickly and tried using an unsterilized metal probe to find the bullet. The
instrument slid down more than three
inches, getting wedged between shattered
ribs and had to be pried out.

When that "Nelaton Probe" failed, the
doctor stuck his pinkie finger in the
wound to widen the hole and find the bullet. That area quickly turned black and
blue. No bullet was found.

Garfield was carried back to the White
House. Soon, leading doctors from
around the nation arrived to play a kind of
"Where's Waldo?" game to find the missing bullet. Many apparently poked and
probed. The great inventor, Alexander
Graham Bell, even helped, rigging up a
metal detector, using two electrical coils
and listening for increase in static to determine the location of the bullet.

Bell and several others clearly heard a hum at the site of the initial black and blue mark. Bell figured the bullet must be deeper. Doctors hesitated, but days later with the President's temperature rising, they reopened the wound and dug deeper. No bullet was found. President Garfield died on September 19, 1881.

An autopsy revealed the bullet cocooned in a protective cyst, and located about *ten* inches from the black-and-blue mark. Some medical historians are convinced—with 20/20 hindsight—that the President would have survived had the bullet been left there.

Instead, weakened by fever and prolonged bed rest, his body couldn't fight the infections caused by all the unsanitary probing.

Joseph Lister pioneered antiseptic operating techniques in the late 1860s in England; unfortunately, his principles weren't embraced by the doctors who treated the President of the United States.

(On a more positive note, Bell's device was later adapted into a land-mine detector.) ❧

ANATOMY: DOCTORS AND BODY-SNATCHERS

A good corpse is hard to find.

During the Middle Ages—when the Church banned dissection—only a few cities such as Florence, Italy, ignored the Vatican and ordered that the bodies of, say, three executed criminals a year be delivered for medical research. But this was a mere handful.

Then Pope Sixtus IV (in office 1471–1484) ended the ban on dissection. This

The corpse shortage led local governments to hand hanged men over to anatomy schools. Satirical artist William Hogarth called this *The Reward of Cruelty* (1751) and graphically showed what a convicted murderer could expect.

bull represented a major turning point in both art and medicine.

Doctors could actually study the insides of bodies, and plenty of Renaissance artists such as Leonardo peered over their shoulders or did dissections of their own. Michelangelo kept open an anatomy salon for twelve years in Florence and Rome. (Renaissance artists' accurate depiction of rippling muscles and bulging veins owes a great debt to Pope Sixtus IV.)

But that's when the trouble began. Where to find enough bodies? Organ donor cards were hardly in vogue, especially when a dismembered corpse would be denied entrance to heaven. While cities increasingly set aside a specific number of condemned criminals to be gently hanged and served up to anatomists, that hardly filled the need.

Christians intent on spending eternity in heaven were a bit leary of seeing doctors and artists up to their elbows in human guts. Were any of these corpses devout Christians plucked from their graves?

DOCTORS' RIOT OF 1788, NEW YORK

While Europeans balked loudly and staged various protests, perhaps the most violent riot against human dissection occurred in New York City in 1788.

The origins are a bit murky. One account states that rumors started circling the taverns that medical students were digging up female corpses and performing lewd exploratory surgery. In another telling, an arrogant medical student held a severed arm out the window and shouted to a youngster

that it was his mother's. The boy's mason dad (i.e., construction worker) rushed to the graveyard and discovered his wife's body missing; the man gathered the mob.

In any case, on April 13, 1788, a mob stormed the medical school at King's College (later Columbia University) and found several human bodies in various states of dissection. In the ensuing riot, at least five and perhaps as many as twenty died; medical students had to be locked in jail to save them. And the next year, a strict statute against grave robbing was passed in New York. ❧

AN UNLIKELY TALE OF RESURRECTION

In Edinburgh in the mid-1700s, medical students of renowned Dr. Alexander Munro were assigned to claim the body of a female murderer after her hanging. As the students watched a boisterous mob gather, they opted to cut the body down the instant it stopped twitching on the gallows. Angry friends and relatives tried to stop them, and during the ensuing melee, as the opposing sides literally tugged at the corpse, she came back to life. "Half-Hang'd Maggie Dickson," as she became known, lived for many years and died at the age of seventy-five. Well, it *could* be true. ❧

BURKE & HARE: THE NO-TELL MOTEL

It was as simple as supply and demand, although a tad messier in practice. As anatomy schools began to flourish in England and Scotland in the 1700s, the demand for corpses ballooned. English law, however, entitled almost all deceased to a Christian burial. So except for a few condemned criminals set aside a year, anatomy schools were hard-pressed to find bodies upon which to instruct their pupils. And as the introduction to the fifteenth edition of *Gray's Anatomy* curtly states: "To study medicine without anatomy [is] folly."

Enter the "Resurrectionists" or "Sack-'em-up Men" or "Body Snatchers" as they were popularly known, ghouls who roamed the graveyards digging up fresh corpses, selling the teeth to dentists and the cadavers to medical schools. In 1828, a fresh corpse might fetch £10 sterling, which is about what a field hand earned *in a year.*

William Burke and William Hare of Edinburgh decided to keep their fingernails clean of graveyard dirt. Hare ran a cheap flophouse at Tanner's Close and the pair conspired to smother some of their poor guests and sell their bodies to a respected anatomist, Dr. John Knox. As a later ditty explained: "Burke's the Butcher, Hare's the thief/Knox the man that buys the beef."

When two well-known local lowlifes, a hulk named Daft Jamie and a prostitute named Mary Patterson, showed up on an anatomy table, investigations began. Hare ratted on Burke, who after a Christmas trial was sentenced to die on January 28, 1829, with the stipulation that his dead body "should be delivered to Dr. Alexander Munro [Professor of Anatomy in the University of Edinburgh], to be by him publicly dissected and anatomized."

The following day the enormous anatomical theater was standing room only as 25,000 persons viewed the remains of the

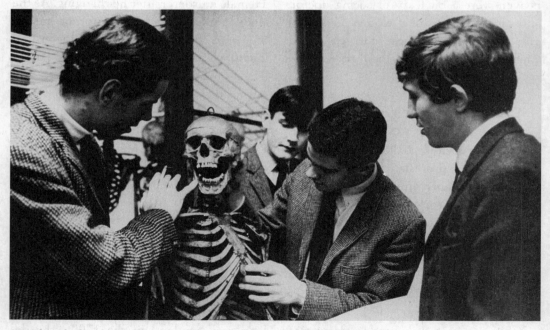

Scottish medical students examine the skeleton of body-snatcher William Burke.

murderer, according to *The Sack-'Em-Up Men* by Dr. James Ball, who adds, a bit shocked, that the witnesses included seven women. Burke's skeleton is still displayed from time to time in the University medical museum. ✺

THE BALLAD OF MARY'S GHOST

'Twas in the middle of the night,
To sleep young William tried,
When Mary's ghost came stealing in,
And stood at his bedside.

O William dear! O William dear!
My eternal rest ceases;
Alas! my everlasting peace
Is broken into pieces.

I thought the last of all my cares
Would end with my last minute;
But tho' I went to my long home,
I didn't stay long in it.

The body-snatchers, they have come,
And made a snatch at me;
It's very hard them kind of men
Won't let a body be!

You thought that I was buried deep,
Quite decent-like and chary
But from her grave in Mary-bone
They've come and boned your Mary.

That arm that used to take your arm
Is took to Dr. Vyse;
And both my legs are gone to walk
The Hospital at Guy's.

I vow'd that you should have my hand,
But fate gives us denial;
You'll find it there, at Dr. Bell's
In spirits and a vial.

As for my feet, the little feet
You used to call so pretty,
There's one, I know, in Bedford Row,
Th' other's in the city.

I can't tell where my head is gone,
But Doctor Carpue can;
As for my trunk, it's all pack'd up
To go by Pickford's van.

I wish you'd go to Mr. P.
And save me such a ride;
I don't half like the outside place,
They've took for my inside.

The cock it crows—I must be gone!
My William, we must part!
But I'll be yours in death, altho'
Sir Ashley has my heart.

Don't go weep upon my grave,
And think that there I be;
They haven't left an atom there
Of my anatomie.
—THOMAS HOOD

THE PRESIDENT'S SON AND FATHER IS MISSING

He was the only man to be the son of one President, the father of another, *and* be publicly dissected.

Soon after a fitting burial in 1878, John

Scott Harrison—a two-time Congressman and the son of President William Henry Harrison—was found on the dissecting table of an Ohio medical college. Some accounts state that his son, the future president Benjamin Harrison, actually discovered dad lying there when he went to visit a friend at college. In any case, the ensuing scandal inspired legislatures nationwide to pass strict anti–grave robbing laws. ✹

MISTREATING THE MENTALLY ILL

CRUEL TO BE KIND? OR CRUEL TO BE CRUEL? OR JUST PLAIN BAFFLED?

Over the centuries, mankind's treatment of insane persons often appears, well, insane.

In times of plague in ancient Greece, lunatics—forced to live on the outskirts of town—would be stoned to death as part of ritual purification for the city, called "pharmakos." (Hence our modern words pharmacy, pharmaceutical, etc.)

And one of the more popular amusements in England through the Victorian era was to go buy a ticket to wander the halls at the Royal Hospital of Bethlem in London (better known as "Bedlam") to view the lunatics firsthand and chat them up. " 'Tis a very undecent, inhumane thing," complained Thomas Tryon in 1695, "to make . . . a show of those unhappy [patients] (by exposing them, and naked too perhaps of either sex) to the idle curiosity of every vain boy, petulant wench or drunken companion."

While day-to-day care could be cruel (chains, whippings, etc.), attempts at curing the patients could be even crueler or fatal, everything from medieval chiseling of the skull to let the devil escape to the 1940s ice-pick lobotomies of Dr. Walter Freeman, president of the American Board of Psychiatry. Dr. Benjamin Rush, a pillar of early American medicine, recommended relentlessly swinging the patient to shake out the madness. Pope John XXI (in office 1276–1277), who wrote several medical treatises, recommended that "a roasted mouse eaten doth heal frantick persons."

Perhaps on no single group has experimentation been more widespread than on the destitute insane in state-run institutions. (What's surprising, though, is the stellar reputation of many of the doctors devising these Torquemada-like cures.)

In hindsight, the experiments appear cruel and useless, but at the time perhaps they were well-intentioned efforts to eradicate one of mankind's most perplexing maladies. Perhaps not. There's an old proverb: "A surgeon experiments on the heads of orphans."

DROWNING THE MADNESS

Jan Baptista van Helmont (1577–1644), a Flemish physician and chemist, earned widespread respect for identifying gases as distinct from air and analyzing the processes of digestion and nutrition. He also argued that water shock, to the brink of death, could extinguish a mad person's "too violent and exorbitant form of *fiery* life."

Dr. van Helmont discovered this cure by observing that "many Fools . . . who accidentally fall into water and are dragged out for dead and remain so for a long time . . . that when a dagger's sheath with the tip cut off is thrust in their fundament [i.e., anus], and someone blows through it till water gushes out of the drowned person's mouth, they are not only restored to life . . . but also to the full use of their understanding."

Concludes his biographer (his son Francis): "The Doctor did cure several distracted persons this way, there are many in Holland that can verify."

BLOOD-LETTING, ENEMAS, ETC.

Dr. Daniel Oxenbridge (1576–1642), a well-respected London physician, employed the latest techniques in 1628 when trying to cure Mrs. Miller, the twenty-four-year-old mad wife of a clothier.

First he gave her an enema, then he bled her using veins in the shoulder, both arms, both feet, her forehead, under her tongue and by applying "leeches to the hemmorhoide vein" at the anus. He had her drink fresh homemade cider, laced with herbal purgatives, causing "a general evacuation." He adds: After that, "once every three or four days, I either bled her or vomited her strongly or purged her . . .

she would vomit twelve times, and purge two or three times downward."

After his attempt to remove all the harmful fluids, he then "shaved off all the hair of her head" and soaked her pate in an herbal lotion of rosemary, sage, lavender; he anointed her head with mandrake oil, and to help her sleep soaked her feet in warm water and gave her opiates such as laudanum paracelsi or white poppy seed. He rubbed her with flowery oils and to her shaved head, he "applied the warm lungs of lambs, sheep, young whelps, pigeons alive."

TRANSFUSION OF SHEEP'S BLOOD

British and French doctors tried transfusing sheep's blood into humans, hoping that the life force of a docile creature might tame mad passions. In France, Dr. Jean Denis tried it on a wife-beater, with at first good results.

Over in England, on November 23, 1667, a daft impoverished clergyman's helper, named Arthur Coga, was paid twenty shillings to undergo the experiment, receiving up to twelve ounces of blood from the woolly four-footed beast. "Some think it may have a good effect upon him as a frantic man by cooling his blood," wrote famed diarist, Samuel Pepys. A large crowd of experts gathered at the Royal Society to observe.

Pepys was pleased to note that the following week, the man addressed the Royal Society in Latin. "He is a little cracked in his head, though he speaks very reasonably," added Pepys a bit cryptically.

Dr. Richard Lower, a "dextrous anatomist" who presided over the test, stated that he "decided to repeat the treatment several times in an effort to improve [the man's] mental condition." Coga, however, either refused or more likely disappeared. Opined Dr. Lower: "I have no doubt that this discovery . . . will be employed with great profit for the human race, if it is practiced with due consideration and care."

Over in France, in January of the following year, Dr. Denis performed his third sheep transfusion on the wife-beater, who'd had a relapse to his brutal ways. The man died and the doctor was accused of murder. Sheep transfusion fell out of vogue for a couple hundred years. ✺

EARLY ELECTROSHOCK

The ancient Greeks sometimes applied an electric eel to numb pain or cure persistent headache, according to Galen. In fact, the Greek word for "electric ray or eel" was "narka"; hence our whole word family of narcotics, i.e., drugs that stun or dull.

In the 18th century, Benjamin Franklin, who suffered two great electric shocks himself inflicting minor retrograde amnesia, suggested "trying the practice on mad people."

Dr. John Birch (1745–1815), a British doctor, did just that in 1787, trying to aid a popular but suicidal singer suffering from extreme melancholy and "depression of spirits."

"I began by passing shocks through the head, about six in number, and di-rected him to call the next day," wrote Birch. "The shocks were repeated daily and his accounts were daily more favourable." The singer attended some rehearsals in hopes of being able to sing on the summer theater circuit. "I electrified him after the first fortnight every other day." After a month, the patient told the doctor that he felt remarkably refreshed and stopped walking by rivers or picking up razors. "After this conversation, I dismissed him, and he fulfilled his summer engagement that summer with his usual applause." ✺

REMOVAL OF BODY PARTS

Dr. Henry Cotton (1886–1933), acting on his theory that a physical "focal" infection caused mental illness, surgically removed potentially "infected" body parts.

Dr. Cotton—riding the wave of his successful 1921 lecture series at Princeton University—claimed an 87 percent cure rate and was hailed by media and scientist alike as a pioneer on the verge of a major breakthrough.

"The insane are physically ill," he stated, arguing that if a doctor could locate and remove the infection, he could abruptly stop the lunacy. "It takes patience and ability," noted Cotton, "to stick to the work of elimination."

Dr. Cotton ordered 11,000 teeth removed from 1919–1921 from his patients at Trenton State Hospital in New Jersey. When the patient wasn't cured by the dental work, the doctor surgically removed parts of the stomach, bowels, or genitals. Four of five female mental patients needed their cervix "enucle-ated," i.e., scooped out whole.

"It was awful to work there," recalled one hospital employee. "There was a young girl [who] worked in the office right by the door where they had to roll the baskets past that carried the bodies and organs and stuff . . . one day she ran out screaming she couldn't take it any longer."

Almost all the patients walking the halls were toothless, since the state budget didn't include any dentures.

After mounting criticism, an investigation revealed a success rate closer to 20 percent, adding "the *least* treatment was found in the recovered cases and the most thorough treatment in the *unimproved* and *dead* groups." The mortality rate hit 43 percent among those treated. The doctor persevered, cutting and lecturing around the world, until his sudden death in 1933.

Cotton's obituary in the *American Journal of Psychiatry* lauded his work as "a most remarkable achievement of the pioneer spirit . . . an extraordinary record of achievement [by] one of the most stimulating figures of our generation."

The doctor's widow in 1951 helped fund an annual award at the Trenton hospital to be given to the finest mental health staffer; it's called the "Cotton Award for Kindness."

THE NOBEL PRIZE FOR APPLE-CORING THE BRAIN

The year 1935 marked a return to the medieval art of brain surgery, with some techniques similar to those used 800 years earlier to drive out the devil. Here is a de-

scription of the *modern* approach by Elliot Valentstein in his excellent *Great and Desperate Cures* (1986).

"After drilling two or more holes in a patient's skull, a surgeon inserted into a patient's brain any of various instruments—some resembling an apple corer, a butter spreader, or an ice pick—and often, without being able to see what he was cutting, destroyed parts of the brain."

In the mid-1930s, Dr. Antonio de Egas Moniz—a Portuguese neurologist suffering from gout of the hands—orchestrated a young colleague to perform the surgery on twenty patients (scooping out little pats of prefrontal brain matter), then with little follow-up interviews, Moniz rushed out articles in six countries claiming success.

Dr. Duchenne—studying the physical display of emotions—gave electrical jolts to a slightly retarded man in 1854. (Nadar)

The idea didn't gather much momentum until Dr. Walter Freeman and Dr. James Watts pioneered lobotomies in America, and were hailed nationwide as saviors by the likes of *Time, Life,* the *New York Times. Life* trumpeted: "The results were spectacular: about 30 percent of the lobotomized patients were able to return to everyday productive lives."

With the world now dazzled, pioneer Dr. Egas Moniz won the Nobel Prize in Medicine in 1949 for his "apple corer" technique for prefrontal lobotomies. This further stamp of approval ignited a rush to operate. The *New York Times* gushed in an editorial: "Surgeons now think no more of operations on the brain than they do of removing an appendix."

By 1951, more than 18,000 lobotomies were performed in the U.S. and tens of thousands more worldwide.

However, by this point, Dr. Freeman—a goateed, abrasive, energetic showman—had refined his technique. Instead of coming in from the side of the head with a tubelike instrument, he preferred to use an ice pick to enter above the eyelid through the eye socket and into the brain where he

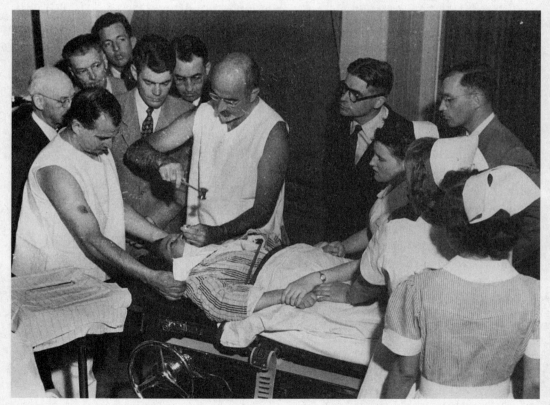

Dr. Walter Freeman performs a through-the-eye-socket lobotomy at Western State Hospital in Washington on July 11, 1949. Waggling the tool inside was supposed to cut *only* harmful nerve connections in the brain. It didn't.

RESEARCH: HUMANS AS LAB RATS

Congratulations! Nobel Prize winner, Dr. Egas Moniz, awarding the "Academy Chain" to Dr. Walter Freeman in 1950, during the heyday of lobotomies.

would make the lateral cut by "swinging" the tool side to side. Unlike our image of delicate "brain surgery," it took strength to penetrate the orbital bone and then to maneuver the tool. (The word "ice pick" used above is not figurative; the handle of Freeman's first tool was embossed with the words "Uline Ice Company.")

By the 1960s, brain surgery was once again considered a barbaric approach to curing mental illness, replaced primarily by drug therapy. A statue to Dr. Egas Moniz — Portugal's only Nobel winner — stands in Lisbon. Visitors to the Egas Moniz museum can buy Egas Moniz postage stamps. ❧

TUSKEGEE SYPHILIS EXPERIMENT

The letter in a clean white envelope embossed with a government letterhead arrived at the run-down shacks of hundreds of sick black men in rural Alabama. It invited them to be examined by government doctors, and closed: REMEMBER THIS IS YOUR LAST CHANCE FOR SPECIAL FREE TREATMENT. BE SURE TO MEET THE NURSE.

Those words helped lure several hundred dirt-poor, uneducated black men in the middle of the Depression to participate in what would become the longest nontherapeutic experiment on human beings in medical history, according to *Bad Blood* by James H. Jones.

The U.S. Public Health Service (forerunner of the Center for Disease Control), with the blessing of the various Surgeons General, from 1932 to 1972 studied the long-term effects of syphilis on 399 black men who were already infected. Government and local doctors periodically examined those men, routinely denied them any treatment for venereal disease, even when "miracle cure" penicillin became widely available in the 1950s. The families received a fifty-dollar burial allowance in exchange for allowing autopsies to be performed and the men, while alive, received minimal medical care for other ailments, such as receiving pink aspirin tablets and red iron tonics. At least twenty-eight of the men died from syphilis-related complications.

The Tuskegee Syphilis Experiment arguably marks the ugliest stain on the public health record of the United States.

It took an outraged federal employee, Peter Buxtun, leaking details to the Associated Press to finally blow the whistle, and the U.S. government later settled a class action suit, paying $10 million to the victims.

In hindsight, it seems clearly unconscionable that an American government could authorize such a racist and cruel experiment.

How could it happen here?

Contrary to most reports, the Tuskegee Syphilis Experiment was *not* top secret. Doctors wrote numerous articles on it in medical journals, and the medical community at large never protested until Dr. Irwin Schatz wrote a scathing letter in 1965. "I am utterly astounded by the fact that physicians allow patients with a potentially fatal disease to remain untreated when effective therapy is available." Dr. Anne Yobs of the U.S. Public Health Service stapled a note onto it and filed it away: "This is the first letter of this type we have received. I do not plan to answer this letter."

The original rationale was to track long-term effects of untreated syphilis on black men, just as an earlier Oslo study had tracked the long-term effects on white European men. The enormous difference between the two studies: the Oslo re-searchers checked on untreated men who arrived at various clinics; the American study involved *withholding* treatment so as to study the men.

The experiment was facilitated by the collaboration of the prestigious Tuskegee Institute, a pioneer of African-American higher education.

Finally, once the plug was pulled, on March 3, 1973, Caspar Weinberger, secretary of Health, Education and Welfare, authorized treatment for the survivors.

Jones states in his book that none of the white male doctors who founded and fought for the continuation of the experiment ever officially apologized. ✺

BIZARRE BREAK-THROUGHS

HIGH POINTS IN MEDICINE
While many of the preceding items would have to be classed as medical low points, the following are high points; just *very odd* and generally overlooked high points.

INDIAN NOSE JOB IN 450 A.D.
Ancient Hindu surgery equaled the Greeks in many areas, with the great Sus-

ruta in the 5th century A.D. writing detailed descriptions of how to remove tumors off the neck and stones from the bladder, among other procedures. Their biggest innovation—surpassing even the Greeks—lay in reconstructive or "plastic surgery," according to *The Early History of Surgery* by W. J. Bishop.

Adulterers in ancient India had their noses cut off. Susruta—great physician—has left behind his surgical procedure for rhinoplasty.

First the leaf of a creeper, long and broad enough to fully cover the whole of the severed or clipped off part, should be gathered, and a patch of loving flesh, equal in dimensions to the preceding leaf, should be sliced off (from down upward) from the cheek and after scarifying it with a knife, swiftly adhered to the severed nose. Then the cool-headed physician should steadily tie it up with a bandage decent enough to look at and perfectly suited to the end for which it has been employed. The physician should make sure that the adhesion of the severed parts has been fully effected and then insert two small pipes into the nostrils to facilitate respiration, and to prevent the adhesioned flesh from hanging down after that, the adhesioned part should be dusted with the powders of Pattanga, Yashtimadhukam, and Rasanjana pulverized together; and the nose should be enveloped in Karpasa cotton and several times sprinkled over with the refined oil or pure sesamum . . . Adhesion should be deemed complete after the incidental ulcer had been perfectly healed up, while the nose should again be scarified and

bandaged in the case of a semi or partial adhesion. The adhesioned nose should be tried to be elongated where it should fall short of its natural and previous length, or it should be surgically restored to its natural size in the case of the abnormal growth of its newly formed flesh.

Debate ensued whether plastic surgery was undermining the punishment for adultery. ❧

AN ASSHOLE HELPS THE STATUS OF SURGEONS, 1685

Since doctors weren't allowed by the medieval Church to perform surgery, someone had to, and barbers, with their portmanteau of sharpened instruments, inherited the business. These barber-surgeons cut hair, pulled teeth, removed warts, arrows, and gall stones, almost all without using anesthesia or antiseptic. "The miracle is that any patients survived these horrors," comments medical historian W. J. Bishop. But during and after the Renaissance, a new class of more educated surgeons started to emerge, and these fellows wanted to separate themselves from their haircutting brethren. But achieving higher status was tough. University-trained doctors—quick to bleed, purge, and theorize—received the big fees while surgeons were the lowly practitioners, manual craftsmen often forced to follow doctor's instructions. But an asshole helped change their lot. King Louis XIV's asshole.

King Louis XIV, the so-called *"Le Roi*

Soleil" (i.e., "Sun King"), felt pain while shitting, and considering the extraordinary number of purges he took (more than 2,000 dutifully recorded during his fifty-nine years on the throne), this was a major problem.

His anus was probed and a small lump detected, which none of the court doctors or apothecaries could dispel with their lotions and ointments. A surgeon was called in, one Charles François Félix, who diagnosed an anal fistula and agreed to remove it . . . in six months.

Félix's clandestine practice sessions on the anuses of the poor allegedly led to several fatalities and midnight burials.

However, on November 18, 1686, Félix operated on Louis at Versailles, while the king's new wife, Madame de Maintenon, looked on; the operation was deemed a success. Louis was so pleased with his repaired asshole that he showered Félix with money and titles. The year of 1686 — in this Louis-centric universe — was dubbed *"L'année de la fistule"* ("The Year of the Fistula").

Several eyewitnesses reported that brown-nosing courtiers requested that Félix perform the same operation on them. Some of those deprived of fistula woes nonetheless strolled the halls of power, with their derrieres swathed in bandages.

On a more impactful note, the powerful king's trusting and rewarding of a lowly surgeon greatly raised the stature of surgery in France. Over the next century French surgeons exported worldwide many of their breakthroughs in surgical techniques. ❧

THE BARBER'S POLE

In the 1700s, surgeons all over Europe wanted to distance themselves from their lowly brethren, the barbers. In England, for instance, the Barber-Surgeon's Company (i.e., Guild) split up in 1745. But what to do with the guild symbol, a red-and-white-striped pole, meant to represent bloody rags hung out to dry, topped by a brass basin which would catch the blood during bloodletting. (Patients used to grasp the pole to make their veins swell for easier puncturing.) As Charles Panati put it in his *Extraordinary Origins of Everyday Things*, "When surgeons and barbers split, the barbers got the pole." ❧

CREDIT FOR INOCULATION: COTTON MATHER'S SLAVE?

At the time of the American Revolution, as many as half the inhabitants of the colonies and of Europe had faces scarred from bouts with smallpox. And those were the survivors.

So, it was a medical breakthrough of giant purport when in 1796 Dr. Edward Jenner perfected a technique of inoculating a person with a dose of less virulent cowpox, which would make them immune to smallpox.

Jenner deserves huge kudos, but what's often overlooked is that he didn't invent immunology, he fine-tuned an existing practice. Doctors in China and Turkey had already learned to give patients mild forms of smallpox so that they wouldn't later contract it.

In the colonies, the slave of Cotton Mather explained to the minister how African natives took a sharpened stick or bone and pricked the smallpox pustule and then "inoculated" others to prevent them from getting the disease later. A Brooklyn doctor later tried it, and both Washington and Franklin had their households inoculated, all before Jenner "discovered" smallpox vaccine.

Jenner's breakthrough was to use a pustule from the less virulent cowpox (vaccinia), and not from smallpox, and avoid the risk that the latter might flower into the full-blown disease and kill off the patient.

The prestigious Royal Society in England rejected Jenner's manuscript on his pox vaccine, although years earlier it had published his research on the cuckoo bird.

THE STOMACH FOR RESEARCH

In one of the odder forays in medical research, a U.S. Army surgeon kept a human guinea pig on retainer for several years, dangling bits of food into his stomach through a small hole.

The year was 1822 and Michigan had not yet joined the United States. A shotgun blast rang out at the trading post on Mackinac Island.

The fort surgeon rushed to aid a young French Canadian fur trader, who lay bleeding, his lung poking out through cracked ribs while his break-

fast literally dripped onto the floor through a hole in his stomach. Dr. William Beaumont (1785–1853) gave seventeen-year-old Alexis St. Martin little chance of survival (the blast coming from so close that it caught his shirt on fire), but the doctor dutifully pushed the lung back in and cleaned and bandaged the wound.

St. Martin lived—although for the next seventeen days, "all that entered by his [mouth] passed out through the wound, and the only means of sustaining him was by means of nutritious injections per anus," according to Beaumont.

After a year of intensive care by Beaumont, the young man had healed up except for one irregularity: He had a hole in his stomach. The wound had never entirely closed. St. Martin simply covered the breech over at mealtime and apparently digested normally.

Army Surgeon William Beaumont in 1822 dangles food via a thread inside the stomach of trapper Alexis St. Martin. Beaumont's unique research revolutionized the understanding of digestion. (Painted a century-plus later by Dean Cornwell.)

Curiosity overwhelmed Beaumont.

The doctor put the frontier youth on retainer to take advantage of this unique opportunity to study the inner workings of the human stomach, experimenting in this "living laboratory."

He tied various foods such as cooked and raw parsnips and various meats onto silken threads and, like an ice fisherman, dangled them into the stomach, minutely recording all digestive information.

His research, which took seven years due to St. Martin skipping off to Canada several times, led to Beaumont self-publishing what is now acknowledged as the classic early study of the physiology of gastric digestion.

At the time, knowledge of the stomach—despite dozens of learned tomes on the topic—could be summed up by one famed surgeon's remark: "Some physiologists will have it, that the stomach is a mill, others, that it is a fermenting vat, others, again that it is a stew pan; but in my view of the matter, it is neither a mill, a fermenting vat nor a stew pan; but a stomach, gentlemen, a stomach."

Beaumont's discoveries landed this frontier surgeon who never went to medical school into the pantheon of great medical researchers.

And what about St. Martin? He married, had children, farmed in Canada, refused dozens of offers to return to Beaumont after 1834. Despite a drinking problem, he lived to be seventy-five.

Can you imagine someone today writing a grant proposal for *that* experiment?

PEERING OVER THE SHOULDER OF EARLY GYNECOLOGISTS

Pagan doctors around the time of Christ used a "speculum" like the one featured at right to peer deep into the vagina, while for most Christian doctors for the next 1,500 years, the vagina remained a closed and mysterious place.

The three-pronged speculum shown at right—resembling a giant corkscrew—was found at Pompeii and dates back to the 1st century B.C. Closed, the instrument's tip measured about a thumb's width, but by turning the crank, the tapered prongs were spread apart and opened the vagina to view.

Male Gréek and Roman doctors were quite unembarrassed about examining women and have left behind descriptions of female genitals. Hippocrates himself, circa 400 B.C., clearly identifies the clitoris as north of the vagina (however, he did apparently think the womb—in Greek *hystera*—could wander inside the female body, causing madness or illness, hence our modern "hysteria," "hysterical female," etc.)

Soranus, a brilliant first-century A.D. doctor operating in Rome, describes menstruation as a cleansing process in the reproductive cycle. "No aspect of this phenomenon runs contrary to Nature," he added, supportively.

On the flip side, male Christian doctors through the Renaissance and as late as the Victorian era, sometimes performed examinations in the dark. Engravings have survived of doctors checking the genitals of female patients by reaching through a slit in closed bed curtains, or by extending their hands up under a long skirt. This prudery was fostered by long-standing attitudes of the Catholic Church regarding female genitals as "pudenda" ("shameful parts"), and the religious views—backed by the likes of Saint Jerome and Thomas Aquinas—that menstruating women were "unclean," unfit for attending Church. (As late as 1878, the *British Medical Journal* carried a half-year long debate on whether a woman in the midst of her monthly flow would spoil a ham by touching it.)

So, female "plumbing" problems and obstetrics in Europe, especially in England, fell mainly to untrained midwives, that is, until Dr. Smellie came along. (Yes, that was his name.) This courageous Scottish doctor, William Smellie (1697–1763) arrived in London in 1739, shocked the community by convincing poor women to let him deliver their babies, and then proceeded to give obstetrics seminars to midwives using leather mannequins to demonstrate various positions of the fetus. One disgusted observer questioned whether Dr. Smellie's male students actually touched the birthing mothers. "These women are treated with less decency than a farmer would his cow," harrumphed the outraged doctor.

British scholars say Smellie single-handedly paved the way for male doctors to become more involved in obstetrics and thereby eventually bring the latest medical breakthroughs to treatment of women's genitals. (This is not to poor-mouth generations of midwives, who blended common sense, traditional methods, *and* superstition to perform deliveries.)

Despite Smellie's breakthrough in obstetrics, research and surgery on women's genitals and reproductive organs lagged far behind the same work on men's midsections. In fact, the vagina had become such *terra incognita* to Western doctors that when an American, Dr. Marion Sims, invented a homemade speculum in 1845 by inserting a bent spoon handle into a woman on all fours, he commented: "I saw everything no man had seen before . . . I felt like an explorer in medicine who first views a new and important territory."

Although Dr. Sims went on to pioneer gynecological surgery, the American medical establishment was soon to stumble into a major pitfall. Around the time of the Civil War a Dr. Hodge campaigned that doctors should look to the position of a woman's womb to find out the state of a female's mind. (Dr. Hodge was reviving Hippocrates's notion about the womb and "hysterical" women.) American doctors convinced droves of females that in order to make their wombs hang in a correct, healthy position, they needed to insert and wear a specially designed rod or pessary. "The young practitioner was inclined [in the 1860s] to make a toy shop out of every woman's vagina," stated a Dr. Kennard in the *St. Louis Medical and Surgical Journal* in 1879. "Our instrument stores are full of pessaries; and it is very entertaining to see the ingenuity displayed by some of our brethren of a mechanical turn of mind in varying their size and shape." Yes, *very* entertaining.

Added Dr. Kennard: "We might well suppose that no two vaginas were constructed upon the same plan if we did not know to the contrary."

This enthusiasm for fitting pessaries was finally doused when several women died from complications from puncture wounds.

The second half of the 19th century marked *man's* discovery of the exact geography of the vagina and female reproductive organs. ✺

MALPRACTICE MISCELLANY

BEFORE AMBULANCE CHASERS

An early king of Babylon (c. 1925 B.C.) left behind his famous Code of Hammurabi. "Concerning the wounds resulting from operations it is written . . . If a physician shall make a severe wound with an operating knife and kill him or shall open an abscess with an operating knife and destroy the eye, his hands shall be cut off.

"If a physician shall make a severe wound with a bronze operating knife on the slave of a free man and kill him, he shall replace the slave with another slave."

PAPAL EYEWASH

Pope John XXI (died 1277), a doctor from a family of doctors, wrote several respected medical treatises before he became pope. In *Liber de Oculo*, he recommends using baby's urine as an eyewash. Elsewhere he recommended a poultice of "goat's dung dissolved in wine" to reduce swollen testicles. For excess lust, he prescribes "hemlock bound to a man's stones" or anointing the member with camphor oil. ❧

A RUSH TO JUDGMENT?

Two centuries after his heyday, Dr. Benjamin Rush (1745–1813) stares out clear-eyed from the seal of the American Psychiatric Association; numerous statues have been erected in his honor and the prestigious Rush Institutes of Chicago still bear the good doctor's name. Without question, Dr. Benjamin Rush, an energetic reformer dominating colonial Philadelphia, was the most influential doctor at the founding of the United States and became the first American to achieve an international reputation. Rush even signed the Declaration of Independence.

And yet, it appears—based on his own voluminous writings—that Dr. Benjamin Rush was a *terrible* doctor. "In the whole vast compass of medical literature, there cannot be found an equal number of pages containing a greater amount and variety of utter nonsense and unqualified absurdity," wrote Dr. Elisha Bartlett in the 1840s, after reviewing Rush's writings and theories.

Dr. Rush prescribed massive bloodletting for almost all illnesses, sometimes siphoning off up to forty or fifty ounces from a single patient at one sitting. If that approach failed, he often called for drugs to induce purges and vomiting; blistering was another favorite treatment. During the yellow fever epidemic of 1793, one observer, disturbed by the quarts of blood that Rush drew from already weakened

Dr. Benjamin Rush, a signer of the Declaration of Independence and a furious bloodletter.

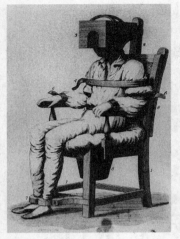

The Rush "Tranquilizer" chair of 1811 was considered the most complete restraint of a patient ever devised (short of death). The head box was packed with padded linen; the body straps were strong leather; the ankle clamps were wooden. Finally, note the stool bucket below "which can be emptied and replaced without removing or disturbing the patient."

patients, accused the doctor of killing more patients than the disease itself. Dr. Rush, a meticulous observer, noted the swarms of mosquitoes pestering Philadelphians that fall, but opted to pin the yellow fever plague on coffee dumped and rotting in the harbor.

Dr. Rush is sometimes called the "father of American psychiatry" and is held in special honor by mental health specialists because, it's said, he pioneered a more humane treatment of the mentally ill. Rush advocated listening to patients and taking notes and he also recommended not beating patients or locking them in squalid cells. These were genuine breakthroughs for that time period.

However, what's conveniently overlooked in tributes to Dr. Rush is that he also drained buckets of blood from those unfortunates and that he put some of his best hope for a cure for mental illness in "swinging." Dr. Rush argued that mental patients should be strapped into "gyration devices," i.e., chairs suspended from the ceiling by chains, and that attendants should swing and spin them for hours. He believed that the spinning would reduce the force of the blood flowing into the brain, and relax muscles and lower the pulse. He also noted other positive side effects from spinning lunatics, contending that vomiting would also create a more healthy circulation.

Today, the prestigious Rush Institute for Mental Well-Being is pioneering new approaches to treat behavioral problems, as is Rush Neuro-Science Institute.

SPERM WAIL

Professor Eugene Steinach of Vienna in the 1920s performed vasectomies on older men as a kind of fountain-of-youth procedure to revitalize them. The logic was that ejaculation of sperm reduced male energy; therefore, preventing sperm loss should increase male energy. (Ancient Chinese doctors recommended lovemaking without ejaculation on the same grounds.)

More than one hundred teachers and university professors underwent vasectomies to revitalize themselves, including Sigmund Freud, and poet William Butler Yeats. The procedure turned out to have no proven value—except to prevent pregnancy.

POPEYE: "STRONG TO DA FINICH"

Good news for Bluto. Spinach doesn't work as an especially potent energy booster. T. J. Hamblin discovered that researchers back in the 1930s had misplaced a decimal point regarding iron content of that smelly leafy vegetable. Their error boosted the value tenfold and it turns out there's more iron in eggs, beef, pork, liver, shellfish, and brown sugar. ✺

DENTISTRY BEFORE NOVOCAINE

THE PURSUIT OF WHITE TEETH: URINE TOOTHPASTE

Throughout the ages, poets have been waxing poetic about the beauties of white teeth. In the Old Testament's Song of Solomon, the beloved's teeth are compared to a flock of sheep, fresh-washed, evenly shorn, all twins.

But how do you get white healthy teeth? It's a pursuit that dates back to the Pharaohs and beyond. Egyptians used to rub their teeth with a chew stick coated with a paste made from granulated pumice stone and wine vinegar. In Europe in the Middle Ages and Renaissance, barber-surgeons filed the surface of the teeth and slathered on aqua fortis, a corrosive nitric acid. A dazzling smile would be followed in middle age by massive tooth decay because the filing and acid took all the protective enamel off the teeth.

Another early popular approach was human urine. In ancient Rome, women gargled and brushed with urine to help keep their teeth sparkling, and most prized was Portuguese urine, reputed to be the strongest. (Actually, the long delivery time might make that claim true.)

Besides making teeth whiter, urine could also be used to fight cavities.

The use of urine in dental hygiene, while not *well* documented, apparently remained in vogue at least through the 1700s. Pierre Fauchard (1678–1761), considered by many to be the father of modern dentistry, wrote an astounding 900-plus page two-volume compendium on all aspects of dentistry, including orthodontics, implantation, cavities, gum disease, extraction. This is a groundbreaking work by a genuine pioneer in a medical field that has significantly reduced human misery. "The keen observant mind of Fauchard," writes Arthur Lufkin in *History of Dentistry,* "collected all that was good in dentistry, catalogued this material accurately and added to it much of original merit."

Here is what Fauchard had to say on urine:

I have brought a great deal of relief to a number of persons who had nearly all their teeth in decay and who as a consequence were often tormented by pains and aches and mouth troubles, by means of the following remedy. It consists in rinsing the mouth out every morning and also every evening before going to bed with some spoonfuls of their own urine just after it has been passed, provided, of course, that one is not ailing in any way other than the teeth.

The urine should be retained in the mouth for some time and the remedy must be used for a number of days. This remedy is of great service but it is true that it is not very agreeable, except inasmuch as it brings distinct relief. Some of those for whom I prescribed this remedy and who have made use of it have assured me that after its employment they were freed from other troubles of various kinds throughout the body to which they had been subject. Most people have some little trouble at the beginning to accustom themselves to it, but what will one not do for relief and for health?

Actually, as for the urine, scientists say that urine would help clean teeth. The natural ammonia molecules present in pee do have cleansing properties. Fauchard was right. ☙

TASTES LIKE SHIT

The *Dictionnaire Universelle des drogues (Universal Dictionary of Drugs)*, written during the Renaissance by Nicolas Lemery, states: "Human excrement is a digestive aid, that helps dissolve, soften and ease; it must be used in dried pulverized form and should be swallowed. A single dose should not exceed one dram (i.e., 3.9 grams). ☙

THE PATRON SAINT OF TOOTHACHES

The Middle Ages, while not known for many breakthroughs, did succeed in producing some of the most disgusting mouths

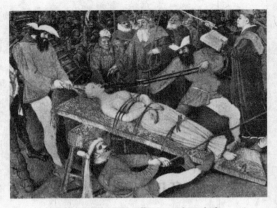

The martyrdom of Saint Apollonia with melodramatic pliers. Miniature by Jean Fouquet (1416–1480).

in the history of the human race. Teeth were at an all-time low: rotting, blackened, cracked, painful.

Sometimes, itinerant teeth pullers in Europe wandered from town to town with a little medicine show, climaxed by the locals watching their brethren writhe in agony while teeth were yanked by long metal pliers. Barbers—along with surgery and hair cutting—did tooth pulling. Remember, there was no local anesthetic.

It's no wonder the Church did a thriving business in devotional offerings to Saint Apollonia, the patron saint of tooth pain.

According to legend, Apollonia—the daughter of a pagan magistrate in Alexandria, Egypt—decided to convert to Christianity. The young woman was tortured to renounce Christ and return to the Roman gods, but she refused. The authorities started pulling her teeth out one by one. Still, she refused. She died a martyr's death at the stake. In 300 A.D., she was canonized. ☙

Replacing Missing Teeth: Human Teeth for Sale

Before the widespread use of porcelain dentures, dentists used human teeth to replace missing ones. The two primary sources: the mouths of the poor and the mouths of the dead.

Much like the blood donors of today, a poor person back in the 1600s and 1700s, pinched for some ready cash, could sell his or her teeth. Emma Hamilton (nee Hart), the mistress of Admiral Nelson and one of the beauties of her generation, was said to have been on the way to the dentist to sell her mouthful of perfect teeth when an old fellow servant steered her toward the sex trade.

A full set of matching fine young teeth was most desirable. Grave robbers when

A 19th-century dentist demonstrates steel forceps to pull a tooth. Was the tooth rotten or was the man trying to raise cash by selling his teeth?

not selling corpses to anatomy schools were selling teeth to dentists. "Every dentist in London [in the early 1800s] would purchase teeth from these men," wrote Bransby Cooper in his memoir.

And a battlefield could turn into a gold mine for a man with a pair of pliers. "Oh, sir, only let there be a battle, and there will be no want of teeth," Cooper quotes one supplier as telling him. "I'll draw them as fast as the men are knocked down."

George Washington's dentist, John Greenwood, returned from a trip to Europe in 1805 with a keg of human teeth.

A whole generation wore "Waterloo" dentures made from teeth yanked from the corpses on the battlefield and the practice continued as late as the Civil War, when thousands of teeth were stolen from bodies moldering at places like Bull Run and Gettysburg. Many teeth of fine young American soldiers were secretly shipped to Europe to correct the crooked smiles of European aristocrats.

In addition, rich people sometimes bought poor people's teeth and had them immediately transplanted into their own gums. Ambroise Paré (1517–1590), sometimes called the father of modern surgery, "heard it reported by a credible person that he saw a lady of the prime nobility who had her rotten tooth pulled, then at the same time had a sound tooth drawn from one of her waiting maids, to be substituted and inserted, which tooth over time took root and grew so strong that she could chew upon it as well as any of the rest."

In the 1700s in the United States as

well as in Europe, the prospect of this simple, relatively quick fix fascinated dentists and patients. A British dentist who came to Williamsburg, Virginia, promised in an ad in 1771 that he could transplant teeth "that will be as firm in the jaw as [those which] originally grew there."

The practice flourished, especially among Parisian dentists catering to aristocrats at the time of the French Revolution, and no doubt roiled the underclass.

Transplantation was actually quite problematic, and the tooth almost never took root. Several dentists noted instances when wealthy patients received several teeth . . . and a dose of syphilis.

"I do not like this method of drawing teeth out of some folks' heads to put them into others," wrote a British dentist back in 1685, "it is only robbing Peter to pay Paul." ☙

Rotten Teeth of History

Kings and queens throughout history, with their pumpkin smiles, would have trouble getting jobs at today's McDonald's.

While we might expect peasants through the 1800s to have had rotten teeth (think "Monty Python and the Holy Grail"), we forget that nobles and even royalty had similar stinking mouths, with missing front teeth, blackened decayed stumps and rotting gums.

Take Queen Elizabeth I (1533–1603) and King Louis XIV of France (1638–1715). (You wouldn't want a whiff of their breath in the morning.)

For the last thirty years of his life, King Louis XIV—the so-called Sun King, maestro of the most magnificent court in Europe—was missing all his upper teeth and his condition was often too painful for him to wear any kind of denture. In 1685, the year he brutally deprived French Huguenots of religious freedom, Louis's dental agony had reached such a climax that he ruptured a hole into his maxillary sinus on the left side. His dentist Dubois cauterized it *fourteen* times with a heated metal instrument.

As for Queen Elizabeth, her teeth and gums started deserting her in middle age. At age forty-five around Christmas of 1578, an excruciating toothache had kept her awake for several nights in a row. But the queen, who could stand up to the Spanish and torture conspirators in the Tower, was terrified of having the tooth pulled. One of her aged advisors, the Bishop of London, volunteered to have one of his remaining teeth pulled in her presence to show her "the pain was not so much and not at all to be dreaded." He did, she did, and the queen lived to torture a few more people in the Tower.

From then on, though, Elizabeth frequently suffered severe dental problems. We have an eyewitness account from a French ambassador who had a long tête-à-tête with the sixty-four-year-old queen in her privy chamber. Elizabeth, wearing a reddish wig, had been ill the night before and, feeling flushed, she kept opening and closing the top of her robe. The ambassador, André Hurault, reported that "her bosom is somewhat wrinkled . . . but lower down her flesh is exceedingly white and delicate as far as one could see."

Hurault *also* examined her face. "As for her face, it is and appears to be very aged. It is long and thin and her teeth are very yellow and unequal. . . . Many of them are missing so that one cannot understand her easily when she speaks quickly."

Go look at Western art, especially portraits, through the ages; you rarely see open mouths or teeth unless the artist is lampooning peasants or depicting hell. That's no coincidence. ✺

GEORGE WASHINGTON GNAWED HIPPO PARTS

George Washington maintained a stiff upper lip throughout his long military career, mostly because he had no choice. The upper half of his ill-fitting bridge of hippopotamus ivory thrust against his lip, giving the father of our country that famous simian jaw and mouth line. In some portraits, it looks as though he has a small American flag tucked between lip and gum.

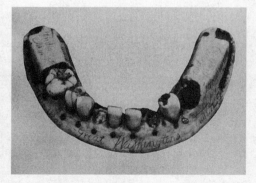

Dead Men's Teeth Helped Washington mouth the Oath of Office

Note in the photo the lower denture that Washington wore the year he was elected President of the United States. Eight human teeth from unknown donors, possibly dead soldiers, were fixed by gold rivets into a denture of carved hippopotamus ivory. A large hole was drilled through to accommodate Washington's *last* remaining tooth, a lower left molar. (That final tooth was pulled later that year.) Etched in the hippo denture is "This Was Great Washington's Teeth" as is the name of the dentist, "J. Greenwood."

Ever since his first tooth was extracted at age twenty-four, Washington (1732–1799) fought a losing and annoying battle with his teeth. He went through six dentists before settling in with John Greenwood for the final decade-plus of his life. During the Revolutionary War, during the battles around New York, Washington once smuggled a French dentist through enemy lines to examine his mouth. To no avail.

Dentures back then were often so ill-fitting that they had to be taken *out* at meal time, and Washington's—while better than most—still gave him problems.

Beyond the functional aspects, the commander-in-chief was quite self-conscious about changes in his facial contour, and maintained his vanity right to the grave. "The principal thing you have to attend to," Washington wrote Greenwood on December 12, 1798, while returning his new dentures for remodeling, "is to let the upper bar fall back from the lower one . . . for I find it is the bars alone, both above and below that give the lips the pointing and swelling appearance . . ." Washington goes into great detail describing his own attempts with a file to correct the previous bridge "or it will have the effect of forcing the lip out just under the nose." Washington closed the letter: "I shall only repeat again, that I feel much obliged by your extreme willingness, and readiness to accommodate me, and that I am, Sir, Your Obedient Servant, Go. Washington."

Greenwood fixed the old and new denture, but in his letter accompanying their delivery took the time to lecture the Founding Father on proper oral hygiene. Greenwood complains that Washington's old pair of false teeth are "very black . . . occasioned either by your soaking them in port wine or by drinking it." Greenwood advises Washington—if he wants to drink port after dinner—to take out his new dentures and put in an old pair. Or if the ex-President can't be bothered with switching dentures, he tells him, "you'll have to clean them right afterwards with a brush and some chalk dust."

Fine-tuning the color was apparently quite important and a bit tricky, since ivory or another man's teeth could be dazzling white. "If you want your teeth more yellower," writes Greenwood, "Soake them in Broath or pot liquer, but not in tea or Acid." He charged Washington fifteen dollars for the additional work, which was about two months' wages for a corporal back during the Revolutionary War.

George Washington's conciseness and pithiness in his day-to-day speech and military commands, traits that made subordinates hang on his words, could have been occasioned by a strong desire on George's part to open *as infrequently as possible* his mouth full of carved hippo and dead men's teeth. ❧

RELIGION

THE INDECENT FORGOTTEN PARTS OF THE BIBLE

ROMANCE AND A BAG OF FORESKINS

Sometimes, you wonder if most Bible-thumpers have ever really read the Bible or if they just keep trotting out the same tired one-liners: "Man doth not live by bread alone." "An eye for an eye."

Racier than any daytime talk show, the Bible packs incest, castration, beheadings, cross-dressing, polygamy, sex slaves, seduction, baby murder, and that's just the first few hundred pages. Smack in Deuteronomy (25:11–12), we learn that a wife who helps her husband in a fight by grabbing his enemy's testicles shall have her right hand cut off. In the Book of Samuel II (16–20), we find the son of King David insulting dad by having sex with *ten* of his father's concubines on a rooftop for all of Israel to see.

Somehow, because of the ponderous marbles-in-mouth King James translation by scholars who had read too much Latin, most people aren't awake or alert to the *good* parts.

King Saul, always leery of David, didn't want the young man to marry his daughter, so he sent him on a quest. It wasn't to slay some dragon or bring back the Ark of the Covenant. "Saul ordered [his officials] to tell David: 'All the King wants from you as payment for the bride are the foreskins of a hundred dead Philistines, as revenge on his enemies.' (This was how Saul planned to have David killed by the Philistines.) Saul's officials reported to David what Saul had said, and David was delighted with the thought of becoming the king's son-in-law. Before the day was set for the wedding, David and his men went and killed two hundred Philistines. He took their foreskins to the king and counted them all out to him, so that he might become his son-in-law. So Saul had to give his daughter Michal in marriage to David." [Saul realized that the Lord was clearly with David.] (I Samuel, 18:24–27; *Bible in Today's English*)

Can you picture the future king of Israel standing there with his bag of foreskins, doling out these little sun-dried ringlets of human skin one by one? Losing count, starting over, making piles of ten, etc.

MOSES' COMMAND TO KILL AND RAPE

Moses laid down the Ten Commandments, of course. He also laid down rules of engagement for battle, and Moses and his troops would today be considered guilty of heinous war crimes. The patriarch would be condemned in the United Nations, in *New York Times* editorials, etc.

In Numbers, we learn that the Lord ordered Moses to raise an army to attack Midian to punish the people there. Moses gathered 12,000 soldiers who sacked the cities of Midian, killed the kings and marched back loaded with the spoils of victory. "Moses became angry with the officers, the commanders of the battalions and the companies, who had returned from the war. He asked them, 'Why have you kept all the women alive? Remember it was the women who followed Balaam's instructions and at Peor led the people to be unfaithful to the Lord. That was what brought the epidemic on the Lord's people. So now kill every boy and kill every woman who has had sexual intercourse but keep alive for yourselves all the girls and all the women who are virgins.'" (Numbers 31:13–18)

Moses, the law-giver.

Moses later tallied up all the spoils. "The following is a list of what was captured by the soldiers, in addition to what they kept for themselves: 675,000 sheep and goats, 72,000 cattle, 61,000 donkeys and 32,000 virgins."

Of course, applying modern standards to Moses isn't fair (although it is apparently okay to apply biblical standards to us today). The killing of male children and the capturing of virgins was pretty typical for biblical warfare. In Judges 20, the assembly sent the soldiers of Israel out with orders to "Kill all the males and also every woman who is not a virgin." The army returned with 400 virgins to give to the men of the tribe of Benjamin. That tally, unfortunately, came up 200 virgins short so the assembly gave the Benjaminites the following advice: "Go and hide in the vineyards and watch. When the girls of Shiloh come out to dance during the feast, you come out of the vineyards. Each of you take a wife by force from among the girls."

CAPTURED VIRGINS

The practice of capturing women for sex during warfare back then was so common that the Bible spells out the detailed ground rules. "When the Lord your God gives you victory in battle and you take prisoners, you may see among them a beautiful woman that you like and want to marry. Take her to your home, where she will shave her head, cut her fingernails and change her clothes. She is to stay in your home and mourn for her parents for a month; after that you may marry her. Later, if you no longer want her, you are to let her go free. Since you have forced her to have intercourse with you,

you cannot treat her as a slave and sell her."
(Deuteronomy 21:10–14)

In biblical times, a woman, in effect, was the property of her father and then of her husband. She was a servant with certain privileges, and many responsibilities. The single greatest responsibility of a girl was to preserve her virginity. This was no fond wish by her parents. This was the law, and a very harsh law.

VIRGIN BRIDES

Parents of a bride accused of being not a virgin were expected to bring proof, i.e., a bloodstained wedding sheet, to court to disprove the charges. "But if the charge is true and there is no proof that the girl was a virgin, then they are to take her out to the entrance of her father's house, where the men of her city are to stone her to death. She has done a shameful thing among our people by having intercourse before she was married, while she was still living in her father's house. In this way, you will get rid of this evil." (Deuteronomy 22:20)

Some authorities on punishment claim that stoning to death ranks among the most horrible forms of execution, a far slower and more painful death than, say, hanging, guillotine, firing squad, or electrocution.

GOD'S STRANGEST PUNISHMENT

In Ezekiel, God, in a lather over their wicked ways, ordered the children of Israel to eat human excrement: "And thou shalt eat it as barley cakes, and thou shalt bake it with dung that cometh out of a man, in their sight. And the Lord said: Even thus shall the children of Israel eat their defiled bread among the Gentiles, whither I will drive them." (Ezekiel 4:12–13)

The prophet Ezekiel, claiming a history of good dietary practices, asked for leniency for himself. And the Lord allowed him alone to bake his barley bread mixed *with cow dung* instead.

Thomas Paine, in his *Age of Reason,* said he thought the passage meant that God ordered the people to eat a "turd."

MISCELLANEOUS LAWS: SO GOD WON'T STEP IN IT

There were rules for soldiers out on a raid: "You are to have a place outside the camp where you can go when you need to relieve yourselves. Carry a stick as part of your equipment, so that when you have a bowel movement you can dig a hole and cover it up." (Deuteronomy, 23:12–14; *Bible in Today's English)*

And what is the reason for defecating outside the camp? "For the Lord thy God walketh in the midst of thy camp, to deliver thee and give up thine enemies before thee; therefore shall thy camp be holy: that he see no unclean thing in thee, and turn away from thee." (Deuteronomy 23:12–14; *King James Version)*

WHY NO RAISED ALTAR

"Do not build an altar with steps leading up to it; if you do, you expose yourselves as you go up the steps." (Exodus 20:24)

This tells us something about the lack of biblical underwear (i.e., loinclothes and short robes could be quite revealing) and makes us realize how easy it was for David to circumcise those two hundred Philistines.

A MANLY MAN

A man is sometimes referred to as he "that pisseth against a wall." This euphemism, this circumlocution is used five separate times in the Bible. (I Samuel 25:34; I Kings 14:10; I Kings 16:11; I Kings 21:21; II Kings 9:8)

There is no female equivalent such as she "that splattereth in the dust."

BRUTAL TREATMENT

The Bible accepts that Israelites may own slaves, preferably not fellow Israelites. And there were standards of behavior: "If a man takes a stick and beats his slave, whether male or female, and the slave dies on the spot, the man is to be punished. But if the slave does not die for a day or two, the master is not to be punished. The loss of his property is punishment enough." (Exodus 21:21)

LOVE THY SISTER-IN-LAW

Polygamy was sometimes very actively encouraged. When a man died, it was the duty of a surviving brother (married or not) to impregnate his sister-in-law, so she could name her next son after the dead man. When Onan spilled his semen on the ground instead of inside his late brother's wife, the Lord killed Onan (Genesis 38:1–10).

In Deuteronomy (25:5–10), however, a different punishment is specified. "If he still refuses to marry her, his brother's widow is to go up to him in the presence of the town's leaders, take off one of his sandals, spit in his face, and say, "This is what happens to the man who refuses to give his brother a descendant.""

A COUPLE MORE RULES FOR HAPPY POLYGAMY

☞ "If a man takes a second wife, he must continue to give his first wife the same amount of food and clothing and the same rights that she had before." (Exodus 21:10)

☞ "No man is to disgrace his father by having intercourse with any of his father's wives." (Deuteronomy 22:30)

You never know what you might find in the Bible if you stray from the usual passages and especially if you read it in a colloquial translation. I hope the references above will be accepted in the spirit of Robert Frost's little couplet:

Forgive, O Lord, my little jokes on Thee,
And I'll forgive Thy great big one on me.

HOLY RELICS: JESUS' FORESKIN

During the Middle Ages, French King Louis IX paid a fortune of 10,000 gold pieces to buy Jesus' crown of thorns, and all of Paris turned out for the triumphal parade through the streets.

Relics — snippets of the flesh and bones of saintly men and women — have fascinated the Christian faithful since the death of Jesus Christ. Along the pilgrimage routes, church after church promised a ghoulish glimpse and the chance to pray and make donations. Relics were big, big business and the faith-healing powers of a relic could make or break a church. (Actually relics were probably often *safer* and more effective than the prevailing medical practices of head-drilling and cow-dung poultices.)

The pursuit of relics (and profit-potential) turned into a European obsession. Two churches had a bloody dispute over whose head of John the Baptist was authentic. "How does it come to pass that eighteen apostles are buried in Germany when Christ chose only twelve?" complained Martin Luther. And reformer John Calvin weighed in, "Had the Virgin Mary been a wet nurse all her life, she could not have produced more milk than you can see in various parts of the world." If relics depended on the saintliness of the deceased, then the ultimate faith-heal-

ing relic would be the actual body of Christ. There was a problem, though. The New Testament clearly stated that after his resurrection, Jesus traveled with the disciples to Bethany and "while he blessed them, he was parted from them and carried up to Heaven."

If Jesus was transported to heaven, then no part of his body remained on earth. That is, until some astute scholar realized that Jesus — as a faithful Jew — had been circumcised. Where was the foreskin? Who had the foreskin of the Savior?

Thus began a frantic search, a kind of twisted Holy Grail saga, that yielded not one, but a dozen competing ringlets of holy flesh.

Let's pick up the tale from James Bentley's spirited *Restless Bones: The Story of Relics*.

"Charroux in the diocese of Poitiers [in France] insists that Charlemagne gave its abbey the holy prepuce. In the early twelfth century the monks of Charroux carried their most precious relic in triumph to Rome, exhibiting the foreskin (alongside a piece of the true cross and Jesus's sandals) before Pope Innocent III. Yet, at that time another foreskin, also claiming to be Jesus's, was on show in the parish of Calcata, a medieval village in the province of Viterbo north of Rome. Another was displayed in the abbey of Coulombs in the diocese of Chartres. A fourth rested at Puy, a fifth at Metz, a sixth at Anvers, a seventh at Hildersheim, and an eighth holy foreskin in the church of Notre-Dame-en-Vaux, Chalons-sur-Marne.

"Naturally enough each religious foundation possessing such a relic disputed the authenticity of the others. Pope Innocent III refused to judge the issue, declaring that only God could know the truth about something so delicate."

Can you picture the pope and his learned advisors peering into the reliquary, trying to decide in those pre-DNA days? By smell? By texture? The pope's refusal to pick a winner wound up opening the door to the discovery of another half-dozen holy foreskins.

But over time, Charroux (whose very name derives from "Chair Rouge" or "Red Flesh") won out in the relic battle. Pope Clement VII (in office 1523–1534) issued a bull granting indulgences to anyone viewing the foreskin at Charroux.

Then tragedy struck. The relic at Charroux disappeared, was thought stolen, and was missing for centuries. Then, in 1856, a workman found a reliquary hidden inside a wall, perhaps to protect it during the many religious wars. A new church to house it was built, and Monsignor Pie at the dedication ceremony told the adoring crowd that on careful scrutiny he could still see coagulated blood on the bit of holy flesh.

Over time, though, the Vatican came to frown on foreskin relics, stating in 1900 that they encouraged "irreverent curiosity." And although holy foreskins haven't made the news lately, one church in Italy defiantly did keep up the worship through the 1980s. Each year in Viterbo, the relic was exposed, appropriately enough, during the Feast of the Circumcision. But in 1983 thieves broke in and stole the three-hundred-year-old jeweled relic case, and the holy flesh within. "We would prefer

not to have too much publicity about the affair," Monsignor Rosina told relic expert, James Bentley. The police never solved the case. Another Holy Grail, anyone? ◉

BAD POPES AND VATICAN BORDELLOS

Taking potshots at pontiffs has become a popular sport, although modern critics will probably never exceed the concentrated venom of Martin Luther, who called Julius II a "blood-drinker" and the "anti-Christ."

However, in the spirit of fairness (before we take what might be construed as potshots), here is how devout Catholic Jerrold Packer described the popes in his *St. Peter's Kingdom*. (FYI, he noted of the current cardinals that "it would be difficult to find a more esteemed group of men anywhere in the world.")

On the popes: "The diversity of station, character and ability of the 262 men who have legitimately occupied Peter's throne is almost boundless. Their backgrounds have ranged from the heights of landed nobility to the poverty of itinerant monkhood, their private lives from unarguable saintliness to bottomless venality, their discharge of the office from a level equal to history's greatest heroes to a point where only the institution's momentum saved the Holy See from disintegration. At the time of their election, the popes have covered an age span from the eighty-six-year-old Gregory IX to eighteen-year-old Benedict IX. In terms of academic achievement, 'hey range from scholarly graduates of the world's great universities to utter illiterates . . . The story of the Vatican is, in great part, the accumulated story of the pope's lives, stories that have filled libraries."

Pope Stephen VII
(In Office 896—897 A.D.)

The living pope interrogated the dead pope, then sentenced him to die.

Pope Stephen VII—furious with his predecessor, Pope Formosus (in office 891–896), over the man's pick for Holy Roman Emperor—had Formosus's corpse dug up from the grave where it had lain for eleven months. He then had it carefully dressed in full pontifical vestments and placed upon the papal throne in the Lateran to stand trial for his capital crimes. Scholars have dubbed the event "The Cadaveric Synod," which almost sounds respectable.

Pope Stephen VII—an unhinged young man—glowered at the rotting corpse, the skeletal caricature of a pontiff, and shouted: "Why did you usurp this See of the Apostle?" And a teenage deacon, crouched nearby, replied: "Because I was evil." The synod convicted the former pope, invalidated his appointments; soldiers hacked off his blessing fingers (i.e., first three on his right hand), stripped him to a hair shirt, and tossed his body in the Tiber.

Pope Stephen VII was strangled soon after. 🕭

John XII
(In Office 955—963)

In his mid-20s, the heir of one of the wealthiest families in Rome, John XII was a bon vivant able to shock even the jaded Romans. Besides the high life, he had even approached the dreaded Huns and Saracens about forming an alliance.

At a trial orchestrated by the pope's enemy, Holy Roman Emperor Otto, a bishop and a cardinal "declared they had seen the Pope ordain a deacon in a stable . . ."

"Benedict, cardinal deacon, with his fellow deacons and priests, said they knew the Pope had been paid for ordaining bishops . . . On the question of sacrilege, they said, inquiries were hardly necessary because it was a matter of eyesight, not of hearsay. As regards the pope's adultery, they knew he had copulated with Rainier's widow, with Stephana, his concubine, with the widow Ana, and with his own niece. He had gone hunting in public, had blinded his spiritual father Benedict, and caused the death of cardinal sub-deacon John by castrating him . . ."

Those are a few highlights of the charges as recorded by *Otto's* secretary, Liudprand. John XII, not surprisingly, refused to come to Rome to answer the charges. Pope Leo VIII was installed in his stead but when Emperor Otto returned north, John rushed back to Rome and reclaimed the Vatican. It was his turn now to call a synod and thirty of the hundred high Church officials who had attended the previous one showed up again. Those who had made specific charges against him were rewarded. One had his tongue yanked out; another his hand cut off; a third lost nose and fingers.

Pope John XII was back in power for his eighth year, and Emperor Otto was too embroiled in war to pay a visit to Rome to reinstall Leo. But Otto caught a break.

John XII was sporting with a married woman when her husband came home. He bashed the pontiff's head in with a hammer, and John XII died a few days later. Another version of the tale has John XII suffering a stroke during the adulterous act and dying eight days later. Whatever, he was certainly dead and Otto, unlike Stephen VII, didn't dig up his bones. 🍂

PICKING A POPE:
TORTURE THE CARDINALS

The medieval and Renaissance popes were sometimes the most powerful men in the world, de facto arbiters of disputes among the militant kings and princes of Europe. So when the papacy was temporarily vacant between the death of one pope and the election of the next, the tumultuous times were even more tumultuous. Hence, the conclave.

The term "conclave" literally means "with key," and back in the 1200s for the first time, the cardinals were actually locked up under austere conditions until they could agree on a new leader. The cardinals often represented various warring factions of Italy and Europe; many were promised huge sums of money for their vote and the election could easily get deadlocked.

Banking houses such as the Fuggers regularly sent representatives to Rome during the time of elections. "The invention of the Sacred College has been, on the whole, perhaps the most fertile source of corruption in the church," wrote T. A. Trollope in *The Papal Conclaves*.

Perhaps the ugliest papal election dates back to 1241. Gregory IX died, while in the midst of a power struggle with Holy Roman Emperor Frederick II. Very influential, Senator Matteo Orsini of Rome wanted to force a quick decision by the ten cardinals in Rome who could elect the next pope.

Orsini had his men lock up the aging cardinals in a delapidated thousand-year-old Roman temple, the Septizonium. Some accounts have it that his soldiers first tied the cardinals hand to foot, beating them and cursing them. The cardinals were stuck in a room, all windows blocked, with a few pieces of broken furniture, and ordered to choose a successor. Spartan food was shoved through a grate.

When the defiant cardinals after weeks still refused to make a choice, Orsini ordered his guards to start urinating and defecating through holes in the roof; summer squalls turned the floor to a grotesque soup. (Another account states the roof guards merely used the gutters as a latrine, which later collapsed into the temple during a storm.) All the cardinals fell ill; when one English cardinal died in the heat, he was hastily shoved in a wooden coffin, which remained in the room.

Finally, after two months, the weary churchmen elected Godfrey of Sabina as Celestine IV. Orsini was pleased, he allowed the cardinals to leave, and they scattered pronto. But Celestine IV died sixteen days later from the ordeal.

And nothing could convince the cardinals to meet again. For two years, from November 10, 1241, to June 25, 1243, there was no pope. 🌀

RENAISSANCE POPES AND ROMAN PROSTITUTES

Not only did Renaissance popes tolerate prostitution in Rome, they at times taxed it and even regulated it. One estimate pegged in 1490 that 6,800 of Rome's population of 100,000 were "respectable courtesans"—many catering to the heavy pilgrim/tourist trade. "In Italian Renaissance society," states historian Geoffrey Parker, "prostitutes as a class flourished and were granted an increasingly respectable and honoured place."

The pope at that time had complete control over the civil government of Rome, and, in effect, set the local laws. Here, according to French historians Augustin Cabanes and Emmanuel Rodocanachi, are some of the acts of various Renaissance popes:

Pope Sixtus IV (in office 1471–1484) openly taxed prostitutes.

Pope Alexander VI (in office 1492–1503) rented out several buildings to be used as bordellos, according to an act of June 23, 1496, and these pleasure houses continued to service customers for almost a century, according to a later eyewitness, Pompeo Tigonio.

Pope Julius II (in office 1503–1513) issued a papal bull on July 2, 1510, that, to prevent bordellos close to the papal palace, authorized the creation of a bordello in a section of Rome, set aside for prostitution, i.e., a Prostitute's Quarter.

Popes Leo X (in office 1513–1521) and Clement VII (in office 1523–1534) confirmed that the bordello could continue, on the condition that one fourth of the possessions of the prostitutes, upon death, would go to the convent of Santa Maria Magdalena.

Prostitutes were at various times during the Renaissance charged a fine for riding in carriages; and at other times to obtain an annual license, they had to pay a sum equal to 10 percent of their gross income.

As stated above, prostitutes had their own quarter (just as the Jews) and under various popes, there were strict rules regarding when streetwalking was allowed. Under Pius IV (in office 1559–1565) a bull was announced which forbade "women of bad character" from living near churches and stopped girls under *seven* from "selling chicory in the street." (Apparently, this was a euphemism: Just as street corner flower girls during the Victorian era were sometimes themselves for sale, so too were chicory sellers during the Renaissance.)

Streetwalking times were generally limited to certain hours on *un*holy days. A violation meant a whipping—sometimes in the prison courtyard, sometimes in public. The famed courtesan, Nina, reportedly drew a large crowd on her way to punishment on the bridge at St. Angelo.

Despite the regulations and penalties, prostitutes were still too visible for Pope Pius V (in office 1566–1572), who authorized the building of a wall around the Prostitutes' Quarter—mirroring one built a decade earlier by Pope Paul IV around the Jews' Quarter. The first stone was cast, er, placed on October 19, 1569, and the wall completed a month later, with only two gates. Now, the pope would decide when prostitutes could exit and when clients could enter; the gates were locked at nightfall.

Pius V decided that the gates should remain locked throughout the springtime weeks of Lent. "The intention was praiseworthy," states Augustin Cabanes in *Les Indiscretions de l'histoire* (1906), "but in effect, it also deprived the young ladies of their livelihood and condemned them to die of hunger." The pope couldn't expect such a sacrifice, so he announced on February 8, 1570, that he would grant a daily allowance of food as long as the gates remained locked.

During the Renaissance, Roman prostitutes had a guild; they paraded, had patron saints, and during Christmas week celebrations, they had a traditional footrace through the streets, which always drew big crowds, much bigger even than the Jewish race or the old man's race. ❧

THE POPE'S MISTRESS

Pope Alexander VI (1431–1503) divided the Atlantic in half in his famous bull giving most of the western New World to the Spaniards and Africa to the Portuguese. He also found time for women.

Cardinal Rodrigo Borgia (soon to be Pope Alexander VI) was fifty-seven years old when he chose gorgeous fifteen-year-old Giulia Farnese as his mistress in 1489. She had spectacular long golden hair which in a few years would reach all the way to the marble floors of the Vatican. Giulia was already married to Orsino Orsini. "He was a good husband," states papal antihistorian E. R. Chamberlin. "He was blind in one eye, he knew how to wink with the other."

It became an open secret in Rome that the pope had chosen this giddy, joyous, spectacularly beautiful teenager as his mistress. Her friends called her "La Bella";

Pope Alexander VI, father of Lucrezia Borgia and lover of Giulia Farnese.

Giant fig leaf. This Renaissance sculpture of Giulia Farnese, Pope Alexander VI's mistress, is still in St. Peter's. The famed beauty was originally portrayed *in the nude* and remained so for three hundred years but Victorian-era Pope Pius IX (1846–1878) was sooooo scandalized that he ordered her covered in a metal drapery, which was then painted white to match the marble.

the people dubbed her the "Bride of Christ." To call it an "open secret" is perhaps too cautious; everyone knew, and very few cared—except the pope's master-of-ceremonies, a German, Johann Burchard, who kept a diary that has survived. "From the greatest to the least," wrote Burchard of the top church officials in 1491, "they took on concubines in the fashion of marriage, and indeed they did this publicly." He added: "Unless God provides, this corruption will spread to monks and those in religious orders, although the convents of Rome have almost become all brothels even now, since no one forbids it."

In these modern days of a reputable papacy, whose temporal power controls an area the size of a college campus, it is very difficult to get a handle on these Renaissance popes.

They fought wars, had mistresses, fathered bastards, sold Church offices, and yet at the same time mouthed pieties. This was *accepted* behavior.

Giulia Farnese (1474–1524) attended the wedding of the pope's thirteen-year-old daughter, Lucrezia Borgia; Giulia was not skulking in the corners, but dazzling in the front of the wedding party. Lucrezia, whose long white gown's train was borne by a young black, entered the appointed room in the papal palace, and Giulia Farnese and 150 other women followed her to where the pope sat on the great papal throne with eleven cardinals. The doors were shut for about an hour to the male wedding guests. Burchard—a stickler for protocol—records of the women that "despite my admonishments, none of them genuflected, except for the pope's daughter and a few others close to her." He adds, though, that later when the pope's son kissed his father's foot, all the

"The convents of Rome have almost become all brothels," complained Pope Alexander VI's master-of-ceremonies, Johann Burchard, in 1491.

The pope's daughter, Lucrezia Borgia, was married at the Vatican at age thirteen. Apparently, her later reputation as a poisoner was greatly exaggerated.

150 women followed suit, performing the traditional greeting of kissing the cross on the papal slipper.

The men were allowed to enter about halfway through the ceremony, which ended with a huge celebration. The pope offered up fifty silver urns of sweets, about one hundred pounds of expensive candy. A miffed Burchard reports that "for a sign of great happiness the candies were thrown into the bosoms of many women, especially the beautiful ones," adding, testily, "and this was done for the honor and praise of God and the Roman church."

Giulia Farnese bore the pope two sons, which he acknowledged openly, and one of her descendants from their union became Pope Innocent X (in office 1644–1655). More immediately, her brother Alessandro Farnese was made cardinal, and wags called him the "Petticoat Cardinal," that is, until he became Pope Paul III (in office 1534–1549). Giulia was portrayed in several religious paintings, including a *Transfiguration* by Raphael. Some scholars also contend that she was the model for the Virgin Mary painted by Pinturicchio in the papal apartments. ❧

THE ORIGIN OF NEPOTISM

Many early popes rushed to appoint relatives to highly lucrative posts such as cardinal. "Ten papacies wouldn't have sufficed to satisfy all his cousins," complained one writer of Pope Alexander VI.

Since popes—i.e., unmarried churchmen—were not in theory supposed to have children, many of these appointments went to their nephews—some actually were offspring of the pope's brothers and sisters, but many so-called "nephews" were actually their own illegitimate children. The Italian word for nephew is "nipote," which became bastardized to "nepotism." ❧

KISSING THE POPE'S FOOT

The proper way to greet a medieval and Renaissance pope was to kiss the pope's foot. The practice dates back to the strong medieval Pope Gregory VII (in office 1073–1085), who decreed that popes had the absolute authority to crown emperors and kings. He wanted to bring all temporal power under his spiritual power, and he listed twenty-seven papal rights, including:

- "The Roman Church has never erred nor can it err until the end of time."

- "The pope can be judged by no one."

- "The pope alone offers his foot to be kissed by princes."

- "A rightly elected pope, is, without question, a saint, made so by the merits of Peter."

While the sainthood line fell away, the foot-kissing survived. Casanova, the notorious rake, met Pope Benedict XIV (in office 1740–1758) in 1743. He was told to enter the room where the pope awaited him alone. "I kiss the holy cross on the most holy slipper, he asks me who I am and I tell him." Casanova made some witty small talk about a lusty cardinal, and was invited to come again. Before he left, Casanova asked a favor. "I asked him for permission to read all the forbidden books, and he granted it by giving me his blessing and saying that he would have a written permission sent me gratis; but he forgot to do it." ❧

THE UNHOLY CRUSADES

RICHARD THE LYIN'-HEARTED LOSES THE TRUE CROSS

The Crusader knights played a strange game that hot summer of 1191 in the Holy Land. King Richard the Lion-Hearted (1157–1199) offered his men first one gold coin, then four gold coins to race across the open plain beneath the eyes of the Saracen bowmen and hot oil-slingers and pull a single stone from the thick wall of Acre. Richard, who preferred derring-do, was growing annoyed as the siege of this key Mediterranean seaport castle dragged into its second year.

Finally, though, supplies inside Acre ran out and the Saracens surrendered. Richard (and the Crusaders) negotiated hard terms: the delivery by Saladin of 2,000 Christian captives, the payment of 200,000 dinars, and the populace of Acre must leave with nothing but the clothes on their back. And, most importantly, Saladin must return that holiest of relics, the True Cross. In exchange, the Crusaders would release their Moslem prisoners.

The Crusader knights were impressed by the defeated people of Acre. "Their appearance as they emerged empty-handed from the city was, nonetheless, amazing in its gracefulness and dignity," wrote one chronicler. "They were unconquered by their adversities."

Richard for his part ordered his men not to insult the Moslems or throw stones at them. Warfare back then had its *strangely* polite rules. Saladin, during the siege of Acre, had been sending gifts to his royal adversaries, King Richard and King Phillip II of France: plums from Damascus, pears, and other delicacies. High-ranking prisoners were never executed, but held for ransom. That century, the Vatican ruled that high tech crossbows could be used only against *non*-Christians.

On August 11, the Crusaders met the Saracens to accept the first of three installments of prisoners and money. The number of prisoners was correct, but the Crusaders claimed certain specified noblemen were to have been included in the first batch. The Saracens denied that. Both sides refused to budge. The exchange didn't take place.

Through August 20, the stalemate continued, when King Richard grew tired of waiting—he had received no money and no prisoners—and ordered all 2,700 Moslem prisoners brought shackled outside the walls of Acre, in plain sight of the enemy flanked in the distance. He circled the prisoners with his infantry and cavalry and ordered his troops to kill every last man. And they did, with fury "avenging their fallen comrades who had died at Acre." (Another account states King Richard had the prisoners all beheaded, yet another has them all hanged. Some say it was only prisoners of war; others that there were men, women, and children.)

Whatever the method, close to three thousand unarmed Moslems died that summer day in the Holy Land, a clear violation of the code of chivalry and the rules of medieval warfare. Saladin was stunned by the boorishness of the man. When a rumor spread that the Moslem prisoners had swallowed gold and gemstones, Crusaders started slicing open their bellies looking for treasure. Saladin's troops rushed from nearby positions but arrived too late to stop the further butchery.

Saladin, now himself enraged, ordered the death of all 1,600 Christian prisoners, and he hid the True Cross somewhere where it has yet to be found—some said under the doorway of the Mosque in Damascus.

For several centuries after King Richard the Lion-Hearted had left the Holy Land, Moslem women would frighten their children into behaving by threatening them: "King Richard is coming to get you!" Our *"Coeur de Lion"* was *their* bogeyman.

And maybe those women were right. King Richard's résumé—despite the *great* nickname—is quite spotty. Twice, he mounted armed rebellions against his own father, the king. And when he was returning home from this third Crusade, he carelessly allowed himself to be captured by the Austrians. (His phony beard fooled no one.) And the enormous ransom of 100,000 marks put a massive dent in the wealth of England. ❦

ILL-FATED CHILDREN'S CRUSADE

It was a scene out of a fairy tale or a gospel. A fifteen-year-old shepherd boy named Stephen was walking through the French countryside in 1212 A.D., followed by thousands of children, carrying a letter from Jesus to the king.

Stephen, who had offered bread to a weary pilgrim, said the man revealed himself as Jesus and gave Stephen a letter bidding him preach a children's Crusade to recapture the Holy Land. The children would travel armed with only their innocence; they would succeed where the greatest warriors of Europe had failed; the seas would part and they would walk to the Holy Land. Purity would triumph.

A fervor swept France, which two centuries later would embrace a shepherd girl named Joan of Arc. The Saracens had reconquered the Holy Land and something must be done.

More than thirty 13th-century chroniclers wrote of the Children's Crusade, but few could agree on the details. In any version, it was a tad dark.

Matthew Paris wrote: "They abandoned their fathers, mothers, wet nurses and friends; locked doors wouldn't hold them back, nor the prayers of their parent." Imagine a tidal wave of preteens on an ecstatic mission, carrying crosses and candles, sweeping through town after town on their way to Paris to help Stephen deliver his letter to the king. They chanted: "Free the Holy Land! Return the True Cross!" Estimates of their numbers varied from 15,000 to "infinite."

And what did the king say, when he took a break from building Notre Dame? He consulted with high Church officials in Paris at the University and he told the children to go home to their parents. He *ordered* them to do so.

According to some accounts, that's where it ended. But quite a few other chroniclers state that Stephen led them south to Marseilles. And Pope Innocent III reportedly enthused: "These children put us to shame; while we sleep they go forth joyfully to conquer the Holy Land."

At Marseilles, two merchants decided to part the waves for the little ones. For the love of God, they said, they would offer free passage on seven ships. The men's names were Hughes Ferri and Guillaume de Porqueres.

Then no word from the children. No sighting in the Holy Land. For almost twenty years, no one knew what had happened to them until one day in 1230, a priest returned from the East and said he had been on that sea voyage with them.

Two of the ships got caught in a storm, he said. "Huddled together below the decks, the little Crusaders heard the waves strike blows upon the frail planks, which threatened each moment to yield, and they were thrown from side to side as the vessel pitched and rolled," amplified 19th-century historian George Gray.

Those two ships crashed on the rocks near the tiny island of San Pietro, off Sardinia. (The pope would later commission a shrine to them there.)

Those were perhaps the lucky ones. The other five boats were delivered to North African ports and the children were sold into slavery, some sold to the "eunuch makers and the purveyors for the harems," others sent to work in the fields.

It's said that eighteen died of various tortures refusing to renounce their faith. No one knows what happened to young Stephen, the leader. A German boy named Nicholas the same year raised a similar Children's Crusade which ended just as badly.

One bright spot, though: The chroniclers claimed to have found out what happened to the double-crossing merchants, Hugh Iron and William Pig (for that's what their names meant), who probably sold the children into slavery. They were hired by the Saracens to kidnap Holy Roman Emperor Frederick II, but were caught and hanged side by side. ❧

THE PROFIT MOTIVE BEHIND THE INQUISITION

The darkest secret of the Inquisition is perhaps not the sadistic pleasure some priestly torturers felt, but rather the enormous financial incentive that drove the Inquisition, perhaps as much as the desire to root out heresy. *A convicted heretic had his or her property confiscated.* This was a solid moneymaker for the Vatican, right up there with the sale of indulgences and divorces. Families in the Middle Ages were sometimes turned out of doors as soon as someone was accused of heresy.

Not even death could protect heretics. The Inquisition sometimes prosecuted the dead (who had perhaps even more difficulty than the living in defending themselves) and then confiscated the property of their heirs. (The moldering corpse was sometimes dug up, dragged through the streets, and then burned.) The heirs of one wealthy Gheraldo of Florence lost their property sixty-five years after his death, because Gheraldo allegedly confessed to heresy on his deathbed. For a period in the Middle Ages, real estate contracts in Florence came with a "Heretics' Clause," promising the buyer reimbursement if the Inquisition later confiscated the property.

Formulas for splitting the proceeds varied, according to H. C. Lea in *The History of the Inquisition of the Middle Ages*, but it was often, especially in Italy: one third for the Vatican, one third for the local Inquisitor, one third for the local lay authorities. In 1343, for instance, Pope Clement VI had to send an armed contingent to the Inquisitors of Florence and Lucca to get them to pay their full share.

Families wronged by the Inquisition could not even take comfort that Inquisitors would one day roast in hell. The job title came with the promise of "plenary indulgence," i.e., forgiveness of sins. A bona fide perk in a hell-fearing world.

When Americans think of the Inquisition, their first thought is generally the Spanish Inquisition; that was merely the latest and one of the more vicious in a series of Catholic Inquisitions to root out heresy. Popes—starting with Lucius III in 1184—parceled out *local* Inquisitions almost like religious franchises throughout Europe. There were Inquisitions—really, a traveling investigative committee—in regions of France, Germany, Italy, and elsewhere, and local Inquisitors were often hard-pressed to meet their goals in terms of heretics burned and property confiscated. It is hard for a modern-day American to imagine the terror that a visit from the Inquisition could cause.

The Inquisitors were granted enormous powers to help them find and punish heresy. Here are the basic ground rules, which give you a glimpse why so few accused people ever escaped the Inquisition. According to scholar Rossell Hope Robbins, "the Inquisitorial method, which developed slowly, may be summarized as follows:"

- Presumption of guilt, not innocence.

- Gossip or hearsay accusations acceptable.

- Accusers and precise accusations not revealed to the accused.

- No right to a lawyer. (Since the lawyer would, in effect, be defending heresy.)

- No right to defense witnesses.

- Torture to obtain confessions allowed.

- Every accused must reveal the names of other heretics.

- All property confiscated.

There are many Great Lies of History, from Nixon's "I am not a crook" on back in time, but one of the greatest was *"Ecclesia abhoret sangue."* "The Church abhors blood[shed]." In practice, this meant that the tortures of the Inquisition were just as painful but simply not as bloody, and that civil authorities handled the actual executions.

The standard phrase when Inquisition officials handed over heretics was: "We urgently beg the secular court to reduce its sentence so that the spilling of blood and the risk of death may be avoided."

Yet, when secular courts fulfilled their request, the Vatican came down hard. When the Senate of Venice in 1521 refused to execute heretics delivered by the Inquisition in Brescia, Pope Leo X (Michelangelo's patron) blasted them in a papal bull: ". . . It is indecent and contrary to the disposition of law and the sacred canons, prejudicial to the liberty of the Church, that laymen interfere in ecclesias-

tical proceedings and refuse to carry out an execution ordered by us . . ." He rages: "The only thing they have to do is do as they are told and perform the execution," which he later notes is "for the salvation of souls." Pope Leo closes, "From this order there is no appeal."

FREE AND OPEN CONFESSION

Even several attempts by genuinely compassionate popes to reform the system fell flat. For instance, the papacy in the late Middle Ages forbade the use of a confession made *during* torture. The prisoner must be willing to repeat and sign whatever he had said on the rack *later,* during a "free and open confession."

Savonarola, the fanatical reformer of Florence, was brutally tortured *seven* times, until his arm hung down burned and lifeless before he later "freely and openly" confessed, as the Ecclesiastical Court record clearly states. He was then hoisted in chains and roasted alive at the stake.

Another merciful pope decreed that torture could be repeated only three times. But the Holy Inquisition cleverly avoided that cap through another nicety of language, by stating that the next round of torture was merely a "continuation" of the first session.

In fact, this entire area of torture, i.e., inflicting pain, is shrouded in a nicety of language, a kind of gauze to protect the bullies from the brutality of their actions.

One punishment applied to nuns committing heresy in medieval France was sentencing them to live out their lives *"in pace*" (i.e., "in peace"), which meant locked in a small dark cell with food pushed through a grate. No human contact was permitted until death, not even a syllable of conversation. *"In pace."* 🌀

MORE INTOLERANCE

PURITANS: MAKING THE QUAKERS QUAKE

The Puritans escaped religious persecution in England, traveled to America and promptly began persecuting all other religions. This much, most of us know. (As historian Thomas Macaulay put it: "The Puritan hated bearbaiting, not because it gave pain to the bear but because it gave pleasure to the spectators.")

The theocracy in New England was fanatically intolerant, basically on a par with, say, an Ayatollah Khomeini. This is an unpleasant fact for most Americans who would like to believe the Puritans generally did little more than put Sunday drunks in the stocks and make adulterous wives sport a garish A on their dresses.

The intolerance was far more brutal than that. There was, of course, the Salem witch trials, but wasn't that a short-lived madness, later apologized for? Perhaps,

but here are the laws that were on the books for how to punish a person for arriving in New England and being a Quaker, i.e., a member of another Protestant faction.

The general court at Boston on October 14, 1657, enacted the following law: "Every male Quaker for the first offense, shall have one of his ears cut off, and be kept at the House of Correction to be sent away at his own charge; and for the second offense, shall have his other ear cut off, and every woman Quaker, that has suffered the law here, that shall presume to come into this jurisdiction, shall be severely whipped." A woman's return a second time would draw the same punishment again.

"And for every Quaker, he or she, that shall a third time, herein again offend, they shall have their tongues bored through with a hot iron, and be kept at the House of Correction close to work, until they be sent away at their own charge."

The Quakers, unlike other sects, were quite conspicuous. Their interpretation of the Bible required that Quakers use scriptures' "Thee" and "Thou," that they not remove their hat in greeting, that they not pay church "tithes" (a Jewish custom, they believed), and that they not fight ("Love thy enemies").

"Within four years of their first appearance [in 1656], scores of Quakers had been stripped naked, whipped, pilloried, stocked, caged, imprisoned, laid necks and heels, branded, and maimed," wrote Alice Earle in *Curious Punishments of Bygone Days.* She also noted, "Four had been hanged in Boston."

They were punished solely for having different religious beliefs. An eyewitness described what happened to a Quaker in New Haven: "The Drum was Beat, the People gather'd, Norton was fetch'd and stripp'd to the Waist, and set with his back to the Magistrates, and given in their View, Thirty-six cruel stripes with a knotted cord, and his hand made fast in the Stocks where they had set his Body before, and burn'd very deep with a Red-hot Iron with H. for Heresie."

Four Quaker women were caught. Their names were: Anna Coleman, Mary Tompkins, Alice Andrews, and Alice Ambrose. Their sentence was forwarded to the constables of twelve Massachusetts and New Hampshire towns.

"You are enjoined to make them fast to the cart-tail & draw them through your several towns, and whip them on their naked backs not exceeding ten stripes in each town, and so convey them from constable to constable at your peril."

Apologists like to point out that three thousand religious dissidents died in prison in England under Queen Elizabeth so the local Puritan theocracy was comparatively mild. Hmm.

William Penn—after many stints in jail—founded a safe haven for Quakers in 1681 in what would become Pennsylvania.

One advantage, perhaps, of the Quaker dress code was that with their long hair and hats pulled down it would cover the holes where their ears used to be.

THE RELIGIOUS FAT THAT ROCKED THE BRITISH EMPIRE, 1857

Out of all the thousands of stories of religious beliefs sparking wars, this one must rank among the stranger.

"Blowing from Guns in British India." This *painting* by V. Verestchagin (1890) shows a notorious form of punishment.

The spark that lit the Indian Mutiny of 1857—which rocked the British Empire and led to thousands of deaths including two hundred British women and children massacred near Cawnpour—was animal grease.

A report started circulating among the hundreds of thousands of native Indian troops—armed and trained by the British—that the British had issued them rifle cartridges coated in animal grease, *made from a mixture of cow fat and pig lard.*

Not only would the soldiers have to touch the greased cartridges, but they would have to bite the tips before loading them into the new Enfield rifles.

In India, the cow is, of course, sacred to Hindus and if a Brahmin (highest caste of Hindu) eats any portion of a cow, he must struggle through several lifetimes to regain his high caste with all its privileges. "The sepoys [Indian soldiers] became alarmed," wrote Field Marshal Lord Roberts in his *Forty-One Years in India* (1898), "and determined to suffer any punishment rather than pollute themselves by biting the contaminating cartridge." The man's family would literally be shunned to the lowest circles of society.

As for Moslems, pork is considered unclean and it is forbidden to eat it.

The British, in one insensitive move, had succeeded in uniting dire enemies, Hindus and Moslems, against a common villain: Queen Victoria. Religious leaders inflamed the men, telling them that the greased cartridges were part of a British plot to destroy native religions and convert the entire nation to Christianity.

Concludes Field Marshal Roberts: "Incredible disregard of the soldiers' religious prejudices was displayed in the manufacture of these cartridges."

Of all the sparks helping to ignite rebellion—from stamp tax in the American colonies to "Let-them-eat-cake" propaganda in the French Revolution—these greased cartridges stand as one of the odder ones . . . that is, unless you happen to be a Hindu or a Moslem. And that's just the point.

ODD CULTS: CASTRATION, FLAGELLATION, AND EARLY WITHDRAWAL

One man's cult is the next woman's Anabaptist Revival. So, after scrupulously studying tens of thousands of cults, memorizing each and every obscure theological tenet, I have chosen three of the stranger cults ever to have lured the blessedly open-minded. (In fact, their minds were so open, one can almost still feel the draft.)

THE SKOPTZY

This cult, which flourished for about a hundred years in Russia from the mid-1700s, fascinated early anthropologists and scholarly articles about it have dotted academic journals in French, German, and English as late as World War II.

They called themselves "White Doves." (Cynics called them "madmen" and worse.)

The Skoptzies were a fanatical Christian sect who believed the only way to become pure enough and chaste enough for heaven was through castration. They wooed converts quoting the New Testament lines from Matthew (19:12) "and there be eunuchs which have made themselves for the kingdom of Heaven's sake" and from Luke (23:29), "blessed are the barren."

Their castration of men and their breast and genital slashing of women signified a kind of voluntary and terribly painful martyrdom to purify themselves. "Sin is so profound that the only way to Heaven is through iron and fire" was one of their sayings.

The 1700s marked a period of religious mysticism in Russia. The founder, Kondrati Sseliwanow, who split his group off from a flagellant sect, was shipped off by the authorities to a Siberian labor camp. Nonetheless, there were supposedly quite a few converts at the Russian court, including the future czar Peter III, the bumbling, insane first husband of Catherine the Great. (This not-so-happy couple was estranged almost from the start, due to Pe-

ter's impotence; Catherine started plotting his death and taking lovers.)

Skoptzies believed that Peter III was not assassinated but that a guard was killed in his stead, and that Peter escaped to preach the Skoptzy cult, demanding of converts a "baptism by fire," i.e., emasculation.

(Historians, *on the other hand*, believe that soon after Peter III assumed the throne in 1762, he was strangled on the orders of Catherine and a clique of noblemen.)

Skoptzy rituals were very secretive. French anthropologist Eugène Pittard

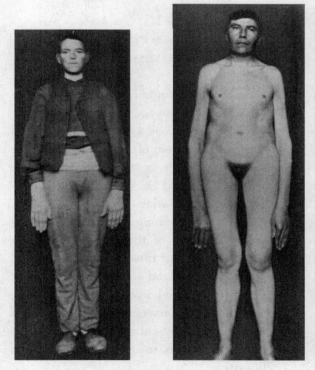

Holy castration. The man on the right, Ivan Gregor, age twenty-four, was castrated in the name of God at age five. Anthropologists note the long arms and the feminine pubic region. The young cult member, on the left, shows a similar body type.

Holy slashing. A drawing of a twenty-year-old Skoptzy woman who had her nipples cut off and her breasts drastically reduced.

five hundred still practicing their beliefs in Romania as late as the 1930s. ❧

FLAGELLANTS

Long processions of flagellants snaked through the streets of Paris, their backs bare even in winter, the metal-tipped whips hanging from their belts. Crowds gathered to watch the whippings, and chronicler Jean Froissart tells us that "foolish women" raced to catch the blood of these devout martyrs "and smear it on their eyes."

As the Black Death swept through Europe unchecked, defying the best efforts of the two main healers of the day, i.e., doctors and priests, there arose a new cure: mass public flagellation.

If the sinful world purified itself through painful penance, perhaps God would end the plague, the pious logic ran. Maybe the suffering of these voluntary martyrs could stay the onslaught.

Pope Clement VI in Avignon personally oversaw a procession of male and female flagellants in May 1348. The rules for ascetic sects varied, but the main tenets were as follows: never speak to a woman, never sleep on a feather bed, never spend more than one night in a parish; wear a holy cross on robes and hats. To join the French branch, one must have pocket change of four "sols" a day (so as not to have to beg); one must have confessed his sins, forgiven his enemies, and like Crusaders going off to the Holy Land, "have received the permission of his wife."

claimed that Skoptzies would emasculate themselves by the age of fourteen by placing their genitals on a fallen tree trunk and then lopping them off with an axe. Other experts, judging by the neatness of the scars, suspected a trained priest performed the operation.

The purest among the Skoptzies were called "bearers of the Imperial Seal," a term reserved for those who had removed penis, testicles, and scrotum, leaving only a crinkly scar and a pouty urethra hole.

Women underwent various types of mutilation from cutting off the clitoris, labia, or nipples to deep scarring of the breasts.

The Skoptzies—perhaps by winning new converts with children, or perhaps by delaying castration till after fatherhood—survived into the 20th century with about

Almost all the flagellants were male, and the movement spread to Italy, the Low Countries, and *especially* Germany.

Here is an eyewitness account by Robert of Avesbury of a march of flagellants through the streets of London in late September 1349, as they stopped to enact a painful leapfrog ritual.

About Michaelmas 1349, over six hundred men came to London from Flanders, mostly of Zeeland and Holland origin. Sometimes at St. Paul's and sometimes at other points in the city they made two daily public appearances wearing clothes from the thigh to the ankles, but otherwise stripped bare. Each wore a cap marked with a red cross in front and behind. Each had in his right hand a scourge with three tails. Each tail had a knot and through the middle of it were sometimes sharp nails fixed. They marched naked in a file one behind the other and whipped themselves with these scourges on their naked and bleeding bodies. Four of them would chant in their native tongue and another four would chant in response like a litany.

Thrice they would all cast themselves on the ground in this sort of procession, stretching out their hands like the arms of a cross. The singing would go on, and the one who was in the rear of those thus prostrate, would in turn step over the others and give one stroke with his scourge to the man lying under him. This went on from the first to the last until each of them had observed the ritual . . . Then each put on his customary garments and always wearing their caps and carrying their whips in their hands they retired to their lodgings. It is said that every night they performed the same penance.

The flagellant mania snowballed in Germany as people started to worship these "Armies of Saints," who in turn flushed with their newfound power, started to attack anyone they considered enemies of God. They massacred Jews at Mainz, Cologne, Frankfurt, and they even seized church property and attacked monks.

At this point, not surprisingly, Pope Clement VI reversed field and issued a bull banning the flagellant sect, and officially calling it a heresy, punishable by death. A number of leaders were tried, and burned as heretics.

The movement faltered, but it did enjoy another brief vogue in the late 1500s when the flamboyantly gay king of France, Henri III — always surrounded by his minions — decided to reintroduce it to Paris as a kind of S&M masquerade parade. For a night procession, hundreds of "penitent" men and women, young and old, boys and girls wore midthigh nightshirts, a pointy white hood with two eyeholes, and *nothing* else even though it was January, according to the diary of Pierre de l'Estoile. When the servants at the palace were caught mocking the king, he had eighty footmen — appropriately enough — whipped. ❧

No Penalty for Early Withdrawal

Pundits dubbed upstate New York the "Burnt Over Region" because the fires of so many revivals had flared there. Of all the many sects that came and went, none aroused the national fury like John Humprey Noyes's Perfectionist movement at Oneida, New York. (The press called it more of a "Free Love" movement.)

Noyes (1811–1886), the well-educated son of a wealthy Vermont family, preached a good many things about how to create a Utopian Christian community—communal property and public criticism sessions (a forerunner of group therapy)—but very few people looked beyond his theories on Christian love.

Noyes's wife, the daughter of a Vermont governor, had suffered through five pregnancies during the first six years of marriage with four of those ending in stillbirth, and Noyes, during a period of self-enforced abstinence, had a bit of a revelation.

He divined that there were two aspects to sexual intercourse: the procreative and the spiritual. "The sexual conjunction of male and female," he later said, "no more necessarily involves the discharge of the semen than of the urine." In practice, Noyes recommended that Christian couples enjoy intercourse for up to an hour or more at a time but that the male should not allow himself to orgasm. He stressed the love, not the procreation, and a revolving selection of partners.

Taking his theories to the hilt, Noyes founded a utopian community near Lake Oneida in 1848 that eventually swelled to three hundred members. Men and women could ask Noyes and his ruling committee for permission to have spiritual intercourse (i.e., nonprocreational sex) with any other partner. Women were always free to say no. And for almost twenty years, Noyes and the community had barely a baby or two a year.

Outsiders charged the cult with practicing "Free Love," and Noyes, who had been hounded out of his original settlement in Vermont on adultery charges, was being investigated again. He was lampooned nationwide; curiosity (and no doubt jealousy) was piqued. While Noyes produced a whole pamphlet on *Male Continence,* he was a bit Victorian in describing sex practices. Apparently, the method was quite simple. Men over time through practice learned to pace themselves so as not to have orgasms. His pamphlet conjures a boatman approaching a waterfall: He must learn to guide the boat in still water and then control it in the rapids without letting himself be cast over the falls. With Niagara nearby it was good scary imagery.

In 1869, almost twenty years after founding Oneida, Noyes started a eugenics program called Stirpiculture. Fifty-three women signed a pact agreeing to procreate with a partner chosen by Noyes. The pact opens: "1. That we do not belong to ourselves in any respect, but that we first belong to God, and second to Mr. Noyes as God's true representative. 2. That we shall have no rights or personal feelings in regard to childbearing which shall in the least degree oppose or embarrass him in his choice of scientific combinations. 3. That we will put aside all envy, childishness, and self-seeking and rejoice with those who are the chosen candidates;

that we will, if necessary, become martyrs to science . . . we offer ourselves "living sacrifices" to God and true Communism." (We're talking "commune" here.)

Over the next decade, fifty-eight children were born, to be raised in the communal Children's House. John Humphrey Noyes proudly fathered nine of the fifty-eight before moving away to Niagara Falls during controversy in 1876 and later fleeing to Canada to escape adultery charges. Within a few years, the Utopian experiment died and the Oneida community set itself up as a for-profit business, issuing $600,000 worth of stock certificates to 226 men, women, and children.

And the business venture thrived; to this day, Oneida, Ltd., sells its much esteemed "Community" silverware, among other products, and in 1995 reported annual sales worldwide of $514 million. ✎

SEDUCING THE FAITHFUL

Erotic Church Art

Competition was fierce along pilgrimage routes in the Middle Ages, as churches tried very hard to lure pilgrims (and their purses) into their shrines.

Some churches paid dearly to buy faith-healing relics—a saint's finger or the milk of the Madonna—and then build reputations as the best shrine to cure, say, madness or infertility. Others had renowned choirs or living holy men or nearby monks famed for fasting. Yet others carved sex acts and naked bodies onto their outer walls.

While scholars disagree over the exact purpose of the carvings, attracting the faithful certainly played a part. Apparently, the idea was to portray the world in all its sinfulness and temptation on the *outside* of the church so that the *inside* would be a blessed sanctuary and place of salvation.

These carvings—generally over doorways, supporting columns, or as part of gargoyle gutters—can be found all over Europe and the British Isles, although art history books have tended to ignore them. The genre especially flourished at Romanesque churches in western France and northern Spain from 1000 to 1200 A.D. along the pilgrimage route to St. James of Compostela.

For instance, as pilgrims approached San Pedro de Cervatos, they could see a couple copulating upside down, or a man and a woman exposing their genitals to each other. Or, to cap it off, they could view a man who has guided his enormous erect penis into his own mouth.

These are startling images to discover on a church, and were so disturbing to many of last century's Victorian renovators that they were taken down and mothballed in storage or purposely allowed to rot. Eight hundred years of weather will take a toll on even gargantuan stone genitalia.

Women having sex with snakes was portrayed at more than sixty churches in France. Here's a weathered but still explicit one from the Church of Oô in the Haute Garonne region. The sculpture is now indoors . . . at the Toulouse Museum.

Art historians are just now prying their blinkers off and starting to explore this long ignored trove of erotic sculpture. "We suggest," write Anthony Weir and James Jerman in their excellent *Images of Lust,* "that the function of [these] sexual exhibitionists is not erotic but rather the reverse, that these extraordinarily frank carvings were probably an element in the medieval Church's campaign against immorality."

Acceptable sexual behavior (i.e., husband-on-top-of-wife intercourse) was not portrayed, but rather exhibitionism, masturbation, autofellatio, rear-entry sex, and bestiality. These practices were all strictly taboo and their enactment on the walls of a church could serve as a reminder for a largely illiterate audience of what *not* to do. (On the other hand, they must have planted a few ideas among church-going teenagers and preteens.)

But you have to put it all in context. People in the Middle Ages were more frank about scatological and sexual matters than their counterparts in the 20th century. One of the more popular entertainments back then were the fabliaux, or rhymed short stories, packed with vignettes such as the one about the fisherman who cut off his own penis to find out whether his wife would still love him as much. (She didn't . . . but he hadn't really cut it off, you see, he had accidentally hooked a corpse while fishing and . . .)

Nudity was less shocking since both sexes often dressed in the same room and

An acrobat attempts autofellatio at Saint-Servais in Brittany. Is that a grin or whitish bird droppings?

Punishment of the damned at Bourges Cathedral, 14th century. Be warned: Ecstasy can lead to agony.

sometimes bathed together. People often used the great outdoors as a privy and street names sometimes featured words such as "Gropecuntlane" in England or the equivalent *"Grattecon"* in France. The French *cul*, as in "ass," has survived in now polite words such as "cul-de-sac," a dead end.

And the clergy during that period had a reputation for firsthand knowledge of the seven deadly sins. Popular French sayings included: "Vice in their acts; virtue on their lips" or "Hock the church valuables to settle up at the whorehouse."

But back to the medieval carvings. No reliable inventory has yet been made of all the sexual sculpture on holy Christian walls, but scholars Weir and Jarman have made a start. Their categories include "Acrobats pulling Vulvas" and "Women with Toads." And modern-day pilgrim Jack Hitt in his *Off the Road* wasn't shy about describing the photos he observed in the

private collection of a Spanish curator in Palencia. "At the Colegiata de Santillana del Mar is a man and a woman splayed crotch to face, a primitive 69 position," recounts Hitt. "At San Martín de Elines is a man exhibiting his penis while tightening a garotte painfully around his neck."

So, let's time-travel for a moment. Imagine you have your cockleshell around your neck and you're wandering down the pilgrim route to St. James of Compostela. You look and you see a woman with a snake emerging from her vagina with its fangs clamping down on her breast; you might be enticed to linger. And if, while you're there, someone starts preaching about hellfire and damnation and walks you around to see the boiling cauldron and the devils slow-roasting sinners, you might decide to walk inside. And while you're there, you might drop a few coins for a candle or a few more coins for the promise of a few decades of prayer on your behalf. You can't be too careful when the eternal dinner menu features devil's *merde*. 🌀

RELIGIOUS WORD ORIGIN: BUGGER

The Brits still say "Bugger off," which is perhaps slightly less insulting than "Fuck off."

Strictly speaking, to bugger someone is to screw him or her in the ass. As a noun, the word means a "sodomite," according to Webster's Collegiate Dictionary (1947). And don't forget Bulgarians.

All these words date back to an 11th-century religious sect called the "Bulgars."

These Christian "heretics," who had left the Roman Catholic Church, were accused of all kinds of foul behavior (roasting babies, orgies, blasphemy), and, significantly, of sodomizing their wives as a means of birth control. (Both the sodomy and the birth control were sins.)

Over time, the other religious technicalities of their faith were forgotten and the sodomy remained, and became broadly applied to various sects of heretics and to sodomites in general. Words can have a strange afterlife.

Brits today will still call a charming rogue "a handsome bugger," regardless of the man's opinions on sodomy. ❧

THE MORNING AFTER: PENANCE FOR SEX

A criminal in the Middle Ages might be punished severely by the state but that didn't clear him or her with God. That was the job of the Church, and priests were trained to ask elaborate series of questions during confession and then dole out the proper punishment.

A series of now mostly forgotten books called *Penitentials* helped the priest to uncover sins and dictate penance, which might include extra prayers, a liquid diet, the lash, and in some cases, pilgrimage.

The length of penance imposed clearly reveals the heinousness of a given sin in the eyes of the theologian.

> • "Anyone who kills a pagan or a Jew shall do penance for forty days."—Penitential of Cuidad (Spanish), c. 1410

> • "Any woman who paints herself with white makeup or other pigment in order to please men, she shall do penance for three years."—The Milan Penitential (Italian) c. 1700

> • "Anyone who kills a priest shall do penance for twelve years."—The Milan Penitential (Italian) c. 1700

Some of the penitentials tried to anticipate *all* possible foul deeds.

> • "If he vomits the host, [penance] for forty days."—Penitential of Cummean (Irish) c. 650

> • "If a dog laps up this vomit, he who has vomited shall do penance for one hundred days."—Penitential of Cummean (Irish) c. 650

> • "He who eats the skin of his own body, that is, a scab, or the vermin which are called lice, or his own excreta—with the imposition of the hands of the bishop he shall do penance for an entire year on bread and water."—Penitential of Cummean (Irish) c. 650

Not surprisingly, the penitentials came down quite hard on sex outside of marriage. A masturbating male was looking at anywhere from forty days to a year or more of penance, while a homosexual act usually drew seven years or more. (Bestiality and homosexuality were often equated.) Marital sex was dangerous as well. A couple of glasses of mulled wine, a bit of passion, some creativity . . .

- "Whoever discharges semen into the mouth shall do penance for seven years: this is the worst of evils." — Penitential of Theodore (English) c. 675

- "A husband who has intercourse with his wife from behind, he shall do penance for forty days the first time." — Penitential of Theodore (English) c. 675

- "A wife who mixes her husband's semen into dinner so as to make them more amorous shall do penance for three years." — Penitential of Theodore (English) c. 675 ✎

THE SEDUCTION TECHNIQUES OF THE MORMON PROPHETS

Now that Brigham Young University has a solid football team, most of the fight over Mormon polygamy has been forgotten. But there was a time in this country before the Civil War when wiping out the polygamy of the Latter-Day Saints roused almost as much righteous fury as abolishing slavery. Harriet Beecher Stowe *(Uncle Tom's Cabin)*, for one, crusaded loudly against both.

Despite endless public denials at the time, the inner circle of Mormon leaders practiced "plural marriage" for half a century, from the 1840s to the 1890s. The original prophet, Joseph Smith, a charismatic preacher who found a new gospel buried on gold plates, had approximately fifty wives over the course of his life (including twelve already married women, five sets of sisters, and one mother-daughter pair), according to Fawn Brodie's award-winning biography, *No Man Knows My History*. "When I see a pretty woman," he once commented to a friend, "I have to pray for grace."

Brigham Young, for his part, had nineteen wives in the 1870s, according to Mrs. T. B. Stenhouse, a Mormon Englishwoman who was then living with the faithful in Utah. "Now these are the Prophet's wives — his real, living wives — nineteen in all," she wrote in her autobiography in 1882. "How many spiritual wives, it would be impossible to say; probably he himself does not know their number."

(Now, it should be said, whatever their views on wives, Joseph Smith and Brigham Young were very successful at laying the foundations of a new religion; today, more than ten million Mormons practice their religion worldwide.)

Joseph Smith (1805–1844) was six feet tall and strong, with piercing blue eyes framed by very long lashes. He kind of looked like Elvis.

Joseph Smith's résumé — as viewed by an outsider — bears more than a few smudges. At seventeen, on trial for being a "disorderly person and an imposter," he admitted in a New York court that he had told people he had visions from staring at a "seer stone" revealing to him where to dig for buried treasure. And Smith a decade-plus

Mormon founder Joseph Smith (1805–1844) married at least *forty-nine* women (including twelve already married women, five sets of sisters, and one mother-daughter pair).

later set up a bank in Ohio and issued Mormon money that his accountant later admitted was backed by strongboxes filled with sand and metal bolts, topped by a layer of silver coins. And he frequently claimed that he was a great linguist since he had translated the Book of Mormon from "reformed Egyptian" pictographs. (Mark Twain once called the book "chloroform in print.") But when Smith spied a future Promised Land in Illinois, he named it "Nauvoo," which he said in Hebrew means "beautiful plantation"—only there's no word like that in Hebrew. To cap off the ineptitude, Smith once wrote an unintentionally hilarious letter in which he claimed to quote from seventeen foreign languages including Chaldean ("Keed'nauh"), Syrian ("Zaubok"), and Saxon ("Hwaet").

So, the prophet engaged in necromancy, financial chicanery, and linguistic puffery, all with moderate success, but he was absolutely inspired when it came to seduction. "But Joseph was no careless libertine," writes Fawn Brodie in her biography. "There was too much of the Puritan in him, and he could not rest until he had redefined the nature of sin and erected a stupendous theological edifice to support his new theories on marriage."

Besides the obvious problems of being a minister and convincing young Christian women to share his bed and keeping it secret in a small close-knit community of Nauvoo, Illinois in the 1840s, Smith had the added (and extremely ironic) difficulty that his hot-tempered first wife, Emma Hale, was *very* jealous.

Here's how thirty-seven-year-old Joseph Smith "married" seventeen-year-old Lucy Walker, a motherless girl living in Smith's home. (Walker, who remained a devout Mormon, later wrote the incident up in a memoir.) Smith's wife Emma went to St. Louis on a shopping trip in late April 1843, conveniently taking along Lucy's brother.

Smith abruptly told Lucy, "I have been commanded of God to take another wife, and you are the woman." He then briefly explained "celestial marriage" and the everlasting glory it would bring her and her family.

When she balked, he added, "I have no flattering words to offer. It is a command of God to you. I will give you until tomorrow to decide this matter. If you reject this message the gate will be closed forever against you."

"This aroused every drop of Scotch in my veins," she wrote. "For a few moments, I stood fearless before him, and looked him in the eye. I felt at this moment, I was called to place myself upon the altar a living sacrifice." Smith stared deeply into her eyes and promised that she would soon see that it was God's will.

That night, Lucy recalled, as she lay sleepless, her room became engulfed in celestial light and she received "the powerful and irresistible truth of plural marriage." She secretly married Smith the next day, just before Emma returned.

To an already married woman named Mary Rollins, Smith reported that he had been visited three times by an angel telling him to marry her, and the last time the angel had held a sword over his head and threatened to kill him. She succumbed.

Brigham Young was one of the early converts to the Mormon creed back in 1832 and, rising in the Church, he followed Smith to Nauvoo. One of Brigham Young's courtships has also come down to us, from an eyewitness account. Young took an eighteen-year-old pretty English girl, Martha Brotherton, to a room over Joseph Smith's store in Nauvoo and locked the door. Young explained to her, "Brother Joseph has had a revelation from God that it is lawful and right for a man to have two wives . . . If you will accept of me I will take you straight to the celestial kingdom, and if you have me in this world, I will have you in that which is to come, and brother Joseph will marry us here today, and you can go home this evening, and your parents will not know anything about it."

Martha kept stalling, so Brigham called for reinforcements. Joseph Smith came upstairs and told her, "Just go ahead, and do as Brigham wants you to do," adding with a chuckle, "he is the best man in the world, except me." Smith grew serious. "If you will accept of Brigham, you shall be blessed—God shall bless you and my blessing shall rest upon you . . . and if you do not like it in a month or two, come to me and I will make you free again; and if he turns you off, I will take you on."

Brotherton still refused, and eventually escaped the room, fleeing with her outraged parents to St. Louis where her account was published in the *St. Louis Bulletin*, July 15, 1842.

Brigham Young adamantly denied the charges and Smith blasted adultery from the pulpit. Plural mar-

Brigham Young with his seventeenth wife, Margaret Pierce, whom he married in 1846 in Nauvoo, Illinois.

riages were then still a deep secret known only to the Church hierarchy and a handful of women, including the local midwife. But there was one person who knew and was not amused, and that was Smith's wife, Emma.

In 1843, Smith, with fortuitous timing, revealed that he had had a revelation on "plural marriages," which he instructed his brother to read directly to Emma. Boiled down, the long document stated a married man could take another wife, if the first wife consented and if the next wife was a virgin, vowed to no other and she herself consented to the union. "And if he have ten virgins given unto him by this law, he cannot commit adultery, for they belong to him." The revelation added with Old Testament vigor: "If she [i.e., Emma] will not abide this commandment, she shall be destroyed, saith the Lord; for I am the Lord thy God, and will destroy her if she abide not in my law."

That day, Emma cursed out Joseph's brother, but she eventually agreed and later handpicked several of her husband's other wives.

Is polygamy all it's cracked up to be? Seven of Brigham Young's wives (actually his widows) posed for this group photo in 1899. Young died in 1877.

Polygamy would contribute to Smith's premature death. A band of disgruntled Mormons printed a detailed list of grievances against Smith in the *Nauvoo Expositor:* headlining polygamy, followed by tyranny, land speculating, etc. Smith—via the city council—had the printing press destroyed, an act for which the Illinois governor demanded he stand trial. While in custody in Carthage, Illinois, a mob burst past the jailers and shot Joseph Smith, who fell out of a second-story window and died.

He became a martyr. And Mormons soon after followed Brigham Young to Utah, where the pioneer community sur-

vived via hard work and where polygamy flourished for almost half a century despite a spate of federal laws against it. In 1890, Mormon President Wilford Woodruff issued an order to Mormons to "refrain from contracting any marriages forbidden by the law of the land." Then in 1904, the Church put teeth in the law by promising to excommunicate any Mormon husbands who took a new plural wife.

A book on polygamy published in 1987 by University of Utah Press in Salt Lake City concludes: "While other studies have emphasized the negative aspects of Mormon polygamous life, pointing to jealousies between husbands and wives and between the wives themselves, husbands being absent and wives having to be self-sufficient, and families being divided, this study shows that while those experiences did occur, they were the exception rather than the norm. Because they believed they were obeying a higher commandment of God, Latter-Day Saints practicing polygamy had fewer negative experiences than have generally been reported."

Remember Lucy Walker, the seventeen-year-old who had the vision and married Joseph Smith? A year after Smith's "martyrdom" in 1844, she married a Church dignitary, Heber C. Kimball, who over time had forty-three wives and fathered sixty-five children. Lucy herself pitched in nine youngsters. Observed Kimball, "I have noticed that a man who has but one wife . . . soon begins to wither and dry up, while a man who goes into plurality looks fresh, young and sprightly." ❧

VOLTAIRE ON MUHAMMAD

"He is admired for having raised himself from being a camel-driver to be a pontiff, a legislator and a monarch; for having subdued Arabia, which had never before been subjugated; for having given the first shock to the Roman Empire in the East; and *I* admire him still more for having kept peace in his house amongst his wives." ❧

MARK TWAIN ON HEAVENLY JOY

Mark Twain's *Letters from the Earth* remained unpublished for half a century after the great humorist's death, until Twain's daughter Clara could finally be convinced they weren't blasphemous or especially misleading about her father's views. He wrote them late in life when he was putting more sting in his humor.

Twain here assumes the voice of Satan writing letters back to the other immortals and describing man's cockeyed idea of heaven: "He has imagined a heaven, and left entirely out of it the supremest of all his delights, the one ecstasy that stands first and foremost in the heart of every individual of his race—and ours—sexual intercourse!"

Twain later drives home how much mankind prizes sexual intercourse. "The very thought of it excites him; opportunity sets him wild; in this state he will risk life, reputation, everything—even his queer heaven itself—to make good that opportunity and ride it to the overwhelming climax. From youth to middle age all men and all women prize copulation above all other pleasures combined yet it is actually as I have said: it is not in their heaven; prayer takes its place."

Twain jabs at a few other ironies of man's conception of heaven: *"Everybody sings . . .* all day long, and every day, during a stretch of twelve hours. And *everybody stays;* whereas in the earth the place would be empty in two hours."

Finally, Twain also complains about the seating arrangements. "The inventor of their heaven empties into it all the nations of the earth, in one common jumble. All are on an equality absolute, no one of them ranking another; they have to be "brothers"; they have to mix together, pray together, harp together, hosannah to-gether—whites, niggers, Jews, everybody—there's no distinction. Here in the earth all nations hate each other, and every one of them hates the Jew. Yet every pious person adores that heaven and wants to get into it. He really does. And when he is a holy rapture he thinks he thinks that if he were only there he would take all the populace to his heart, and hug, and hug, and hug!" ❧

DIVINE CATCHALL

HOLD THE CHAIRS AT THE LAST SUPPER

The apostles took the Last Supper lying down. It wasn't that they didn't treasure every moment with Jesus, but everyone with a few shekels to spare back then in ancient Judea ate in a reclining position. The poor ate sitting on benches or the floor.

We really don't have a good word in English for the body position in which apostles ate. They had their legs and torsos stretched out on couches with their heads propped on their hands, which were supported by their elbows. Some of the couches of that period had a raised cushioned portion at the table end to save the

fellow the trouble of hoisting himself up for hours.

We associate lying down with Roman orgies. So apparently have two millennia of painters who have steadfastly painted the Last Supper with diners *sitting* at a table. The New Testament in John (13:23–25) clearly identifies future Saint John as "lying close to Jesus' breast."

This is tough to do if Jesus is seated; has John rolled up a port-a-bed and angled it next to Jesus' chair? Of course not.

Artists have wriggled to stick to the letter of "lying close." Many artists depict John napping. Renaissance painter Andrea del Castagno has John dozing with his head cradled in the crook of his arm on the table. The problem here is that John at that very moment, according to the Bible, must ask the identity of the betrayer, with his famous question: "Lord, who is it?" A tough question to ask when you're sleeping. ❧

FAT MONKS AND BABY RABBITS

During the Middle Ages, in many monasteries, the eating of meat was forbidden not only on Fridays but on most days of the year.

However, some of the more canny brothers concocted some excellent fudges. They lobbied hard that the fetuses of rabbits, just like the eggs of chickens, be not considered meat. At various times and places, this was approved. In fact, monks were apparently the first to domesticate and breed rabbits in their monasteries in order to have a steady supply of "unborns" for dinner.

"Later in the medieval period," states Reay Tannahill in *Food in History*, "the Church became subject to attacks of extreme asceticism—brought on, very often, by the sight of too many plump abbots—and at such times not only eggs, meat and rabbit feti were banned on fast days, but milk and butter as well."

And for those days when fish only could be eaten, some monks turned to the monastery ponds and hauled out . . . frogs and beaver, which "conveniently . . . were counted as fish." ❧

Saint Joan

Joan of Arc was certainly a Christian martyr, inspired by heavenly voices to lead her people, but unlike most Christian martyrs, she was condemned to death by her own Church.

Most Americans don't realize who actually judged Joan; they assume because the English held her captive that they tried her. They didn't. A Catholic court of the Inquisition, with the judges all French Church officials, tried and convicted nineteen-year-old Joan of Arc of heresy and other crimes.

After her death, her mother petitioned the pope for a retrial and twenty-five years later in a process known as the Rehabilitation, Joan was acquitted. She was named a saint in 1920. ❧

They Celebrated Christmas a Bit Differently

During the rule of Renaissance Pope Alexander VI (1492–1503), here is one part of the Christmas festivities, as recorded in the diary of the pope's master-of-ceremonies, Johann Burchard.

On the first day of Christmas, 30 masked men with long thick noses in the form of enormous phalli (i.e., penises) proceeded after dinner to the palace of Saint Peter. Before them a cardinal's chest was borne, to which was affixed a shield with three dice. Then came the masked fellows and behind them someone rode in a long coat and an old cardinal's hat. The fellows also rode on donkeys, some of them on such small ones that their feet touched the ground and they thus walked astride together with the donkeys. They went up to the little place between the portal of the palace and the hall of audience, where they showed themselves to the Pope, who stood at the window above the portal in the Loggia Paulina. They then made a procession through the whole city. (tr. Geoffrey Parker) ❧

St. Peter's Splits the Church

It's a tad ironic that St. Peter's in Rome—that ultimate monument to Catholic grandeur and awesome ceremony—also helped splinter the monolithic Church into a hundred sects.

The magnificent rebuilding of St. Peter's during the Renaissance, an extremely expensive project overseen by the likes of Michelangelo, Bernini, and Bramante was in main financed through the sale of indulgences, which in turn helped spark the Reformation.

Martin Luther at age fifty by Lucas Cranach.

Martin Luther hammered his ninety-five theses in Wittenberg in 1517 to protest the indulgences peddled by Dominican monk John Tetzel. Luther didn't wake up one morning and say, "Okay, boys, let's start the Reformation." He had a deep heartfelt abhorrence of the sale of indulgences as the signal example of papal greed and sin. "By this way of purchasing pardons," raged Martin Luther, "any notorious highwayman, any plundering soldier, any bribe-taking judge, shall gain exemption for some part of their unjust gains, and think all their grossest impieties atoned for."

His ninety-five theses—mostly focusing on narrow points of theology—were meant as a challenge to debate, a call to rouse Catholic scholars to prove the justness of selling indulgences. Instead of debating the issues, the pope tried in effect to kill the messenger, excommunicating the defiant Luther.

What was Luther protesting against? You could call it a divine protection racket.

The Catholic vision of hell was used for more than a thousand years as a threatening way to force Catholics to pay up, whether it be in cash contributions to the local church or in day-labor penance in building glorious cathedrals.

In fairness, the threat of hell has unquestionably motivated many to genuine good deeds and helped the Catholic Church finance many good works. However, during the Renaissance, the process degenerated into: "When coin in coffer rings, a soul from purgatory springs."

Almost any sin could be pardoned through the purchase of a slip of paper and the sinner would be spared the torments of hell, so graphically displayed on the walls of medieval churches. Why have a spear thrust through your eyeball? Just take a second job and fork over a few extra soldi.

St. Peter's stands glorious, an awe-inspiring building, one might say a *heavenly* building, with the dome of Michelangelo, the bronze canopy of Bernini. However, as devout Catholic Jerrold Packard states of the rebuilding project in *Peter's Kingdom:* "To help meet its costs, income from the sale of indulgences was applied toward financing this most massive and expensive of papal whims and was to portend a major cause for the coming cataclysm in Western Christianity." 🕮

SCIENCE

WRONGLY CREDITED INVENTIONS

Repetition doesn't make it right. Many important inventions are credited to the wrong person, according to the *Dictionary of Misinformation* by Tom Burnam.

ELECTRIC LIGHT

It wasn't Thomas Alva Edison. About half a century before Edison was born, Sir Humphry Davy (1778–1829), who had already discovered the euphoria of inhaling nitrous oxide, produced an arc lamp in 1802, which used an electric current "arcing" between two posts to produce light. Frenchman Jean Foucault (1819–1868) refined the process to light a massive city square, Place de la Concorde in Paris in 1844.

Edison wasn't even first with the carbon filament incandescent light bulb (the electric charge passing through a narrow wire and glowing to give off light). Sir Joseph William Swan demonstrated a carbon filament lamp in Newcastle in 1878, about ten months before Edison made his "discovery."

STEAMBOAT: FULL STEAM BACKWARD

Steamboat Willie, the Disney character, deserves about as much credit as Robert Fulton for *inventing* the steamboat. James Rumsey and John Fitch beat Fulton's launch in 1807 by a good twenty years. "Particularly sad is the case of John Fitch," laments debunker Tom Burnam. "Few have so obviously pioneered and been so obviously overlooked by succeeding generations."

Fitch fine-tuned his boat in 1785 and had it cruising on the Delaware River within a year. By 1790 he was running a steamship line, with a regular schedule, advertisements, etc., hauling freight and passengers between hubs of Philadelphia and Trenton. Fitch even landed exclusive franchises from several states to operate steam-propelled boats.

"But unfortunately he was ahead of his time," concludes Burnam. "He could neither survive financially nor persuade anyone to back him. He died both broke and broken at Badstown, Kentucky, in 1798."

Fulton *invented* his steamboat in 1807, and it wasn't called the *Clermont*, it was called the *North River Steamboat*. Fulton was a canny entrepreneur who cashed in on someone else's breakthrough.

PHOTOGRAPHS: A DAGUERRE IN THE BACK

Louis Jacques Daguerre (1787–1851) of Daguerreotype fame was much in the same mold as Fulton. He really didn't invent the process but he put his stamp on moderate changes and basked as the world credited him with the invention. Joseph Nicéphore Niepce (1765–1833) took the world's first photograph in 1826 in a *"camera obscura."* Niepce used a small darkroom with a hole in one wall; the image was projected onto a pewter plate covered in chemicals mounted on the opposite wall. Eight hours later, an "image" was ready. A couple of famous Parisian opticians, the Chevalier brothers, hooked up Niepce with a showman/doctor named Daguerre.

The rest, as they say, is larceny.

After Niepce died in 1833, Daguerre came out with his improved process using silver-plated copper sheets instead of pewter. "Daguerre had few scruples," observes Guy Breton in *Curieuses histoires de l'histoire,* "and he baptised the invention simply: 'daguerreotypie,' monopolizing thus the glory and the profit of a discovery to which he contributed only the most minimal improvements."

George Eastman truly revolutionized photo taking in 1888 with his box camera and roll film.

AUTOMOBILE: MODEL Z

Not Americans Henry Ford or Charles Duryea. The Germans won the race to invent a car. Karl Benz, in 1885 in Mannheim, took out a patent for the Benz Patent Motor Car and the same year Gottlieb Daimler, working in nearby Cannstatt, patented an auto in Stuttgart. The Duryeas brought out America's first automobile in 1894, a year after Benz was marketing his "Velo," which could hit *twenty-five* miles an hour.

Another innovation should be snatched from Henry Ford: the assembly line in auto factories. Ransom E. Olds, who gave us the Oldsmobile, put in an assembly line in 1902, boosting production fivefold. Olds had wooden platforms on wheels roll between crews of workmen adding parts until the car was complete.

Ford took the concept and put in a brilliant refinement: the conveyor belt. "Ford's method cut the time needed to produce a Model T from a day and a half to ninety-three minutes," says Burnam, who adds: "Nevertheless, his contribution was a modification of another's idea."

TELEPHONE STATIC

In the history of invention, the telephone ranks as one of the most disputed patents. Five cases went all the way to the U.S. Supreme Court. One country inventor, Daniel Drawbaugh from rural Pennsylvania, was asked by a Supreme Court judge to explain how he had discovered electric speech. "I don't remember how I came to it . . ." replied Drawbaugh. "I don't remember getting it by accident either . . . I don't remember anyone telling me of it."

Not all claims were so ridiculous. German Phillip Reis invented a bare-bones telephone fifteen years before Bell squawked his famous "Mr. Watson, come here, I want you." Reis's device could transmit the sound of the human voice and reproduce it at the other end. Unfortunately for him, the prototype failed to work during the Supreme Court session. His flustered attorney blurted out, "It can speak, but it won't." Elisha Gray (1835–1901) of Chicago also patented a form of a telephone before Bell, but he had once admitted in a letter to Bell back in 1877: "I give you full credit for the talking feature of the telephone." And Italian Antonio Meucci patented a "teletrofono" in 1871.

Nonetheless Bell swept them all, winning all five cases. His only loss was an out-of-court settlement early on with Western Union, granting the giant company one fifth of the patent royalties. At the time, Bell was short of funds and couldn't finance a long legal fight.

Edison with a very early phonograph on June 16, 1888. The mythmakers claimed the inventor had been awake for five straight days refining the device. Don't look for a turntable: Edison's design called for a cylinder.

SCIENTIFIC GENIUS! COMMERCIAL DUNCE?

EDISON SITS ON THE PHONOGRAPH

Thomas Alva Edison (1847–1931), perhaps America's greatest inventor, did not see much practical use for a machine that could record and play back sounds. "The disc phonograph will never amount to anything anyway," he groused, when his U.S. patent application was rejected on a technicality. Edison viewed the device as mainly a stenographer's aid to help in writing down tele*phone* messages, hence the name he gave it: *phono*graph.

Note what Edison stressed in his first press release for the device in 1877: "Mr. Edison the Electrician has not only succeeded in producing a perfect articulating telephone, far superior and much more ingenious than the telephone of Bell but has gone into a new and entirely unexplored field of acoustics which is nothing less than an attempt to record automatically the speech of a very rapid speaker upon paper from which he reproduces the same speech immediately or years afterward."

Swift came the response from the experts. A Yale professor reading a description in the *New York Sun* called the writer a "common penny a liner in the incipient stages of delirium tremens. The idea of a talking machine is ridiculous."

One Senator Beck, after trying a bit of Robert Burns on the machine, was convinced that Edison must be a clever ventriloquist and asked the inventor to please leave the room for the next demo.

The one story people usually know about the invention of the phonograph is that Edison's first words into it were: "Mary had a little lamb, its fleece was white as snow." While it's true that Edison used the nursery rhyme for one of his earliest tests, he and the other naughty boys in the lab started mad-libbing the lines. One variation we know about: "Mary has a new sheath gown, It is too tight by half/Who cares a damn for Mary's lamb, When they can see her calf!"

Edison could never quite figure out the practical use for the device. At one point he suggested putting a giant phonograph in the mouth of the statue of the "Goddess of Liberty," soon to be erected in New York Harbor.

He steadfastly linked its use to the telephone. Since he expected the telephone to wind up *not in every home* but rather in city message stations, he thought his "phonograph" could help the clerks log the thousands of messages, without having to scribble them all down right away.

Despite incorporating a phonograph company in 1879, Edison let the device languish, and in 1885, he even failed to renew his British patents on it. Other companies started muscling in and it wasn't until 1895 that Edison finally tried to market a home phonograph player for twenty dollars. The venture failed; people at the time still preferred dropping a nickel in a "juke box"–type device out in public with friends.

EDISON FAVORS THE PEEP SHOWS OVER MOTION PICTURES

Edison succeeded in projecting moving pictures onto a screen with synchronized sound as early as 1888, but mothballed the device for almost a decade, figuring individual peep show machines would find a greater commercial market. That's according to *A Million and One Nights*, the definitive history of early motion pictures by Terry Ramsaye.

The Edison peep show device was called the kinetograph and within a couple years gave birth to the nickelodeon, the five-cent-a-peep machine set up in parlors in cities nationwide. Movies were at first limited to the fifty-foot strips of celluloid then available. Edison in 1891 took out a U.S. patent on his kinetograph and his lawyer asked if he wanted to file in England and France as well. "How much will it cost?" Edison asked. "Oh, about $150." Edison decided to pass. "It isn't worth it."

That mistake would open the door to hundreds of competitors building movie devices. Edison also didn't file any patent at the time for any device that could project images onto a screen.

On April 23, 1896, the first American public display of a *projected* motion picture took place at Koster & Bials Music Hall in Herald Square, New York City.

NAKED BASEBALL AND THE BIRTH OF MOTION PICTURES

Batter up.

When Thomas Edison was first struggling to record and project action in the late 1880s, he purchased a series of ninety sequential-action photo plates from an eccentric English photographer. These photos showing movement were part of scientific research conducted under the auspices of the University of Pennsylvania. So it's a bit surprising to learn that many of the images featured *completely nude men and women* playing baseball, climbing ladders, having tea parties, drop-kicking a hat.

Both the images and the photographer, Eadweard Muybridge, played a strange but key role in the technical development of the movies.

It all started with a bet.

Leland Stanford (1824–1893), railroad magnate and ex-governor of California, stood on his sprawling horse farm in Palo Alto in 1872 and bet a rich friend the hefty sum of $25,000 that at full gallop, all four horse's hooves leave the ground. This proposition contradicted five thousand years of art.

Now Stanford, whose namesake university would one day stand on that very property, needed to prove his point. He hired respected (though eccentric) English photographer, Eadweard Muybridge (1830–1904), who had won some acclaim for photographing Alaska for the U.S. government.

Muybridge was a piece of work—outlandishly scruffy in appearance, midforties, flowing beard, and flaming eyes, a showman with a beautiful twenty-two-year-old blond, blue-eyed wife. He had cleverly transformed his name from Edward Muggeridge to Eadweard Muybridge.

Now, Muybridge tried hard to rig all kinds of trip-action devices, but given the slow speed of the "wet plate" photography

The All-American pastime. In the 1880s, Eadweard Muybridge took thousands of sequential-action photos, while studying human and animal motion. The University of Pennsylvania funded the research, which was strictly clothing-optional, and Thomas Edison later bought a set.

of that era, he produced more blurs than bet winners.

Then his research, despite the enthusiasm and bank account of Stanford, came to an abrupt halt.

Muybridge shot his wife's lover in the heart.

A midwife had come to Muybridge's darkroom in San Francisco demanding a hundred dollars in payment for helping with the recent birth of Muybridge's son. When Muybridge balked at paying, the woman, perhaps in an attempt to blackmail him, blurted out that Colonel Harry Larkyns was the real father; she even produced a baby photo with the name "Harry" scrawled on the back in Muybridge's wife's hand.

Muybridge plucked his revolver and sailed to the Calistoga baths to seek the Colonel, a dashing English-Irish adventurer type. Muybridge tracked him down near midnight. When Larkyns came to the door, the photographer called out: "My name is Muybridge—here is a message from my wife." The bullet entered the man's heart and Larkyns was dead in half a minute.

The trial in Napa County courthouse in 1875 was going badly for Muybridge, who had confessed but was pleading "temporary insanity." He could actually point to a bump on his head he had received years earlier in a brutal stage coach accident in England. His Kentucky lawyer, W. W. Pendergast, spoke of adultery and the unwritten law of reprisal. Then he looked into the eyes of the jury. "I cannot ask you to send this man forth to family and home—he has none. Across the arch of his place where once were written the words Home—Wife—Child Content and Peace, there now appears as a substitute for all, the black letters, placed there by the destroyer, the single awful word DESOLATION. But I do ask you to send him forth free—let him take up the thread of his broken life and resume that profession on which his genius has shed so much lustre, the profession which is his only true love."

After a tense night, the jury acquitted him.

Muybridge resumed his quest for four flying hooves. With photo equipment improved during the several-year lapse, Muybridge came closer to the prize, but it took Governor Stanford hiring a brilliant young railroad engineer named John D. Isaacs to invent an electric trip-wire device that would sequentially set off two dozen cameras.

Stanford, who had spent about $40,000, now had his proof in several series of photos, and presumably collected his $25,000 winnings.

The former governor, soon to be U.S. senator in 1885, delighted in globe-trotting and showing off these unique stop-action photos. In 1880, he took them to Paris. The following year, Muybridge, now hailed as a world-class scientific genius, also took them to Paris. He was feted at a gathering that included the likes of Alexander Dumas and top painters such as Jean-Léon Gérôme.

An artist-scientist named Jean Louis Meissonier exhibited the Muybridge pictures via a revolving photo projection device, called a praxinoscope.

Now, according to film historian Terry Ramsaye, Muybridge was a talented photographer who could aim a camera and print pictures. He didn't develop the tripwire device for shooting the pictures; he didn't invent the projector for displaying them. No fool, however; he took credit for it all, dubbed *his* projection device, a zoogyroscope or zoopraxinoscope. The polysyllables were very impressive.

Just before Christmas 1887, about six years later, one W. P. Garrison of the culture-loving New England Society, asked Edison for permission to run a lecture series at Edison's new state-of-the-art West Orange laboratory. On February 25, the eccentric charismatic, much-feted Muybridge showed up with his series of sequential-action plates.

He did his polysyllabic presentation, including a sort of fast slide show of the photos on a zoopraxinoscope. Some credit these displays as the birth of motion pictures. Some credit this particular display with inspiring Edison to invent motion pictures. Some think the Lumière brothers of France, projecting in 1895, deserve all the credit. And others . . .

Let's skip the "me first" controversy. What's incontrovertible is that Edison bought a set of ninety plates from Muybridge for a dollar each and each contained a stop-action series of about three dozen pictures.

(Muybridge had had a falling out with Stanford over credit, but had fortunately hooked up with the University of Pennsylvania, where he'd been stop-action photographing since 1883.)

As the fine Edison bio, *Streak of Luck* by Robert Conot, puts it:

Muybridge titled them "Animal Locomotion," and there were remarkable and Disneyesque pictures of trotting and jumping horses, deer, kangaroo, camels, jaguars, and eagles in flight. But, very much aware that art was a great deal more marketable when spiced, Muybridge concentrated on animals that were human, and as naked as their counterparts in nature. Of the 733 plates he offered, 219 were of animals and birds; 211 of men, of whom 205 were mostly or entirely unclothed; and 303 of women, of whom 243 were totally or transparently nude. They included a naked baseball player and a naked cricketer taking batting practice; naked boxers and jujitsu combatants; naked fencers; a naked tumbler; a diaphanous-gowned fan dancer; innumerable bare, buxom women performing a variety of tasks; two nudes frolicking in their Saturday night bath; and a mostly unclad mother receiving a bouquet of flowers from her naked daughter. These pictures were, of course, not displayable in mixed company, but they made great conversation pieces for men of wealth in their smoking rooms, and subscribers included Cornelius Vanderbilt, J. P. Morgan, Augustus Belmont, and Anthony Drexel.

Edison and assistant W. K. L. Dickson took those ninety series of photos and tried to reproduce some of them in pinhead-size ($1/32$ of an inch) images on a spiral winding around a cylinder. This technique was similar to Edison's approach at the time to the phonograph.

It would take Edison and Dickson several years and the help of celluloid strips from George Eastman to perfect the kinetoscope peep show device. Their research was kept quite hush-hush, even from the rest of the staff. "It was the beginning of a profound secrecy about the motion picture which continued for many and many years after there were no secrets to be kept," observes Terry Ramsaye in his definitive *A Million and One Nights*. One wonders if part of the reason for constantly shutting the door was that Edison and Laurie were still using copies of Muybridge's nudes.

Eadweard Muybridge spent a decade at U Penn, photographing his nudes and doing lecture series. By the turn of the century, some devotees deemed him the father of motion pictures. He eventually retired and spent his last years comfortably in England.

While his technological contributions to early motion picture history are debatable if not negligible, Muybridge certainly added spice a decade before the Lumière brothers unveiled their Cinematographe projector in 1895. The Frenchmen publicly debuted with one Mrs. Lumière spoon-feeding her baby daughter, a far cry from naked baseball. ☙

SECRET LIVES OF THE SCIENTISTS

TAKING A BITE OUT OF NEWTON'S APPLE

Isaac Newton sat in the summer heat in 1666; the twenty-four-year-old pondered; he scratched his nose. An apple konked him on the noggin and he discovered gravity.

That story makes it into almost every textbook.

Voltaire, one of the world's wittier and more mischievous men, spread the tale in his brief bio of Newton. The philosopher said he heard it from Newton's niece, Catherine Barton Conduitt, who lived with Newton for twenty years.

However, Sir Isaac never once recorded the story in his voluminous published works or letters.

And Newton never mentioned the falling pomme to two learned men who interviewed him extensively on the development of his gravity theory.

One German astronomer, Karl Friedrich Gauss, gave perhaps the best explanation of where the apple story came from.

Sir Isaac Newton (1642–1727)

Wrote Gauss: "The history of the apple is too absurd. Whether the apple fell or not, how can anyone believe that such a discovery could in that way be accelerated or retarded? Undoubtedly, the occurrence was something of this sort. There comes to Newton a stupid importunate man who asks him how he hit upon his great discovery. When Newton had convinced himself what a noodle he had to do with and wanted to get rid of the man, he told him that an apple fell on his nose; this made the matter quite clear to the man, and he went away satisfied."

Splinters from that apple tree have been sold as "holy relics" in England.

THE REST OF NEWTON'S LIFE

The plague struck in 1664, soon closing Cambridge University for eighteen months. Twenty-two-year-old Isaac Newton—instead of trying to tan that pale body or play tennis—used the forced recess to make some of the most startling scientific discoveries in the history of the human race: the law of gravity, laws of motion, the binomial theorem and method of fluxions (roots of calculus), and spectrum theory in optics (that would lead to the reflecting telescope).

But what did Newton (1642–1727) do with the rest of his long life? He lived to be eighty-five. Certainly, he pursued further work on some of the above, but his two major preoccupations for half a century were alchemy and theology. (Minor interests were checking prophecies and determining the chronology of the long lost kingdoms.)

Isaac Newton wrote more than one million words on religion—almost all unpublished and never intended for publication,

according to *The Religion of Isaac Newton* by Frank Manuel.

"For two hundred years thereafter most of the manuscripts were suppressed, bowdlerized, neglected or sequestered, lest what were believed to be shady lucubrations tarnish the image of the perfect scientific genius," observes Manuel. ("Lucubrations" are overwrought studies).

Newton wrote such page-turners as *Paradoxical Questions Concerning the Morals and Actions of Athanasius and his Followers, A Treatise on Revelation,* commentaries on Latin translations of the Talmud, investigations into the apocalypse, and much more.

In a word, Newton's obsessive religious investigations and fractious Bible study have proved disturbing to biographers and fellow scientists wanting to celebrate the man's remarkable scientific achievements.

As Robert Frost remarked, well-rounded figures roll, and Newton was anything but, being rather a mass of spiky extremes.

Here's a taste of Newton's more accessible religious thoughts from a fragment, *Of the Faith which was Once Delivered to the Saints:*

"If God be called . . . the omnipotent, they take it in a metaphysical sense for God's power of creating all things out of nothing whereas it is meant principally of his universal irresistible monarchical power to teach us obedience."

There is absolutely no way to summarize Newton's million words on religion, to boil them down to some pithy phrase on the relation of science and religion, of reason and faith. Most of his biographers have ignored the challenge, and a glance at some of the text makes it a pardonable offense.

For instance, published after his death was *Observations upon the Prophecies of Daniel and the Apocalypse of St. John*. In it, Sir Isaac—who was raised an Anglican—put his awesome mathematical powers to work to compute when the Church of Rome would become the eleventh horn of the fourth beast in prophet Daniel's vision. Newton's tally came to 1,260 solar years and he therefore predicted the Catholic Church's downfall between the years 2035 and 2054. Being a seasoned scientist, he left a margin of error.

ALCHEMY

Although alchemy is now considered greed-driven quackery, in the midseventeenth century, it was still a fairly respected branch of study. Among Newton's unpublished writings, scholars have found more than 650,000 words on alchemy. "Its evident appeal to generation after generation of adepts is inaccessible to the modern critical intellect," observes Betty Jo Teeter Dobbs in *The Foundations of Newton's Alchemy*. Here, here.

Newton's notes are packed with the confusing symbols alchemists employed in their research.

Here are some experiment notes: "Its fumes strangely open & volatize minerall bodys as of Antimony in making it Butter, and *[45 degree forward upward angle arrow]*

grosly beaten Venetian Sublimate opens *[45 degreee backward downward arrow]* Copper cemented with it so as to . . ."

Some scholars have speculated that Newton's alchemy experiments might have caused him to suffer from long-term lead and mercury poisoning. Newton's life is packed with surprises for the modern reader—perhaps the most surprising of all is that he died a virgin, and proud of it. ❧

KEPLER PREDICTS COLD WEATHER AND LOTS OF TURKS

Johann Kepler (1571–1630), one of the greatest astronomers ever to live, made more money doing horoscopes than he did from his research. Although he had misgivings about *charlatans* performing astrology, he ultimately justified his own work: "It still remains that people are distinguished from one another more by heavenly bodies than by institutions and habit." And he stated that the alignments of the planets at birth stamped a person's character for life, and he "boasted" that he could discern future behavior and opportunities from checking planetary positions.

One of Kepler's first career breaks came when his "astrological calendar" for 1595 predicted extreme cold and a Turkish invasion. He was right on both scores. (Some peasants, it was recorded, blew their frozen noses right off their faces; and no one could deny the onslaught of the Turks.)

The Holy Roman Emperor Rudolph

II—who appointed Kepler "Imperial Mathematician"—gave Kepler plenty of astrology homework; Rudolph wanted to know about the planetary alignment at the birth of Augustus Caesar and Muhammad; he wanted a critique on astrological predictions about a battle raging between Venice and Pope Paul V; he wanted to know the meaning of the New Star of 1604 that sparked "Day of Judgment" predictions.

One of Kepler's horoscopes begins: "I might truthfully describe this man as one who is alert, quick, industrious, of restless disposition, with a passionate . . ."

Astrology was taken very seriously at the time. (Nancy Reagan would have been deeply respected for turning to Joan Quigley.) Many university-trained doctors turned to astrology to know when and how much to bleed a patient, or when to schedule an operation. A patient's astrological sign (denoting fieriness or earthiness) might also dictate the proper treatment.

Kepler, for his part, tried to downplay the telling the future side of his job. Nonetheless, having grown accustomed to daily meals, Kepler filled volumes with his "calendars," horoscopes, special astrostudies, and yes, even predictions. He also found time to discover his three planetary laws that paved the way for Newton and gravity. For those of you who snoozed that afternoon, those laws are: the elliptical path of the planets, increased orbital speed closer to the sun, and the relation between orbital duration and distance from the sun. 🜨

FRANCE CUTS OFF ITS MOST BRILLIANT HEAD, 1794

Antoine Lavoisier (1743–1794), often called the "father of modern chemistry," used precise laboratory methods to identify and name hydrogen and oxygen. His research helped debunk the reigning phlogiston nonsense and his *Elementary Treatise on Chemistry* (1789) paved the way for chemical research. In May 1794, Lavoisier inserted his head through the window of Dame Guillotine, the heavy slanted blade descended, the crowd roared . . . But why did the Republic execute its leading scientist?

Lavoisier, an aristocrat, had invested his inheritance in buying a share in tax farming, a business that had nothing to do with raising crops. These rich entrepreneurs harvested taxes, collecting royal duties from the people on numerous goods including tobacco and salt in exchange for a percentage. (Imagine a privatized IRS run by a clique of wealthy Americans.) They literally carved the country up into districts and had a standing army of 20,000 often brutal men, who, upon the merest suspicion, had the

Aristocratic tax-collector Antoine Lavoisier (1743–1794) with his wife. (Painted by Jacques-Louis David.)

legal right to pole-ax doors and search homes.

Lavoisier, truth be told, *did* apply his considerable genius to various tax-farm problems, and even helped design and build an enormous wall around parts of Paris to thwart smugglers. On the flip side, Lavoisier used his profits from tax collecting to finance his chemistry experiments.

Of all the villains hated by the French working class, these tax farmers, especially the so-called Farmers-General, probably topped the list since they set prices for all kinds of daily food items.

It was at one of the more crowded public executions that Antoine Lavoisier—along with fellow tax farmers—was guillotined. Their remains, including Lavoisier's body and head, were tossed in unmarked mass graves in the cemetery of Parc Monceaux.

Nobel Prize Adultery: Madame Curie

When Madame Curie (1867–1934) was accused of adultery in 1911, her good friend Albert Einstein rose to her defense: "She is not attractive enough to become dangerous for anyone," he declared. Thank you, Albert.

The Nobel Prize committee reacted a bit differently. One committee member begged her *not* to come to Stockholm to accept her upcoming unprecedented *second* Nobel Prize, advising her to stay in Paris and clear her name. Madame Curie refused. "The prize has been awarded for the discovery of radium and polonium," she wrote back. "I believe there is no connection between my scientific work and the facts of my private life." How charmingly naive.

This scandal has largely been forgotten in the glare of Madame Curie's halo, her enshrinement on everyone's short list as one of the world's most brilliant, most accomplished women.

She belongs on that list, and part of the reason is how she reacted to that scandal. She could have let the Nobel committee bully her into not accepting her award; she could have given up research. She could have moved back in with her family in Poland. While she sat in her apartment that November 1911, pondering these decisions, she could hear French crowds outside chanting: "*A bas l'étrangère, la voleuse de maris!*" "Down with the foreigner, the thief of husbands!"

Manya Sklodowska, native of Poland, married her teacher, Pierre Curie, and the two of them, in perhaps the most successful marital collaboration in history, did pioneer research in discovering radioactive elements, key breakthroughs in the route to atomic energy. While Pierre focused more on the theoretical, Marie spent years shoveling and stirring *tons* of pitchblende in a

Long before she become world famous Madame Curie, Manya Sklodowska was a governess.

warehouse-like lab to isolate a precious decagram of radium. *Her* chemical experiments would prove *their* theoretical physics.

The genuinely enamored couple had no idea of the dangers of radioactivity. In fact, they sent samples by mail to a handful of choice friends around the world. A scientist in Iceland commented on how nicely it glowed. Pierre even tried wrapping a barium-laced bandage around his arm for ten hours and then carefully observing the fifty-two-day healing period that followed.

The Curies were rewarded with a joint Nobel Prize for Physics in 1903, the first time a woman had ever received the then fledgling prize. The popular press fussed over her, and the Women's Movement not surprisingly embraced her as a hero.

The Curies's collaboration, and their happy marriage was suddenly cut short when absentminded Pierre stepped off the curb and was run over by a horse-drawn wagon in 1906, his skull crushed by a wheel of the six-ton vehicle hauling military uniforms.

Devastated, Marie immersed herself in work, and that work would lead to her being selected in 1911 to become the first *person*—male or female—ever to win a second Nobel Prize.

In France, at the time, successful men could take mistresses so long as they appeared in polite society with their wives. That was acceptable, but Marie Curie, a successful forty-three-year-old widow, taking up with thirty-eight-year-old Paul Langevin, a dapper, married, father of four, was apparently not.

The story broke in purple prose on November 4 in *Le Journal.* "The fire of radium lit a flame in the heart of a scientist and the scientist's wife and children are now in tears."

Madame Curie's married lover, scientist Paul Langevin.

Langevin's wife, who had been suspicious for a while, had somehow gotten a hold of the couple's love letters. Perhaps her fury was a bit aroused when she read that Madame Curie had written Paul to make sure to avoid getting his wife pregnant, since another baby would dishonor Marie in the eyes of their friends who knew about their affair. Her love letters, which sparkle with desire, reveal that she had hopes they could one day live together openly.

Langevin's wife, Jeanne, sued for divorce and leaked documents to the media, but before the trial, scheduled for early December, both sides agreed to a settlement.

The French press for the most part hammered Madame Curie, whipping up some xenophobia about Polish émigrés breaking up French homes; the French Academy of Sciences, legendary for pigheaded snobbery, acted true to form and voted not to elect her. But she defied the Nobel Prize committee, which had already selected her, and despite being ill, traveled to Stockholm to accept her award.

A bit anti-social at age fifty-five, Madame Curie was photographed as she arrived in New York in 1922.

However, she devoted the last two decades of her life exclusively to research, and colleagues say that Madame Curie, by nature intense and taciturn, often became downright dour and dictatorial. She only acted more warmly with her family and a very tight circle of friends.

Paul Langevin eventually reconciled with his wife, Jeanne, who later gave her blessing to Paul's keeping a mistress, this time an acceptable one, a secretary. 🐦

SILLINESS OF PRIZES

Ben Franklin's Fart Experiment

Benjamin Franklin (1706–1790), American extraordinaire, helped start America's first public library, fire brigade, police force; he invented the lightning rod, bifocals, a new stove. During his decade-plus as ambassador to France, he was hailed there as one of the world's preeminent geniuses. Yet, somehow, the Academy of Science in Brussels dared to criticize some of his work.

Franklin was annoyed and dashed off a response. He never sent it; the genius was venting by cooking up a mock contest for the Academy to run. For about 150 years after Franklin's death, the text of this letter was available only to scholars who chose to suppress it. Here it is:

To the Royal Academy of Brussels

Gentlemen:

I have perused your late mathematical Prize Question, proposed in lieu of one in natural Philosophy for the ensuing Year . . . I was glad to find . . . that you esteem *Utility* an essential point in your Enquiries, which has not always been the case with all Academies . . .

Permit me then humbly to propose one of that sort for your Consideration, and thro' you, if you approve it, for the serious Enquiry of learned Physicians, Chemists, etc., of this enlightened Age.

It is universally well-known, that in digesting our common food, there is created in or produced in the Bowels of human Creatures a great quantity of Wind.

That the permitting this Air to escape and mix with Atmosphere, is usually offensive to the Company, from the fetid smell that accompanyes it.

That all well bred People therefore, to avoid giving such offense, forcibly

Scientific fart research. This lampoon, which even identifies the locale as a "Royal Institution," seems to capture Franklin's odoriferous drift.

restrain the Efforts of Nature to discharge that Wind.

That so retained contrary to Nature, it not only gives frequently great present pain, but occasions future Diseases such as habitual Cholics, Ruptures, Tympanies, &c., often destructive of the Constitution, and sometimes of Life itself.

Were it not for the odiously offensive smell accompanying such escapes, polite People would probably be under no more Restraint in discharging such Wind in Company than they are in spitting or blowing their Noses.

My Prize Question therefore should be: To discover some Drug, wholesome and not disagreeable, to be mixed with our common food, or sauces, that shall render the natural discharges of Wind from our Bodies not only inoffensive, but agreeable as Perfumes.

That this is not a Chimerical Project & altogether impossible, may appear from these considerations. That we already have some knowledge of means capable of *varying* that smell. He that dines on stale Flesh, especially with much Addition of Onions, shall be able to afford a Stink that no Company can tolerate; while he that has lived for some time on Vegetables only, shall have that Breath so pure as to be insensible to the most delicate Noses; and if he can manage so as to avoid the Report, he may anywhere give vent to his Griefs, un-noticed. But as there are many to whom an entire Vegetable Diet would be inconvenient, & as a little quick Lime thrown into a Jakes will correct the amazing Quantity of fetid Air arising from the vast Mass of putrid Matter contained in such Places, and render it rather pleasing to the Smell, who knows but that a little Powder of Lime (or some other thing equivalent) taken in our Food, or perhaps a Glass of Lime Water drank at Dinner, may have the same Effect on the Air produced in and issuing from our Bowels? This is worth the experiment. Certain it is also that we have the Power of changing by slight means the Smell of another Discharge, that of our Water. A few stems of Asparagus eaten, shall give our Urine a disagreeable Odour; and a Pill of Turpentine no bigger than a Pea, shall bestow on it the pleasing smell of Violets. And why should it be thought more impossible in Nature, to find means of making a Perfume of our *Wind* than of our *Water?*

For the encouragement of this Enquiry (from the immortal Honour to be reasonably expected by the Inventor) let it be considered of how small importance to Mankind, or how small a Part of Mankind have been useful those Discoveries in Science that have heretofore made Philosophers famous. Are there twenty men in Europe this day the happier, or even the easier for any knowledge they have pick'd out of Aristotle? What Comfort can the Vortices of Descartes give to a man who has Whirlwinds in his Bowels! The knowledge of Newton's mutual *Attraction* of the particles of matter, can it afford ease to him who is racked by their mutual *Repulsion,* and the cruel distentions it occasions? The Pleasure arising to a few Philosophers, from seeing, a few times in their lives, the threads of light untwisted, and separated by the Newtonian Prism into seven colours, can it be compared with the ease and comfort every man living might feel seven times a day, by discharging freely the wind from Bowels? Especially, if it be converted into a Perfume; for the pleasures of one Sense being little inferior to those of another, instead of pleasing the *Sight,* he might delight the *Smell* of those about him, and make numbers happy, which to a benevolent mind must afford infinite satisfaction. The generous Soul, who now endeavours to find out whether the friends he entertains like best Claret or Burgundy, Champagne or Madeira, would then enquire also whether they chose Musk or Lilly, Rose or Bergamot, and provide accordingly. And surely such a Liberty of *expressing one's scent-iments, & pleasing one another,* is of infinitely more importance to human happiness than that Liberty of the *Press,* or of *abusing one another,* which the English are so ready to fight & die for.

In short, this Invention, if completed, would be, as *Bacon* expresses it, *Bringing Philosophy home to Men's Business and Bosoms.* And I cannot but conclude, that in comparison therewith for *universal* and *continual Utility*, the Science of the Philosophers abovementioned, even with the addition, Gentlemen, of your [mathematical prize], are, all together, scarcely worth a

Fart-hing

THE NOBEL DYNAMITE BLASTING CAP AWARD FOR PEACE

What about the Exxon award for environmental safety? Or the Adolph Hitler award for ethnic tolerance? Or the John F. Kennedy award for marital fidelity? They have a certain irony, if not outright hypocrisy.

It is the same with the Nobel Peace Prize, only most of us have forgotten who Alfred Nobel was.

On April 13, 1888, the Swedish engineer woke up in Paris and read his obituary. The French newspaper had accidentally run an obit for him when actually it was his brother *Ludwig* who had died.

Alfred was shocked to see himself portrayed as the Merchant of Death, the man responsible for escalating the arms race. Nobel had invented dynamite, blasting caps, smokeless gunpowder, and blasting gelatin; he had made high-powered explosives much easier and safer to use and he was quite proud of how this power had been unleashed to mine precious minerals and to build roads, railways, and canals. "Despite nine centuries of gunpowder," states Donovan Webster in *Aftermath: The Landscape of War*, "weaponry had not really

Alfred Nobel in the 1890s, near the end of his life.

changed until Nobel's discoveries boosted the bloody art of war from bullets and bayonets to long-range high explosives in less than twenty-four years, forever altering the way armies killed one another."

Nobel (1833–1896) was horrified to see himself portrayed as some kind of bellicose monster. He came up with a shrewd spin control plan for the family name. With his vast wealth and 350 patents, he decided he would create prizes to be awarded in physics, chemistry, medicine, literature, and peace. In a world now overrun with awards (mostly commercial self-promotion disguised as meritocracy), the Nobel Prizes have evolved into perhaps the planet's most prestigious prizes.

Past winners in various categories have included Einstein, Sartre, Schweitzer, Faulkner, Martin Luther King, and darkly humorous picks like Henry Kissinger.

Of the billions of people who have heard of the Nobel Prizes, very few nowadays ever think of long-range artillery shells or of the estimated 100 million deaths by war in the century since Alfred Nobel first helped revolutionize the art of killing.

REJECTEES WIN NOBEL PRIZE

The world-respected scientific journal *Nature*, taking advice from its panel of experts, chose to refuse to publish Enrico Fermi's research on beta-decay, H. C. Urey's work on heavy hydrogen, and Hans Krebs's work on the citric acid cycle. All three went on to win Nobel Prizes. The same happened to Rosalyn Yallow at *Science*, where her future Nobel Prize work on radioimmunoassay was tossed in the circular file. Her process is now used in almost every hospital lab. ❧

Darwin see, Darwin do. This cartoon of the famed naturalist with the receded hairline appeared in 1874 a few years after his *Descent of Man*.

DARWIN: NO RUSH TO PUBLISH

Imagine working on a research project for eighteen years, finally being on the verge of collecting your material to publish it and you receive an envelope from someone you barely know living in the Malay Archipelago. Inside is an article outlining that very theory you've been hatching for almost two decades.

That's what happened to Charles Darwin (1809–1882).

He received in June 1858 a copy of a paper that twenty-four-year-old Alfred Russel Wallace had written, entitled *On the Tendency of Varieties to Depart Indefinitely from the Original Type*.

Darwin reacted like the perfect Victorian gentleman.

He had Wallace killed by blow dart.

No, just joshing. After much agonizing, he was convinced by his inner circle of fellow scientists that he should give a reading from his own work in progress on July 1, 1858, at London's Linnaean Society, the same night that Wallace's paper would be read there.

(One geologist wondered whether Darwin would have *ever* gone public with his research without the hemi-circum-globular prick from Wallace.)

While some contrarians delight in giving Wallace equal credit, the younger man never made that claim for himself, and Darwin, for his part, had several times shown his far more extensive research to colleagues over the preceding decade, including a detailed letter the year before to American botanist Asa Gray.

And Darwin never claimed to have completely originated the theory of "survival of the fittest." In fact, that very phrase he openly borrowed from Herbert Spencer and the heart of Darwin's work represented synthesizing the piecemeal efforts of Aristotle, George Buffon, Jean Lamarck, William Wells, Patrick Matthew, and others. Theories like that don't spring whole from a burning bush.

Finally, Bible thumpers like to hammer Darwin for his blasphemous *Origin of Species* (1861) in which he supposedly traces man's family tree back to the monkey. They're a bit confused. Darwin expounded on that idea in his decade-later *Descent of Man* (1871), and what he said was that man and ape and other mammals *shared* a common ancestor. ❧

SEX

CAST A GIANT SHADOW: PENIS SIZE

One of the best-known lines from one of the world's most famous poets has been routinely misinterpreted. Sappho wrote a wedding song that opens: "Raise high the roofbeam, carpenters, here comes the bridegroom." This song was meant to be sung by the wedding party as they guided the newlyweds to the bridal chamber. The poetess from Lesbos is playfully suggesting the eager groom will become so aroused that his manly tool is going to hit the ceiling.

The ancient Greeks and Romans were very comfortable in joking about oversize organs. In Greece and Rome, in the days before Christianity, you couldn't spend a day walking the streets of a city without seeing a giant penis depicted somewhere. In Greece, clay pots used every day boasted satyrs with oversize organs; many cities had annual parades toting around giant phalluses; in ancient Rome, there were wise-guy herm statues in gardens with giant erect organs to ward off thieves; in Pompeii, a penis in bas-relief was carved on the outside of many houses as a good luck charm. In the baths and gymnasia throughout the ancient world, naked men were everywhere, and many poems have survived showing that the well-endowed liked to strut: One mentions a fellow whose tool casts a giant shadow like a lance; another mentions that when you hear clapping in the baths, you know some fellow with a giant organ has arrived. The Greeks and Romans, so accustomed to nudity, displayed an amused preoccupation with giant penises. Christianity, however, brought a change to all that as the erect or

The duel. A Japanese woodcut.

oversize organ became a symbol of sin or the devil himself. "The devil, whether he assumes the form of a man or a goat, always has the member of a mule," wrote theologian Pierre de l'Ancre in 1612. "The member of the devil is about half a yard long, of medium thickness, red, dark, crooked, very rough and almost pointy."

It was also around the time of the Renaissance that the belief spread in Europe that Africans as a race boasted the world's largest penises. Some of the earliest maps by the Portuguese in the 15th century depicting the newly discovered coastline of Africa featured clip art of well-endowed Negro kings. And the first anthropologists tended to echo that view.

"It is generally said that the penis of the Negro is very large," wrote German anthropologist Johann Friedrich Blumenbach in 1795. "And this assertion is so far borne out by the remarkable genitory apparatus of an Ethiopian which I have in my anatomical collection."

Famed Orientalist Sir Richard Burton chimed in during the following century. "I measured one man in Somali-land, who, when quiescent, numbered six inches." And a 19th-century French army doctor, who wrote under the pseudonym of Dr. Jacobus X., delighted in describing giant organs he discovered. "I often came across a penis of $9^3/4$ to 10 inches, by $2^1/4$ inches [in diameter], and once, in a young Bambara [in Mali], barely twenty years of age, found a monstrous organ $11^3/4$ inches long by $2^3/5$ inches in diameter at the circumcision mark . . . This was a terrific machine, and except for a slight difference in

At the Temple of Luxor, the god Amon-Ra punctuates a wall of hieroglyphics.

length, was more like the penis of a donkey than that of a man. This unfortunate Sharpshooter [i.e., a soldier] who possessed this "spike" could not find a Negress large enough to receive him with pleasure and he was the object of terror to all the feminine sex."

While organ oversize hasn't exactly been a major focus of clinical study, the topic does pop up in a surprising number of forgotten love manuals dating back to the 1500s. Dr. Nicolas Venette, whose *Tableau de l'amour conjugale* went into a dozen editions in the late 1600s, even cites a remedy for the overendowed husband. He prescribes a *"bourlet,"* which is a donut-shape piece of cork covered in padded silk to be slipped over the husband's penis before intercourse. (He adds the concerned wife might want to carry one around in case her husband forgets it at home.)

Not surprisingly, this attention to size has led some men to seek penile enhancement, which dates way back beyond today's ads for surgical procedures promising two additional inches. Various inflammatory lotions are described as "aphrodisiacs" in medieval medical books both to increase size and maintain erections. One Dr. William Earl of New York City advertised an enlarger in 1848 that apparently consisted of a "congester" ring and a *manure*-based cream. Dr. Jacobus X. found natives in 19th-century Guyana inserting their penises into an eggplant loaded with a paste made from ingredients such as pimentos, peppercorns, and cloves.

All of this preoccupation with organ size leads one to recall the wise words of the Roman satirist, Juvenal: "If you've run out of luck, it doesn't matter how long your penis is."

THE BIG PENIS IN PRINT

The Chinese pillow books fill pages with descriptions of the gargantuan man terrifying the little woman, waggling his organ like a weapon. In *The Golden Lotus*, Moonbeam is afraid of the hero, Hsi-Men. "This is the first time we are together, you ought to be merciful and put only half of it in," she pleads. "If you put all of it in, you'll kill me."

The English language's most famous erotic novel, *Memoirs of a Woman of Plea-*

sure, i.e., Fanny Hill, seems to punctuate every major scene with an organ exclamation point. Says Fanny: "I saw with wonder and surprise, what? not the plaything of a boy, not the weapon of a man, but a maypole of so enormous a standard that, had proportions been observed, it must have belonged to a young giant."

And De Sade, not surprisingly, delights in tormenting his victims with similar weapons. "Oh heavens!" says the girl. "Yours is thicker than Dolmance's . . . Chevalier, you are tearing me apart! Go softly, I beg of you!" And the chevalier replies, "Impossible, my angel!"

Page after page of this battering gets tedious—especially without that ancient Greek or Roman sense of humor. Much of it also seems deeply misogynistic, rather than erotic.

As an antidote to the clichéd hammering of the porn novels, here is an authentic, fairly restrained scene from that suppressed Victorian classic, *My Secret Life*. First published in a very limited edition in 1888, these are purported to be the sexual memoirs of an anonymous Victorian gentleman. (Most scenes in the twelve volumes have a diarylike ring of authenticity.)

The writer, Walter, has paid a prostitute named Sarah to guide an especially well-endowed client into a room equipped with a spying hole. Walter can see and hear them through a hole pierced in a murky second-rate painting on the wall.

Sarah undressed to her chemise.—His back was towards me, his hand was evidently on his prick.—"ain't you going to take *your* clothes off, you had better—you can do it nicer."—He evidently had not intended that, but yielded to her suggestion. When in his shirt he went up to her, she gradually turned round so that *her* back and *his* face were towards me, and her movement was so natural that no one could have guessed her object, altho' I did.—Moving then slightly on one side, she put her hands to his shirt, lifted the tail, and out stood the largest prick I ever saw. "Oh what a giant you've got," said she.—He laughed loudly.—"Is it not, did you ever see a bigger?" "No, but your balls are not so big." "No, but they are *big*." "No," she said. "You can't see them,"—and he put one leg on a chair,—Sarah stooped and looked under them.—Whilst doing so, he tried to give her a whack on her head with his prick—and laughed loudly at his own fun.—"Why," said Sarah, "if your balls were equal in size to your prick, you wouldn't be able to get them into your trousers."—He laughed loudly, saying, "They're big enough—there is plenty of spunk in them."

Sarah went on admiring it, smoothing it with her hand, pulling up and down the foreskin and keeping it just so that I had a full view. "You are hairy," said she, rubbing his thigh. Then I noticed he was hairy on his legs, which was very ugly.—"Yes, do you like hairy-skinned men?" "I hate a man smooth like a woman—take your shirt off and let me see." "It's cold." "Come close to the fire then."—She talked loudly, purposely, tho' it was scarcely needed. His voice was a clear and a powerful one. Without seeming anxious about it, but flattering him, she managed to get his shirt off and he

stood naked.—He was a tall man, very well built, and hairy generally. Masses hung from his breasts, it darkened his arms. It peeped out like beards from his armpits, it spread from his balls half way up his belly, he had a dark beard and thick black hair.—In brief, he was a big, powerful, hairy, ugly fellow, but evidently very proud of his prick, and all belonging to him. Her flattering remarks evidently pleased him highly and as he turned round as she wished him, to let him see her well all over.—His prick which had been stiff had fallen down, for instead of thinking of the woman, he was now thinking of himself, but it was when hanging, I should say, six inches long, and thick in proportion. "Damn it, it's cold, we are not accustomed to strip like you women." Then he put his shirt on and began business.

He made her strip and told her to go to the bedside. She went to the end and leaned over it with her backside towards him.—He tucked his shirt well up, came behind her, and with his prick which had now stiffened and seemed nine inches long (I really think longer), hit her over the buttocks as if with a stick. It made a spanking noise as it came against her flesh. Then he shoved it between her thighs, brought it out again, and went on thwacking her buttocks with it.—"Don't it hurt you?" she asked him turning her head round towards the peep hole.—"Look here," said he. Going round to a small mahogany table and taking the cloth off it—he thwacked, and banged his prick on it, and a sound came as if the table had been hit with a stick.—"It does not hurt me," he said.—I never was so astonished in my life. ✦

SEXUAL ACCIDENTS: LOST AND FOUND

These kind of accidents rarely make it into print outside the medical journals, i.e., masturbatory mishaps, sex games gone sour, articles lost *inside* the human body. A German gynecologist in the 1890s cited forty-seven instances of women losing objects inside the bladder. Apparently, it was popular for some women to titillate the clitoris by twanging the nubbin with a dull

Accidents can happen when a woman masturbates with strange objects, such as a comic mask, especially if her husband suddenly surprises her. (Japanese woodcut)

hairpin which at the moment of orgasm could accidently slip into the urethra and on into the bladder. In fact, Italian Dr. Francesco Plazzoni mentions just such a case in 1621, the first recorded instance of this type of accident. Thésée Pouillet in his 1897 bestseller on female masturbation mentions that doctors have also aided patients to retrieve from vagina and anus the following: broken candles, corks, thimbles, wine flasks, shot glasses, an egg, or even a compass.

In all the research it took to write this book, which led to all kinds of very odd byways of scholarship, perhaps the strangest document uncovered was an article in the *Journal of the Royal Academy of Surgery* in Paris, dated 1743.

The article by M. Morand was entitled "A Collection of Several Singular Accounts of Foreign Bodies — Some Applied to the Genitals, Others Insinuated into the Bladder and Others into the Anus."

Some of the two dozen accounts are mind-boggling, from the nun who lost a perfume bottle to the man whose mistress advised him to slip his penis through his wedding ring. (When he arrived at the hospital, he told the doctor examining his swollen penis that he had been stung by a bee.)

"However ridiculous these mishaps might appear," wrote article author Dr. Morand, "they would have wound up far more tragic had not Surgery come to the rescue."

Case number twelve involved a handsome young man who before going to bed passed his penis through the metal loop at the top of a skeleton key. The key rested against his pubic bone and tickled his tes-

The vegetable in dangerous play is a turnip. The finger on nose is open to interpretation in this French photo, c. 1860.

"The spot where the foreign body had made the greatest impression was threatened with mortification, and was dressed with a mixture of spirit of camphor and theriac. The urethra of the patient had to be probed the next day, and this wasn't done without difficulty . . ."

Healing progressed but "the scar which formed tended to leave the penis bent down and to one side. That was counteracted as best as possible by a lead plomb in the urethra. However, in spite of that, the young man's penis retained a very strange shape, although his wounds healed completely within two months." ✏

ticles. The fellow awoke during the night with a painful erection and in trying to slip the key off gave himself a larger and more painful erection.

"The examining doctor found the penis of such an enormous thickness that he could hardly see the metal ring. The first idea he had was to pour oil all along the penis, and to wait a bit, which fortunately allowed him to slide the loop of the key forward to the crown of the penis, but he couldn't go beyond that.

"The condition of the patient seemed dangerous, so he decided to lance several tiny holes at the location of the key. By this means, he removed it.

AMERICAN PROSTITUTION: RED, WHITE, AND VERY BLUE

THE FORGOTTEN ST. LOUIS EXPERIMENT

Prostitution is now illegal in the United States except for a handful of counties in Nevada, but about a century ago, two major American cities experimented with open regulated prostitution: New Orleans and, a bit more surprisingly, St. Louis.

On July 5, 1870, the city council of St.

Louis set up six districts for open prostitution and required prostitutes to register permanent addresses and identify themselves in one of three categories: brothel, independent room, or "kept woman," i.e., mistress of a wealthy client.

This remarkable experiment, the so-called "Social Evil Ordinance," was set up to stop the spread of venereal disease, and doctors were appointed to each district to examine the women on a regular basis. Any women who tested positive for V.D. were confined to the "Social Evil Hospital" until cured. After four years, though, a petition drive featuring young girls in spotless white dresses drew 100,000 signatures and prodded the Missouri State Legislature to repeal the ordinance.

Around the same time, several other major American cities, such as New York, Philadelphia, and Chicago, came close to passing similar laws but failed primarily due to lobbying efforts by the newly empowered women's groups, fighting for the vote and against liquor.

Despite crackdowns, prostitution, which needs a concentrated base of male clientele, has flourished in American cities basically since the founding of American cities. Take Puritan New England. In 1672 in Boston, convicted brothelkeeper Alice Thomas was punished by being whipped through the city streets and sentenced to indefinite jail sentence. Local politicians were so upset that they passed a law that year that featured punishment by harnessing the pimp or madame to a cart full of garbage or manure and forcing them to make a circuit of several nearby New England cities. Right-minded citizens presumably threw rotten eggs at the guilty ones.

The California gold rush of 1849, which drew thousands of lone men westward, set off a boom for bordellos. During the Civil War, Union officers cordoned off districts in conquered Southern territories such as Nashville for prostitution. "At pay time," wrote a Union officer, "the lines before these houses are appalling and men often fight each other for a place." He added: "The average charge is three dollars and on pay days some [women] make as much as $250/$300."

Since narcotics trafficking became a crime only in the 20th century and since gambling has cycled in and out of legality in the United States, prostitution easily ranks as the oldest, most successful illegal industry in American history.

STORYVILLE, NEW ORLEANS

At the turn of the century, there was a huge thirty-eight-block red-light district in New Orleans called Storyville, crammed with bordellos of every shape, featuring piano-playing "professors" singing dirty lyrics and trying out new jazz riffs. "Hundreds of men were passing through the streets day and night," recalled pianoman Jelly Roll Morton. "The chippies in their little-girl dresses were standing in the crib doors singing the blues. Some were real ladies in spite of their downfall, and some were habitual drunkards, and some were dope fiends."

New Orleans through the early 1900s

was America's Las Vegas, its Sodom by the Sea. Its debut in so-called sin was abetted by the fact that the French—before Napoleon sold Louisiana to Jefferson—helped increase the female population early in its colony's history by sending over convicted prostitutes. When the authorities back in France sent a message in 1715 to governor Lamonthe Cadillac to reform the place, he replied: "If I expel all the immoral females, there will be no women left here at all, and this would suit neither the wishes of the king nor the inclination of the people."

Back in the antebellum South, one of New Orleans's biggest tourist attractions was an annual "Quadroon Ball," in which light-skinned women were auctioned off for the night to the highest bidder.

By the 1890s, prostitution was flourishing so much that prostitutes worked almost all the quarters of the city. This led reform-minded alderman Sidney Story to fight for the creation in 1897 of a regulated district, which was promptly dubbed by wise-guy journalists Storyville, much to the horror of the crusader.

CONFESSIONS OF AN AUTHENTIC "PRETTY BABY"

Louis Malle immortalized Storyville in his film, *Pretty Baby* (1978), starring Brooke Shields as the underaged prostitute whose virginity is auctioned off. (The publicity campaign noted the starlet was too young to see the R-rated film.) The movie, with its Lolita overtones, painted a fairly glamorous portrait of life in the district.

Al Rose, for his remarkable book *Storyville, New Orleans* (University of Alabama Press, 1976), tracked down a prostitute who lived a life very similar to the Pretty Baby. Here is her authentic unvarnished account.

"Violet" reminisces about her start in Storyville, New Orleans.

I was born upstairs in the attic of Hilma Burt's house on Basin Street. A lot of kids was born in that attic and in the Arlington attic and other places like that. There was a midwife used to come for all the girls who got caught. Why do people think whores can't have kids?

I read in a book one time about one of the houses that was selling a mother and daughter combination for fifty dollars a night. The man that wrote the book acted like that was some kind of a freak act or something. Well, you can write the truth is that I remember fifty combinations like that and I was one myself, and I know two girlfriends, both still living, that were in the same kind of an act. I ain't ashamed of what I did, because I didn't have much to do with it. I don't blame my mother much either. I ain't no more ashamed of that, anyway, than I am to be a member of the human race. The johns can't help it either, you know. It ain't their fault. Just seems like the good Lord ain't got good sense.

Nobody ever stopped me from seeing my mother and the rest of the girls turn tricks. I don't remember anytime when I didn't know what they did, and what a man's prick looked like. Sometimes I'd watch through them portiers like they had

A young unidentified prostitute in New Orleans. Around 1912. Ernest Bellocq, a short, misshapen French photographer, took pictures of the prostitutes of Storyville Red-Light District. These photos—after decades in a trunk and later abuse by Bellocq's preacher-brother—were eventually rediscovered in the late 1960s by Lee Friedlander.

then, and other times I'd walk right in the room and nobody said nothing.

I got to know what a "yen pok" [part of preparation for smoking opium] smells like cookin' and knew it put people to sleep before I was five years old . . .

We moved into a smaller house on Conti Street. The madame was Edna Hamilton. She had three girls and then my mother and me. There was one big parlor and a piano. I only remember the name of one piano player, Sammy Davis. He was colored and he played the piano faster than anybody I ever heard. All the piano players was colored fellows.

One night when I was ten years old I walked into the bedroom where my mother turned her tricks. The john was in there with her and he had his pants off. She was, you know, washing off his prick with a wash cloth. She said this is my kid. He said don't

I think a good little girl ought to help her mother. They both laughed. My mother asked me if I wanted to help and she held up the wash cloth. I didn't think nothin' of it. You know, like I said, I seen so much of this from the time I was born. So I took the wash cloth and washed him off, and they both laughed and he gave me a dollar. Well, that routine went over so big, pretty soon all the other girls were laughing about it, and then my mother used to get me to do the wash-up act everytime she turned a trick. I'd get one and two dollar tips nearly every time, and then the other girls started gettin' me to wash off their tricks, too, before and after, and Edna got the word around and it sure helped business. I was takin' in maybe a hundred dollars a week myself, and the other girls was gettin' more johns.

The johns never bothered me. I didn't

have nothing even to feel yet. But they liked to have me around in the room when they fucked. One time, Cora, one of the girls, had a john and she was sucking him off. It was nothing new to me. I'd seen it plenty of times before but only lately I'd be in the room while they were doing it. I said "I can do that." So we took turns. Then he fucked her while I felt his balls. I made five dollars for my end of that one, and then I started turning tricks myself just by blowing. I was still only ten years old and not very big so I didn't fuck. It was two years more before I did that. So I was a virgin for two years.

But after I found out what the johns would pay for, I started all kinds of stunts with 'em except fuckin'. One time Edna called me down to the parlor. There were four johns sitting there about half-juiced. I had on a white party dress to make me look about four years younger than I was. That was Edna's idea. She said to blow all of them. One of them was feeling my cunt while I did this. None of them seemed to want to come. Everybody just laughed. Then one of them, a thin, bald one, asked me how I'd like to go upstairs with him and I did. In the bedroom he asked whether I ever had my cunt sucked, and I said no, because that was the truth. So he went ahead and did it to me and it felt real nice, you know—but nothing happened because I was too young. Anyway I made fifty that night by myself, which was pretty good for a ten year old kid.

The first time I ever got fucked wasn't at Edna's but Emma Johnson's—you know they called it the Studio on Basin Street next to the firehouse. I was twelve and Edna had been sendin' me over there nights to be in the circus. I don't need to explain what that is do I? Well, I was in the circus two or three nights a week. There was another kid my age Liz she's still alive. Oh yes! that's right. We used to work together. By this time we were gettin' a little figure and looked pretty good and neither one of us was afraid to do them things the johns liked, so we'd get a hundred a night to be in the circus. My mother was in the circus too. She's the one who used to fuck the pony. Emma kept a stable in the yard and a colored man, Wash, used to take care of the two ponies and the horse. In the daytime, me and Liz rode the ponies around the yard. Ain't that somethin'?

So this one night Emma had some live ones in the house and she says to me she thinks I'm ready to fuck, and will I do for half of what she gets for me. Usually I never talked anything over with my mother anymore, but this time I did. She said that since I was getting hair on my cunt, I might as well go ahead. So, Emma, she had a big mouth—a loud voice, made a speech about me and Liz and how everybody in the District knew we was virgins, even though we did all these other things and that if the price was right, tonight was the night and she'd have an auction. Some snotty kid bid a dollar and Emma had one of the floor men slug him and throw him out in the street. One man bid the both of us in, honest to God, for seven hundred and seventy five dollars *each!* A lot of johns bid and he wasn't gonna be satisfied with just one. He bought us both. Well, we went upstairs with him. He wanted us both together, and you know how it is, we thought he ought to be entitled to somethin' for all that money, so we came on with everything we could think of, includin' the dyke act which we been doin' anyway in the circus and we got to like it so much we'd lots of time do it when we was by ourselves. We did a dance we had worked out where we jerked ourselves and each other off and we started to play with him but I didn't hardly touch him when he came. Well right away he went to sleep with us on the bed with him and in a little while, maybe an hour, he woke up, and the three of us fooled around until he got in shape to do something and we managed to get him into Liz. I could tell it hurt her and she bled pretty good too, but afterwards she said it wasn't so bad and she was glad it was over. But the john didn't have enough left to do nothin' with me so he arranged with me and Emma to hold me over to the next night.

The next night he came around to Edna Hamilton's and that's when I got broke in. It wasn't bad, and he really thought all around, he had his money's worth . . .

I know it'd be good if I could say how awful it was and like crime don't pay—but to me it seems just like anything else—like a kid whose father owns a grocery store. He helps him in the store. Well, my mother didn't sell groceries.

During World War I, when the U.S. set up a major naval base in New Orleans, the department of the Navy ordered Storyville shut down in 1917. Commented the mayor: "Our city government has believed that the situation could be administered more easily and more satisfactorily by confining prostitution within a prescribed area . . . but the Navy Department of the Federal Government has decided otherwise."

CUNNING TIPS FROM FORGOTTEN LOVE MANUALS

Roman Emperor Tiberius kept a copy of Elephantis's love manual by his bed in his country home on Capri; diarist Samuel Pepys records reading *L'Ecole des Filles* (School for Girls) and then burning it so it wouldn't be found in his library; Casanova tried out suggestions from Aretino's *Sixteen Positions*, including the following "Straight Tree."

"I lifted her up to devour her chamber of love, which I could not reach otherwise since I wanted to make it possible for her in turn to devour the weapon which wounded her to death without taking her life." If you can follow the anatomical geography, Casanova is describing a standing 69 position.

Love manuals have been enormously popular throughout history. How many fourth-century Indian classics besides the

Kamasutra can you name that are still in print?

But there's a misconception that there have been only a handful of these type of books: Ovid's *Art of Love, Kamasutra, The Perfumed Garden,* to name the most obvious. This is completely wrong.

There have been hundreds, if not thousands of other titles but erotic bibliography has been a bit of an overlooked scholarly niche.

Dr. Nicolas Venette wrote *L'Amour conjugale* in 1687 and it went into a dozen editions and at least five languages. During the tail end of the Italian Renaissance,

Giovanni Sinibaldi collected every imaginable scrap of sexual advice and folklore into *Geneanthropeia* (1642), which was reprinted again and again.

The most popular sex manual of the 1700s and 1800s in the United States and Great Britain was called *Aristotle's Masterpiece,* and during the Civil War era, it helped drive the birth of the fledgling mail-order business. The book—which was most definitely *not* written by Aristotle—was advertised for sale in newspapers. (Vendors guaranteed it would arrive in plain brown wrapping.)

"This is beyond all comparison, the

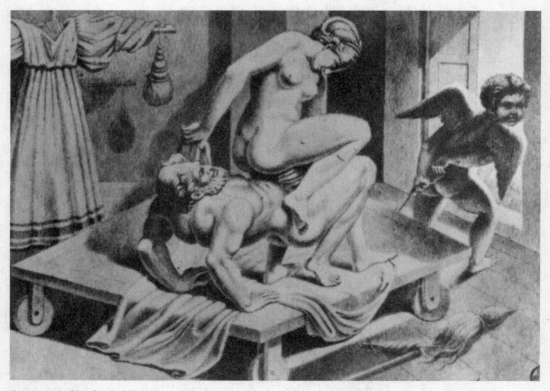

Position 14 of *"Seidici Modi"* (Sixteen Positions). Good luck. In the accompanying sonnet by Pietro Aretino, the man complains that in this position even a mule would become exhausted and that he also can't stop farting. He ends, though, on a high note, reveling in the close view he's getting of his partner's *"cul di latte"* (i.e., her milky ass).

most extraordinary work of Physiology ever published," promised the monthly newspaper *Ormsby's New-York Mail Bag*, dated September 1863. "There is nothing whatever that married people can either require or wish to know, but what is fully explained. Illustrated with some Twenty Descriptive Plates, mostly colored." The paper lists more than a dozen other sex manuals—*The Wedding Night, Male Generative Organs, Woman & Her Secret Passions*—among ads for nudie pictures and "French safes," i.e., condoms.

In addition, the Arabs and Chinese of course produced many volumes of sex manuals. The Chinese, especially in their so-called Bedchamber books, offer advice for men to learn how to control themselves, to prolong the joust. Taoists believe that man shouldn't squander his yin energy in orgasm after orgasm but rather let it build up, while in turn he should unleash his partner's yang by giving her many many orgasms. (You know: yin and yang.) This required control.

Some of that advice for control includes imagining that the man's partner is ugly, or having him gnash teeth or concentrate on complicated breathing patterns à la Lamaze. But of the distraction techniques perhaps the most provocative is the following: The man must try to imagine a red disc at his head and a yellow disc at his waist and then meditate on the two discs gradually moving closer and closer to each other until they merge to form an orange disc around his chest. (It's better than stock prices or batting averages.) Over time, the man can also learn to do various plunges:

Advice or social commentary? This vintage French postcard explains how a woman should savor a banana at various ages and then promises that "she will thus experience delights and exquisite consolation." (That last word is loaded in the French, since a dildo was sometimes called a "*consolateur*," i.e., something that "soothes in distress," and Diderot himself referred to the sexual act as "consolation.")

nine shallow, one deep, then working to three shallow, one deep. Keeping track will keep his mind off other things.

As for the Arab manuals, many are spiced with erotic stories, because those writers believed that a dramatic tale could teach as well or better than cold advice.

Erotic manuals also provide a window to the sexuality of the times. Sinibaldi, that Renaissance Italian, for instance, includes advice for stopping impotency caused by a witch's spell ("urinate through a wedding ring") while a Victorian advice book from 1897 warned that a wife might die and her husband get cancer of the tongue because he "had the fatal habit of applying the tongue and lips to his wife's genitals to provoke in her a venereal orgasm." ❧

Techniques from a French Revolutionary, 1783

Comte Mirabeau was an aristocrat who played a crucial role in the French Revolution. He also wrote an impishly witty book, *Erotica Biblion* (1783), one-quarter love manual, three-quarters history of sex.

Here is Mirabeau's advice for how a woman should stroke a man's penis.

The girl . . . should occupy herself only with creating, exciting and maintaining a plateau of pleasure . . . and then make every effort to suspend sensation at that level, and to delay accelerating it, or even worse, to provoking climax. All her caresses should be calibrated with infinitely delicate nuance . . .

Imagine the two actors naked in an alcove surrounded by mirrors and on a bed tilted on an angle. At first, the adept young woman takes the greatest care not to touch the man's genitals; her approaches are slow, her embraces gentle, her kisses more tender than lascivious, her tongue strokes are measured, her glance voluptuous, the intertwining with his limbs full of grace and gentleness; she uses her hands to excite a light tingling on the tips of his nipples; once she perceives that his "eye" is moist, and she feels that his erection is quite solid, then she gently puts her thumb on the tip of the head of the penis which she finds bathed in lymphatic liquid; from the tip, the thumb gently descends to the root, returns, re-descends, makes a tour of the crown; then the stops, if she perceives that the sensations are building too fast. She then uses only light general caresses, and it is only after the simultaneous and immediate touches of first one hand, then of both, and the approach of her entire body, it is only then, just then once the erection has become too violent that she judges that it's the instant to let nature act its course or help it along. That's because the orgasm that is building in the man is becoming so lively and his hair-trigger craving so intense that he would faint away if someone doesn't bring on the grand finale.

Mirabeau defends this type of manual caress as an alternative to intercourse, especially, say, when the wife is pregnant. The Frenchman also has a curiously apt way of stating that men need sexual release: "If all men's penises become as hard as oak trees, then the world will turn into a forest where it would be impossible to move."

EARLY PSYCHIATRY EXPLORES THE FIRST "DEVIANTS"

The stories are hilarious, pathetic, titillating, profoundly disturbing. They are the sexual case studies of the pioneers in the study of psychology, written from the

1880s to the 1930s, during the heyday of Sigmund Freud. The doctors who zeroed in on sex are Magnus Hirschfeld, Richard von Krafft-Ebing, Havelock Ellis, Alfred Binet, among many others. With literally thousands of case studies to choose from, here are a few of the odder ones as well as some notes on some of the scientists who brought them to you.

HAIR FETISH:
RICHARD VON KRAFFT-EBING

"X., aged twenty, inverted sexually. Only loved men with a large bushy mustache. One day he met a man who answered his ideal. He invited him to his home, but was unspeakably disappointed when this man removed an artificial mustache. Only when the visitor put the ornament back on the upper lip again, he exercised his charm over X. once more and restored him to the full possession of virility."

So begins a typical case study (no. 99) in *Psychopathia Sexualis* by Dr. Richard von Krafft-Ebing. The Latin title of the book was purposely chosen to scare off the general reading public. Don't be scared. Just get a modern edition that translates all the hard-core sexual descriptions out of Latin and into English.

As it says in the introduction to a 1939 edition of *Psychopathia Sexualis* in describing Dr. von Krafft-Ebing: "Through his hands, in consulting-room, clinic and law court, passed a succession of the undersexed, and the hypersexed, rapists, stranglers, rippers, stabbers, blood-sucking vampires and necrophiliacs, sadists who

hurt their partners, masochists who thrilled at the sight of the whip, males in female clothes and females in male clothes, stuff-fetishists dominated by a shoe or a handkerchief, lovers of fur and velvet, slaves of scatology, defilers of statues, despoilers of children and animals, frotteurs and voyeurs, renifleurs and stercoraires, pageists and exhibitionists, paedophiliacs and gerontophiliacs, satyriasists and nymphomaniacs, and again and again male-craving males and female-craving females, and the endless army of men who lusted after Woman in perverse ways but had no desire for her vagina." ❧

UROLAGNIA: HAVELOCK ELLIS

British sex researcher Havelock Ellis received this letter from a forty-four-year-old Englishman, and was quite pleased to publish it.

Before marriage, though I had a certain amount of sexual experience, I had none of urination in company with a woman. In fact it was not until I had been married some little time that I discovered the delights of it. Not that there had been any shyness between us. On the first night we were married my wife sat down for this purpose quite simply and naturally and I followed. And if we were in the country together we would water the roadside side by side. Then one day in the country, when we had been married about four months, I invited her to sit on my knees to urinate, as I sat on the ground with my knees hunched up. When the smoking golden stream gushed forth, she was irresistible, and it hardly ceased when, to my wife's astonishment, I pulled her eagerly back into my lap and bestowed a different libation on her.

Afterwards, we often repeated the experience in lonely country spots, and to this day, though we have been married eight years and I have seen her make water every day (except when parted during the War) such an experience never fails to excite me powerfully. When we are in bed, I sometimes ask her to urinate a little on my hand or penis. This induces excitement and also lubricates the vulva. Many may think this practice "filthy" but it is an exquisite delight to feel the flow gushing out and little harm is done to the bed-clothes. I should add that while my wife shares this pleasure, she tells me she does not find any sexual excitement in the casual spectacle of men and boys urinating, she thinks because the sight is too common.

Havelock Ellis (1859—1939) was a more talented writer than Krafft-Ebing and much more capable of synthesizing case studies into grand overviews. Ellis's seven-volume *Studies in the Psychology of Sex* is credited with helping to undemonize masturbation and adolescent sexual urges; he noted women's intense sexuality, multiple orgasms, and perceived the cosmic side-splitter that men's sexual peak occurs a decade or so before women's. He also explored the role of the *five* senses in sexual urges. Perhaps one reason that Havelock Ellis was more tolerant of diversity than most of his colleagues was that all his life he was a passionate devotee of golden showers, i.e., his deepest sexual thrill came from watching women urinate.

AXILLARY AROMA: CHARLES FÉRÉ

French doctor Charles Féré (1852–1907) describes a friend's predelection.

It was twenty years ago, I used to hunt often with a man already in his sixties, very healthy, without any apparent defects and whose family . . . didn't present any grave neuropathic taints. This man had the habit of pestering girls and women, sometimes even quite old women, in a manner that surprised me greatly. He attacked only women who worked in the fields, in short sleeved shirts. He would creep close enough to them so that he could put his hand in their armpit. Once he had achieved his goal, which baffled his victims, he would leave satisfied. But for a long time, he would lift his contaminated hand to his nose with an expression of evident pleasure. After hesitating for a long time, I finally asked him to explain why he did it. He answered me as though it was the most natural thing in the world. "It is a smell that resurrects me and makes Lazarus ready for a long bout." And he told me when he was young, the women whose juices had strongest scent were capable of inspiring him to perform amazing sexual exploits, and that during recent years, they were the only ones who could obtain anything from him. ☙

La Femme Petomane:
Magnus Hirschfeld

Magnus Hirschfeld (1868–1935), until Hitler dismantled his world-renowned institute in Berlin, studied all manner of sexual oddities.

"To prove that what may have a fetishistic influence far exceeds everything one may imagine, is the fact that even the intestinal gases can have an attracting effect. Thus, in a Montmartre nightclub in Paris, I saw a girl who called herself *"La Femme Petomane"* and her large audience was in part amused and in part excited because from time to time, amidst witty remarks, she produced flatus of varied strength and length. Those who wished to derive the full pleasure of the odor sat in the front rows, those who were content with the acoustical charm sat in the other rows." 🌀

THE CHALLENGES OF MASTURBATION

Self-love dates way back. Egyptian queens were buried four thousand years ago with

A Greek vase shows a hetaira (i.e., a courtesan) with dildos. The most popular models back then were made of *leather*.

all the objects they would need in the afterlife, such as clothes, combs, and . . . dildos.

The Bible, of course, mentions masturbation. No, not the passage about Onan; he was in trouble for spilling his seed on the ground and not fulfilling the ancient law to impregnate his brother's widow. No, the more apt biblical passage is in Ezekiel 16:17, when the prophet rails: "Thou hast taken thy fair jewels of my gold and of my silver, which I had given thee, and madest to thyself images of men, and didst commit whoredom with them."

The ancient Greeks, on the other hand, were quite amused by dildos. The playwrights mention them in their comedies and the artists depicted them on their jars and pitchers and bowls. The city of Miletus grew famous throughout the Mediterranean for its leather dildos. Aristophanes has a woman in *Lysistrata* complain about a dildo shortage. "Why, since those beastly

Masturbator! The book *Boyhood's Perils & Manhood's Curse* (1858) clearly shows what happens to young men who flog the bishop, choke the chicken, etc.

Milesians revolted and cut off the leather trade, that handy do-it-your-self kit's vanished from the open market."

Masturbation, how-ever, fell out of favor in Europe with the birth of Christianity. Anyone spilling their semen in their palm was missing the proper spot: the womb of their wife. The-ologian after theologian deemed self-love a sin, and medieval penance manuals are filled with the appropriate punishments, which usually, though, were relatively mild: on the order of thirty days of special prayers and fasting.

By the Victorian era, doctors began to echo theologians in viewing masturbation as the root of many of the world's problems. Many medical books in the 1800s describe the dire effects of masturbation, from insan-ity to torpor to hair loss. Some even deemed it a potentially fatal practice. "In my opin-ion," wrote Dr. Réveillé-Parisé in 1823, "neither the plague nor war has had more disastrous effects for mankind than the mis-erable habit of masturbation." A rush to cure this dread malady swept doctors all over Europe and in the United States. Patents were taken out on devices such as a sharp-toothed nocturnal penis ring to pre-vent unwanted erections. Sylvester Graham (1794–1851) invented his bland graham cracker in part to reduce the body's pas-sionate urges toward self-love.

However, sometimes the zeal of the re-formers took a sinister turn. Dr. John Kel-logg of Battle Creek, Michigan, the man who originally invented corn flakes, de-voted himself to campaigning against mas-turbation by women. He prescribed cool baths, a cool enema, and a spare diet as remedies. He also stated that in 1880, he performed a clitorectomy on a ten-year-old girl "who had become addicted to the vice to a most extraordinary degree." ✎

SEX *AFTER* MARRIAGE

WIVES' ORGASMS

Many people have the impression that it was only during the Women's Lib Move-ment of the 1950s and 1960s that the world first recognized women's sexual needs and that doctors finally discovered the impor-tance of the clitoris in sex and the fact that all women could and should have orgasms.

That notion of sexual history is hooey, and does a great disservice to husbands in prior generations who are somehow pic-tured as greedy slobs who took their brief pleasure and rolled over and snored.

Doctors such as Hippocrates identified the clitoris as the seat of women's pleasure as far back as 500 B.C., and clearly mentions orgasm. "A tickling sensation overwhelms her genitals," wrote Hippocrates, "and a feeling of pleasure and warmth pools out through the rest of her body."

And the popular notion through the late 1700s in Europe and America was that *a woman must have an orgasm in order to conceive.* Hippocrates and Galen both write of the "female sperm" mixing with the male sperm, and medieval doctors echoed that belief. "When the woman does not emit any sperm, conception cannot take place," wrote Avicenna around 1020 A.D. Think about it. Any European man wanting to be a father, according to this understanding of sex, must give his wife an orgasm. Of course, not every husband could do this every time, but if this was the prevailing folk and medical belief, it certainly must have given wives hours of added pleasure, i.e., innumerable extra diddles and piston strokes, through the ages.

One of the more unusual bits of evidence that wives' needs could be taken seriously occurred during the Norman Conquest of England by William the Conqueror in 1066. After almost two years of having their husbands fight over in England, the wives back in Normandy were fed up. "At this time," wrote the chronicler Ordericus Vitalis, "certain Norman women, consumed by fierce lust, sent message after message to their husbands to return home at once, and adding unless they did so with all speed, they would take other husbands." William the Conqueror tried to bribe the soldiers to stay with promises of land and revenues, but many still returned to the home fires in Normandy.

That belief about women's orgasms facilitating pregnancy persevered. Casanova, a well-educated man, wrote in his memoirs in the late 1700s of one of his partner's orgasms making pregnancy a very real possibility.

But with the advent of improved medical research, doctors in the 1700s and especially the 1800s came to the conclusion that a woman's orgasm was not in fact necessary for conception to occur. This evolved into the Victorian attitude that women were by nature frigid receptacles for man's seed who tolerated the sexual act for the purpose of procreating. "I should say that the majority of women (happily for society) are not very much troubled by sexual feeling of any kind," wrote Dr. William Acton, a very influential family doctor of the Victorian era.

And it was these prudish experts of the Victorian era who foisted that frigid view on many people of the 20th century. (And yes, Women's Lib did help fight to clear these Victorian misconceptions that had addled humankind for a century or so.) Ironically, recent research has shown that a woman's orgasm—with its spasms and lubricating emissions—probably does increase the chances of pregnancy.

HUSBANDS STAND BEHIND THEIR WIVES IN ANCIENT GREECE

When the wives in Aristophanes' play, *Lysistrata,* want to sexually frustrate their husbands into suing for peace, they solemnly vow among other things: "not to

Greek dinner bowl. This position was popular in the more bisexually open ancient world; some doctors back then also thought the deeper penetration achieved in this way would increase the odds of pregnancy.

MARITAL SEX: THE CHURCH VIEW IN THE MIDDLE AGES

The Catholic Church was the single most influential voice in Europe for more than a thousand years and its theologians repeatedly condoned only one form of marital sex: husband above, wife below, for procreation.

Foreplay was generally forbidden, as was oral sex, or any of the many sexual positions. Medieval handbooks helped outline for priests the penance required when a couple strayed from what would one day be called the "Missionary Position." Hands to genitals was generally the most minor offense, while oral sex was more taboo, and, most forbidden of all was anal sex, i.e., "from behind like beasts" which, over time, evolved in the civil courts, into a capital offense.

Pierre Payer, in his wonderful *Sex and the Penitentials*, produces a chart showing when sex was technically allowed during the Middle Ages. Basically, according to the strictest penitentials, you couldn't have intercourse when the wife was menstruating, pregnant, nursing, during holidays, Wednesdays, Fridays, Saturdays, or Sundays, in daylight, naked, or in church, and, of course, not for fun, but only to conceive a child, and only once, and without kissing.

The good news is that we don't have a clue how many people really followed these rules. And, obviously, husbands who believed their wives needed an orgasm to conceive might have bent the rules a bit or else developed incredible stamina in ye olde missionary position. ❧

point their feet to the thatched roofs and not to act like the lioness on the cheese grater." Say what?

That latter position was crouching with head low and derriere raised high, inviting entry from behind.

Judging from vases and wall paintings, this was obviously a popular position in the ancient world, and worth being spelled out in the *Lysistrata* oath.

The Roman satirist, Martial, wrote a long poem complaining that his wife wouldn't let him come at her from behind. "You don't use your voice, body or fingers to show me a good time . . . but worst of all, you refuse to let me plow you from behind. Cornelia used to let Gracchus do it; Julia let Pompey; Portia let Brutus, and right before dinner, Juno let Jove. If you enjoy being a prude so much, be one all day long. But at night, I want you to be my high-priced hooker." ❧

VINTAGE MISCONCEP- TIONS

LESBIANISM: SOME EARLY THEORIES

One of the sillier notions about lesbian- ism—a belief popular in learned circles for at least four centuries—was that lesbians were women with oversize clitorises, some measuring two inches and more. Many leading doctors writing about sex during the Renaissance, many pioneer anthropol- ogists of the 19th century and experts of various disciplines as late as the early 20th century subscribed to the theory.

Some of the first European explorers to Africa claimed that they discovered African women with enormously enlarged clitorises which they could insert like a pe- nis into their female partners. (Africa was uncivilized; ergo a hotbed for lesbian ac- tivities.)

Echoing that view was the likes of Dr. Nicolas Venette in his *L'Amour conjugale* (1687), a popular love manual reprinted into a dozen editions, who wrote: "Sappho the Lesbian would have never gained such a notorious reputation, if she had had a smaller clitoris."

Direct examination finally undermined the lesbian/enlarged-clitoris theory. There was plenty of anecdotal evidence that French prostitutes in the 19th century turned to each other for sexual comfort, so Alexandre Parent-Duchatelet in his de- tailed study of 3,250 prostitutes in Paris tried to test the lesbian-clitoris theory but found only three prostitutes with organs of more than an inch in length. None of this trio was a lesbian, not the small-breasted woman with the three-inch clitoris nor the two other large-breasted prostitutes. "I have known quite a number of girls, given over to this abominable vice [i.e., lesbian- ism]," wrote Parent-Duchatelet, "and they were remarkable, on the contrary, for their youth, their delicacy, the softness of their voice and for their other charms."

The history of lesbian relations is clouded in secrecy and misinformation. Many European countries and the early American colonies nominally had very strict laws on the books against "unnatural relations" between women. However, de- tailed searches by scholars in recent years have turned up relatively few instances of those laws being enforced.

There is one notable exception, an ex- traordinary Prussian case of 1721, in which a woman spent her life masquerad- ing as a man, often as a soldier, so as to be able to have sex with women.

Catharina Margaretha Linck enlisted in a regiment as a musketeer at age twenty. She fashioned a leather penis and had sex with several prostitutes and several wid- ows but never had sexual intercourse. In order to be able to pee standing up with the other men, she fashioned a kind of leather pee cone.

Her legal troubles began when she mar- ried at age twenty-three without inform- ing her eighteen-year-old virginal bride that she was a woman. After several months of painful attempts at intercourse, the bride finally uncovered her husband's secret and fled back to her mother, who later alerted the authorities.

The case devolved into a he/she said, she said with the husband claiming the wife knew her true sex all along. Both also admitted that the husband had once put the leather penis into the wife's mouth.

The judges were quite perplexed how to rule, with the verdict hinging on arcane theories of whether oral sodomy, a capital crime, could be committed without ejaculation. The judges pointed out that the sodomy was committed with a lifeless leather instrument, and the defendant was not like Eastern or African women with an enormous clitoris who could achieve penetration. Also, it was noted that the Bible doesn't expressly decree death for unnatural relations between women as it does for those between men.

Nonetheless, after much legal theorizing, the husband, Catharina Margaretha Linck, was sentenced to be beheaded, while the young wife was sentenced to three years in prison.

The verdict was submitted to King Frederick-William I for final approval, with the proviso that some prosecutors argued that the death sentence should be commuted to flogging and life imprisonment, perhaps in a room spinning cloth.

EARLY CONDOMS

The English called them "French letters" and the French called them "Redingotes

One size does not fit all. In the 1700s, condoms made of animal gut often varied in size. Here, Casanova and friends are blowing some up.

Anglaises," i.e., English riding coats. Casanova (1725–1798), the notorious autobiographer, describes an encounter with a beautiful nun in which he used one in 1760. "I told her to wait a moment, for I, too, had something in a package which should be precious to her. I then take from a portfolio a little jacket of very fine transparent skin, eight inches long and closed at one end, and which by way of a pouch string at its open end had a narrow pink ribbon. I display it to her, she looks at it, laughs and says I had used such jackets with her Venetian sister, and that she was curious about it."

"I will put it on myself," she said, "and you cannot imagine how glad I am."

That condom fit, but, apparently, in

those days before latex factories, the size could vary according to the sheep gut. In another tryst, Casanova's partner kept trying to ensheath him in one ill-fitting condom after another until Casanova accidentally "splashes" her.

Condoms made of animal gut with drawstrings grew in popularity over the 1700s and became increasingly available at European brothels.

And in the United States, an ad in a Civil War newspaper lists "French safes" at twenty-five cents each, which makes them relatively expensive. (A turn with a prostitute back then cost as little as fifty cents.) Maybe that's why it's been estimated that almost one fifth of the troops on both sides suffered from venereal disease.

And it was in fact fear of disease that actually inspired the first condom, which was, surprisingly, made out of linen. Gabriello Fallopio (1523–1562), the anatomist who discovered the eponymous tubes, wrote that he had devised a small medicated linen sheath to fit over the head of the penis and *under* the uncut foreskin; he also said it could be placed in the vagina—all to help prevent contracting syphilis, which had started spreading in 1493. "I tried the experiment on 1,100 men, and I call immortal God to witness that not one of them was infected."

But did they fully enjoy themselves?

As the French aristocrat Madame de Sevigné (1626–1696) put it so succinctly: "[Condoms] are gossamer against infection, steel against love." 🌀

THE SEXUAL SIDE OF SLAVERY

Slaves were almost never raped. That's because in the history of slavery, slaves had almost no rights. To be raped implies a law against such behavior. If a master wanted to have sex with a slave, a master had sex with a slave.

Of the hundreds of books on slavery, very few focus on this aspect of that peculiar institution. When the famous Athenian lawgiver, Solon, wanted to set up brothels to cut down on adultery in Athens, he simply bought foreign slaves and stocked the brothels. He didn't ask the slaves' permission. The orator Demosthenes stated matter-of-factly that Athenian men have "slaves for their daily sexual needs." And the Romans, both men and women, were notorious for using their slaves in all manner of sex games.

When American slave owners wanted sex with their slaves, they simply did what they wanted. It is always dangerous to make blanket statements, but apparently there was not a single prosecution of an American slaveholder for raping a slave. "The body of the black female slave was the master's for the taking," states Beth Day in *Sexual Life Between Blacks and Whites* (1972). "Sexual rights over the body of the black woman also became the privilege of the master's sons, the plantation overseers, and, by extension, to any white male around."

Wrote Mary Boykin Chesnut in her famous *Diary from Dixie:* "Like patriarchs of old, our men all live in one house with their wives and their concubines; and the mulattoes one sees in every family partly resemble the white children. Any lady is ready to tell you who is the father of all the mulatto children in everybody else's household but her own."

VIRGIN SLAVES IN CONSTANTINOPLE, c. 1600

"These slaves are bought and sold as beasts and cattle are, they being viewed and reviewed and felt about their limbs and bodies, and their mouths looked into as if they were so many horses. They are

How much? Fit for the sultan? A virgin slave is sold in Constantinople. (Painted by 19th-century artist Jean-Léon Gérôme.)

examined of what country they are and what they are good for, either for sewing, spinning, weaving, or the like. . . . Now, when there is a virgin that is beautiful and fair, she is held at a high rate and sold for far more than any other. As for security for her virginity, the seller is not only bound for restitution of the [purchase price], if she prove otherwise, but for his fraud is fined a great sum of money."—Ottaviano Bon, Venetian ambassador to the Ottoman Empire from 1604–1607.

HAREM GIRLS AND CUCUMBERS

Of all the images of foreign lust, perhaps none incited the Europeans' envy and spurred more pornographic fancy than the sultan's harem: three hundred exquisite young women bought at slave auction, and on call to suit the sultan's every whim. "Most of us still imagine," wrote N. M. Penzer in *The Harem* (1930), "that the Sultan is—or, rather, was—a vicious old reprobate, spending all his time in the harem, surrounded by hundreds of semi-naked women, in an atmosphere of heavy perfume, cool fountains, soft music, and over-indulgence in every conceivable kind of vice that the united brains of jealous, sex-starved women could invent for the pleasure of their lord."

The reality is a bit different, though not without its charm for the sultan. The Turkish harem, founded by Muhammad II in 1454 and surviving through 1909, did indeed house hundreds of women, but many of the women slept in dormitorylike

The naked Harem, as imagined/fantasized by British artist Thomas Rowlandson (1757–1827).

rooms on simple cots with one older woman matron per ten young ones. They were guarded over by black eunuchs purposely chosen for their ugliness. Though fashion changed over half a millennium, they generally wore clothes that covered them up from head to toe, with loose-fitting pants (of thin but *not* diaphanous material), sometimes with four- or five-inch platform slippers.

The seraglio was a city unto itself with strict rules for everything from eating to bathing to clothes. This walled off community was ruled generally by the sultan's mother and the mother of the sultan's first son. The rest of the women were subservient.

"When the Grand Signior [i.e., sultan] is pleased to call for some of the young ladies to the Garden of Love," wrote Paul Rycaut back in 1668, "the cry *Helvet* is raised, and bells ring through the seraglio, at which signal people withdraw from the area and eunuchs are posted at every entrance and pathway, it being Death at that time for anyone to linger near the garden. Here, in this beautiful landscape, the damsels dance and sing, hoping to make

The habit of a Lady in the Seraglis

A harem girl's *authentic* outfit, as recorded in 1668 by eyewitness, ambassador Paul Rycaut for his *State of the Ottoman Empire*.

themselves mistress of the Grand Signior's passing affection, then, abandoning all modesty to this end, let themselves loose to all kinds of lascivious gestures and wanton carriage."

If one of the harem girls caught the sultan's eye, tradition has it that he would toss his handkerchief to her. She would then be prepared for the sultan's bed by being bathed, perfumed, shampooed; every hair would be scrupulously removed from her body as sultans followed Near Eastern tastes regarding body hair, preferring their women to look prepubescent.

That night she would be escorted to the sultan's giant bed, where tradition also has it she would lift the covers at the foot of the bed, and then crawl reverentially forward up along the sultan's body. Reliable accounts of what they did next haven't survived although the fripperies of some notorious sultans included fur bedspreads, giant mirrors, and aphrodisiac cocktails.

In the morning, the young woman was entitled to all the jewels and money in the sultan's pockets, and could expect another gift later in the day.

Any woman who had sex often with the sultan, and especially those who had borne him a son, were often granted a private room, thus escaping the dormitory or the cell-like rooms.

Given these ground rules, most of the women were desperate to catch the sultan's eye, and most were sexually frustrated. Caught so much as kissing another man, even a eunuch, meant instant death, tied in a weighted sack and tossed in the Bosporous. When the women were sick, doctors examined them through bed curtains, with the absolute minimum of flesh exposed. "She lies there closely covered from head to toe with blankets, and holds out her arm only, so that the doctor may touch and feel her pulse," wrote one observer. "After he has given orders about what should be done . . . he takes his leave immediately."

Even masturbation was denied to these women. Ottaviano Bon, an emissary from Venice who attended the sultan's court from 1604–1607, wrote in one of his dispatches: "Nor is it lawful for anyone to bring anything to them, with which they might commit foul deeds of lechery; so that if they eat cucumbers, they are sent into them sliced, to deprive them of the means of playing the wantons."

GUARDING THE HAREM

Who can be trusted to guard three hundred beautiful, sexually deprived women, many of them virgins? three hundred of the choicest women of the Mediterranean who *might* have sex with the sultan once a year? An ugly black man with no testicles or penis, that's who. At least, that's what the Turkish sultans decided.

"White eunuchs are not permitted to [go into the Harem], nor can any man that is white (but the Sultan only) see and come amongst the women," wrote Venetian ambassador Ottaviano Bon in 1605. "All the eunuchs in the Seraglio, in number about 200, what with old, middle-aged and young ones, are not only gelded but have their yards cut clean off."

The black eunuchs chosen are the ones "with the worst features to be found among the most hard-favoured of that African race," stated Paul Rycaut in his *State of the Ottoman Empire,* published in 1668.

Cunning eunuchs in the Ottoman Empire, Byzantine Empire, and in China sometimes achieved great political power in the royal court, and amassed huge wealth. It was thought their lack of family ties and disinterest in sexual pleasures would free them to become the ultimate loyal bureaucrat. And conveniently, at their death, however, with no heirs, all their riches would return to the state.

One such eunuch named Hali commanded the Ottoman troops during the Renaissance. One day in 1556, a messenger arrived to tell him that the Christian forces had captured a major Turkish city, against all odds. The bringer of bad news trembled in fear. Hali put a hand on his shoulder and told him: "I have known greater losses than that of a single city. Set your eyes on this, young man." The eunuch Hali opened his trousers. "This is what is a truly deplorable loss because it is something I may never be able to recapture."

And perhaps no amount of wealth or power could compensate for the deep wound in their souls, in their manhood. Though some eunuchs were literally de-sexed by their hormonal changes, quite a few were not. This poignant poem from a eunuch during the Ming Dynasty (1368–1644) has survived:

I awoke from a dream of Paradise
In which I was like other men
And knew the delights of Yin. [i.e., of women]

Now, again myself, I find she was a
   rainbow,

A beauty seen but never touched.
I know life only in my dreams
And perhaps in that longer sleep
That promises so much with Death.
—Hu-Yung-hsi 🐚

PAINFUL FETISHES

CHINESE FOOT BINDING: SWALLOWING HER TINY FOOT

Chinese love manuals recommended that *her* foot for *his* optimum erotic enjoyment should be four inches long and two inches wide, the toes scrunched completely under the sole and the heel so bent down that it creates almost vaginal folds in the fleshy underside.

For almost a thousand years until the 1920s, the erotic centerpiece for hundreds

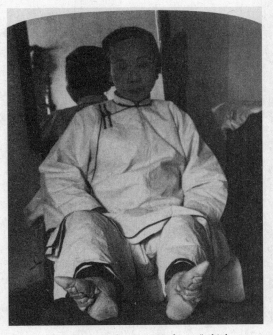

Reality. A stereoscope shot in 1900 shows "a high caste Lady's" feet, unbound and out of the perfumed slippers.

of millions of Chinese men was the tiny, severely bound Lotus foot of his lover.

And of all the fetishes passed down from other cultures and ages—from sadism to watersports—foot-binding ranks high among the toughest for an outsider to grasp.

Parents would start binding the feet of girls around the age of five when the bones were still malleable, and over time, the girl would be unable to walk without a long pole or someone's help. It's estimated that as high as 40 percent of the billions of Chinese women living from 1100 to 1902, when an Imperial decree banned it, had their feet bound with ten-feet-long strips of cloth.

The entire sexual culture in China revolved around these tiny feet. Marriage

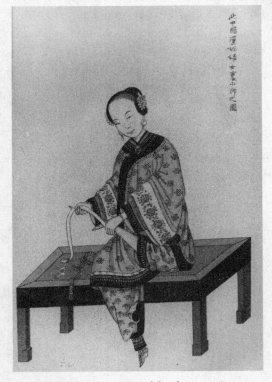

Ideal. A Chinese artist's view of the elegant petite "Lotus Foot."

dowries were often based on the tininess of the bethrothed's shoe. Only husbands could see their wives feet unbound. All Chinese prostitutes had bound feet, as did cross-dressing male prostitutes catering to homosexuals.

The origin of the custom is lost in the mists but the popular version is that 11th-century Empress Taki was born with a club foot and decreed that all aristocratic ladies should imitate her foot shape.

Historians, on the other hand, tend to trace the custom back to court dancers who were admired for their tiny feet as they danced on a carpet of lotus petals. Desire to emulate these women led others to try to reduce the size of their own feet.

The practice grew to a national obsession. "For the husband, the foot is more interesting than the face," wrote Dr. J. J. Matignon, who spent thirty years in China around the turn of the century. Sex manuals abounded with the proper techniques for maximum foot pleasure. "When I loved a woman, I went all the way and wished I would swallow her up, but only the tiny feet could be placed in my mouth," one Chinese man told interviewer Howard S. Levy for his book, *Chinese Foot-Binding.*

Another spoke reverentially of the aroma. "Every night I smell her feet, placing the tip of my nose by the smell, which is like no identifiable aroma of perfume." (Before you scoff, remember the women didn't wear leather shoes, they wore scented silk slippers and they didn't exercise a lot.)

When they did walk, it was dubbed the "willow walk" because of the way they swayed along. And connoisseurs enthused that the unnaturally pointed foot and suspended heel forced the thighs forward, plumped out the buttocks, and, it was said, tightened the vaginal muscles. "The smaller the woman's foot, the more wondrous became the folds of the vagina," claimed Sun Mu-han, a 19th-century ambassador to Russia. "There constantly developed layer after layer of folds in the vagina . . . those who have personally experienced this in sexual intercourse feel a supernatural exaltation."

Sex in the fleshy arches of the foot was also popular, as was eating seeds or nuts from between the toes. Some women were said to achieve orgasm from having their feet licked.

Whatever the pleasure, foot-binding caused severe pain for Chinese girls that lasted for four to six years, and was followed by a sedentary life as a sexual plaything. That tens of millions of Chinese women did it for a millennium is a tad mind-boggling, at least to a Westerner.

Mao Tse-Tung finally drove out the last vestiges of the practice with his Communist Revolution. ❧

HERMAPHRODITES: IN ART AND REAL LIFE

Imagine a voluptuous, full-breasted woman with the ample genitals of a man. Sexual paradise or hell? Joke or dream date? To the ancients, who were much more open to bisexual urges, this was a provocative, amusing question. Clients en-

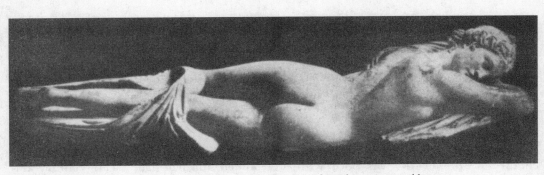

The peaceful sleepy backside view of a famous hermaphrodite statue from the ancient world . . .

tering the bordello in Pompeii were titillated by hermaphrodites painted on the walls. And an ancient door handle has survived showing a busty man/woman with an erection.

In the Louvre, there's a Roman copy of a famous Greek 5th-century B.C. statue of a hermaphrodite. At first glance, the sculpture appears to be a stunningly beautiful woman lying down with her head resting in the crook of her arm and her breasts nestled in the covers; but if you walk around to the other side, you see a knee raised slightly propping up the body and revealing the extended penis of a man.

When Théophile Gautier saw it, the 19th-century French author described it as "an enigmatic statue of *disturbing* beauty." "Is it a young man or a woman? a goddess or a god?" he asked. "Love, afraid of being base, hesitates and suspends its judgement."

In the Middle Ages, theologians deemed these men/women "beasts." In the

. . . and the startling front view.

early 1990s, a visitor to New York's Times Square before the wave of censorship could see aisles in the porn shops dedicated to "trans-sexuals," surgically enhanced creatures with silicon breasts towering over impressive male genitals.

This is a baffling topic; for some, hermaphrodites are the ultimate sexual one-stop shopping; for others they are a pitiable hodgepodge, a human Picasso.

In real life, according to medical studies, natural hermaphrodites (i.e., without cosmetic surgery or hormone injections) are *extremely* rare in the human species. (And no, they cannot impregnate themselves.)

Doctors, especially since the Renaissance, have been fascinated by the concept. "There are few subjects of anatomy, which have been more studied than hermaphroditism," states the *Grand Larousse*, the French equivalent of *Encyclopedia Britannica*. And the *Grand Larousse* article goes on to cite "among numerous researchers" sixteen distinguished doctors by name. It's a very complicated medical topic because hermaphrodites never have *all* the fully formed sexual characteristics of both sexes: such as ovaries, vagina, clitoris, penis, two testicles, etc.

Basically, hermaphrodites fall into three types: ones that have slightly more of the sexual organs of the male, those with slightly more female sexual characteristics, and finally, those that have an almost equal balance of the two—even if some of those organs are malformed. For instance, a case reported in 1924 as one that "more nearly approximates the perfect hermaphrodite than any other which has been reported" featured a patient with a penis, a single testicle on one side and an ovary on the other.

While medical categories can quickly seem arcane, the ancient myth, tracing the origin of hermaphrodites, is much more accessible (and titillating).

Ovid recounts that Hermaphroditus was the exquisitely beautiful *son* of Hermes and Aphrodite, and was bathing in a spring, watched over by a nymph named Salmacis. She fell passionately in love with the young man swimming naked in the water. "At the sight, Salmacis was spellbound. She was on fire with passion to possess his naked beauty and her very eyes flamed with a brilliance like that of the dazzling sun . . . She could scarcely bear to wait, or to defer the joys which she anticipated."

She stripped naked and dove in after him; he tried to fight her off as she kissed and caressed him. Though he struggled hard, she succeeded in twining her body around him like ivy, like a serpent, like an octopus. "You might fight, you rogue, but you will not escape," she shouted. "May the gods grant me this: may no time to come ever separate him from me or me from him." And the gods granted her wish.

Plato in the *Symposium* argues that there used to be three genders: male, female, and the union of the two. "They once had a real existence, but it is now lost, and the name (*'androgynos'*) only is preserved as a term of reproach." So, apparently the Greeks, who were much more open to homosexuality, when they wanted to insult someone, called him or her: "You %$^%$^# androgyne!" As slurs go, there's something very advanced about it, especially since there were so few hermaphrodites to feel the sting.

Paradise or hell? Joke or dream date? You decide.

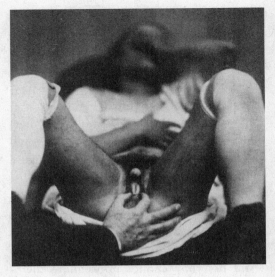

HERMAPHRODITE CASE HISTORIES: BEARDED MARY, c. 1560

Ambroise Paré (1517–1590), dubbed the father of modern surgery, recounts a case he encountered while traveling in the Champagne region of France. A fifteen-year-old girl named Marie was tending to her herd of piglets when one escaped. Marie leaped a ditch to catch the little porker, when she felt something rip in her crotch and Marie ran home to her mother, saying that her guts were falling out. When her mother examined her, she found a penis and two testicles had descended through a rip in the skin. Marie was eventually taken to the bishop of Chalons who rechristened him/her "Germain." (The locals started singing a song warning girls against leaping ditches lest they become boys.) Paré describes Germain, a decade later, as being an athletic young man of medium height with a thick red beard.

NADAR'S HERMAPHRODITE

The early French photographer, Nadar, took portraits of many of the famous men of his generation. He also captured a hermaphrodite in 1860 in the only series of photographs he ever copyrighted. The surgeon, Jules-Germain Maisonneuve, assisted in the demonstration. This rare photo is now on display at Musée D'Orsay in Paris. ✺

DOUBLE PENIS

In 1869, doctors in Paris decided to photograph one of the most unusual genital anomalies ever observed: the fully functional double penis of Juan Battista de los Santos, a thirty-four-year-old Portuguese man. The doctors noted that the subject has "two penises of imposing caliber, each free and independent" . . . that he uses "the slightly larger one for sexual intercourse." They added, though: "It frequently occurs that he profits from the richness of his means to use each of the organs one after the other, and sometimes even simultaneously." De los Santos could

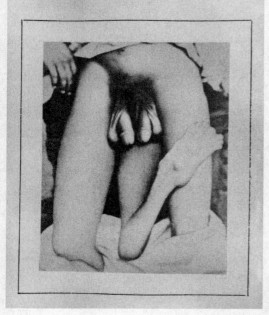

REVUE PHOTOGRAPHIQUE

DES HOPITAUX

achieve erection and ejaculation simultaneously in both; he could also urinate at the same time through both.

What is that strange item in the center of the photo? De los Santos also had a third leg, with ten webbed toes, which he strapped to his thigh when walking. The man was said to be cheerful, lusty, and of above average intelligence.

THE FATHER OF MASOCHISM

Leopold von Sacher-Masoch (1836–1895), a minor German novelist, begged his wife to dress up in furs and beat him. She finally left him when he kept demanding that she, though pregnant, have affairs with strangers he found through "Help Wanted" ads.

Although his fiction will be justly forgotten, his name will live on, since sexologist Richard von Krafft-Ebing used it to coin the term "masochism." Von Sacher-Masoch's most notorious work, *Venus in Furs,* profiles a very literate man who agrees to become the slave of a stunningly beautiful and cruel woman, named Wanda. Here is the first scene after the hero has signed the binding contract, handed over his passport and money to Wanda, and then has been tied by "negresses" to a pillar. Wanda addresses him.

"You are no longer the man I love, but *my slave,* at my mercy even unto life and death."

"You shall know me!"

Thank you, my Venus in Furs. Novelist Leopold von Sacher-*Masoch* is shown getting inspiration in this "Weiner Figaro" cartoon of 1879.

"First of all you shall have a taste of the whip in all seriousness, without having done anything to deserve it, so that you may understand what to expect if you are awkward, disobedient or refractory."

With a wild grace she rolled back her fur-lined sleeve and struck me across the back.

I winced, for the whip cut like a knife into my flesh.

"Well, how do you like that?" she exclaimed.

I was silent.

"Just wait, you will yet whine like a dog beneath my whip," she threatened, and simultaneously began to strike me again.

The blows fell quickly, in rapid succession, with terrific force upon my back, arms and neck; I had to grit my teeth not to scream aloud. Now she struck me in the face; warm blood ran down, but she laughed and continued her blows.

"It is only now I understand you," she said. "It really is a joy to have someone so completely in one's power, and a man at that, who loves you—you do love me?— No—Oh! I'll tear you to shreds yet, and with each blow my pleasure will grow.

Now, twist like a worm, scream, whine! You will find no mercy in me!"

Finally, she seemed tired. She tossed the whip aside, stretched out on the ottoman, and rang.

The negresses entered.

"Untie him!"

As they loosened the rope, I fell to the floor like a lump of wood. The black women grinned, showing their white teeth.

"Untie the rope around his feet."

They did it but I was unable to rise.

"Come over here, Gregor."

I approached the beautiful woman. Never did she seem more seductive to me than to-day in spite of all her cruelty and contempt.

"One step farther," Wanda commanded. "Now kneel down and kiss my foot."

She extended her foot beyond the hem of white satin, and I, the suprasensual fool, pressed my lips upon it.

"Now, you won't lay eyes on me for an entire month, Gregor," she said, seriously. "I want to become a stranger to you so you will more easily adjust yourself to our new relationship. In the meantime you will work in the garden and await my orders. Now off with you, slave!" ✺

EROTICA: NAPOLEON, LINCOLN, AND OTHERS

NAPOLEON READS ALOUD HIS OWN EROTIC ADVENTURES, 1817

Napoleon didn't exactly have a fun time when in exile on the tiny island of Saint Helena, stranded there from 1815 after

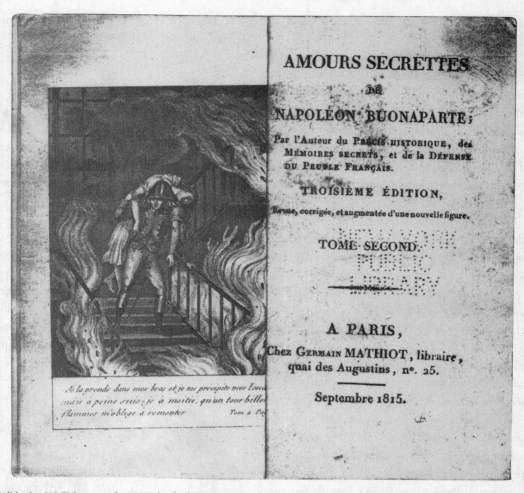

I did what?!? Title page of an 1815 book claiming to reveal Napoleon's love life. The former emperor enjoyed the faux memoirs.

Waterloo till his death in 1821. But one winter evening in 1817, he and a few choice friends certainly enjoyed themselves. "At 7:30, I go into the drawing room," wrote Napoleon's longtime companion, General Baron Gourgaud in his private journal. "His Majesty is busy, reading to Bertrand and O'Meara the *Amours secrettes de Buonaparte*. He is laughing heartily, and says he knows none of the women mentioned. 'They make a Hercules of me!' he exclaims."

The illustration above is from a rare edition of that phony memoir, *Amours secrettes*, and shows a young Napoleon carrying a pretty woman down the stairs of a burning building. The caption refers the reader to page 22, where he or she can read the fictional scene that no doubt amused the former emperor.

Young Napoleon has rushed into a burning building.

"What a sight displays itself before my eyes! a young unconscious woman, stretched out on the floor and wearing nothing but her nightgown. I have no time to lose: I scoop her up in my arms and race towards the stairs; but when I am half way down, a whirlwind of flames forces me to re-ascend. I am lost, a cruel death would be my reward for bravery."

But Napoleon escapes by breaking through the wall and on into the next building, where he finds himself safe in a locked empty room.

"I examined the person that I had saved: what good luck! she is young, she is *charmante!* I was eighteen years old: for a long time I had been deprived of the pleasures of love; no witness could reach me here; a young woman, beautiful and undressed, was at my disposal. Ah! it would have been too much at that moment not to manhandle modesty and take advantage of the situation. I approach my fainting beauty: a very passionate kiss roughly applied to her mouth rouses her a bit. She wants to fight my desires but is too weak to repel them; my victory is complete before she has even entirely regained consciousness. I rush to break the lock and carry this young woman to safety. At the bottom of the stairs, she tells me: 'For pity's sake, *monsieur,* cover me up.'"

Napoleon is welcomed as a hero by his fellow soldiers. He concludes: "In love, as in battle, few men know better than I how to keep a secret."

You can still hear the boys laughing on St. Helena. 🌀

EARLIEST EROTIC PHOTOS

At the birth of every new medium of expression, from cave-paintings to CD-ROMs, some canny fellow has rushed to try out erotica. Here are two little known stories from the early days of photography.

ABRAHAM LINCOLN AND NUDIE PHOTOS

One day in 1863, his mind reeling from the pressures of the endless war, Abraham Lincoln opened an envelope in the White House and out tumbled an ad for girlie photos. The handbill touted that photos could be ordered by mail for twelve cents a piece

French photos like this one circulated among Union soldiers during the Civil War.

or $1.20 a dozen, twelve-inch-by-fifteen-inch pictures suitable for framing. Choices included "Indian Maidens," "Wood Nymphs' Frolic," or "Circassian Slavegirls."

One Union Captain M. G. Tousley had written this letter directly to President Lincoln complaining about the deluge of pornographic photos and pictures being passed around by soldiers and even officers. To drive his message home, Tousley had slipped into the envelope a handbill he had confiscated, called "New Pictures for Bachelors."

There's no record of Lincoln's response—either to the captain or to the mail-order company. ✸

PARIS: BEFORE THE ZOOM LENS

Dr. Ambroise Tardieu, France's leading expert in the fledgling science of legal medicine, was called in to help in a rather unusual investigation of nude photos. Let's listen to the doctor's own description of the situation:

Middle of August 1861. The authorities— amid a truly bottomless stack of pornographic photos seized—found a series that depicted women . . . the exposure of whose genitals seemed to have been complicated by a refinement of singular obscenity. One's eye could penetrate so far that it seemed that the "spread-eagling" might have been achieved through some artificial process.

This circumstance, since it would have added to the criminal charges against the photographer, needed to be explored. At the invitation of the presiding judge, I was compelled to examine the seized images.

My mission was to determine whether the position in the photographs could have been achieved through a natural pose, or if, on the contrary, it was more likely to believe that a foreign object had been inserted to keep the genitals gaping wide for view.

. . . I went to Saint-Lazare—where Doctor Costilhes very generously let me be present at the "exam" of a very great number of women placed in exactly the same position as the models in the photographs. The results of these observations quite plainly confirmed my first impression . . .

In all the photographs, the "spread-eagling" of the genitals resulted either from the natural conformation of the women, or the position in which they had been placed.

This "spread-eagling" does not exceed the natural limits reached by certain women, who simply open their thighs and pull back the labia minora. There is no grounds for assuming that any of them used an artificial means—notably the introduction of a foreign body in the sexual parts.

The photos have not survived. ✸

COMSTOCK: DEATH GRIP ON VICE

Benjamin Franklin was purportedly the first American to own a copy of *Fanny Hill,* and up to the 1840s, Americans with a letch for the lewd read books imported from England and Europe. Although many states had laws on the books against "indecent" or "obscene" material, "as in

Europe, enforcement was so lax as to be non-existent," states Walter Kendrick in *The Secret Museum.*

Then in 1846, an enterprising Irishman, William Haynes, publishing out of New York City, began to hire American writers to churn out book after smutty book set in uniquely American locales, with titles such as *Bertha: Memoirs of a New England Spring Mattress* or *The California Widow* or *Gay Girls of New York.*

American erotica was born. Haynes made a mint, and by 1871, his yearly sales were pegged at 100,000 copies.

Enter Anthony Comstock (1844–1915). The early history of erotic writing in America is dominated by this one fat, bald-headed YMCA crusader.

Born to Puritan stock in New Canaan, Connecticut, Comstock moved to Brooklyn, where he landed a job as a dry-goods store clerk and eventually headed up the YMCA's "Committee for the Suppression of Vice." Finding New York City and State officials not eager to enforce antiobscenity statutes, he lobbied hard in Washington for tougher federal laws. On March 3, 1873, President Grant signed "An Act for the Suppression of Trade in, and Circulation of, obscene Literature and Articles of immoral Use." A federal salary was set aside enabling the Postmaster General to appoint a "special agent" to enforce the law, and that agent was Comstock, who held the post and wielded *extraordinary* power until his death (a la Hoover, later in the FBI) to determine what was obscene and whom to prosecute. He was a fearless, bribe-proof, self-righteous, one-man vice squad who fought nudity in classical art, outlawed the likes of Boccaccio, and even prosecuted store clerks for dressing a mannequin in a store window. "If you open the door to anything," he later wrote, "the filth will all pour in and the degradation of youth will follow."

By January 1874, Comstock estimated he had already destroyed 134,000 pounds of "improper" books, and 194,000 pictures and 60,300 "rubber articles" and 5,500 indecent playing cards. Near the end of his career in 1913, he bragged to the *New York Evening World* that he had destroyed 160 tons of obscene material and convicted "persons enough to fill a passenger train of sixty-one coaches, sixty coaches containing sixty passengers each and the sixty-first almost full." (Comstock always retained a clerkish knack for tallying.)

Comstock and his colleagues in virtue were so effective that very few copies of *any* erotic books authored by Americans during his reign have survived. One of the few to live beyond Comstock and earn a bit of notoriety is *The Memoirs of Dolly Morton*, a novel about a young girl's sexual adventures with abolitionists and slave owners during the Civil War. One early scene, which would have made Comstock apoplectic, features a pale stern Quakeress abolitionist and the young heroine, Dolly Morton, caught by a proslavery lynch mob. To punish them for helping runaway slaves, the men strip the women and prepare to whip them. "The men pressed closer to the ladder, and I could see their eyes glisten as they fixed them with lecherous looks on Miss Dean's half-naked body. [Ringleader] Stevens, after gazing for a moment or two

Cartoonist's delight, Anthony Comstock, seen in this 1915 Robert Minor cartoon. The caption read: "Your honor, this woman gave birth to a naked child!"

at her straight figure, exclaimed with a laugh: 'Je-ru-sa-lem! What a little bottom she's got. It ain't no bigger than a man's. Perhaps she is a man!' The men then turn her around and are astounded. 'By gosh!' exclaims one. 'I've never seen such a fleece between a woman's legs. Darn me if she wouldn't have to be sheared before a man could get into her.'"

The novel features flagellation and in-terracial orgies, as Dolly a la Fanny Hill discovers sex. (There's even a chance this lone American "classic" was not written by an American but by a Brit in Paris and survived only because it was published abroad.)

Comstock wasn't content to ban out-right erotica like the above, he also confis-cated birth control literature, Suffragette newspapers, and plays.

When he tried to close George Bernard Shaw's play *Mrs. Warren's Profession*, the acerbic playwright commented: "Comstockery is the world's standing joke at the expense of the United States . . . it confirms the deep-seated conviction of the Old World that America is a provincial place, a second rate country town."

Although many Americans grew fed up with Comstock's prudery (and cartoonists had a field day with him), Comstock was still potent enough to be appointed by President Wilson in 1915 to be U.S. representative to the International Purity Congress. Comstock died that year and the United States headed on its bumpy course towards relative freedom of expression, a battle that was capped by the 1966 Supreme Court decision on obscenity, *Memoirs vs. Massachusetts*. That decision, a victory for Fanny Hill over New England prudes, effectively took erotic books from under the counter to the shelves of mainstream bookstores.

"Comstockery," however, tried to make a comeback in the 1990s as Congress passed and President Clinton signed a law in 1995 to prohibit "indecent" material as tame as *Playboy* from the Internet. The politicians' cry of "Save the children" almost seemed quoted from Comstock's *Traps for the Young* (1883). "Our youth are in danger," he wrote in the preface. "Mentally and morally they are cursed by a literature that is a disgrace." ✸

CHEESECAKE ON THE MOVIE MENU

The first productions made in the 1890s at Edison's Black Maria studio relied heavily on physical comedy, such as Fred Ott's sneeze, and *cheesecake*. The serpentine dance of Annabelle was a big hit on the movie industry's opening night in 1896. A Biograph catalogue from that era lists *How Bridget Served the Salad Undressed*, and *The Pretty Stenographer, or Caught in the Act*. A 1905 hit was *The Flatiron Building on a Windy Day*. As many current New Yorkers know, this triangular building at Twenty-third Street and Fifth Avenue acts like a wind tunnel, generating great updrafts. "It is at this corner where one can get a good idea of the prevailing types in hosiery and lingerie," boasts the catalogue of Crescent Films. "This is the finest picture that has ever been taken at this corner, and we can safely recommend it as something exceptionally fine." ✸

WORLD HISTORY

DEFENDING DEMOCRACY IN ANCIENT ATHENS

Some "politically correct" modern critics have complained that democracy in ancient Athens did not extend to women, slaves, or foreigners. That's true: out of a population of about 140,000 total, perhaps 30,000-plus free Athenian males over eighteen could vote. But the criticism is a bit silly, since slaves never voted anywhere back then and women got the vote, say, in the United States in 1920, about two-and-a-half millennia after Athens's noble experiment.

The system in Athens was *very* revolutionary and *very* participatory. You didn't just vote and forget about it till the next election. In Athens, every male citizen over eighteen was entitled to attend the Assembly, Athens's highest legislative body, which convened at least forty times a year. Amazingly, about six thousand men usually showed up for each meeting. From among those over thirty years old who volunteered, five hundred were chosen *by lot* each for the Council of 500, which set the agenda for the Assembly. The Council, in turn, had a core committee of fifty men, and that group changed every thirty-six days. Top officials, even generals, were voted in and out of office; lower officials were chosen by lot. (Playwright Sophocles was once elected to head the military.)

Athenian democracy, though, did have one feature which would seem especially strange to us: ostracism. Once a year, if the Assembly opted to hold an ostracism vote, and if more than six thousand ballots on clay shards mentioned one name, that person was banished from Athens for ten years. Imagine voting to exile Donald Trump or Henry Kissinger. The practice sounds rife for abuse and Athens eventually abolished ostracism, which was probably first intended to boot any potential law-abusing tyrant.

With modest variations, the Athenian democracy thrived from 508 B.C. to 322 B.C., when Phillip of Macedonia (Alexander the Great's father) overran the city-state. "During its 180 years of democratic government," writes Greek scholar Robert Browning, "Athens saw an unparalleled flourishing of art, literature, philosophy and science, which has become part of the common heritage of mankind."

Before we all get weepy over how democracy stimulates the arts, let's remember Orson Welles's line in *The Third Man:* "In Italy for thirty years under the Borgias they had warfare, terror, murder, bloodshed—they produced Michelangelo, Leonardo da Vinci and the Renaissance. In Switzerland they had brotherly love, five hundred years of democracy and peace, and what did they produce . . . ? The cuckoo clock." 🌀

IF I RULED THE WORLD . . .

THE ECCENTRICITIES OF POWER

The exchange was either profound or moronic. "The very rich are different from you and me," F. Scott Fitzgerald told Ernest Hemingway, who replied, with his usual gruffness, "Yes, they have more money."*

They also can afford to enjoy themselves, in ways perhaps out of the reach of most mortals.

- The Medicis kept a fully stocked dwarf mansion as a sort of human dollhouse.

- Pope Leo X had a pet elephant.

- Nero's bedroom ceiling showered rose petals.

---

*The original source of this riposte was apparently one Mary Colum who first said it to Ernest Hemingway. After that, Hemingway and Fitzgerald chiseled the anecdote, creating a maze of slight distortions and wrong attributions, worthy of a couple of fiction writers.

- Genghis Khan demanded one thousand virgins *a year* in tribute from his conquered territories.

- Ivan the Terrible blinded Russia's greatest architect so he couldn't design buildings for others.

- At Baron Alfred de Rothschild's, the butler would ask guests wanting milk in their tea: "Jersey, Hereford, or shorthorn, sir?"

- Before King Xerxes (in the Bible story) would allow the beautiful peasant girl Esther into his bed, she had to be bathed and perfumed for a year, "six months with oil of myrrh and six months with sweet scents."

- Elvis Presley used to have deep-fried peanut-butter-and-jelly sandwiches flown in to Nashville from Seattle.

- Sultan Ahmet I (1589–1617) had two slaves stand by his bed all night ready to replace his fur covers in case they slipped off.

- Seventeen-year-old Roman emperor, Heliogabulus (A.D. 204–222) once ordered: "Bring me a thousand pounds of cobwebs." 🌀

CLEOPATRA WAS NO LIZ TAYLOR

Cleopatra (69–30 B.C.), the legendary beauty, was apparently no beauty at all, if the coin pictured on the next page is an accurate portrait. (Think Anjelica Huston on a bad day.) "Her beauty was by no means flawless or even remarkable upon

Hollywood: Elizabeth Taylor as Cleopatra in the 1963 mega-budget film costarring Richard Burton.

first meeting," wrote ancient historian Plutarch, "but anyone listening to her but a moment sensed her irresistible charm." He added: "Her voice was beguilingly rich and sweet, and she used her tongue like a many-stringed musical instrument."

Given that Cleo was no stunner, it is even more impressive that she was twice able to seduce the Roman generals who conquered Egypt—first Julius Caesar, then Marc Antony—and thereby save her kingdom. Antony eventually left his wife

"Her beauty was by no means flawless," wrote Plutarch of Cleopatra. Scholars say this ancient coin depicts what Cleopatra probably looked like.

for her and plunged Rome into civil war. Cleopatra, apparently, created a court of exquisite hedonism and had a great sense of naughty play. (One of her pranks: She had a diver tie a teeny salted herring on Antony's fishing line, and then she brought a crowd to watch the great warrior haul it in.) Rumors spread about other uses to which Cleo put her tongue, even a heroic night of servicing one hundred noblemen. But that was all probably just war propaganda and foreigner bashing. When Antony and Cleopatra lost the war at sea against the Roman navy, they both committed suicide. He, it's said, fell on his sword upon a false report of her death. And she let herself be bitten by a poisonous asp—but not probably out of despair over Antony's death but rather to avoid being paraded naked in disgrace through the streets of Rome by Augustus Caesar. ✺

NERO: TRYING TO KILL HIS MOTHER

Nero's attempts to kill his mother play like something out of a *very* dark comedy, like the faux suicides of *Harold and Maude,* or the dog killings of *A Fish Called Wanda.*

Nero (A.D. 37–68), pale and pudgy, deeply resented his domineering mother, Agrippina. For public relations reasons, though, he wanted her death to appear to be by natural causes. This proved surprisingly difficult, according to gossipy Roman historian Suetonius (tr. Robert Graves in *The Twelve Caesars*), who recounted:

Nero (A.D. 37–68)

"[Nero] tried to poison her three times, but she had always taken the antidote in advance; so he rigged up a machine in the ceiling of her bedroom which would dislodge the panels and drop them on her while she slept. However, one of the people involved in the plot gave the secret away. Then he had a collapsible boat designed which would either sink or have its cabin fall on top of her. Under pretence of a reconciliation, he sent her the most friendly note inviting her to celebrate the Feast of Minerva with him at Baiae, and on her arrival made one of his captains stage an ostensibly accidental collision with the galley in which she had sailed. Then he protracted the feast until a late hour, and when at last she said: 'I really must get back to Bauli,' offered her his collapsible boat instead of the damaged galley. Nero was in a very happy mood as he led Agrippina down to the quay, and even kissed her breasts before she stepped aboard. He sat up all night, on tenterhooks of anxiety, waiting for the outcome of his scheme."

Hours later, his mother's freed slave rushed in "joyfully to report" that although a horrible accident had occurred, Agrippina had swum to safety.

"Nero, in desperation, ordered one of his men to drop a dagger surreptitiously behind [his mother's freed slave], Agerinus, whom he arrested at once on a charge of having been hired to kill the emperor.

"After this he arranged for Agrippina to be killed, and made it seem as if she had sent Agerinus to assassinate him but committed suicide on hearing that the plot had miscarried. Other more gruesome details are supplied by reliable authorities: it appears that Nero rushed off to examine Agrippina's corpse, handling her limbs and, between drinks to satisfy his thirst, discussing their good and bad points."

Nero, who never felt guilt, felt guilt for this crime. "He often admitted that he was hounded by his mother's ghost and that the Furies were pursuing him with whips and burning torches; and set Persian magicians at work to conjure up the ghost and entreat its forgiveness."

Nero was certainly unhinged; he married his slave boy, killed his pregnant wife with a brutal kick, and went to the Olympics where he won every event he entered. One thing he didn't do, though. He didn't fiddle while Rome burned; Nero dolled himself up in a costume and sang "The Fall of Troy." 🌀

PAINFUL DEATH OF AN ENGLISH KING

British schoolkids still titter about this bit of history.

King Edward II (1284–1327) was not well loved in England, especially after his repeated failures to capture Scotland. (For those of you who saw Mel Gibson's rousing *Braveheart*, he was the fay son of

King Edward II of England. Director Mel Gibson portrayed him as gay in *Braveheart*. The scepter shown here seems to be an inside joke.

reigning king ["Long Shanks"], a baffled boy with a handsome male lover who married but never appreciated his strong-willed wife, Isabelle of France.)

It was long rumored that Edward II was homosexual and that he elevated his lovers. A coup—engineered by his estranged wife, Isabelle, and her lover—overthrew him and they imprisoned him in Berkeley Castle.

There, a band of conspirators snuck into his cell and shoved a red-hot poker up his ass while strangling him. As the vicar of the castle, John Treviso, put it: "with a hoote broche putte thro the secret place posterialle." This was supposed to be payback for all his sodomy. Historians are divided over the red-hot poker but several contemporary sources repeated the story. Given the medieval mind-set of sometimes castrating sex offenders and chopping off the hands of thieves, it's a much better bet than Catherine and the horse. 🌀

A VERY STRANGE PATH TO THE THRONE OF A VAST EMPIRE

It sounds like something out of the *Arabian Nights*.

A stunningly beautiful thirteen-year-old blond Italian girl was sailing from her home port of Venice across the Mediterranean around 1575 to visit relatives when her boat was captured by Moslem pirates. The captain immediately noticed the beauty of this teenager, a member of the wealthy Baffo family; she was tall, and Turkish historians said she had "a figure that danced as she walked." The captain, who was going to take her to the slave markets of Constantinople, instead judged her fit for the sultan and sold her directly into the harem.

The Turks called her "Safiyeh," or the "Light One," and her name has been corrupted to Sophia Baffo (1562–1603).

Fortunately for her, she bore Sultan Murad III (1546–1595) his first son, which gave her primary position among the 250 or so women in the harem. (The sultans, back then, never married, but produced heirs by slave girls purchased for the harem. Ironically, then, the sultans were always sons of slaves.)

From her position of power, and especially since Murad III spent much of his time fathering 103 children, Sophia was able in effect to rule the massive Ottoman Empire which stretched from North Africa to Persia.

She favored her native Venice, prevented a war against it and smuggled notes back and forth to Europe through a Jewish jeweler named Chiarezza; she even had a secret correspondence with Catherine de Medici and exchanged gifts with Queen Elizabeth.

When Sultan Murad III died, Baffo's son was heir to the throne. The ruling Turks at that time had a unique way of dealing with sibling rivalry and avoiding potential succession wars; the new sultan by law had "the right to execute his brothers."

Sophia, it's said, instructed her son, Mahomet III, to invite his nineteen brothers to the palace, telling them they must be circumcised, but when they arrived, they were instead strangled by silken cord. She now had a continued hammerlock on power for the eight years of his reign.

Her unlikely position atop the empire ended, however, when her son the sultan died. Safiyeh Baffo, the Venetian noble turned slave girl, was strangled in her bed.

LIFE AFTER SOPHIA: THE CAGE

The next sultan, Ahmed I, decided not to kill his brothers and replaced the "Right of Fratricide" in 1603 with the supposedly more humane "Cage" or "Kafes."

All potential heirs were locked up in a luxurious building, served by deaf-mutes and very birth control–conscious slave girls. (The penalty for pregnancy was death; some had their ovaries removed.)

The result of the law, though, was that after a decade or so in cushy isolation, drooling idiots would emerge from "The Cage" to suddenly become ruler of one of

the world's largest empires. One sultan came out and soon made his teen lovers governors of Cairo and Damascus; another liked to practice archery on live prisoners; a third had his entire harem of 280 women drowned in sacks in the Bosporus. As harem expert, N. M. Penzer, pointed out: "To [The Cage] are due the weakness, vices and imbecility of so many of the sultans and, to a large extent, the gradual decay and fall of the Ottoman Empire." ❧

UNHOLY RELICS: CROMWELL'S HEAD

During his lifetime, Puritan Oliver Cromwell, the dour zealot who banned theater a generation after Shakespeare, was rarely the life of the party. But after his death, he often starred at social gatherings, and was in fact quite amusing. His head, that is.

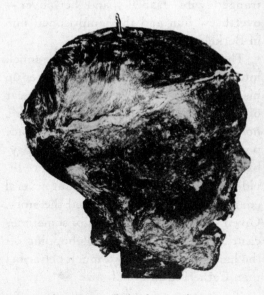

Puritan Oliver Cromwell's head on a spike.

Oliver Cromwell led the Puritan takeover of England, as that bloody Civil War culminated in the beheading of King Charles I. In 1660, when the monarchy was restored, Cromwell's body was dug up and publicly beheaded, and the former Lord Protector's head was placed on a spike on Westminster Hall. It remained there, haggard, bearded, for twenty years, an object lesson for anyone thinking of killing a king.

In the late 1700s, the Russell family ran a small museum, with the zealot's dome as centerpiece. In 1814, one Josiah Henry Wilkinson bought the piece for £230 and started lugging it for show-and-tell at parties. A letter from a woman who attended one of those parties has survived. "Mr. Wilkinson its present possessor doats on it," wrote Maria Edgeworth, "a frightful skull it is—covered with parched yellow skin like any other mummy and with its chestnut hair, eyebrows and beard in glorious preservation—the head is still fastened to a pole."

Ms. Edgeworth describes how the guests took turns standing at the window holding it. She notes she could still see "a cut of the axe" on the back of the head made by the "bungling executioner" and that "one ear has been torn off as it should be." But the final proof that this was truly Cromwell was "the famous wart of Oliver's" over the left eye.

Cromwell finally left the party circuit for good just before the time The Beatles were forming. In a chapel in Cambridge, an unusual plaque reads: "Near to this place was buried on 25 March, 1960, the head of Oliver Cromwell, Lord Protector of England, Scotland and Ireland, Fellow Commoner of this College 1616–7." 🐚

CATHERINE THE GREAT AND THE HORSE

It is probably *the* dirty story of history: that Catherine the Great (1727–1796), the lusty ruler of Russia, was so wild with sexual desire that one day she was screwing a horse when the harness broke and killed her.

It's simply not true. Catherine liked *officers* of the Imperial Horse Guard, not the

The caption reads: "The Empress of Russia Receiving Her Brave Guards." This illustration by British artist Thomas Rowlandson (1757–1827) captures the gossip spread around Europe about this powerful female monarch.

The real Catherine the Great, from a contemporary illustration. She corresponded in French with Voltaire.

horses. Yes, Catherine also liked sex—one her favorite toasts was "God grant us our desires and grant them quickly." This ruler of a vast empire had a dozen documented lovers (really, male mistresses) over her thirty-four years in power. But she had them one after another. This level of sexual consumption would hardly rate a footnote for most male monarchs; in fact, their virility might have been questioned. What was unusual about Catherine was how organized she was in selecting her lovers. She had a lady-in-waiting sample the man's prowess in bed and then she had a British doctor examine him for diseases. The young officer would soon be given 100,000 rubles and a country estate. No doubt what roiled foreign diplomats at her court was that this woman, who was pretty when young, grew stout and gray, and at age sixty-two was still taking the likes of twenty-one-year-old Platon Zuboff to bed. That bred jealous rumormongering, and tales of horses.

Actually, Catherine was one of the greatest and toughest female monarchs of all time: this German-born princess plotted the death of her dotty husband, Czar Peter III, she expanded the borders of Russia, crushed rebellions, built gorgeous palaces, and was a generous patron of the arts, corresponding personally with Voltaire and Diderot.

How did she die? Catherine suffered a stroke on her way to the water closet and died on a straw mat three days later, with eyewitnesses there. ✪

NAPOLEON: FASHION VICTIM

First off, Napoleon wasn't sooo short. He was 5'2" in *"pieds de roi,"* i.e., the Old French measurement system, which equals 5'6" in modern measures, just a tad below average height in those days.

Second, why was Napoleon's hand always tucked in his jacket? This was a common pose for the midsize general who suffered from "neurodermatitis" or "chronic nervous itching" throughout his life. In his constant hyper state of anxiety, he often

scratched sores to the point of bleeding, even ones on his face. He once commented, "I live only by my skin," but it wasn't always the skin on his face that bothered him. An attack of very painful hemorrhoids at Waterloo often kept Napoleon, a brilliant aggressive strategist, from riding out to survey the troops or consult with field commanders during the final two days, when the battle was still winnable. Several sources claim he was high in his tent on painkilling opium for much of that time.

And finally, what about those *tight* pants? Napoleon very clearly set Europe on a fashion trend toward extremely tight pants, requiring men to tell their tailors whether they chose to "dress" to the right or left. Some fat Frenchmen looked truly ridiculous in this style; nonetheless, they wore it out of respect for Napoleon. Unfortunately, for the emperor, in his waning years, either due to a pituitary deficiency or perhaps arsenic poisoning, this revealing style didn't exactly suit him, since his manly organ observed at autopsy by a British doctor was reported to be "extremely small and underdeveloped." Some scholars, however, believe the rumormongering about Napoleon's penis size was one last shot of British revenge.

When Napoleon's personal artifacts were put on auction October 30, 1969, at Christie's in London, included on the roster was one "mummified tendon," loudly whispered by British publicists to be Napoleon's penis. Some war wounds never heal. 🌀

WITCHES: RELIGIOUS MARTYRS? SEXUAL ATHLETES?

Every Halloween, thousands of little American girls troop around in pointy black hats, carry brooms, and pretend to cast evil spells for a few hours. An equally appropriate costume might be to wear a Nazi prisoner outfit with a Jewish star on the breast.

Witches—contrary to the Disney-inspired view of an old warted crone preying on children—were martyrs to religious fanaticism; they were executed for being heretics, prosecuted in mostly Church courts or by roving bands of Inquisitors. Most did absolutely nothing to harm their neighbors, yet suddenly found themselves sadistically tortured, interrogated about their sex lives, sentenced to die. Their relatives were forced to pay court and prison costs, often including the banquet that prosecuting judges and lawyers enjoyed the day following the executions.

From the 1400s to the early 1700s, in Europe and briefly in America, it's been estimated that more than 200,000 innocent men, women, and children (and a few animals) were burned as witches.

"The record of witchcraft is horrible and brutal," observes Rossell Robbins in his authoritative *Encyclopedia of Witchcraft and De-*

A young witch is being taught to fly by an experienced crone in this Goya etching (1799). Spanish art critics long before Freud were convinced that this broomstick wasn't just a broomstick.

monology (1959). "The filthiest passions masqueraded under the cover of religion."

Belief in witchcraft, or spellcasting, dates back to the earliest civilizations, but it wasn't until Pope Innocent VIII issued a papal bull on December 5, 1484, upgrading witchcraft to heresy that it became a capital crime throughout Europe.

The pope lit the bonfires by clearly equating witchcraft with heresy, a death-penalty offense and encouraging his Inquisitors to root it out. The papal bull stated: "Many persons of both sexes, unmindful of their own salvation and deviating from the Catholic Faith, have abused

themselves with devils, incubi and succubi, and by their incantations, spells, conjurations and other accursed superstitions and horrid charms . . ." He accuses them of killing off infants, animals, crops, of tormenting man and beast with pain and disease, of causing impotency and infertility "whereby neither husbands with wives nor wives with husbands can perform the sexual act." He accused them of blasphemy, and of joining in grotesque orgies.

This papal bull was spread throughout Europe, thanks to Gutenberg's printing press. "Whatever punishment we can order against witches by roasting and cooking them over a slow fire is not really as bad as . . . the eternal agonies which are prepared for them in Hell," wrote jurist Jean Bodin, "for the fire here cannot last much longer than an hour or so until the witches have died."

Witchcraft prosecutions tended to follow a certain sadistic pattern, inspired by a Vatican-endorsed handbook called *Malleus Maleficarum,* literally "Hammer of the Witches." (Heinrich Kramer and Jakob Sprenger—German theology professors who were appointed Inquisitors of witchcraft by Pope Innocent VIII in 1484—wrote the *Malleus* in 1486.)

SHAVING WITCHES

Many of the recommendations might surprise modern readers. First off, most witches had all their body hair and head hair removed. "The hair should be shaved from every part of her body," states the *Malleus Maleficarum.* "The reason for this is the same as that for stripping her of her clothes . . . for in order to preserve their power of silence they are in the habit of hiding some superstitious object in their clothes or in their hair, even in the most secret parts of their bodies, which must not be named."

These "superstitious objects" were supposedly charms, some made from powders from roasted bodies of unbaptized babies, charms that would enable witches to withstand torture and remain silent.

The *Malleus* does point out elsewhere that sometimes the local populace rebelled against the idea of Church officials performing *too* much searching. "Now in regions of Germany, such shaving, especially of the secret parts [i.e., the pubic hair], is not generally considered delicate, and therefore we Inquisitors do not do it . . . but in other countries the Inquisitors order the witch to be shaved all over her body, and the Inquisitor of Como informed us last year, that is, in 1485 he ordered forty-one to be burned, after they had been shaved all over."

Another motive for shaving was the search for the devil's mark. Any wart or scar could be viewed as Satan's nipple, the witch's teat, where the devil got his nourishment. These spots were supposed to be insensitive to pain, so witch-hunters would prick them with needles, some three inches long, and watch the woman's reaction. If she showed *no* pain, then she was obviously a witch. England, which forbade torturing witches, nonetheless for a decade or so allowed "pricking" witches, and notorious Matthew Hopkins roamed the countryside, being paid per witch to strip-search and poke. In stubborn cases, Hopkins supposedly used a "cheating prick," in which the needle retracted into the handle, like a toy stiletto. (Hopkins, who caused the death of one hundred or more English witches, was finally discredited in 1645, and died a year later.)

TORTURING WITCHES

"Common justice demands that a witch should not be condemned to death unless she is convicted by her own confession," states the *Malleus Maleficarum*. This meant, for those Inquisitors following *Malleus* (as most did in Europe except England) that physical evidence was never enough. Witches rarely confessed without some form of torture, and here are the guides for torturing witches, according to the Inquisitor's handbook.

First the accused would be asked to confess, then showed instruments of torture and asked again; finally they would be tortured, if necessary.

"Let the guards bind her with cords and apply her to some engine of torture," states the handbook, but adds a warning: "Let the [men] obey at once but not joyfully, rather appearing to be disturbed by their duty." *Appearing to be disturbed.*

The Inquisitors—besides probing the specific accusation of spellcasting—invariably zeroed in on two topics: sex with the devil and witches' Sabbath. Page after page of court testimony revolves around the devil's penis. (Much of it is some of the most outlandish sexual fantasy ever recorded.)

The handbook, *Malleus*, though, warns

about the pitfalls of torture. "Note that if she confesses under torture, she should then be taken to another place and questioned anew, so that she doesn't confess only under the stress of torture." (This is how the court record could indicate that so-and-so made a "free and open confession.")

Witches were usually swiftly handed over to civil authorities for execution. A condemned person who had renounced Satan might be mercifully strangled before the pyres were lit.

One of the uglier aspects of the witch persecutions—just like other Inquisitions—was the profit incentive for the Church and lay authorities. The property of anyone convicted of heresy was confiscated, and split according to varying formulas between civil and ecclesiastical authorities. Rossell Robbins points out that when the Holy Roman emperor forbade the appropriation of property in 1630, witchcraft prosecutions in Bamberg, to name one town, dropped from one hundred a year in the 1620s to twenty-four in 1630 to zero in 1631.

By the 1700s, during the age of the so-called Enlightenment, witchcraft was finally decriminalized. Great Britain, whose laws greatly influenced the American colonies, took it off the books in 1736. The path toward Disney and Halloween had begun.

THE DEVIL'S PENIS
One of the strangest aspects of witch mania was the obsessive curiosity on the part of prosecutors to hear these witches— some young and pretty—reveal all aspects of their sexual relations with the devil.

According to witchcraft handbooks, most witches agreed the devil was well endowed. One French woman measured his penis at half a yard long, the size of a kitchen utensil; another said the devil's penis "was half iron, half flesh." Yet another compared sexual intercourse with the devil to giving birth.

According to court records, young chambermaid Françoise Fontaine testified in 1591: "[The devil] had a black *membre virile* very stiff, and so thick that I experienced considerable pain when he copulated with me, because the said *membre* was as hard as flint and extremely cold. As [he] was leaving me, he kissed me repeatedly and fondled my breasts and private parts."

At another trial, Marie de Marigrane, age fifteen, a resident of Biarritz, "affirmed that she had often seen the devil couple with a multitude of women, whom she knew both by name and surname, and that it was the devil's custom to have intercourse with the beautiful women from the front and with the ugly from the rear."

Sometimes Satan appeared in the form of animals, everything from roosters to deers to goats. The relentless sexual descriptions grow mind-boggling. One eyewitness, who observed the goings-on at a witches' Sabbath, said the devil's penis was forked like his tongue. "He customarily performed coitus and pederasty [i.e., vaginal and anal intercourse] at the same time, while on occasion, a third prong reached up to his lover's mouth."

THE ORGY AT THE WITCHES' SABBATH

Witches allegedly flew through the air to attend secret twisted conclaves, while good Christians slept. The oldest surviving detailed description of a diabolical sabbath dates back to a letter by Pope Gregory IX in 1234. (This was before the mass burnings, when witches were as likely to be men.) "When this novice enters their assemblages for the first time, he sees a toad of enormous size, the size of a goose or larger. Some kiss it on the mouth, others on the behind. Then this novice meets a pale man with very black eyes and so thin that he is nothing but skin and bones; he kisses him and at once feels cold as ice. After this kiss, he easily forgets the Catholic faith. Finally, they make a feast together, after which a black cat descends behind a statue . . . The novice first kisses the cat on the behind; then he kisses the one who presides over the assemblage . . . After which they put out the lights and commit among themselves all sorts of indecencies."

In the 1500s and 1600s, the "indecencies" would fascinate the Inquisitors. The sabbath featured singing and dancing, a feast of foul food, boasting about evil

The traditional greeting given by a young female witch to her master Satan.

deeds and climaxed with the obligatory orgy. "At first the presiding devil put [his member] in the natural orifice [of the neophyte], and ejaculated the spoiled yellowing sperm, collected from nocturnal emissions . . . then he put it in the anus, and in this manner inordinately abused her."

The initiation rite to join the cult of a witch named The Sibyl of Norcia was even a bit more twisted. "At night, the men and women as well as The Sibyl turn into horrifying snakes. And whoever wants to enter the cave must first share lascivious pleasures with those revolting serpents."

MARIE-ANTOINETTE'S DOG OF A LOVER

The blue collar anger that boiled over in the French Revolution was certainly sown in bread shortages, worthless money, abusive treatment by noblemen, etc.—all duly noted in textbooks. Yet another force helped percolate that rage. Perhaps it wasn't a decisive force but it added to the incendiary climate of the times. In the late 1780s, writers released a floodtide of pornographic propaganda depicting the royals—especially Marie-Antoinette—engaging in strange sex acts. The people of France would tolerate a few discreet affairs but not this kind of conduct.

Cheap pamphlets crammed with obscene poetry were hawked on street corners, and read aloud. Starring by name in more sex dramas than any other was the queen herself. This native of Austria was accused of masturbation, lesbianism, nymphomania, and even bestiality—the events often taking place while her impotent husband, King Louis XVI, lurked in the shadows.

One pamphlet, *The Uterine Furies of Marie-Antoinette,* shows a color illustration of a limp Louis and a masturbating queen. The defining line near the queen explains, with crisp French wit: *"Le vit fut remplacé par un doigt libertin."* "The penis was replaced by a libertine finger."

Perhaps the strangest book to come out against her was a spinoff from her nickname. The people mockingly called her *"L'Autrichienne"* (i.e., "The Austrian") with punning emphasis on the end. The French word *chienne* means a female dog, i.e., a "bitch." In 1790—a couple centuries before Millie or Socks would write their White House confessions, came the kiss-and-tell-all by the queen's pet spaniel, spelling out in vivid detail all the creative sexual games, enjoyed by both dog and mistress.

All rubbish, of course. If anything, Marie-Antoinette might have been a bit undersexed. Her marriage to King Louis had started off miserably. The primary duty of a queen back then was to provide a male heir, further cementing the bond between two countries. For the first seven years of their marriage (from age fifteen to twenty-two for Marie-Antoinette), she was childless and it wasn't her fault. Somewhat baffled by sexual intercourse, the king confided his problems to Marie-Antoinette's brother, Joseph II, when the latter visited in 1777. Thanks to Teutonic thoroughness, the king's whispered words have survived. Joseph II described the problem in a secret diplomatic missive home: "[Louis] has strong well-conditioned erections, introduces the member, stays there without moving for perhaps two minutes and withdraws without ejaculating but still erect and says goodnight; this is incomprehensible because he says he sometimes has nightly emissions but once in place and going at it, never—he says plainly he does it from a sense of duty." (Quoted in *Citizens* by Simon Schama.)

It turned out Louis suffered from phimosis, a malformation of the foreskin causing a kind of strangling of the head of the penis, making erections painful.

Minor surgery two months after Joseph's report cured the king. Marie-Antoinette duly produced the proper princeling four years later.

"Let Them Eat Cake"

So how about her reputation as perhaps the most insensitive monarch ever to rule? Piffle, although she certainly had her failings, like going to a miniature dairy farm built near Versailles where she and friends could play peasant a la Rousseau and milk cows into porcelain bowls. She was a giddy, spoiled Austrian who nonetheless actually tried to avoid many of the elaborate conventions of French court life.

As stated back in the first chapter, there's no evidence she ever said "Let them eat cake." Putting those words in Marie-Antoinette's mouth—this time instead of sex objects—was yet another example of antiroyal propaganda.

And that slander campaign continued right up until her death at the guillotine.

At her trial, she was accused not only of smuggling millions out of France but of also teaching her eleven-year-old son, the formerly future king, to masturbate. The boy was reported to have claimed that he was made to sleep between the queen and her sister-in-law and taught to diddle. One muckraker named Hébert contended the queen did it "to weaken the child's health so they might dominate his mind."

Marie-Antoinette was so disgusted by the charges that she asked with disdain: "Is such a crime possible?"

Many people were surprised by her composure at her trial and then at her execution. "The whore, for the rest, was bold and impudent right to the end," complained Hébert, who would later wind up on the same guillotine. ❧

SPIES WITH A TWIST

THE FRENCH SPY: IS HE OR ISN'T SHE OR PERHAPS HE/SHE?

In late 1776, a few months after the American Declaration of Independence, the British public eagerly awaited military news from across the Atlantic. Was it possible that Great Britain, with its vast armies and navies, would lose its American colonies? Not bloody likely. At the same time, the British were also much concerned with the outcome of another contest: Was it true that the highest profile Frenchman living in England, the diplomat, Chevalier D'Eon, was actually a woman? Was he a she in lifelong masquerade? or was she a he? or perhaps even a true he/she? The question had titillated London for five years.

Although it seems beyond bizarre, the debate over the gender of a decorated French military officer, Chevalier D'Eon, drew more coverage some days in London newspapers of the time than the fight over the American colonies. "The doubts with regard to the sex of Mons. d'Eon," wrote *The Morning Post*, "which have prevailed these some years past, appear to be destroyed, as it is absolutely decided that . . ." And London gamblers and investors had embraced the proposition with gusto, as stock speculators underwrote vast betting pools (called "policies"). The Chevalier had opened in March 1771 as a 3–2 favorite to

be a man, then climbed swiftly to 10–1 for male, but by 1776 the odds had reversed. Chevalier was now a 7–4 favorite to be a woman.

The British—who have a tradition of legalized bookmaking on everything but royalty—"invested" (i.e., wagered) as much as £280,000 over the Chevalier's gender. A glimpse of the diplomat's genitals could be worth a fortune.

Chevalier D'Eon (1728–1810) was born in Tonerre, France, studied law, entered the military, and wound up commanding a company of dragoons and winning the coveted Order of St. Louis for his bravery against Austria. Of Peter Pan-ish physique, he was an expert fencer, although his fellow soldiers were quick to note that he was *not* a swordsman with the ladies.

"I have never wished for wife or mistress . . ." the Chevalier wrote to a colleague in 1771, "and this has given my friends in France, as well as Russia and England, grounds for imagining in their innocence that I was of the female sex."

The Chevalier performed several delicate diplomatic missions and for two decades was a spy in the French Royal Secret Service. When word of his female sex surfaced, all kinds of rumors started making the rounds. During his spy days in Russia, it was said, D'Eon had sneaked into the boudoir of Empress Elizabeth of Russia dressed as a woman and seduced her.

Some French gossips said that the Chevalier had been surprised by King George III at 2 A.M. in the queen's bedroom, and the queen's quick-thinking master-of-ceremonies, to save her honor, had told the enraged king that this lover was, well sire, actually a woman. (The tireless rumormill added this wasn't D'Eon's first visit to the queen and that the Chevalier earlier had fathered the future king of England, George IV.)

Whatever the case, by the mid-1770s, we know for a fact from documents, that D'Eon was marooned in a midlevel diplomatic appointment in England, very deeply in debt and was spending his spare time building one of the world's largest collections of feminist literature. ("It is a unique collection," states D'Eon biographer Gary Kates, who notes: "Outside the largest public collections, such as those in the British Library or the Biblioteque Nationale, we know of no other person who assembled so many historical and contemporary books about women.") The image we have of D'Eon from his *authentic* letters and notebooks is of a serious and deeply conflicted man, who was fascinated by gender. This self-professed lifelong virgin also hated to be the butt of jokes.

The King of France, tired of the controversy, ordered Chevalier back to France, but D'Eon refused, claiming he hadn't been paid for a decade, and this veteran spy had kept as insurance dozens of compromising secret documents, including plans for invading England. Louis XVI sent celebrated playwright Beaumarchais (*Marriage of Figaro, Barber of Seville*) on a secret mission to negotiate a settlement with Chevalier D'Eon to end the embarrassing gender matter and get back those documents.

French portraits of Chevalier D'Eon: the man, the woman, the enigma.

(While there, the French playwright also met with an American named Arthur Lee who convinced him to lobby the French king to supply arms for the upcoming American Revolution; Louis wound up supplying 90 percent of the munitions during the first two years of the war.)

Beaumarchais (1743–1799), a bon vivant with a wicked sense of humor, struck a deal in 1775 with D'Eon. In exchange for the documents, the king would pay Chevalier D'Eon a generous pension *and*, as requested by D'Eon, would issue a statement to the world that the Chevalier was truly a woman. In addition, the French government would pay for the Chevalier's new wardrobe since the Chevalier agreed to spend the rest of his/her life dressed as a woman.

("The notion of becoming a woman for the second half of one's life has no historical precedent," opines biographer Kates.)

Article IV of the agreement states: "I [Beaumarchais] demand, in his Majesty's name, that the disguise which has until today hidden the person of a maiden [i.e., a virginal woman] under the appearance of the Chevalier d'Eon be entirely aban-

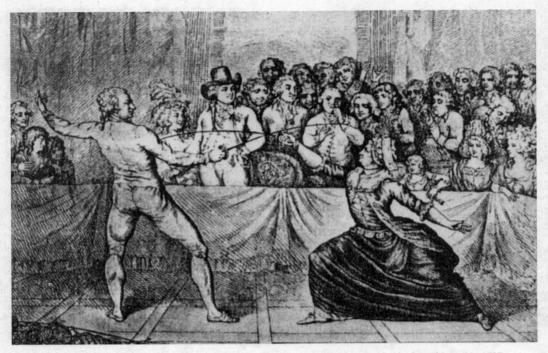

Wearing full woman's dress, the Chevalier D'Eon entered British fencing tournaments, such as this one in 1787, attended by the Prince of Wales. D'Eon, deeply in debt, needed the prize money. Over time, he/she earned the reputation as the best *female* sword fighter in the world.

doned . . . I require absolutely that [to re-solve] the uncertainty about her sex, which until today has been an inex-haustible subject of indecent bets and sala-cious jokes . . . that a public and unequiv-ocal declaration be made of the true sex of . . . d'Eon . . . before her resumption of her woman's clothes . . ."

Last minute niggles surfaced: Could she wear her Cross of St. Louis medal? (Yes, but not in Paris.) Could she carry guns? (No.)

D'Eon and Beaumarchais both signed the document, and now Beaumarchais, armed with inside information about the imminent declaration of D'Eon's woman-hood, proceeded to bet tens of thousands

of British pounds on the sex of D'Eon. To leave nothing to chance, the playwright circulated rumors that D'Eon wanted to marry him, and even wrote little songs about it.

D'Eon—a complicated, well-read, and very Christian individual—was furious and fired off letters to the British newspa-pers saying he/she would never reveal his/her sex. The Chevalier adamantly re-fused to strip naked for the greedy gam-blers of Exchange Alley, turning down £30,000 to bare all. And D'Eon challenged one insulting bettor named Charles Morande to a duel. The *Westminister Gazette* of August, 1776, reported: "Mr. de Morande very politely replied that it was impossible for him to meet d'Eon anywhere but in a bed." The butt, again.

The mass of bettors with thousands at stake grew annoyed at the continued delay in finding out the outcome. A surgeon named Hayes, who had bought a "policy" in 1771 that would pay 7–1 if D'Eon turned out to be a woman, sued the seller, Mr. Jacques. At the trial, a Dr. La Goux testified that he had secretly treated D'Eon for a woman's disorder and Charles Morande (the one D'Eon had challenged to a duel) told the court that one morning D'Eon had allowed him into the bedroom: "I put my hand into [her] bed and was fully convinced she was a woman."

The respected judge, Lord Mansfield, ruled for the British plaintiff Hayes and ordered Jacques to pay the £700, which started a flood of those who had bet female trying to collect their wagers. D'Eon advised no one to pay up and repeated that he/she would never reveal his/her sex. "I took to bed in my depression and isolation," wrote D'Eon, "begging the heavens for relief." (Imagine if Wall Street took bets on whether Attorney-General Janet Reno was secretly a man, and the *New York Times* covered it and every late-night comic riffed on it.)

From 1777 on till death, D'Eon wore women's clothes, and "she" became feted as one of the world's most accomplished women. In 1792, some London literati threw a dinner party honoring both American hero Thomas Paine *(Common Sense, Rights of Man) and* Chevalier D'Eon. "I am now in the most extraordinary position in which man was ever placed," toasted the British linguist, John Horne Tooke. "On the left of me sits a gentleman, who, brought up in obscurity, has proved himself the greatest political writer in the world, and has made more noise in it, and excited more attention and obtained more fame, than any man ever did. On the right of me sits a lady, who has been employed in public situations at different courts; who had high rank in the army, was greatly skilled in horsemanship, who has fought several duels, and at small sword has no equal; who for fifty years past, all Europe has recognized in the character and dress of a gentleman." Did Paine and D'Eon embrace? Did D'Eon now consider writing *Rights of Woman?*

When Revolutionary France in turmoil came under attack in 1792 by outside enemies, D'Eon volunteered to lead a brigade. "Perhaps you are destined to save your country as another Joan of Arc," enthused one legislator to the sixty-four-year-old "woman." "You could raise a column of Amazons who will cut down all oppressors of humanity," imagined another. "Victory will be ours!"

But it wasn't meant to be. D'Eon was too deeply in debt to be allowed to leave England and was forced to auction off his huge six-thousand-volume library at Christie's.

Another general emerged, decimating the enemies of Revolutionary France; his name was Napoleon.

As for D'Eon's sex, baptismal records show that he was born a man, and mortuary attendants confirm that he died a man . . . in woman's clothing. ❧

Mata Hari: An Innocent Femme Fatale? Well, at Least a Not Guilty One

Mata Hari . . . her sensual mouth could coax secrets out of the most hardened officer. Her stupendous buttocks almost changed the course of World War I. When the French came to arrest her, it's said, she opened her dressing gown and tried to seduce her way to freedom. Her name — like that of the Queen of Sheba — has passed into the vernacular, hers meaning a traitorous femme fatale.

That whole myth is a bit ironic, since Mata Hari — a Dutch divorcee with an overactive imagination and libido — apparently did little or no spying. At her trial, it was never proven that she passed a *single* secret to the Germans; on the other hand, high-ranking French officers testified that

Mata Hari (1876–1917), the exotic dancer who shed her veils, captivated Paris in 1905.

she several times tried to deliver reports on secret codes and invasion plans to French Counter-Intelligence. Her prosecutor, André Mornet, stated without apology in an interview forty years later: "There wasn't enough [evidence] to whip a cat."

And a German general concluded: "Innumerable tall tales were concocted about the German secret service . . . like the one about the unfortunate Mata Hari, who, in reality, did absolutely nothing for the German espionage effort."

Mata Hari (Malayan for "dawn") claimed that she was raised in Java by temple priests, taught to dance naked, and then later rescued by an English officer who fell in love with her religious gyrations.

"Mata Hari personifies all the poetry of India, its mysticism, its voluptuousness, its languor, its hypnotizing charm," raved *Le Journal.* "To see Mata Hari . . . is an unforgettable spectacle, a paradiselike dream."

Not everyone, however, was seduced. The writer Colette cattily reported overhearing a spectator say: "She an Oriental? Don't be silly! Hamburg or Rotterdam, or possibly Berlin." Almost none of the breathless men and women worshiping the exotic dancer had a clue about her real origins.

Mata Hari (1876–1917) was actually born Margaretha Geertruida Zelle in Leeuwarden, Holland. She was nineteen when she met her husband, Rudolph MacLeod, through a personals ad in the newspaper — "army officer seeks companion." The wild, liberated girl followed him to his post in Java; she remained there a few years, grew to despise the brutal strict man, and eventually fled to the stages of Paris. All her Orientalism was rehearsed seductive claptrap: a stage persona that didn't end at the stage door. After a few years of dancing success, she tried to segue to the role of Grand Dancer of the Theatre, calling herself "Lady MacLeod." She importuned Richard Strauss to compose a Salome for her; she sought out Diaghilev to let her join Ballet Russe. And while she played a few opera houses in Italy and performed at some notorious private parties, even riding in naked at a lesbian fete in Paris, Mata Hari never made that final leap to serious world-class actress.

By 1915, the thirty-nine-year-old exotic dancer was hitting midlife; her career was waning and she was devolving into a Holly-Go-Lightly or what the French call a *"grande horizontale,"* i.e., a horizontally talented courtesan maintained by a wealthy patron. Despite a parade of wealthy foreign lovers into her bedroom, she was constantly running up debts.

With World War I brutalizing the continent, the British arrested her and accused her of being a spy named Clara Benedix but they couldn't make the charge stick.

The French arrested her and tossed her in St. Lazares. Her valises were searched and they tried to prove that two jars of unusual ointments contained disappearing ink. It turned out that one was a spermicide and the other a morning-after contraceptive douche. Her body was searched because several of her lovers said that even in bed, she never removed her upper garment, a cotton *cache-sein* (breast coverlet). Was there some German tattoo? Some cubby for secrets? No, said her longtime doctor, she has very small breasts with large discolored nipples which she prefers not to reveal to anyone.

Here is how her supposedly unbiased French interrogator later described her in his memoirs: "Had she been pretty? Without a doubt, [judging] from her passport photo. But this woman . . . in my office . . . had suffered many affronts from time." He described her bloodshot eyes as "big as eggs"; she had a "bulbous nose, chapped skin, a mouth that touched the ears, the swollen lips of a negress, teeth as big as plates . . . graying hair no longer covered by dye." (tr. Julie Wheelwright)

Death Row. The last photo of forty-one-year-old Mata Hari, taken at St. Lazares prison in 1917.

The French produced coded messages from the Germans allegedly outlining the hiring of the cash-short courtesan but they never produced any evidence of her having delivered anything to the Germans. Apparently, Mata Hari, who had made a career out of manipulating men, was simply playing the Germans for 20,000 francs. "Commandant von Kalle," she explained, "not wanting to pay for my caresses with his own money, found it easier to let his government pay for them."

In fact, she had delivered information to the French and had been vaguely promised a lucrative assignment to spy for them. Broke yet again, she had returned to France to cash in on that offer.

Instead, she wound up facing the firing squad. She didn't know that French Counter-Intelligence had had two men tail her for six months.

Why was she convicted? Blame it on the desperate mind-set in France in 1917 reeling from a failed offensive and battling outright mutinies among the troops. And blame it on the human nature of a pair of vindictive French officers who seemed to have delighted in crushing this former femme fatale, now forty-one and broke and a bit desperate.

Spymaster Ladoux must produce something after investigating her for six months. Prosecutor Bouchardon couldn't let this bed-hopping spy escape.

Her trial was a sham of preordained military justice; she was forbidden to call any civilian witnesses.

Legend has it that Mata Hari stalled the firing squad by unbuttoning her dress, that at first no man would shoot. Here's what really happened.

On October 15, 1917, at dawn, Mata Hari—clothed in a long pearl-gray dress, elegant buttoned gloves, lace-up boots and a tricornered felt hat—was tied with a single rope around her waist to a post. She refused to be blindfolded or have her hands tied behind her back. She waved to the weeping nuns who had accompanied her from prison.

She died bravely.

When curiosity-seekers went days later to a grave set aside for her, they found it empty. Rumors of her escape began. In later years, Mata Hari sightings would crop up in the press. The truth? In war-torn France, no one was courageous enough to claim her body and pay for a burial. The presiding officers ordered her body delivered to the dissecting room at the University of Paris medical school.

Name another female spy beside Mata Hari.

Ethel Rosenberg? Doesn't quite have the same ring. The Mata Hari myth will die hard.

CHIVALRY: A KNIGHT ON ERRANDS

Ulrich von Lichtenstein (1200–1276) —a well-respected Austrian knight whose family founded that European principality bearing his name—swore his love to a high-born married princess. Standard practice for a chivalrous Christian knight. In his autobiography in verse, *Frauendienst* (or *The Service of Women*), he describes some of the acts he performed over fifteen years to show his devotion: he stole and drank her bath water; he sent her his pinkie, which he said he lost jousting in her honor (actually he had a friend cut it off); he mixed with lepers to beg alms from her.

Forget about Lancelot and the others. If you're going to know about just one knight, make it Ulrich von Lichtenstein, the Inspector Clousseau of chivalrous knights.

Ulrich, after years of frustration, wanted to conceive of some quest that would really impress his unnamed lady fair. So, he cross-dressed in a white ball-gown as "Frau Venus" and challenged all the knights of Europe to joust with him.

From Ulrich's autobiography, April 25, 1227: "At Venice, I lay all winter through; hear now what I did there. I caused ladies' garments to be made; twelve gowns were made for me, and thirty fair ladies' sleeves sewn upon little shirts. With that, I bought two pretty braided tresses of hair, which I richly entwined with some of the plentiful pearls for sale in Venice; also they sewed for me white silk mantles and silver-white were my beautifully carved saddles with trappings of white cloth, long and broad and with expensive bridles."

Over his five-week journey north, Ulrich shattered on average eight lances a day, fighting the cream of Europe. He also took three days off to visit his wife and children. (Most knights were married, so were the princesses they loved: Chivalry was one big game of adultery.) He says he won 307 jousts and was never unhorsed.

Ulrich finally gained permission to be in the same room with his lady love. After a miserable night shivering outside, she allowed him to sneak up to her in the tower. (Her husband was in another part of the castle.) Three times, he was hoisted up in a coverlet and three times crashed back to the ground. Finally he let his servant, who was lighter, go up first and the servant reached the top and was greeted with a warm kiss. Ulrich, upon arriving, found his beloved surrounded by eight stalwart handmaidens. When he complained (very politely) about the crowd, she gave him yet another task: Spend the night waist-deep in a nearby lake. As the handmaidens helped lower him out another window, the princess herself leaned forward to give him a kiss. Ulrich let go of the windowsill to embrace her and fell into the moat.

After fifteen long years, he finally chose another lady fair.

Before you dismiss Ulrich as fiction, as a forerunner of Don Quixote, know that this Austrian knight really lived and breathed. He signed several documents that still exist and his marriage to Bertha was duly recorded, as were the births of their four children. The country bearing his ancestral family name still dots European maps, tucked between Switzerland and Austria. (The pinkie, which he sent his love in a green velvet box, though, has never been found.)

Could the autobiographical poem still be fiction? a satire of a famous knight? Of course, but several scholars have analyzed it and they accept the basic facts although they concede that Ulrich might have exaggerated just a tad. 🌀

SNAPSHOTS OF THE NAZIS

THE TATTOO COLLECTION OF ILSA KOCH

Be prepared. This is a gruesome item, and is included to show the *depths* of Nazi depravity. Perhaps we are sometimes numbed by the repetition of the same footage of emaciated corpses stacked like firewood or the crematoria belching smoke.

The following shows another face of Nazi perversity, the face of a smiling redhead.

Even the Nazis were appalled by this woman's behavior.

Ilsa Koch, the thirty-something flame-haired, green-eyed wife of the commandant at Buchenwald and the mother of two young children, used to ride around

A Nazi family. Ilsa Koch, with husband Karl, commandant of Buchenwald Concentration Camp, and their son and dog.

the concentration camp half naked and then have prisoners severely whipped who dared to look at her. A confidential Nazi S.S. report called her the most hated person at Buchenwald, and "a perverted, nymphomaniacal, power-mad demon."

And swirling around her at her war crimes trial in 1947 was the unproven charge that she collected human tattoos off the bodies of prisoners, the way some people collect pressed flowers or butterflies. Ilsa Koch (1906–1967), pregnant, was given a life sentence.

And Koch's grotesque tattoo hobby might have stayed the stuff of rumor had it not been for the grievous error committed by the military governor of the U.S. Zone, General Lucius Clay. He reduced her sentence for "lack of evidence" and freed her in 1949.

She was immediately rearrested by *German* authorities and at her trial, the seventh accusation stated the following:

"In the summer of 1940 all the tattooed prisoners were photographed. Then the majority of them were killed by lethal injection. Their bodies were skinned in the 'Pathology' lab in order to be made into leather and for other uses. The accused showed a passionate interest in beautiful tattoos. She herself possessed objects made of human skin. Very often, she noted down the number of a tattooed prisoner and had those tattoos lifted by her accomplices in the S.S."

Much collaborating testimony was produced. A French doctor—forced to assist at Buchenwald—stated that tanned human skins were routinely given as pres-

"Section of Human Skin Lampshade, Buchenwald Concentration Camp." That's how American prosecutors identified this piece of evidence. (Those two circles on the far right and left are nipples.)

tend the hanging of a Polish resistance fighter with an elaborate tattoo. "Oh, he's handsome," she exclaimed, as the chair was kicked out from under him, "he's not going to the ovens, he's all mine."

At her trial, Ilsa claimed: "I was merely a housewife." Ilsa Koch was once again sentenced to life in prison; she was found in 1967 hanging from a pipe in her cell, an apparent suicide. ✺

STOP HANDING OUT SHRUNKEN HEADS

An order was issued by the Nazi high command on May 7, 1942, directing the staff at Buchenwald to cease preparing shrunken heads for other than medical reasons. A humane order? Hardly. Visitors were showing up all over Europe with

ents to officers and visitors, to use in binding books. Upon liberation of the camp, thirteen human skins with tattoos were found at Buchenwald including such designs as a woman's head, a pyramid, a dancer with butterfly wings, a knight fighting a dragon, and a broken heart with the words ENFANT DE MALHEUR (CHILD OF MISFORTUNE).

Prisoners testified to seeing in Ilsa Koch's house the following products made of human skin: lampshades, "leather"-bound books, handbags, even a pair of shoes.

An invoice for the shipment of 142 tattooed skins also was found. Finally, one prisoner testified to seeing Ilsa Koch at-

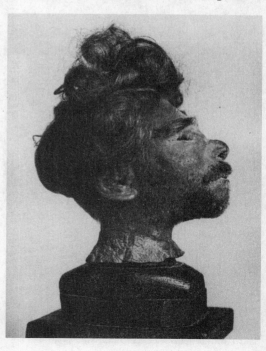

these grim souvenirs and the Nazis feared that word of their genocide might leak out.

Adolph Hitler's Best Friend

Adolph Hitler (1889–1945), the most prolific murderer in the history of the human race, loved dogs. Here, he's pictured in 1935 playing with his Alsatian, Muck, at his mountain retreat in the Bavarian Alps.

Muck, though, died a few years later, and in the summer of 1942, as the pressures of the war mounted, Hitler's aide, Martin Bormann, gave the führer an Alsatian bitch named Blondi. Hitler bonded with Blondi. "The dog remained

Hitler with beloved Muck, in 1935.

the only living creature at headquarters who aroused any flicker of human feeling in Hitler," observed Albert Speer, Minister of Armaments for the Third Reich.

One of Hitler's stenographers recalled how happy the führer seemed when he was running the big dog, training her to leap through hoops and over a six-foot wall, even climb a ladder. Another overheard Hitler say to Blondi when the dog failed to execute a command: "Look me in the eyes, Blondi. Are you also a traitor like the generals of my staff?"

Hitler was a strict vegetarian, and when Blondi was allowed near the dinner table, the dog often tried to beg food from the guests eating meat. Although it sounds more like a scene from Marx Brothers' *Duck Soup*, anyone being nuzzled by Blondi would try discreetly to shoo the dog away, since the führer deeply resented his dog showing affection to anyone but himself. "I avoided, as did any reasonably prudent visitor to Hitler, arousing any feelings of friendship in the dog," recalls Speer, one of the more frequent dinner guests. Luckily for the general staff, Blondi was kept outside most of the time because the big Alsatian used to feud with the two little terriers of Hitler's mistress, Eva Braun.

To celebrate Hitler's fifty-fourth birthday in April 1943, a late-night party was thrown and, as a special treat for the führer, Blondi was allowed indoors to attend. Guests recalled that Hitler coaxed the dog to perform tricks, including "singing" a long solo.

As the tide of war shifted against Germany, Hitler became a very lonely, very irritable man, increasingly alienated from people. Speer—who for years was Hitler's protégé—heard the führer say several times: "Speer, one of these days, I'll have only two friends left, Fraulein Braun and my dog."

Late on April 28, 1945, as Russian ground forces fought their way toward Hitler's bunker in Berlin, Hitler in a brief ceremony was married to his longtime girlfriend, Eva Braun. The following day, Hitler distributed vials of poison to those closest to him. When Goebbels expressed doubts whether the liquid cyanamide would still work effectively, a doctor suggested that Hitler's dog Blondi be given some. Hitler agreed, and the liquid was forced down Blondi's throat. The dog died.

On April 30, the married Hitlers sat alone in their suite. Eva swallowed the poison. She died. Hitler shot himself in the temple with a 7.65-caliber Walther pistol and, as ordered, Hitler's staff scavenged Berlin for every available liter of gasoline to incinerate the two bodies. It's unclear where Blondi was buried. ✖

A MISINFORMED AMERICAN FREES TOP NAZI WAR CRIMINALS

One well-intentioned man, with the squiggle of his pen, helped undermine the verdicts at Nuremberg. In 1951, an American bureaucrat signed an order freeing twenty-eight convicted Nazi war criminals from prison; he also reduced the prison terms for sixty-four of seventy-four

prisoners in his jurisdiction, and postponed the execution of ten of fifteen Nazis condemned to die.

While the hunt for Nazis hiding in South America still makes for riveting TV, it's generally forgotten that the American government through the person of John J. McCloy participated in a mass clemency for Nazi war criminals, including the notorious arms manufacturer, Alfried Krupp.

This was not a bureaucratic snafu; this was the reasoned action of one of the nation's most efficient behind-the-scenes administrators.

John J. McCloy, High Commissioner of American Zone in postwar Germany, authorized a three-person board to review the judgments at the Nuremberg trials. McCloy's panel received extensive *defense* testimony from lawyers and witnesses for the convicted Nazis while it never contacted any of the Allied prosecutors or prosecution witnesses.

This panel recommended reduced sentencing in 85 percent of the cases it reviewed, second-guessing Nuremberg by applying American judicial law to what had been an international tribunal with an almost unique mandate to make examples of a handful of criminals to send a message to the world.

With historical hindsight, many of the clemency decisions seem like obscene acts of charity to some of mankind's foulest villains. Take Alfried Krupp's company. He had been sentenced to twelve years imprisonment and confiscation of his family's $500 million munitions fortune.

(The story is brilliantly told in William Manchester's *The Arms of Krupp*.)

Alfried Krupp's enormous industrial steel and weapons company had lobbied the Third Reich to be allowed to make fuses at Auschwitz, using grotesquely abused slave labor. Krupp's firm negotiated with the S.S. on the exact details of how to mistreat the prisoners.

In another instance, Krupp's staff selected five hundred young female slaves, age fifteen to twenty-five, to do heavy labor at one of his plants in Essen. Those young women wore burlap dresses and most had rags for shoes as they trudged nine miles daily, sometimes through snow, to and from twelve-hour shifts. Their daily meal consisted of one slice of bread and a foul soup. They were beaten and kicked to work faster. A torture chamber was close enough to Alfried's office that his secretary testified she could hear the screams. (Alfried did not testify but was ably defended at Nuremberg by thirty-seven lawyers.) One central casting overseer flicked his whip at the eyes of prisoners. The children born to these slave laborers were raised in a squalid nursery and not a single one of the infants is known to have survived. And on and on . . . as documented in Manchester's book.

The panel recommended that Krupp's sentence be reduced from twelve years in prison to seven and that the confiscation of his property be dropped. John J. McCloy found that too unreasonable. He freed Krupp on February 3, 1951, with time served. He defended his action repeatedly through the years. "We tried him reluctantly and the confiscation troubled me. I consulted my French and British colleagues, and they agreed with me. My feeling—it was a feeling—was that Alfried was a playboy, that he hadn't had much responsibility. I felt that he had expiated whatever he'd done by the time he'd already spent in jail. Oh, I don't doubt that he supported the Nazis early; he was a weakling."

McCloy—a very respected man in Washington, a former Assistant Secretary of War—was so misinformed that it's mind-boggling. Alfried Krupp in a company memo is described in 1943 as sole proprietor of the half-billion-dollar concern. Krupp was a high-ranking Nazi who had volunteered for many party projects. Even the most cursory glance at the Nuremberg testimony would have shown McCloy Krupp's role in recruiting and mistreating slave labor. As for being a "weakling," that was McCloy's biggest misjudgment.

On February 3, 1951, Krupp, his eight-member board of directors and four former Nazi generals, walked out of Landsberg Prison. Krupp was a very talented man and thanks to his daring in flying planes, sailing, driving race cars, and running the vast paternalistic company, Krupp was hailed as a national hero in Germany. (It also didn't hurt that McCloy, to ease postwar transition, had forbidden the Nuremberg trial records from being translated into German.)

Within a decade, Alfried Krupp had rebuilt the Krupp steel empire and become once again *the wealthiest man in Europe.*

John J. McCloy took some heavy heat for the mass clemency, but to his death never admitted he was wrong. "Why are we freeing so many Nazis?" Eleanor Roosevelt had asked him back in 1951. He had never really answered the question.

John J. McCloy became chairman of Chase Manhattan Bank, served as a board member emeritus of Mercedes Benz, Squibb, and other companies, and he received many honors including the Grand Cross Order of Merit from the German government. ❧

EXPLORERS DON'T NEED A WELCOME MAT

FIRST EUROPEANS IN NORTH AMERICA: A GUY NAMED BARNEY?

It wasn't Columbus, but rather some flame-haired Scandinavian named Barney or Leif. We can say that with relative certainty because of some tiny bits of metal found on the northern coast of Newfoundland in Canada. Citing Viking sagas, Scandinavians had long claimed that Leif Ericson had sailed west from Greenland and founded a settlement called Vinland, but where was the physical proof? A couple centuries of hoaxes had led experts to doubt the authenticity of the sagas.

Then Dr. Helge Ingstad dedicated his life to finding physical evidence of Vikings in North America, and finally, after many dry holes, he found in the 1960s signs of a very old settlement at L'Anse aux Meadows in Newfoundland, off the coast of mainland Canada. While digging out the turf-walled houses, Ingstad and crew found traces of iron nails, a bronze pin, a soap-stone spindle whorl of the type used around A.D. 1000 in Iceland, among other even more obscure evidence of Vikings such as iron slag.

They didn't find Viking swords or carved mastheads or horned helmets but these little traces confirm for many leading archaeologists that this was in fact a Viking outpost. The local Indians and Eskimos simply didn't have those metal implements. Carbon dating then placed the artifacts within a window of A.D. 600 to 1200

"Years of summer digging by competent archaeologists have (it seems to me beyond a reasonable doubt) proved this place to have indeed been Vinland, where Leif Ericson spent one winter, and where members of his family founded a short-lived colony," wrote Samuel Morison, one of the most respected historians on the discovery of America.

The Viking sagas, though of course unreliable to folks reared on videotape, tell a more fascinating story than iron slag. An Icelandic trader named Bjarni (Barney) Herjolfsson, around A.D. 985, returned home from Europe to find his father had traipsed to a new settlement on Greenland. Barney wanted to see Dad so he set sail west. Years later, he told anyone who would listen that he had been blown off course in the fog and had hit a new country with lots of trees and small hills. Everyone asked what else he found there, and Barney told them he didn't go ashore, which made Barney a bit of a laughingstock among the Vikings.

Leif Ericson, the son of Eric the Red, who had founded the Greenland colony, bought Barney's boat and sailed in a southwesterly direction from Greenland. Now here it becomes murky exactly where he wound up; some experts claim he went as far south as Florida; others stake that he definitely moored at Cape Cod and others favor Newfoundland. Wherever he landed, he called it Vinland, which means "Land of Grapes" or "Land of Berries" or "Land of Meadows" depending on which scholar you believe. Afterward, other Vikings made the trip from Greenland to the tiny settlement until a war with the "skraelings" (i.e., Indians) forced them to abandon it.

Until Dr. Ingstad found those bits of metal, many scholars thought Vinland might be a tall tale like Valhalla.

A Norse penny from around A.D. 1070 was found at an Indian site in Maine. Keep posted for more signs of Vikings in North America. Can Leif Ericson day be far off? And what about Barney?

COLUMBUS'S SECRET AGENDA

Christopher Columbus had a secret agenda when he sailed west to find a new route to the Indies. He wanted to use the profits to finance another Crusade to regain the Holy Land. On December 26, 1492, Columbus wrote in his journal that he hopes to find gold "in so great quantity that the Sovereigns within three years would undertake and prepare to go and conquer the Holy Places." And in 1502 in a letter to the pope, he proposes that he himself will lead a force of 110,000 men.

COLUMBUS ENSLAVES, THEN DEPOPULATES THE WEST INDIES

Columbus rightly deserves credit for many firsts, but one of his firsts has been routinely overlooked in American textbooks.

Christopher Columbus was the *first* slave trader in the New World. He returned from his first voyage with ten live Indians he had kidnapped, and these were paraded along with parrots through the streets and roads of Spain during his triumphant procession to Ferdinand and Isabella in Barcelona. (Four of the Indians were sick and Columbus left them in the care of his Italian backer, Gianetto Barardi in Seville. It so happens that a fellow by the name of Amerigo Vespucci was living at Barardi's at the time.)

Columbus's second voyage kept him away from Spain for two years and nine months and, as it became increasingly clear to him that he had yet to find gold and pearls in abundance, the Admiral started to dream of a brisk traffic in Indian slaves, according to *The Conquest of America* by Tzvetan Todorov. Columbus wrote to Ferdinand and Isabella in 1496: "We can send from here, in the name of the Holy Trinity, all the slaves and brazil-wood which could be sold. If the information I have is correct, we can sell 4,000 slaves, who will be worth, at least, 20 millions, and 4,000 hundred-weight of brazil-wood, which will be worth just as much . . . I went recently to the Cape Verde Islands where the people have a large slave trade, and they are constantly sending ships to barter for slaves, and ships are always in the harbor . . . Although they die now, they will not always die. The Negroes and the Canary Islanders died at first, and the Indians are even better than the Negroes."

Columbus apparently also saw the value of sex slaves; in a later letter he describes the action of the slave traders and what type of Indian sells best: "There are plenty of dealers who go looking about for girls; these from nine to ten are now in demand, and for all ages a good price must be paid."

Columbus's childhood friend, Michele da Cuneo, very matter-of-factly describes the enslavement of the Indians on Haiti before the return from Columbus's second voyage.

"When our caravels . . . were to leave for Spain, we gathered in one settlement one thousand six hundred males and female persons of these Indians, and of these we embarked in our caravels on February 17, 1495, five hundred fifty souls among the healthiest males and females. For those who remained, we let it be known in the vicinity that anyone who wanted to take some of them could do so, to the amount desired; which was done." (About two hundred died on the voyage and had to be thrown overboard.)

To be sure, selling slaves was standard practice then in the Old World. Five years earlier, King Ferdinand had sent a gift to Pope Innocent VIII of one hundred Moorish slaves, which the pope had shared with cardinals and close friends.

But Columbus's slave sales hit a snag. Theologians argued that these Indians had not been taken in

Columbus off the pedestal.

war and therefore couldn't be enslaved. Columbus, with a desperate need for fresh funds, argued bitterly that he should be allowed to sell slaves.

It's a bit ironic that Columbus pushed so hard for slavery because when he first arrived, he had been very impressed by the local Indians. On December 24, 1492, he wrote in his notebook: "A better race there cannot be, and both the people and the lands are in such quantity that I know not how to write it . . . All here have a loving manner and gentle speech."

However, the whole idea of trafficking in Indian slaves back to the Old World soon became moot with the discovery of gold in the New World. Every able-bodied man and woman would be needed to work the mines. Spain alternated its policy between banning slavery of Indians to consigning them as serfs to local Spaniards to allowing the enslavement of only the "bad" Indians, i.e., the cannibal Carib tribe.

Since most Spaniards couldn't tell one Indian from another, a means of identifying "bad" pagan Indians had to be devised: hence the notorious *"Requerimiento"* or "Requisition." It was decreed that a long complicated speech was to be read to captured Indians, tracing the root of Spanish authority back to Jesus Christ through Saint Peter to the pope to Catholic sovereigns of Spain. If an Indian agrees immediately to convert "to our Most Holy Catholic Faith," he or she will be awarded "many privileges and exemptions." If the Indian refuses, "we shall powerfully enter your country, and shall make war against you . . . and shall subject you to the yoke and obedience of the Church and of their Highnesses; we shall take you and your wives and shall make slaves of them . . . and shall do you all the mischief and damage that we can."

In practice, this reading of the *Requerimiento* was often a formality before enslavement because often no interpreter was present to explain it to the Indians.

Columbus, when he was governor, was obsessed with finding gold. He instituted a kind of tribute system that was described by his son, Ferdinand. "In the Cibao, where the gold mines were, every person of fourteen years or older was to pay a large hawk's bell of gold dust; all others were each to pay twenty-five pounds of cotton. Whenever an Indian delivered his tribute, he was to receive a brass or copper token which he must wear about his neck as proof that he had made his payment. Any Indian found without such a token was to be punished." The punishment, which Columbus's son failed to

mention, was the cutting off of their hands, according to *Lies My Teacher Told Me* by James Loewen.

The Spaniards' greed and cruelty grew worse over time. About a decade after Columbus's death, here is a day in the life of those Indians working in the mines, as described in a report by Dominican monks:

"Each of [the foremen] had made it a practice to sleep with the Indian women who were in his workforce, if they pleased him, whether they were married women or maidens. While the foreman remained in the hut or the cabin with the Indian woman, he sent the husband to dig gold out of the mines; and in the evening when the wretch returned, not only was he beaten or whipped because he had not brought up enough gold, but further, most often, he was bound hand and foot and flung under the bed like a dog, before the foreman lay down, directly over him, with his wife."

Life was also miserable for those Indians who were not enslaved but rather assigned to a Spaniard and, in theory, paid wages. "Since no one has the assurance that he will be able to keep his . . . Indians," wrote eyewitness Bernardino de Manzanedo in 1518, "he used them like borrowed goods, and thus many have perished and are perishing." Kind of like a "rental car" syndrome for humans.

Obviously, not all the exploitation of the Indians can be blamed on Columbus, but he was the first in charge and he set the tone.

Between overwork, underfeeding, and

especially disease, the local Caribbean Indians were wiped out. Wrote a contemporary Spanish historian: "All the Indians of these islands were allotted by the Admiral [Columbus] . . . to all the settlers who came to live in these parts; and in the opinion of many who saw what happened and speak of it as eyewitnesses, the Admiral, when he discovered these islands, passed sentence of death on a million or more Indians, men and women, of all ages, adults and children. Of this number and of those since born, it is believed that there do not survive today, in this year 1548, 500 Indians, adults and children, who are natives and who are offspring of the stock of those he found on arrival."

The pope banned enslaving of *Caribbean Indians* in 1537; the Spanish monarchs followed in 1542. This opened the door to the mass importing of African slaves, which would later almost fracture the United States. ✿

THE NAME "AMERICA"

It's time to stand up and defend "America"—the name, that is.

It has been fashionable since the 1550s and historian Bartolomeo de las Casas to call Amerigo Vespucci a liar and a cheat, a bombastic self-promoter who would have trouble navigating a large bathtub, let alone uncharted waters.

Ralph Waldo Emerson wrote: "Amerigo Vespucci, whose highest rank was boatswain's mate in an expedition that never sailed, managed in this lying world to supplant Columbus and baptize half the earth with his own dishonest name."

Well, not so fast. Columbus thought he had discovered the Indies. It was Vespucci, in his enormously popular letters, who called the discovery a "New World."

Historian Gary Wills states that Vespucci—unlike Columbus who used speed and time to estimate distance—was a navigator who used the latest breakthroughs in astronomy to plot his course and reckon his location and create maps. He perceived that the giant land mass could not be part of Asia.

In 1507, German Martin Waldseemuller created a map using Vespucci's information. He credited astronomer Ptolemy with charting the Old World and Vespucci with identifying the New World and he dubbed the southern land mass (i.e., South America) "America." In the margin of the map was written: "It is fitting that this fourth part of the world, inasmuch as Americus discovered it, be called Amerige, or let us say, land of Americi, that is: AMERICA."

There is no record that Vespucci begged Waldseemuller and the scholars at the little monastery at Saint Die to name anything after him. Vespucci, who was in charge of the voyage that touched the mainland of South America in 1497, was an astute observer, was named Chief of Navigation by Spain (akin to being in charge of NASA now), and could write a thrilling letter.

Wrote Gary Wills of the two explorers: "Each played an indispensable role in breaking out of the geographical confinement of the Western world. But when it comes to naming the new, one must know that it is new. Vespucci, however hazily, did."

If Columbus had had his way, we'd be living in the "United States of West Indies," or something like that, because the Admiral swore to his grave that he had discovered a part of Asia, never swerving from that belief. ❧

Vespucci's Soft-Core Bestseller

Unlike Columbus, Vespucci rarely wrote of finding gold, but, rather, his accounts are spiced with lewd details about the lives of the Indians. No wonder his letters became one of the world's first bestsellers in the fledgling industry of printed word publishing. Some scholars, such as Jack Hitt, contend that some of the more outrageous details were slipped in by printers trying to boost sales. Whatever, it definitely grabs your interest. The following was first printed in 1502, then republished dozens of times, in many languages throughout the 1500s. This English translation, by Gary Jacobson, appeared in *Letters from a New World* (Marsilio, 1992).

First, then, the people . . . a gentle tractable people. Everyone of both sexes goes about

This 16th-century allegory shows Amerigo Vespucci with an Indian maiden representing America. Her nudity helped spur immigration; her hammock spawned knockoffs worldwide.

naked, covering no part of the body, and just as they issued from their mothers' wombs so they go about until their dying day. They have big, solid, well-formed and well-proportioned bodies, and their complexions tend toward red, which happens, I suppose, because in going about naked they are colored by the sun. They also have long black hair. They are nimble in gait and in their games, and have open, pleasant faces, which they themselves, however, disfigure. They pierce their own cheeks, lips, noses, and ears, and you must not imagine that these holes are small or that they have but one of them: indeed I saw several people who had seven holes in a single face, each big enough to hold a plum. They fill these holes with beautiful stones, cerulean, marblelike, crystalline, or alabaster, or with very white bones and other things artfully wrought in their fashion; if you were to see such an unusual and monstrous thing as a man with seven stones just in his cheeks or jaws or lips, some of them half a palm long, you would be amazed. And I often considered this and judged that seven such stones must weigh sixteen ounces. Beyond that, in each ear, which they pierce with three holes, they carry more stones dangling from rings; this custom is only for the men; the women do not pierce their faces, but only their ears. They have another custom that is appalling and passes belief. Their women, being very lustful, make their husbands' members swell to such thickness that they look ugly and misshapen; this they accomplish with a certain device they have and by bites from certain poisonous animals. Because of this, many men lose their members,

which rot through neglect, and they are left eunuchs.

They have no cloth of wool, linen or cotton, since they need none. Nor have they any private property, but own everything in common: they live together without a king and without authorities, each man his own master. They take as many wives as they wish, and son may couple with mother, brother with sister, cousin with cousin, and in general men with women as they chance to meet. They dissolve marriage as often as they please, observing no order in any of these matters. Moreover, they have no temple and no religion, nor do they worship idols. What more can I say? They live according to nature, and might be called Epicureans rather than Stoics. There are no merchants among them, nor is there any commerce. The people make war among themselves without art or order. The elders deliver orations to the young to sway their will, urging them on to wars in which they kill each other cruelly, and they take captives and keep them, not to spare them but to kill them for food: for they eat each other, the victors eat the vanquished, and together with other kinds of meat, human flesh is common fare among them. This you may be sure, because one father was known to have eaten his children and wife, and I myself met and spoke with a man who was said to have eaten more than three hundred human bodies; and I also stayed twenty-seven days in a certain city in which I saw salted human flesh hanging from house-beams, much as we hang up bacon or pork. I will say more: they marvel that we do not eat our enemies and use their flesh as food, for they say human flesh is very savory. Their weapons are bows and arrows, and when they charge into battle, they cover no part of their bodies to protect themselves, also in this respect like animals. We tried our best to dissuade them from these wicked customs, and they promised us that they would give them up. The women, as I said, although they go naked and are exceedingly lustful, still have rather shapely and clean bodies, and are not as revolting as one might think, because, being fleshy, their shameful parts are less visible, covered for the most part by the good quality of their bodily composition. It seemed remarkable to us that none of them appeared to have sagging breasts, and also, those who had borne children could not be distinguished from the virgins by the shape or the tautness of their wombs, and this was true of other parts of their bodies, which decency bids me pass over. When they were able to copulate with Christians, they were driven by their excessive lust to corrupt and prostitute all their modesty.

Amerigo, with his raunchy bestseller, certainly helped entice boatloads of Europeans to the New World. ❧

CANNIBALISM:
PASS A FEW GRAINS OF SALT

From the very discovery of the New World, alleged eyewitness accounts and fearsome rumors of cannibalism floated back to the Old World. Yes, gold awaited the intrepid, so did the cannibal stew pot. Columbus,

himself, described the Carib Indians of the West Indies as ferocious cannibals and Columbus's shipmate and friend, Michele da Cuneo, states that the Caribs castrated teenage prisoners, as we do capons, "to fatten them up and later eat them."

Actually, the word "cannibal" in English (and its equivalents in Spanish, French, Portuguese, etc.) comes from the Spanish *Carib* for the local Indian tribe, which shifted to "calib" to "canib." (That modest linguistic shift saved travel agents from having to try to sell tours to the "Cannibal Sea.")

A French missionary, Father Labat, stood on a beach in Martinique in 1694 as a boatload of Carib Indians glided shoreward. As they waved in greeting to the good reverend, he noticed that there was one extra arm waving at him, that is, one not attached to any body. "It was the arm of a man barbequed in the buccaneer fashion, that is to say, dried with a slow fire in the smoke," observed Labat. "They offered it to me very civilly and informed me it was the arm of an Englishman whom they had lately killed." Labat, being pious, declined to sample smoked Brit.

So what was the best way to prepare human flesh? Cannibal opinion differs.

The Conquistadors reported that some Aztecs liked to cook human meat with roasted peppers and tomatoes, while others opted for a man-and-maize stew. Brazilian cannibals apparently preferred to smoke the flesh over a leafy fire.

And what were the choicest body parts?

A feast of Brazilian cannibals as pictured by Theodor de Bry in 1592.

Some chose buttocks; some chose breasts. A Portuguese Jesuit was a bit surprised when he asked a dying old Indian woman in Brazil if there was anything he could bring her, perhaps some sugar. "Oh, my stomach is upset . . . but if I had the little hand of a tender Tapuya boy, I think I could just pick the little bones," she replied.

THANKSGIVING

The whole Thanksgiving tradition serves up far more bull than turkey. One of the few times a Pilgrim father mentions a turkey in his memoirs of life in early New England, it is to state that a young lad confessed to "buggering" (i.e., having sex with) a turkey, among other animals. (Sixteen-year-old Thomas Granger was hanged for the offense, according to Governor William Bradford.) None of the Pilgrims even mention that turkey was eaten at Thanksgiving; at best, we know that "fowl" and "deer" were consumed.

As for the image that the Pilgrims shared their feast with the Indians, if anything, it was the other way around. The Indians celebrated an autumnal feast, and apparently included the Pilgrims, who never regarded Thanksgiving as a regular yearly affair.

If anyone deserves credit for Thanksgiving besides the Indians, it's Abraham Lincoln. During the Civil War, when the nation needed something to celebrate and something to bring some unity, Lincoln set aside Thanksgiving in 1863 as a national holiday. But even then, the Pilgrims were not part of the tradition. It wasn't until the 1890s that the Pilgrim myth was created.

As for Squanto, that trusty Indian who helped the Pilgrims, yes, he really existed and he really helped teach them to plant corn, and showed them the best places to hunt and fish. But Squanto wasn't just some bighearted local who happened to be good at foreign languages. This Indian was captured by British slave traders in 1614, sold as a slave in Spain, escaped to England, and in 1619 made it back to Cape Cod. When he reached his home village of Patuxet, he found all his relatives and the inhabitants had been wiped out by disease. When the *Mayflower* arrived the next year with thirty-five Pilgrims among its 102 passengers, they were indeed very lucky to find a resourceful English-speaking Indian named Squanto. Governor William Bradford called Squanto "a special instrument sent of God for their good."

So, basically, there's a kernel of truth in our Pilgrim Thanksgiving. 🖋

CHRISTMAS IN OLD NEW ENGLAND

Christmas has the feel of a time-honored American tradition dating back to the zealots who founded the colony at Plymouth. Actually, the Puritans of New England frowned on Christmas as a Catholic gewgaw. "Frowned" is too weak a word; they outlawed it. In 1659, a new law called for a five-shilling fine for anybody "found observing, by abstinence from labor, feasting or any other way, any such days as Christmas." The law stayed on the books for more than twenty years.

And jolly Santa didn't gain his roly-poly figure and white beard until the Civil War, when cartoonist Thomas Nast pictured him that way. In the 1600s and 1700s, the Dutch settlers who first imported Santa showed the future patron saint of retailers as a skinny and dignified man.

American Santa Claus before the Civil War, as he appeared in *Harper's Weekly*, December 25, 1858.

NEW ENGLAND WITCHES WERE ALSO MEN AND DOGS, 1692

The witchcraft hysteria that plagued Salem in the summer of 1692 led to the execution of nineteen people. Contrary to popular belief, the witches were not all women.

Five of the nineteen Salem witches who died were men—condemned for the same pact-with-Satan crimes as the women: casting spells on their neighbors, causing crops to fail, kicking up storms. (The men's names were Rev. George Burroughs, George Jacobs, John Proctor, Samuel Wardwell, John Willard.)

The men, same as the women, were *hanged*, not burned at the stake. And while Salem gets all the publicity, it's mostly forgotten that a witchcraft prosecution was also started in nearby Andover, Massachusetts, that led to the deaths of three women, one man and . . . two dogs.

When the local Andover doctor was unable to cure the long-suffering wife of Joseph Ballard, the husband suspected that perhaps a witch's spell might be involved. Two of the Salem girls—Ann Putnam, the twelve-year-old chief accuser, and Mary Wolcott—were brought to Andover. Since they didn't know the names of the citizens there, another method of inquiry needed to be created. The two girls went into long fits, and suspects were brought forward to touch the girls. If the girls were calmed, it proved that the suspects were witches.

Before long, more than forty persons had been accused when the local Justice Dudley Bradstreet refused to sign any more arrest warrants. Bradstreet, the son of a former governor, soon found himself accused of committing nine murders. His brother, John, was accused of bewitching a dog to hurt people. Someone else was accused of bewitching another dog. The Bradstreets fled the colony. Both dogs were tried for witchcraft and hanged. (Details of the trial and execution unfortunately have not survived.)

The Salem witchcraft trials have turned into a bit of a Halloween cottage industry, from books to movies to local tourist attractions. Here are a few facts that often slip outside the basic story.

• Torture was sometimes used to get witnesses to testify.

John Proctor wrote a letter on July 23, 1692, from prison. "My son, William Proctor, when he was examined, because he would not confess . . . they tied him neck and heels till the blood gushed out at his nose, and would have kept him so for twenty-four hours, if one more merciful than the rest had not taken pity on him." (Proctor senior was executed on August 19; William survived.)

• The families of convicted *and acquitted* witches had to pay for their upkeep in prison and for sheriff's expenses, including executing them. Martha Carrier's husband,

Richard, paid the sheriff fifty shillings and paid the prison keeper £4 and sixteen shillings for the cost of keeping his wife and four children in prison. (When he sued in 1710 for compensation, he asked for the exact amount back, which was eventually granted.)

• Giles Corey, eighty years old, was slowly pressed to death between giant slabs of stone over two days for refusing to plead innocent or guilty. It was a gruesome way to die. "In pressing," wrote a contemporary, "his tongue being prest out of his mouth, the Sheriff with his cane forced it in again, when he was dying." Many have thought that Corey refused to plead so that his property would be inherited by his children and not be confiscated by the state. Witchcraft scholar Rossell Robbins states "in America, property was not confiscated" and cites that condemned witch John Proctor wrote a will, which was honored.

In all, about 150 persons stood accused of witchcraft in 1692–1693; twenty were executed (including Corey), four died in prison. Four years later, the jurors admitted their error, avowing "the guilt of innocent blood." Anne Putnam also later recanted. "It was a great delusion of Satan that deceived me in that sad time." The colony of Massachusetts banned spectral evidence and in 1711 reversed about two thirds of the witchcraft verdicts, providing meager compensation to the families of some of the victims. It wasn't, however, until 1957 that the state of Massachusetts reversed all the remaining verdicts.

If anything good came out of the sorry business, it was a general awakening to the perils of theocracy that could allow religious fanatics to legally murder twenty innocent people. The backlash helped start to break the Church's stranglehold on government and justice, and drive a wedge between Church and State, a fragile hallmark of the United States (where you still cannot buy beer on Sunday morning in New York City). As Sarah Good, a pipe-smoking beggarwoman told Reverend Nicholas Noyes on the gallows: "I am no more a witch than you are a wizard, and if you take away my life, God will give you blood to drink."

HARVARD AND YALE TIED TO RELIGION

It is nowadays hard to imagine how intimately tied both Harvard and Yale were in their early days to Protestant ministries. At Harvard, when Increase Mather was president, scriptures were regularly read out loud to the students in the Hall.

The college that would become Yale was founded in part to stem the so-called "liberal" irreligious trends at Harvard. Cotton Mather in 1718 convinced diamond merchant and Connecticut native Elihu Yale to endow Yale College "to serve the great interests of education and so of religion."

Mather had had to convince Yale, an Anglican (i.e., Church of England), that it was okay to underwrite an institution run by Calvinists. Mather wrote to Yale that New England is based on "Catholic and generous principles of Christianity and . . . beyond the Narrow spirit of a party." Yale was convinced and he sent a shipment of goods worth £562, which would finally allow the school to have some permanent buildings.

Three years later, the rector of Yale College, Timothy Cutler, a protégé of the Mathers, closed his commencement speech by saying: "and let all the people say, Amen."

The Mathers were dumbfounded, appalled. Those were the words to close an Anglican service, not a service of Boston Congregationalism. Mather dubbed him a "treacherous Rector." Cutler resigned, and left immediately for England.

And Cotton never stopped criticizing Harvard after being passed over for the presidency. He complained in his diary about July 2 "being the Day of the senseless Diversion they call the Commencement at Cambridge, one of my special errands unto Heaven was to ask the Blessings for the College, and the Rescue of it from some wretched circumstances in which it is now languishing." 🍂

SCALPING THE INDIANS

DISEASE: A REAL ESTATE OPPORTUNITY

Most textbooks gloss over or omit the single most dominant factor in allowing Europeans to conquer the New World: disease. It wasn't gunpowder or superior technology that quickly opened up huge tracts of land to settlement, it was smallpox and other diseases.

Disease wiped out more than 90 percent of the Indian population of coastal New England in the early to mid-1600s. The Puritans, ever alert to see the hand of God shaping their lives, saw it as divine justice. John Winthrop, governor of Massachusetts Bay Colony, wrote a friend in 1634: "But for the natives in these parts, God hath so pursued them, for 300 miles space the greatest part of them are swept away by the smallpox which still continues among them. So as God hath thereby cleared our title to this place, those who remain in these parts, being in all not 50, have put themselves under our protection."

King James I of England thanked God for sending "this wonderful plague among the savages."

In Manhattan's tight real estate market in the 1990s, the long-standing joke advice to newcomers desperate for an apartment is to tell them to read the obituaries.

That's in effect what the original Puritans did; they listened for rumors of wide-spread death among the Indians. ✦

SCALPING: DEBUNKING THE DEBUNKERS AND MONEY FOR HAIR

For much of the late 20th century, it became fashionable among some liberal scholars to state that *Europeans* taught American Indians how to scalp. This notion has made its way into politically correct history books and documentaries.

It's simply not true.

Indians invented scalping, and had elaborate rituals surrounding it which were documented by the earliest explorers arriving in North America in the 1500s. Linguists point out that many Indian dialects had specific words for all aspects of the process, while explorers kept fumbling with circumlocution. Archaeologists have found ancient Indian graves with skulls showing clear signs of bashing and scraping.

On the other hand, while they didn't invent it, Europeans helped promote the practice. The French and British, during their North American wars against each other and the Indians, offered bounties, i.e., rewards for scalps. Colonists sometimes hunted Indians for their scalps, to gain a nest-egg for life in the New World.

Since we've been fed a steady diet in Westerns, both movies and TV shows, of Indians scalping the pioneers, it's only fair to serve up a few documented instances of colonists scalping Indians.

SCALPING: A NEW ENGLAND COURTSHIP, 1725

Young Jonathan Frye attended Harvard, class of 1723. He fell in love with Susanna Rogers, the thirteen-year-old daughter of a minister. His father had the usual objections: the girl was too young and how could the young fellow possibly hope to support her.

Frye was nonetheless determined to raise a fine sum of money quickly, and win his bride. So he decided he would try to scalp a few Indians, and collect the hefty bounties then being paid by the colonial government of Massachusetts: £100 for scalps of Indian men and warrior youths; £10 for women and children over the age of ten.

Frye succeeded in getting himself appointed chaplain to Captain Lovewell's band of rangers. "While he was praying before the company at daybreak on May 9, 1725, the troop spotted a lone Indian hunter in the woods near Pigwacket, Maine, and ambushed him," according to *Sibley's Harvard Graduates (Class of 1723)*. Frye hacked off his first scalp but soon a larger band of Indians attacked and the colonists were pinned down in a fierce ten-hour fight in which some of the rangers fired their guns "more than 20 times," according to contemporary coverage in the *Boston News-Letter* of May 27 of that year. Frye—who the *News-Letter* states "fought with undaunted courage"—bested another Indian and scalped him too, but Frye was wounded. He died soon after and became a New England folk hero, celebrated in ballads with lines like:

[He] was our English chaplain; he many
   Indians slew;
And some of them he scalped when bullets
   round him flew.

One vintage New England historian, Parson Symmes, who wrote up the incident, engaged in a mild cover-up. He changed the date of the attack to Saturday May 8 to hide the fact that Frye had been scalp-hunting on the Sunday Sabbath. Young Susanna waited almost a decade before marrying.

HANNAH DUSTON: TEN SCALPS, 1697

Indians raided her farmhouse in Haverhill, Massachusetts, and dashed her week-old baby to death against an apple tree. Hannah Duston, the mother of twelve, was dragged, wearing only one shoe, through the snow on a fifteen-day trek to an Indian camp. The night of March 30, 1697, Hannah and widow Mary Neff and fourteen-year-old Samuel Leonardson were kept prisoner on an island in the Merrimack River. They had been told they were going to an Indian village in Canada where they would likely have to run the gauntlet, being beaten by the entire tribe. Afterward, they might die, standing as targets for young hatchet-throwing teens.

At midnight, this unlikely colonial threesome—two women and a boy—gathered up the hatchets and killed ten of their twelve Indian guards. The captives fled but then decided to return to take the scalps; they then grabbed a canoe and floated back toward Haverhill, where they were welcomed as heroes. On June 8 of that year, the General Court of Massachusetts awarded Mrs. Duston £50 for the scalps of two Indian men, two women, and six children.

REVOLUTIONARY WAR, 1775

British loyalist Peter Oliver, who was in Boston during the war and whose memoirs were written in 1781, claims that American patriots scalped British soldiers during the fierce Battle of Lexington.

"Many lives were lost this Day; the King lost about 90 men, and the Rebels at least as many. Many were wounded on each side. Two of the British Troops, at fewest, were scalped, and one of those before he was dead. Let Patriots roar as loud as they please about the Barbarity of an Indian Scalping Knife; but let them know, that an Indian Savage strikes the deadly Blow before he takes off the Scalp. It is reserved for a *New England* savage, only to take it off while his Brother was alive."

Oliver wrote his memoir in London, quite bitter that he had lost his American home and had been forced to flee.

Oliver noted that New Englanders for a century had boasted of their piety while paying "premiums" for scalps. "And I have seen a vessell enter the harbor of Boston, with a long string of Indian scalps strung to the rigging, and waving in the wind."

UNSUNG AMERICAN "PIRATES" HELPED WIN THE REVOLUTIONARY WAR

During the Revolutionary War, privately financed American ships—sanctioned by Congress to act like pirates—attacked and captured as many as one thousand British cargo ships, loaded with spices, rum, and other goods, severely disrupting trade. And the investors and sailors split the booty.

Naval historian Edgar Maclay argues that this form of economic terrorism against British merchants had more to do with Great Britain yielding the colonies than the victories of Washington over forces of mercenaries fighting on faraway soil. Maclay points out that page after page of British newspapers during the so-called "American war" complained about the phenomenal success of American privateers in rupturing British trade, even along the coasts of England, while there was comparatively little mention of the land war.

"What produces peace?" asked Thomas Jefferson. "The distress of individuals." And Jefferson added: ". . . every possible encouragement should be given to priva-

teering in time of war with a commercial nation."

British merchants, and their aristocrat investors, lost millions in goods, as well as 16,000 captured seamen—always a labor force in short supply. Insurance rates skyrocketed. Complained Alderman Woodbridge in the House of Lords in February 1778: "that the number of ships lost by capture or destroyed by American privateers since the beginning of the war was seven hundred and thirty three, whose cargoes were computed to be worth over ten million dollars." He added: "Insurance before the war was two percent to America . . . but now that insurance has more than doubled, even with a strong escort, and, without an escort, fifteen percent."

The price of insurance might seem like an obscure point to make regarding the end of the war, but is it? If the insurance costs wipe out the profits, the powerful merchant class will be screaming for peace.

The *London Statesman* at the time of the War of 1812 reminisced bitterly: "Everyone must recollect what [privateers] did in the latter part of the American war. The books at Lloyd's will recount it, and the rate of assurances at that time will clearly prove what their diminuative strength was able to effect in the face of our navy, and that when nearly one hundred pennants [i.e., British war ships] were flying on their coast. Were we able to prevent their going in and out, or stop them from taking our trade and our storeships, even in sight of our own garrisons? Besides were they not in the English and Irish Channels picking up our homeward-bound trade, sending their prizes into French and Spanish ports, to the great terror and annoyance of our merchants and shipowners?"

What exactly is a privateer? Basically, he's *our* pirate. The countries of Europe, especially England with its national hero, Sir Francis Drake, have a long tradition of encouraging privateers to attack the enemy in times of war. In 1776, Congress passed an act, which begins "Instructions to the commanders of private ships or vessels of war, which shall have commissions or letters of marque . . . You may, by force of arms, attack, subdue and take all ships and other vessels belonging to the Inhabitants of Great-Britain." Signed by order of Congress, John Hancock, president, April 3, 1776.

Elaborate rules explain about towing the vessel to port, not ransoming prisoners, not selling goods until a local court can rule whether it's a "legitimate prize."

Within four months after the Declaration of Independence, businessmen in New York had outfitted twenty-six speedy privateers, manned by over two thousand seamen. Besides being a patriotic move, this was a *great* business opportunity: to prey at will on the prosperous merchant ships of England and keep the booty. The shares of these expeditions were actually publicly traded like stock, based on the daring of the captain, the number of guns, etc. "Shares in privateers were widely sold, traded, discounted and used as collateral not only by merchants but by military officers and government officials as well," states Richard Kaufman in *The War Profiteers*. He also points out

that as many as 90,000 sailors manned these privateer vessels, almost as many as served in the Continental Army.

What's also little realized is that when the handful of government battle ships, directly commissioned by the fledgling Congress (i.e., the Continental Navy), captured British ships, the sailors aboard also shared in the wealth. (Who wouldn't fight harder for their country if he stood to make a handsome profit?)

In 1779, three Continental Navy ships captured eight heavily laden British merchant ships in the space of a few weeks. It's recorded that a fourteen-year-old cabin boy, aboard the Continental Navy ship *Ranger*, who had left the family farm but one month earlier, received as his share: "one ton of sugar, from thirty to forty gallons of fourth proof Jamaica rum, some twenty pounds of cotton and about the same quantity of ginger, logwood and all-spice, besides seven hundred dollars in money."

By contrast, a soldier in the Continental Army, at the outset of the war, earned seven dollars a month.

Privateering was profitable. "Large fortunes were secured by many of the owners, and some of them are enjoyed by their descendants at the present day," stated *Harper's Monthly* in a historical piece in July of 1864. The article goes on to state of privateering: "Divested of all its specious habiliments of necessity, expediency and law, it stands revealed in all the naked deformity of black PIRACY."

It simply hasn't suited our national myth to give American pirates (or privateers) their due in winning the Revolutionary War, although perhaps in many ways, these brave, *investment-oriented* warriors truly represent our national character. ❧

THE FIRST PRESIDENT

Even George Washington acknowledged this man to be the first President of the United States. When Maryland ratified the Articles of Confederation in 1781, John Hanson signed the document for Maryland, and then was elected "President of the United States in Congress Assembled." Hanson sent George Washington a letter of congratulations after the general's big victory at Yorktown, and Washington dashed off a note back to the "President of the United States." ❧

PRESIDENT FOR A DAY: DAVID RICE ATCHISON

His presidency ranks right up there with that moment when Secretary of State Alexander Haig erroneously declared himself in charge the day that Ronald Reagan was shot.

Here's how it happened for President David Rice Atchison.

President James Polk's term ended on Sunday March 4, 1849; his Vice President had already resigned. The incoming President Zachary Taylor refused to be sworn in on a Sunday, so technically the chain of command left the President Pro Tempore of the Senate as acting President of the United States. The man's name was David Rice Atchison, and he told a newspaper

that he spent most of his one day in office sleeping late and napping. His tombstone reads: "President of U.S. one day." ❧

PRESIDENTIAL SEX SCANDALS

In the years after JFK's death in 1963, journalists started to document Kennedy's sexual liaisons, and that seemed to pave the way for more snooping into the love lives of presidents. When Gary Hart was caught with Donna Rice in 1988, that seemed to open the floodgates to prying into presidential candidates' love lives. Actually, *some* members of the press have been doing this kind of reporting all along.

Here, since textbooks tend to skip this material, are highlights of the presidential sex scandals, and some provocative evidence about one First Lady.

WASHINGTON: HIS SEXLESS LIFE

He might have been the father of our country, but he wasn't the father of any children, at least no documented ones.

Martha had four children in seven years with her first husband, who died leaving her a rich widow, and then she had none with George, although the couple said they wanted children.

As for his supposed tryst with a slave girl, the one he supposedly confessed to in a letter, that letter was a forgery by the British, a clumsy ploy during the Revolutionary War.

And that great love affair with Sally Fairfax; yes, letters have survived and they are about as flowery and affectionate as you can get. However, if George and Sally dallied, they covered their tracks well, because no proof exists.

JEFFERSON: BREEDER OF SLAVES?

This song appeared in several newspapers around the country in 1802, supposedly written by the "Sage of Monticello," with lyrics such as:

> You call her slave—and pray were Slaves
> Made only for the galley?
> Try for yourself, ye witless knaves—
> Take each to bed your Sally.
> Yankee doodle, whose the noodle?
> Wine's vapid, tope me brandy—
> For still I find to breed my kind,
> A negro wench the dandy!

Thomas Jefferson was accused of fathering some if not all of Sally Hemings's seven children. What you should know is who first went public with the accusation: one James T. Callender, a drunken Scot whom Jefferson had overlooked for a postmaster job. Callender never did any reporting, just echoed rumors he had heard. "This African Venus is said to officiate as housekeeper at Monticello . . ."

However, proving the source unreliable does not make the charge untrue. Sally Hemings was a beautiful mulatto and it is extremely likely that she was the half-sister of Jefferson's late wife, Martha, born from the same father, John Wayles. Sally probably resembled her. Jefferson took Sally, when she was fourteen, along to France as a companion to his daughter. And the only slaves that Jefferson freed were Sally's children, including her eldest, named Tom.

Short of DNA analysis on the bones, though, we'll probably never know.

ANDREW JACKSON MARRIED A MARRIED WOMAN

His political opponents accused Andrew Jackson's wife, Rachel, of bigamy and adultery, because her divorce hadn't been finalized when Jackson married her. The future President (from 1829–1837), when he discovered the mistake, had to remarry her. The campaign against him featured: "Ought a convicted adulteress and her paramour husband to be placed in the highest offices of this free and Christian land?" The resounding answer by the American public was: Yes!

GROVER "BIG STEVE" CLEVELAND (1885–1889; 1893–1897)

During the presidential campaign of 1884, Grover Cleveland did an unthinkable

Grover "Big Steve" Cleveland, a ladies' man and two-term president.

thing when accused of fathering a child out of wedlock. He told the truth.

On July 21, that election year, the *Buffalo Evening Telegraph* broke the story under the headline, A TERRIBLE TALE. When he was a sheriff in Buffalo, beside officiating at two hangings, Cleveland partied with friends at a clubhouse on Niagara Island. "Big Steve," as he was known then, got a pretty widow pregnant. Cleveland supported both mother and child, forced the mother to quit drinking, then later got the child adopted into a wealthy family. Opposition Republicans chanted at his rallies: "Ma, ma, where's my pa?" And the Democrats would supposedly reply: "Goin' to the White House, ha ha ha!"

And they were of course right.

Scandal hit "Big Steve" again once there, though. When his law partner Oscar Folsom died, Cleveland had taken care of the widow and her pretty teenage daughter, Frances, even had himself declared her legal guardian. She called him "Uncle Cleve." In 1885, when

Frances Folsom, twenty-two years old, was married in the White House in 1886, the year this photograph was taken.

she turned twenty-one, the forty-seven-year-old bachelor President proposed. The whole thing was kept fairly hush-hush, but some newspapermen thought they had dug it out and linked Cleveland to the girl's *mother*. "I don't see why the papers keep marrying me to old ladies," he groused at the time.

Grover and young Frances were married June 2, 1886, in the Blue Room of the White House. At first the reaction was unfavorable, but it's said that when photographs of the lovely, statuesque, refined young woman began to circulate, that public opinion shifted. Not until Jackie Kennedy would the American public again be so seduced by a President's wife.

WARREN HARDING: REGISTERED AT HOTEL AS "HARDWICK"

Warren Harding, running for Ohio governor in 1910, was having an affair with his good friend's wife when another friend's fourteen-year-old daughter started climbing on his lap at campaign strategy meetings. Harding's flinty and often ailing wife, Florence, who was five years older than Warren, chased the girl away. Apparently not far enough.

The pair met again in a Manhattan hotel seven years later in 1917, and fifty-two-year-old Senator Harding took twenty-year-old starstruck Nan Britton's virginity, before a couple of house detectives burst in and quickly escorted the couple out a side exit, Harding slipping one of the men twenty dollars. "Gee,

Nan," said Harding in the taxi cab, "I thought I wouldn't get out of that for under $1,000!"

Harding would become very savvy about the price of illicit affairs. When Harding received the Republican nomination for President in 1920, his longtime relationship with a local Marion, Ohio, married woman, Carrie Phillips, almost derailed his bid for the Oval Office.

Harding had started sneaking afternoon visits to tall strawberry-blond Carrie, mother of five, as early as 1905 (neighbors would note the sheets hanging to dry) and judging from the 250 passionate letters he sent her, she was the love of his life. Florence, whom Harding nicknamed the "Duchess," once stood on the porch and threw a feather-duster, a waste-basket, and finally a piano stool at the woman. But Carrie, after fifteen years of hearing Warren promise to divorce his wife and never doing it, had had enough, or perhaps her cuckolded husband had. During the campaign, threats of blackmail caused the Republican National Committee to send advertising mogul, Albert Lasker, to offer the Phillips family $20,000 and generous monthly expenses if they would leave the country as long as Harding was in office. They accepted and scooted off to Japan.

Harding—despite his brush with disgrace—had his priorities firmly in order. After being elected President in 1920, he continued to see young Nan Britton, who in 1919 had given birth to a daughter, Elizabeth Ann.

The pair continued their affair in a soon-to-be notorious White House coat closet. Here are Nan's own words of a private White House tour the President gave her: "He introduced me to the one place where, he said, he thought we might share kisses in safety. This was a small closet in the anteroom, evidently a place for hats and coats, but entirely empty most of the time we used it, for we repaired there many times in the course of my visits to the White House, and in the darkness of a space not more than five feet square the President of the United States and his adoring sweetheart made love."

When Harding died suddenly in office in 1923 amid the Teapot Dome oil lease scandal, the Phillips family returned from exile and Nan Britton tried to convince the Harding estate to continue monthly support payments for Harding's illegitimate daughter.

But the family refused, even after the death of Flossie Harding in 1924. So Nan Britton wrote a book, *The President's Daughter*, which she succeeded in publishing in 1927, even after government Vice Squad

Warren Harding (1865–1923) stepping out with his wife, Florence, nicknamed "The Duchess." The President often stepped out *without* his wife.

Fruits of love. Harding's mistress, Nan Britton, seen here with her/their daughter, Elizabeth Ann. The year is 1931 and Britton has endured eight hard years after the President's sudden death. The girl, by the bye, bears a striking resemblance in the cheekbones, mouth, and eyes to younger Harding.

agents had tried to suppress it and no major publisher would handle it.

The book was prudishly ignored by the national press until fearless caustic H. L. Mencken reviewed it for the *Baltimore Sun.* Sales took off and it hit the bestseller list.

Flossie Harding was buried alongside her husband, leading wags to note that this was probably the first time in years that the couple had slept together.

ELEANOR ROOSEVELT: FIRST LADY TO LADY LOVES?

This is a topic that makes some people *very* uncomfortable: the alleged lesbian affair between saintly philanthropic Eleanor Roosevelt and Associated Press reporter Lenora Hickok. It is inconceivable to some, undeniable to others.

Over thirty years from 1932 on, Eleanor Roosevelt wrote "Hicky" more than 2,300 letters, all of them affectionate, some quite passionate. Hickok saved them but stipulated they not be published until ten years after her death.

Eleanor Roosevelt cuts birthday cake with a bevy of beauties. That's Lana Turner (second from left) and Deanna Durbin (third from left).

For Eleanor's birthday in March 1933, Hickok gave Eleanor a sapphire ring, which had been given to Hickok by an opera singer. "Hick, darling," wrote Eleanor. ". . . Oh, I want to put my arms around you. I ache to hold you close. Your ring is a great comfort. I look at it and think she does love me, or I wouldn't be wearing it."

Then in December 1933, Eleanor wrote: "Dear, I've been trying to bring back your face—to remember just how you look. Funny how even the dearest face will fade away in time. Most clearly I remember your eyes, with a kind of reassuring smile in them, and the feeling of that soft spot just northeast of the corner of your mouth against my lips. I wonder what we'll do when we meet—what we'll say. Well, I'm rather proud of us, aren't you? I think we've done rather well."

Hicky was a frequent guest at the White House and had a small room assigned to her near Eleanor's suite. White House staff often found Hicky asleep on the daybed in Eleanor's rooms and the pair frequently drove off for outings, with Eleanor refusing Secret Service protection. Hicky was chubby, squat, wore her hair in a bun, favored dark suits, dark stockings, and flat shoes. Eleanor and FDR were a very loving couple but apparently not physically affectionate.

Long after FDR died, Hicky moved into the Roosevelt estate in Hyde Park in the 1950s and was living there when Eleanor died in 1962. "The intensity of their passionate sentiment only proves how overwhelming Eleanor's deep love and sexual feeling, at last found, must have been for this woman," contends Michael Sullivan in *Presidential Passions*. Many Roosevelt scholars categorically deny the affair.

IKE AND HIS JEEP DRIVER, KAYE SUMMERSBY

Ex-President Harry Truman told an interviewer in 1961 that General Eisenhower was so in love with his Irish staff driver, Kaye Summersby, that right after World War II Eisenhower wrote General Marshall asking to be relieved of duty so he could divorce Mamie and marry Kaye. Marshall wrote a ferocious reply, threatening to "bust" Ike out of the army if he tried such a thing and to "see to it that his life was a living hell." Ike broke off the relationship.

Kaye Summersby wrote a congenial memoir in 1948 mentioning nothing of the affair but dying of cancer in the mid-1970s, she wrote *Past Forgetting*, and detailed their love. "His kisses absolutely unraveled me," she revealed. And photo after photo from WWII shows pretty Kaye at Ike's side. She said they wanted to consummate the affair, but that Ike failed to perform. She quoted him as saying his marriage to Mamie had "killed something in me. Not all at once but little by little."

Truman said that he destroyed the Eisenhower-Marshall letters filed over at the Pentagon and they certainly didn't surface during the 1952 presidential election, which Ike won. The Eisenhower family has stoutly denied the affair. ❧

THE STOLEN ELECTION OF 1876

An American, a Republican by the name of J. Madison Wells, once tried to sell the presidency, and almost succeeded. Read on.

In 1876, a scant dozen years after the Civil War, the country was still sorely divided along racial lines, with the whites in the Southern states bridling at the so-called "carpetbagger" governments imposed on them by the federal government.

In the presidential election that year, the Democratic candidate, Samuel J. Tilden, representing the interests of the Southern whites, won the election—both the popular vote and the electoral college.

So the Republicans stole the election. "Stole" is the correct verb.

They finagled Rutherford B. Hayes into the White House through voter fraud, election board commandeering, bribery, forgery, and perjury. It is certainly one of the uglier chapters in presidential politics and one routinely forgotten by most Americans.

On November 8, Tilden woke up to see that he had received 4.3 million votes to Hayes's 4 million votes, and apparently 193 electoral votes to Hayes's 173. Enter Republican fixer, Daniel Sickles, a one-legged decorated military officer, who telegraphed Republican leaders in South Carolina, Louisiana, Florida, and Oregon to have the Republican-controlled election boards keep the voter tallies fluid. "With your state sure for Hayes, he is elected.

Hold your state." Federal troops—during this Republican-dominated post–Civil War era—were still stationed in the Southern states.

Hayes remained aloof from the maneuverings, but his party stalwarts manipulated the Republican-controlled election boards in those states to throw out enough Democratic votes to shift the balance to Hayes. South Carolina, with all five election board members Republican, threw out the results in two counties; in Florida, agents from the Justice, Treasury, and Post Office all "helped" in the recount.

However, with Louisiana still in doubt, the election board chairman there, a Republican named J. Madison Wells, tried to sell the presidency. According to *The Presidency of Rutherford B. Hayes* by Ari Hoogenboom, first Wells approached the Democrats, demanding $250,000 ($100,000 for each white board member and $25,000 for each black board member; all were Republicans); that failing, he tried to extort money from his own party; finally he contacted Tilden's nephew, Col. William Pelton, asking for $200,000. Pelton, the acting secretary of the Democratic National Committee, negotiated with Wells but never struck a deal. Wells failed in his outright sales but apparently received some compensation from his own party. The results were now 185–184 for Hayes, but the Democrats were crying foul.

The disputed electoral college results wound up before a special Congressional commission in early February, with eight Republicans and seven Democrats, who voted—surprise, surprise—strictly along party lines.

It's said, then, that with a Democratic filibuster brewing and Democrats threatening to delay or disrupt the inauguration—that in a smoke-filled room at the Wormley's Hotel in D.C. a clique of Republicans agreed to pull federal troops out of the South in exchange for Democrats agreeing not to further fight Hayes's disputed victory. This sealed it for Hayes, and . . . for the voting rights of blacks in the South for the next ninety years.

Hayes was sworn in on March 5, pulled the troops out and whites regained a stranglehold on Southern politics. ❧

CIVIL WAR: SECEDING FROM CONVENTIONAL WISDOM

ABRAHAM LINCOLN AND SHIPPING OUT THE EX-SLAVES
Abraham Lincoln was strongly in favor of having the millions of freed slaves leave the United States after the Civil War. He investigated founding a new colony somewhere in the world as a haven for freed American slaves. "Your race suffers

Gentlemen allow me to introduce to you, this illustrious individual in whom you will find combined, all the graces, and virtues of Black Republicanism, and whom we propose to run as our next Candidate for the Presidency.

How fortunate! that this intellectual and noble creature should have been discovered, just at this time, to prove to the world the superiority of the Colored over the Anglo Saxon race, he will be a worthy successor to carry out the policy which I shall inaugurate.

What, can dey be!

Entered according to act of Congress, in the year 1860, by Currier & Ives, in the Clerk's Office of the District Court for the Southern District of N.Y.

AN HEIR TO THE THRONE,
OR THE NEXT REPUBLICAN CANDIDATE

Published Currier & Ives.   152 Nassau St. N.Y.

This racist cartoon was published by Currier & Ives after Lincoln won the 1860 election. Lincoln cheers the fact the man in the middle will be the next Republican candidate for President and "will prove to the world the superiority of the Colored over the Anglo-Saxon race."

greatly, many of them, by living among us, while ours suffers from your presence," he told a group of prominent free blacks in August, 1862. "If this is admitted, it affords a reason why we should be separated."

The Lincoln administration sent inquiries to many South American and African governments, but found two ac-

ceptable places for freed slave colonies: Panama and the Caribbean island of Ile à Vache.

As the Civil War progressed, the nation debated what should be done with all these freed uneducated slaves. In April 1862, Congress had passed a bill freeing the slaves in the District of Columbia, and set aside the large sum of $100,000 to pay passage for former slaves wanting to emigrate to Haiti or Liberia.

On January 1, 1863, Abraham Lincoln issued the Emancipation Proclamation. It was a noble document and a very courageous political move, but it did not free a single slave, since it applied to slaves only in "rebellion," i.e., the Confederacy. Not surprisingly, the Confederate states in the middle of the Civil War chose to ignore Lincoln's directive.

And, the Emancipation Proclamation specifically did *not* apply to 800,000 slaves in slave-holding states (Delaware, Maryland, Kentucky, and Missouri), which chose to remain with the Union.

The slaves in the Confederacy were freed when the South lost the war in April 1865. Slaves in the four Union slaveholding states were freed by the 13th Amendment, adopted December 18, 1865.

As for any plans Lincoln might have had for repatriating slaves, they were cut short by an assassin's bullet on April 15, 1865. ✲

JEFFERSON DAVIS'S OFFER

After losing the battle of Vicksburg, Jefferson Davis proposed letting the slaves fight for the Confederacy in exchange for their freedom. In 1865, the Confederate government contacted England and France and offered to abolish slavery in exchange for being recognized as a separate nation. The war ended before either country responded. ✲

LINCOLN ASSASSINATION CONSPIRACY THEORY

President Lincoln was shot on April 14, 1865, at Ford's Theater. Just as the Kennedy assassination brought the conspiracy theorists out of the woodwork this century, so did the Lincoln assassination bring them out in the 19th century. And, yes, their books sold too.

Actor John Wilkes Booth shot Lincoln and jumped down ten feet to the stage below. He shouted *"Sic semper tyrannis"* ("Thus always to tyrants"). When British essayist and critic Matthew Arnold heard of the remark, he reportedly commented that Booth's use of Latin "offered a ray of hope in the United States's otherwise bleak cultural outlook." (Don't miss the pinkie ring.)

As late as 1907, a brisk 70,000 copies were sold of a book entitled *The Escape and Suicide of John Wilkes Booth, or the First True Account of Lincoln's Assassination, Containing a Complete Confession by Booth, Many Years after His Crime.* A Booth character even traveled the lecture circuit.

But conspiracy theory wasn't the exclusive field of the quick-buck artists. The federal government had hoped to prove that the plot to kill Lincoln could be traced directly to the Confederate diplomatic corps based in Montreal, Canada. Besides the eight live prisoners in Washington, including Dr. Samuel Mudd and boardinghouse keeper Mary Surratt, the indictment listed Jefferson Davis as well as eight Confederates operating out of Canada: Jacob Thompson, Beverly Tucker, George Sanders, and Clement Clay, the last four being members of the Confederacy's "Canadian Cabinet" in Montreal. Also indicted were William Cleary, George Harper, and George Young, who were agents working with the so-called diplomats.

At the trial, the testimony against this latter group of eight was a mind-boggling mishmash of hearsay and coded letters. All eight of them and "others unknown" were convicted by this military tribunal but never sentenced.

Ironically—according to Theodore Roscoe, author of *The Web of Conspiracy* (1959)—if the testimony of some of these Civil War spies and shady characters were true, then several of them had clearly warned the United States government that Lincoln was in serious danger long before the assassination. It was as though,

This unrepentant twenty-year-old, whose real name was Lewis Powell, confessed to trying to kill Secretary of State William Henry Seward. (He *is* handsome, but actually Lewis had very bad teeth dating back to being kicked by a mule when he was twelve.) In prison on this Union ironclad ship, *Saugus*, he was kept mostly in darkness under a hood. After his death by hanging, Powell's remains went unclaimed for reburial in 1869 and his skull turned up in a U.S. Army medical museum exhibit in of all places . . . Ford's Theater in 1885. It was more recently rediscovered by accident in 1992 among various Native American skulls in the Smithsonian's Anthropology Department.

states Roscoe, the trial proved the army had failed to listen to its own spies such as Richard Montgomery, who testified that Confederate bigwig Jacob Thompson had told him in January 1865 in Canada "that a proposition had been made to him to rid the world of the tyrants Lincoln, Stanton, Grant, and some others."

Roscoe also points out that Louis Wiechmann, who was staying at Mary

The execution was held July 15, 1865, in the courtyard of the federal penitentiary in Washington, D.C., just eight days after the sentencing. Forty-five-year-old widow, Mary Surratt, would be the first woman ever executed by the federal government. The audience was by invitation only, and among the celebrity crowd was the U.S. Army's only female surgeon, Mary Walker. (The press corps found space to chastise her for riding her horse astride to the execution.) As the prisoners mounted the scaffold, they could see very nearby four freshly dug graves, each four feet deep, and four pine coffins. With a hanging, we picture a lever releasing a trapdoor. Actually, soldiers steadied tall "props," which supported the planks under the prisoners' feet, and then yanked the "props" at the proper moment.

Mrs. Surratt and George Atzerodt died quickly, their necks snapping, but David Herold and Lewis Payne took longer; Payne's athletic six-foot body jerked and twitched for close to eight minutes in the sweltering D.C. heat.

Surratt's boardinghouse, on February 20, 1865, informed the War Department that a conspiracy was brewing. Nothing was done to investigate. And . . .

One of the stranger, more recent conspiracy theories comes from Charley Shively, the biographer of Walt Whitman.

Shively states the "circle of conspirators, if they were not a gay study group, were certainly held together by bonds of manly affection." He notes: "Booth wore a pinkie ring on his little finger." He adds: "The group of men sharing rooms in Mary Surratt's boardinghouse were tied together by their love of John Wilkes Booth. Perhaps they were not all gay but some of them clearly were."

On the other hand, a wealth of information shows that Booth was engaged to be married to a *woman* and that he had a long history of frequenting female prostitutes. All of which might prove that Booth was more secretive about his homosexuality than his attempts to assassinate Lincoln.

This bog of conspiracy awaits an Oliver Stone to get it completely wrong. 🌀

RACIST RELATIONS

PRANKS OF THE ORIGINAL KKK

The induction ceremony of the original "Kuklux Klan" in 1866 in Pulaski, Tennessee, was to blindfold a prospective member, put a hat with giant donkey ears on his head, and then take off the blindfold in front of a mirror. Besides riding around at night in white sheets, like Halloween ghosts, the first Klan members would also sometimes carry a spare head (a gourd with makeup) and ask former slaves "to hold my head a minute." Another of their sophomoric pranks included pretending to drink a gallon of water by siphoning it off into a hidden receptacle beneath their robe. "That's the first drink I've had since I was killed at the Battle of Shiloh, and you get mighty thirsty in hell," the hilarious fellow would say. However, once the ferocious ex-Confederate General Nathan Bedford Forrest became Grand Wizard in 1867, the group grew more sinister and violent. 🌀

LYNCHING: OUT OF THE SHADOWS

Photographs of lynching and smiling lynch mobs have been systematically excluded from American history textbooks. It can be argued that they're too horrific to show; it can also be argued that suppressing them distorts history and allows a generation of lynch mobs to walk off scot-free as their crimes are hidden and forgotten.

This was a horrendous chapter in American history and should be faced straight on.

From the dismantling of Reconstruction in the 1880s through the 1930s, America was a country with profoundly racist attitudes, and this is a very disconcerting fact to most Americans today. This is not white liberal guilt speaking or political correctness; it is a statement of historical fact.

Jackie Robinson was not the first black man to play in the Major Leagues. A handful of blacks played in organized major leagues, such as the American Association, in the 19th century until they were banned in the late 1880s. Black jockeys won fifteen of the first twenty-eight Kentucky Derbies until they were ousted in

Not all lynch mob victims were black. Rapist Frank McManus was taken from jail and lynched by this well-dressed crowd in Minneapolis in 1882.

1911. The majority of blacks were *legally* disenfranchised in Southern and border states from 1890 to 1907. In 1896, the Supreme Court upheld segregation. Enormously popular minstrel shows barnstormed the country depicting blacks as toadying fools. An African pygmy was exhibited behind bars at the Bronx Zoo. In 1921, whites in Tulsa, Oklahoma, dropped dynamite from a plane onto a black ghetto, killing seventy-five people and wrecking more than 1,100 homes.

During this period, there were many lynchings. From 1889 through 1930, at least 3,724 people were lynched in the United States, according to *The Tragedy of Lynching* by Arthur Raper. Just under 80 percent of these were blacks, and almost all the lynchers were American-born whites. "Although a few lynchers have been indicted, tried, convicted and sentenced, the courts usually deal with them in the most perfunctory fashion," according to Raper, who wrote his landmark study in the early 1930s. This tolerance of lynching by local, state, and federal governments reveals the nation's attitude. When strikers threatened Big Business, the federal government intervened; at lynch mobs, it looked the other way. The national press generally criticized lynching, but never roused the public to a national fury.

Contrary to popular notion, lynchings were rarely about rape; only one sixth of the lynchings involved a sex crime.

Also, our impression of lynchings have been somewhat whitewashed by our image of frontier justice, of outraged cowboys stringing up some murderer and saving the courts the trouble. There's a perception that lynch mobs merely sped up the execution of criminals.

Lynch mobs, especially in the rural South, often ran a *kangaroo* court, then engaged in extreme sadism. States Raper: "Mobs are capable of unbelievable atrocity. James Irwin at Ocilla, Georgia [in 1930] was jabbed in his mouth with a sharp pole. His toes were cut off joint by joint. His fingers were similarly removed, and his teeth extracted with wire pliers. After further unmentionable mutilations, the Negro's still living body was saturated with gasoline, and a lighted match was applied. As the flames leaped up, hundreds of shots were fired into the dying victim. During the day, thousands of people from miles around rode out to see the sight. Not till nightfall did the officers remove the body and bury it."

Irwin was accused *on circumstantial evidence* of having raped, mutilated, and killed a sixteen-year-old white girl, and tossed her dead body in a hog wallow. Local white citizens kept Irwin's fingers and toes as souvenirs. One of the investigators of the lynching picked up a hitchhiker, a twenty-one-year-old high school dropout, blond-haired, blue-eyed, Baptist, married. He was carrying a toe. ✸

THE GREAT BLACK HOPE AND WHITE WOMEN

Jack Johnson rose from being a "colored boy" fighting "Battle Royals" literally for the pennies tossed in the ring by the all-white crowd in Galveston, Texas, to heavyweight champion of the world.

He was a white bigot's worst nightmare. When Johnson hit the big time, he hired a *white* chauffeur and a *white* butler, and he married two *white* women, and he cheated on them with dozens of *white* prostitutes. The Ku Klux Klan openly fostered the idea of lynching him, but it was actually the United States government that brought him down on a thin, racially motivated charge. (It wasn't the Feds' finest hour.)

Jack Johnson had the broadest smile and the most unrepentant almond eyes. He flaunted it, especially the "it" that perhaps some white men feared most. Sometimes while training for a fight, he'd wrap his penis in gauze bandages to increase its size, and wear tight trunks, according to the excellent biography *Papa Jack* by Randy Roberts.

In 1908, Johnson became the first black boxer to get a shot at the World Championship. With the fight hyped openly along racial lines, Jack Johnson beat Tommy Burns in Sydney, Australia. "The fight," Jack London wrote, "there was no fight. No Armenian massacre could compare with the hopeless slaughter that took place in the Sydney stadium today." Johnson baited Burns throughout the fight, always smiling, taunting him that his wife wouldn't recognize him later.

London's piece in the *New York Herald* ended with a call to the retired heavyweight champion, big Jim Jeffries. "But one thing now remains. Jim Jeffries must now emerge from his alfalfa farm and remove that golden smile from Jack Johnson's face. Jeff, it's up to you. The white man must be rescued."

But Jeffries, a hulk of a man, thirty-three years old and three years out of the ring, wouldn't take the bait. The search for the Great White Hope was on. "Well-muscled white boys more than six feet two inches were not safe out of their mother's sight," joked one newspaperman.

In view of some whites of that era, Johnson became the Bad Nigger, like Stagolee in that blues song: "What do I care fo' yo' children, what do I care fo' yo' wife,/You've taken my new Stetson hat, an' I'm goin' to take yo' life."

Johnson—though carousing heavily—easily beat several white hopefuls, then Jeffries finally agreed to come out of retirement. It was arguably the most anticipated fight in boxing history, and it was billed as civilization versus the savages. In a reflection of the attitudes of that era, a writer in the *New York Times* observed: "If the black man wins, thousands and thousands of his ignorant brothers will misinterpret his victory as justifying claims to much more than mere physical equality with their white neighbors."

Fourth of July, 1910. Reno, Nevada. Twenty thousand mostly white spectators. A brass band played "All Coons Look Alike to Me." The fighters, by prearrangement, did not shake hands before the fight.

By round twelve, Jeffries's face was a bloody mass. In the fifteenth, Jeffries hit the canvas for the first time in his career. The hulking white boxer struggled to his feet at the count of nine; Johnson buried him again; once again at the count of nine, he got up. After another flurry, with Jeffries hanging over the ropes, the fight was stopped. Jack Johnson had done it.

In Georgia, three celebrating blacks were shot dead; in Houston a black man had his throat slit from ear to ear; race ri-

The fight. Jim Jeffries came out of a five-year retirement to save "white man's honor" and wrest the heavyweight belt back from the first "negro" champion, Jack Johnson. The dateline is July 4, 1910, in Reno, Nevada. Twenty thousand white people attended the fight.

The smile. Jack Johnson, on the comeback trail, still flashes that trademark smile in Washington, D.C., in 1922, even after serving a year in Leavenworth. The white man is unidentified.

ots ensued, blacks were beaten in cities around the country.

Johnson refused to back down and he celebrated wherever he went. With historical hindsight, it seems as though the United States government then tried to intervene, to squelch this exuberant Negro. The district attorney in Illinois charged Johnson with violating the White Slave Traffic Act, i.e., transporting a woman across state lines "for the purpose of prostitution or debauchery, or for any other immoral purpose." The law, called the Mann Act, was aimed at pimps, profiting by perverting young girls. Prosecutions of private citizens with prostitutes were *extremely* rare.

"For Jack Johnson, the government was willing to make an exception," understates author Randy Roberts. Johnson was accused, among other charges, of paying to have a veteran prostitute and longtime lover of his, Belle Schreiber, come meet him while he traveled, going once from Atlantic City, New Jersey, to Pittsburgh. At the trial, Assistant District Attorney Harry Parkin, trying to add to the outrage, thundered: "It will appear that those women who he carried about the country with him — very very many times, when he either had a fit of anger, or when the girls refused to do some of the obscene things he demanded of them — that he practiced the manly art of self-defense upon them, blacking their eyes and sending them to hospitals."

Johnson didn't shuffle at the trial or do a Stepinfetchit; he spit his answers in the face of his accusers. And he smiled that golden smile. An all-white jury in Chicago, after an hour's deliberation, convicted him on May 13, 1913. He was sentenced to a year in prison and $1,000 fine, but Johnson — out on bail at the sentencing — fled to Canada and on to Europe.

Being an escaped convict, he had trouble drumming up fights in foreign countries, especially after he lost his title to Jess Willard in Mexico in 1915; Johnson was forced to do mostly wrestling and vaudeville, until he returned in 1920 to serve his one-year sentence in Leavenworth. By the 1933 World's Fair in Chicago, the former champ was doing rounds with children for a dollar a pop, a sideshow attraction. Jack Johnson died in 1946 in a car crash at age sixty-eight.

Jack Johnson was no Martin Luther King but he advanced the civil rights movement in his own way; he was a tough, angry black man with a screw-you smile who defied the shuck-and-jive, "Yes, Boss" order of the day. "Taken as a whole, his life inspires respect," sums up biographer Roberts. "He faced a sea of white hate without fear." Look at the photo of the Jeffries fight on page 376. Look at all those white faces. Imagine trying to go into that arena and win that fight. ❧

This sick racist joke was acceptable in the United States c. 1900. This stereoscopic image—copyrighted by a photographer in New Hampshire—was entitled: "Terrors of the Alligator Swamp, Fla."

Marcus Garvey: Hero or Con Man?

"If Jesus was the accountant or president of the Black Star Line, He could not have done better than I or the accountant did, because the men had the disposition to steal and hide."

So wrote Marcus Garvey in his defense, in a little known autobiography that ran serialized in the *Pittsburgh Courier* in 1930. Garvey was writing from his Caribbean home in Jamaica. What many Americans forget about charismatic Marcus Garvey is that he was convicted of mail fraud, and sentenced to five years in prison and afterward deported back to his native Jamaica.

The name Marcus Garvey (1887–1940) is sometimes mentioned in the same reverential breath with Martin Luther King, Malcom X, and other champions of black civil rights. His Universal Negro Improvement Association, founded in 1914, was the "first mass black nationalist separatist movement," according to civil rights historian Julius Lester. Garvey didn't push simply "Back to Africa," but endorsed the revitalization of black Africa as a haven for blacks worldwide. At a convention held in New York, Garvey—clad in a fancy military uniform—was elected "Provisional President of Africa" and he compared himself to Napoleon in his dream of controlling a reenergized continent.

To realize that dream, Garvey created the Black Star Line, to be a worldwide shipping conglomerate run by and for blacks, serving primarily to transport African-Americans back to Africa. Garvey was selling a dream and many bought shares.

He told of one man who invested $160. "You might think that I have money," he quoted the man as saying, "but the truth, as I stated before, is that I have no money now. But if I'm to die of hunger it will be alright because I'm determined to do all that's in my power to better the conditions of my race."

The advertising literature for the Black Star Line proclaimed: "The Black Star Line corporation presents to every Black Man, Woman and Child the opportunity to climb the great ladder of industrial commercial progress. If you have ten dollars, one hundred dollars, or five thousand dollars to invest for profit, then take out shares in the Black Star Line, Inc. This corporation is chartered to trade on every sea and all waters. The Black Star Line will turn over large profits and dividends to shareholders, and operate to their interest even whilst they will be asleep."

Investors, most of them poor hard-working blacks, never received a dime back on their investment. The company did succeed in launching a few run-down ships (one for rum-running cruises), but assets gradually disappeared and the company went belly-up. Garvey blamed his fellow officers. "I had Americans on the directorate," he wrote in his serialized autobiography. "I had West Indians, I had South Americans, I gave everybody a chance and the sad story is that very nearly every one that I placed in a responsible position fleeced the Black Star Line." He

W. E. B. DuBois once described Marcus Garvey as "a little, fat black man, ugly, but with intelligent eyes and big head . . . dressed in a military uniform of the gayest mid-Victorian type, heavy with gold lace, epaulets, plume and sword."

points out that "the handling of the money took place when I was 2,000 or 3,000 miles away." He also said that he "talked" for the company but never "sold" a single share.

The United States government's prosecution of Marcus Garvey is open to many interpretations, from a covertly racist attempt to sabotage a black leader to a legitimate fraud prosecution to every shade in between.

Toward the end of Garvey's American career, one of his most impassioned enemies was W. E. B. DuBois, the eloquent champion of the NAACP.

"Marcus Garvey is, without a doubt, the most dangerous enemy of the Negro race in America and in the world," wrote DuBois in 1924. "He is either a lunatic or a traitor."

DuBois stated that he thought that Garvey had had a fair trial. "He convicted himself by his own admissions, his swaggering monkey-shines in the court-room with monocle and long-tailed coat and his insults to the judge and prosecuting attorney."

DuBois concluded: "The American Negroes have endured this wretch all too long with fine restraint and every effort at co-operation and understanding. But the end has come. Every man who apologizes for or defends Marcus Garvey from this day forth writes himself down as unworthy of the countenance of decent Americans. As for Garvey himself, this open ally of the Ku Klux Klan should be locked up or sent home."

Garvey was in fact sent home, and spent his last decade in Jamaica. ☙

Maybe it's all those years of Hollywood costumes, but somehow most of us don't picture American Indians dressing this way. These are the summer outfits of two young Wichita women, photographed in 1870 by William Soule.

THE NOT SO WILD WEST

QUICK-DRAW MCGRAW WAS A CARTOON, SO WAS BILLY THE KID

Perhaps in no one area has Hollywood spread more misperceptions than in the Wild West.

High noon. Two men in Main Street ready for a quick-draw shoot-out. Sorry, never happened, or at absolute most a couple of unrecorded times in the history of the West. If it did happen, the guy who flicked his gun out of the holster and fired was undoubtedly the guy who died. Wyatt Earp said the fighter who survived in any gunfight was the one who took his gun out, took a second to aim, and then fired.

And the body count is greatly inflated, thanks to the dime novels that first brought Western badmen to the American public and then to the movies that repeated all the lies. Billy the Kid didn't plunk twenty-one men before he was twenty-one, perhaps three or four. Bat Masterson's tally of dead men must be reduced from twenty-plus to three. One story has it that

Bat was so annoyed by a collector who wanted his gun that he went to a pawnshop, bought an old Colt and carved twenty-two notches in the handle as a joke. Buffalo Bill Cody wasn't wounded 137 times in Indian fights; his wife said a more accurate tally would be exactly once.

As for general day-to-day violence in frontier towns, if you watch old Westerns, you'd expect a shoot-out every couple days. The real Dodge City had five shooting deaths in 1878, and that was its worst year for violent deaths.

CUSTER'S DOWNFALL

In this rare photo, you can see scout Bloody Knife who very much against his own will might have contributed to Custer's fiasco at Little Big Horn.

Charismatic George Armstrong Custer was the most controversial U.S. military officer post–Civil War. Headstrong, he al-

"Custer's Revenge?" This Indian was paid to re-create the "Snake Dance" for tourists staying at the Ingleside Inn in Phoenix, Arizona in 1924.

most flunked out of West Point for disciplinary reasons and his tactics at Little Big Horn were typically aggressive. President Ulysses S. Grant despised Custer: "I regard Custer's Massacre as a sacrifice of troops, brought on by Custer himself, that was wholly unnecessary—wholly unnecessary."

During Custer's last stand at the Battle of Little Big Horn, the scout Bloody Knife was on the flank with Major Marcus Reno, who was second in command and was in his first major Indian fight. During a hasty retreat, Bloody Knife was struck in the head and killed, and his blood and brains splattered all over Reno, which seemed to unnerve him, according to *Custer and the Little Big Horn* by Dr. Charles Hofling. Major Reno ordered his troops to dismount, then immediately to remount. Reno's troops finished their hasty retreat with heavy casualities and then later didn't rush to support Custer. Custer's haste and

General Custer with his first grizzly, 1874.

Reno's delay became major issues in later inquiries into the disaster. The splattering of Bloody Knife's brains might be a gruesome footnote or—on a more human scale revealing the way individual men act on a battlefield—a very important detail. (Reno was later given lukewarm clearance for his actions by a Court of Inquiry.)

When Custer died on the battlefield, contrary to myth, the Sioux—out of respect for a great enemy warrior—did not mutilate his body or take his scalp, unlike the rest of Custer's men, however, who were horrendously carved up. ❧

the press untouched, to be exercised in its full extent, force and vigor," he wrote in 1789, "but to permit the liberty of the cudgel to go with it." Franklin explained: "My fellow citizens, if an impudent writer attacks your reputation, dearer to you perhaps than your life, you may go to him openly and break his head."

The history of American journalism is packed with aggressive reporting, from the *Washington Post*'s Watergate coverage to the *New York Times*'s Pentagon Papers to *60 Minutes*'s Vietnam coverage.

We'll leave all that to the textbooks. What concerns us are lies, curse words, and thuggish attempts at censorship.

(This section leans heavily on Stephen Bates's excellent *If No News, Send Rumors* [1989].)

FROM THE ANNALS OF AMERICAN JOURNALISM

Our Founding Fathers had a keen sense of the role of the press in a free society, yet they weren't naive ninnies about what trash some journalists might print.

Thomas Jefferson once suggested that newspapers be divided into four sections: Truths, Probabilities, Possibilities, and Lies.

And Benjamin Franklin, a printer himself, offered a unique remedy for libel. "My proposal then is to leave the liberty of

THE OUTRAGEOUS LIES (I.E., HOAXES) OF SOME FAMOUS AMERICANS: BEN FRANKLIN

Ben Franklin in 1747 wrote a long uplifting article for a British newspaper about Polly Baker, an unwed New Englander prosecuted for giving birth to her fifth illegitimate child. Franklin reported that Baker delivered an impassioned plea before the judges, saying she was just following the Bible's command to "multiply" and arguing that she deserved a statue for helping to populate the colonies rather than yet another whipping and a fine. The judges, Franklin stated, were so impressed that they acquitted Polly Baker and one of the judges married her the next day.

Franklin, about three decades later, admitted that he had made the whole incident up and said that he had done it to defend women from unjust persecution on "moral" grounds. ❧

Edgar Allan Poe

Poe wrote *The Raven* in 1844 to some literary acclaim (if little money); that same year, he ghosted an article in the *New York Sun* that proclaimed: "The Atlantic has actually been crossed in a balloon." Poe penned an unsigned extra to the Sunday paper describing how that famous aeronaut Monck Mason and seven others had traveled across the ocean in a balloon in seventy-five hours. "The air, as well as the earth and ocean, has been subdued by science." It was all a hoax. Poe died in poverty five years later, only to be rediscovered by French literati and reintroduced into America. ❧

Zoo Animals Escape in Manhattan

The *New York Herald*, one of the more respected newspapers in post–Civil War America, ran this headline on November 9, 1874: AWFUL CALAMITY/Wild Animals Broken Loose from Central Park/TERRIBLE SCENES OF MUTILATION/ . . . Awful Combats between the Beasts and the Citizens.

The story included an incomplete list of the dead as well as a mayoral proclamation, ordering all but the National Guard to stay off the streets. As word spread, mothers raced to schools to save their children, the editor of the *New York Times* lathered a carriage horse to speed downtown to yell at the police commissioner for favoring the *Herald* with an exclusive.

But the whole thing was a hoax, perpetrated by one Irish playwright, Joseph Clarke, who was working the night desk, and who did it with the blessing of management. The piece's last line was: "Of course, the entire story given above is pure fabrication." But, apparently, nobody read that far. ❧

Libel on a Cow

Mrs. Leary's cow did *not* start the Chicago fire. Reporter Michael Ahearn admitted later that he simply fabricated the bit about Mrs. Leary's cow kicking over the lantern to add color to the piece. ❧

H. L. Mencken Out of the Bathtub

Curmudgeon H. L. Mencken in 1917 detailed the history of the bathtub in a feature for the *New York Evening Mail*. Mencken tracked the first tub back to Cincinnati, where it had been installed by cotton dealer Adam Thompson, who had discovered the pleasures of bathing while visiting England. Widespread use in America was slowed because the medical profession suspected that tubs might be bad for health, and forbade bathing except under supervision of a doctor. When President Millard Fillmore risked a bath in the White House, opposition dwindled.

Cincinnati for years ballyhooed itself as the home of the American bathtub and reference works cited Thompson and Fillmore.

A decade later, Mencken admitted the hoax without any apology. He called the piece a "tissue of absurdities, all of them deliberate and most of them obvious" which made him wonder how much of the rest of history is "bunk." 🌀

BROADWAY FIGHTS FREE SPEECH (AND BAD REVIEWS)

Broadway theater owners once fought all the way to the Supreme Court for the right to ban venom-spouting critics from their theaters. Although the idea now seems patently un-American, in 1915, the Shuberts—then and still one of Broadway's most powerful entities—thought it their right to amass a hit list of critics to forbid entry to their shows. Reasoned Jake Shubert: Newspapers that receive tens of thousands of dollars a year in Shubert advertising money shouldn't be allowed to hammer the company's sincere and mostly successful efforts to entertain the public.

Columnist Walter Winchell hit back: "A certain critic, barred from Shubert openings, says he'll wait three nights and go to their closings."

Channing Pollack of the *New York Morning Telegraph* started using nose putty and false mustaches, while in Boston, critic George Holland had himself appointed acting fire marshal and at every opening would announce that it was time for yet another fire inspection.

But the battle turned uglier when the Shuberts tried to muzzle the acerbic new critic for the *New York Times*, Alexander Woollcott. The twenty-seven-year-old reviewer had written that Shubert's recent play, *Taking Chances*, was "quite absurd" and there are "moments when a puzzled audience wonders what it is all about."

When Woollcott—after paying for a ticket—was refused entry to the next Shubert play, *Trilby*, the *Times* sought and received an injunction allowing him in. Woollcott gave *Trilby* a passing grade and said the play was worth seeing—"even if you have to get in by use of an injunction."

Months later, an Appellate Court backed the Shuberts, ruling that while a theater owner couldn't bar someone on the grounds of race, creed, or class, it could bar someone for any other private reason.

During the dispute, with Woollcott barred on twenty-three separate occasions, the *Times* refused to accept any Shubert advertising. After about a year, the Shuberts caved and agreed to allow the *Times* to send any critic they chose. Ironically, they had helped make young Woollcott into a star. (He would later go on to say: "All the things I really like to do are either immoral, illegal or fattening.")

The New York State Legislature passed a bill requiring theaters to admit any sober person with a ticket. The Shuberts fought the law all the way to the United States Supreme Court, but lost. 🌀

ANOTHER WHAT IF?
KARL MARX OVERPAID
HAPPY CAPITALIST?

Angry visionary Karl Marx, whose words helped ignite the rebellion of the underclass, was the London stringer for the *New York Tribune*, writing regularly from 1851 to 1862. The coauthor of *The Communist Manifesto* (1848) not surprisingly groused about low pay and crummy working conditions. "I think myself as a fool . . . I have given these fellows too much for their money." Engels, his coauthor, agreed, saying that the *Trib* had squeezed Marx like a lemon and was now looking for "new fruit" to exploit.

Marx also grew annoyed that the paper repeatedly bumped or compacted his pieces during election years. "The *New York Tribune* can be approached seriously only when the Presidential-dung is at an end," Marx wrote to Engels.

After a tumultuous decade of delivering Marx's socialist-tinged news accounts to the American public, the *Tribune* fired Marx. The newspaper claimed that the man who had complained about low wages had actually billed the *Trib* for nineteen articles he had yet to deliver, accord-

Karl Marx. There are plenty of images of Karl floating around, but this one seemed the most unusual. Long after Marx's death, the Nazis in their quest for racial purity maintained this biographical index card in their archive.

ing to Charles Dana, managing editor, who dismissed Marx in 1862. "The *Tribune* has behaved in this matter like a true penny paper," commented Engels angrily. "Its socialism ends in the most miserable, petty bourgeois passion for cheating." Marx and Engels went on to collaborate on *Das Kapital*, finally completed in 1895, long after Marx's death.

John F. Kennedy, a century later, twitted a group of newspaper publishers. "If only this capitalistic New York newspaper had treated him more kindly," Kennedy mused. "If only Marx had remained a foreign correspondent, history might have been different." 🐚

ALL THE FOUR-LETTER WORDS THAT ARE FIT TO PRINT

It took Richard "Dick" Nixon to get "shit" regularly into the *New York Times*. When the President was caught uttering "shit" and "fuck" on the Watergate tapes, some of those four-letter words actually made their way into the verbally conservative *New York Times*. "We take 'shit' from the President but from nobody else," Executive Editor A. M. Rosenthal was quoted as saying.

And Rosenthal's counterpart at the *Washington Post*, Ben Bradlee (Jason Robards in *All the President's Men*) told the *Wall Street Journal* in 1976 that his paper would certainly print obscenities uttered by the President or Vice President. However, he added: "It gets harder and harder when you come to cabinet members."

All of which leads to one of the more bizarre obscenity wrangles in the history of American journalism. Secretary of Agriculture Earl Butz resigned abruptly on October 4, 1976, and newspapers pioneered dizzying forms of circumlocution. The *New York Times* said the secretary resigned "Amid Rising Protests About Racist Remark." Several newspapers explained murkily that Butz's remark insulted black people's "sexual, dress and bathroom predilections."

Although the Associated Press had reported the remark in full in its wire copy provided to newspapers, only two nationwide reported it verbatim: *Madison Capital Times* in Wisconsin, and *Toledo Blade* in Ohio.

So what insensitive trash did Butz utter that hurled him from office? "I'll tell you what coloreds want. It's three things: first, a tight pussy; second, loose shoes; and third, a warm place to shit. That's all."

So *that's* what he said! Because of the media squeamishness in 1976, most Americans were mystified as to why Butz left office. On the bright side, as David Shaw, media critic of the *Los Angeles Times*, pointed out: Courageously, at least no editors changed "shoes" to an "article of footwear."

Of course, standards change regarding what's fit to print and what isn't.

James Gordon Bennett had scandalized his *New York Herald* readers in the 1830s when he printed "shirt" instead of "linen" and "leg" instead of "limb." In 1954, a photo editor at the *New York Times* was fired for choosing to publish an openmouthed kiss of newlyweds Joe DiMaggio and Marilyn Monroe. In 1980, the *Times* primly reported that Jimmy Carter said if Ted Kennedy entered the race, Carter would "whip his —." That same year, the paper quoted the commander of the failed hostage rescue mission as saying he didn't want to participate in a "half-assed" mission. Some *Times* staffers decided—and rightly so—that half an ass but not a whole ass was then fit to print.

Fast-forward to the 1990s, Clarence Thomas's nomination for the Supreme Court puts "pubic hair" on the lips of many commentators and on the pages of many papers. (Remember the Coke can and Anita Hill?) But that vocabulary stride pales compared to the quantam leap forward that soon after occurred. It's rare that one can pinpoint the date so precisely but in this case we can. On June 23, 1993, Lorena Bobbitt sliced off her sleeping husband's penis with a twelve-inch kitchen knife. For weeks, you couldn't flick open a newspaper or spin the dial without being bombarded by "penis, penis, penis." ◉

RESPINNING TWO NOTORIOUS SCANDALS

PREACHER ON TRIAL

Susan B. Anthony, the stern Suffragette lady who would one day be found on a U.S. silver dollar, stood in a bedroom in Brooklyn in 1871. She shouted at a friend's irate husband as the man pounded on the door trying to get at his wife. "If you enter this room, it will be over my dead body!"

And the husband, Theodore Tilton, who was furious over his wife's admitted love affair with a famous preacher, sulked away. The inability of the

Nationally prominent preacher Henry Ward Beecher (1813–1887) was accused of adultery. Newspapermen rejoiced.

Suffragettes and others to keep this delicious secret led to one of the most notorious sex scandals of the 19th century, a case bannered for half a year across the pages of the leading newspapers.

Cartoonists delighted in depicting a Brooklyn husband locking his wife in a vault as protection against fire and *clergymen;* another showed a new Brooklyn hat style: a top hat with cuckold's horns.

The Suffragettes told the secret to Victoria Woodhull, a flamboyant women's rights crusader, and she put it in 1872 into her weekly newspaper, financed by Cornelius Vanderbilt.

The article accused Henry Ward Beecher, one of the leading clergymen of his day, as well as

Victoria Woodhull ran for President in 1872; she also broke the Henry Ward Beecher scandal, publishing it in her newspaper.

a nationally popular lecturer and columnist, of having an affair with Tilton's wife, Elizabeth, of having seduced her while consoling her over the death of her young son. "Every great man of Mr. Beecher's type has had in the past, and will ever have, the need for and the right to, the loving manifestations of many women," wrote Woodhull, who was a leader of the Free Love movement. (She had an agenda too: she considered marriage slavery for women.)

Beecher indignantly denied the charge: "Anyone is likely to have a bucket of slops thrown upon him." The *New York Times* upbraided Woodhull for having "disgraced and degraded . . . the female name."

The Beecher-Tilton scandal turned into a national morality play, featuring a who's who of the Gilded Age.

Beecher's sister, Harriet Beecher Stowe, abolitionist author of *Uncle Tom's Cabin,* took to tarring Woodhull in print. (Brother Henry once held a mock slave auction in his church to help promote her book.)

And Anthony Comstock, the holier-than-thou censor working for the U.S. Postal Service, filed federal obscenity charges against Woodhull, who, with her sister-in-law copublisher, wound up spending much of the next six months in jail before being acquitted. (This was an inconvenience since she was running for President at the time on a Free Love platform.)

The Plymouth Church, rallying behind their pastor, voted to boot the allegedly injured husband, Tilton, out of the congregation by a vote of 210 to 13.

So Tilton decided to sue Beecher for $100,000 for alienating him from his wife's affections. The Beecher-Tilton trial ran from January 11 to July 2, 1875, filling three thousand pages of trial transcripts, hotly covered from coast to coast.

Based on letters, court testimony, deathbed revelations, etc., there is absolutely no doubt that Henry Ward Beecher had an affair with Libby Tilton and several other married women.

But the jury, after fifty-two ballots, couldn't reach a verdict, deadlocking at nine to three in favor of Beecher.

His congregation embraced him as though cleared of all charges, and his newfound notoriety sent his lecture fees up dramatically, bringing him a small fortune over the next decade. (Beecher also would endorse Pears' Soap: "If Cleanliness is next to Godliness . . .")

But not everyone was snowed. One editorial branded him a "dunghill covered with flowers." Another reporter wrote: "Mankind fell in Adam and has been falling ever since, but never touched bottom until it got to Henry Ward Beecher."

COKE BOTTLE RAPE?
THE SKINNY ON
FATTY ARBUCKLE

This was the O.J. trial of Prohibition America: a murder by a huge celebrity.

The press had a field day, portraying Virginia Rappe as an innocent ingenue brutalized by Hollywood while tabbing one of the nation's biggest box office stars, Roscoe "Fatty" Arbuckle, as a drunken monster who, it was hinted, used a jagged piece of ice or a Coke bottle to rape her, then left her to die.

What's clear is that Fatty had just signed a $3 million contract with Paramount, and was in the mood to celebrate. He rented a huge suite for Labor Day at San Francisco's St. Francis Hotel. The party, fueled by cases of bootleg liquor, rolled over the weekend into Monday, when twenty-six-year-old Virginia Rappe showed up.

Events from here on are in dispute. At some point, Rappe—with three gin-and-orange-juice cocktails in her system—desperately sought a vacant bathroom, which happened to be the one adjoining a room where Arbuckle was changing his clothes.

Screams soon echoed from the room. Arbuckle came out, with Rappe's flouncy hat perched on his head and did a little comic shuffle on the carpet. Friends rushed in and one reported hearing the half-nude Rappe say: "What did he do to me? Roscoe did this to me." And she kept screaming. One guest then claimed that Fatty then lost his temper, shouting: "Get her out of here, she makes too much noise."

For the next three days, Rappe lapsed in and out of consciousness. Various doctors and nurses attended her but most blamed the bootleg liquor. She was finally taken to a hospital where she died on Friday.

The autopsy revealed peritonitis from a burst bladder. An obvious scenario was that the three-hundred-plus-pound comic, in attempting to mount the girl had exploded her full bladder, like a popped balloon. Arbuckle claimed he found her vomiting in the bathroom and had lifted her onto the bed.

Rumors started swirling that his massive organ had torn her apart or that he used ice or a Coke bottle. The press played it as corrupt Hollywood raping a wholesome American girl.

The first jury believed Fatty and not the press, deadlocking at ten to two to acquit; the second jury voted ten to two to convict, while the third jury the following year quickly acquitted him: "We feel a grave injustice has been done him and there is not the slightest proof in any way to connect him with the commission of a crime."

What really happened? Two excellent investigative books go a long way toward solving the mystery. Rappe, who was cer-

Fatty Arbuckle and friends in happier times, before he was accused of murder in 1921.

tainly no virgin, apparently had recently had a "back-alley" abortion. When she was finally taken to a hospital, she was taken to the Wakefield Sanitarium, where the abortion had probably been performed.

After she died, the doctors there performed a rushed illegal autopsy without consulting the local coroner's office, and preserved the ruptured bladder as evidence. But they also removed her uterus, part of her rectum, her ovary, and Fallopian tubes, and these they destroyed. One doctor overseeing the autopsy was Dr. Melville Rumwell, long rumored to perform secret abortions.

An impartial panel of three independent doctors appointed by the court at the first trial ruled that her bladder had indeed burst, but found no evidence of force. Doctors who had treated Rappe for the decade prior reported she suffered from chronic cystitis of the bladder, which could weaken the walls of the organ.

Several eyewitnesses told Andy Edmonds (author of *Frame Up!*) that at the party earlier, the drunken guests had had a high-kicking contest and Rappe at one point started tickling Fatty who in the hijinx kneed her in the stomach. Soon after she rushed to the bathroom.

It seems very likely that Fatty had accidentally damaged her already diseased bladder and that the doctors at the Wakefield Sanitarium then tried to cover up both a botched abortion and their later incompetence in treating her.

Most of the vitriol of the charges against Fatty stemmed from a fanatical district attorney in San Francisco who hoped to be governor some day and the yellow journalism of the Hearst newspaper chain.

Fatty never recovered; he was blacklisted and the American public—fed a diet of tabloid rumor—refused to laugh at his antics again. He tried producing films under the name William B. Goodrich as in "Will B. Good," but he died suddenly in 1933, just on the verge of pulling himself out of debt from all his legal problems.

Ironically, all that he is remembered for is the Coke bottle.

PARTING SHOTS

DICKENS HAWKS A LOUIE ON THE U.S. SENATE

Prior to the Civil War, chewing tobacco was extremely popular. Far more popular than spittoons, apparently. Quite a few European visitors to America lamented how treacherous a mere walk across a room could become thanks to the greasy gobs of spittle everywhere.

Novelist Charles Dickens (1812–1870) visited the United States in 1842 for five months, and was less than amused by quite a bit of American behavior, especially the following activities he observed at the United States Senate.

The Senate is a dignified and decorous body, and its proceedings are conducted with much gravity and order. Both Houses are handsomely carpeted; but the state to which these carpets are reduced by the universal disregard of the spittoon with which every honourable member is accommodated, and the extraordinary improvements on the pattern which are squirted and dabbled upon it in every direction, do not admit of being described. I will merely observe, that I strongly recommend all strangers not to look at the floor; and that if they happen to drop anything, though it be their purse, not to pick it up with an ungloved hand on any account.

It is somewhat remarkable too, at first, to say the least, to see so many honourable members with swelled faces; and it is scarcely less remarkable to discover that this appearance is caused by the quantity of tobacco they contrive to stow within the hollow of the cheek. It is strange enough, too, to see an honourable gentleman leaning back in his tilted chair, with his legs on the desk before him, shaping a convenient "plug" with his penknife, and when it is ready for use, shooting the old one from his mouth as from a popgun, and clapping the new one in its place.

I was surprised to observe that even steady old chewers of great experience are not always good marksmen, which has rather inclined me to doubt that general proficiency with the rifle, of which we have heard so much in England. Several gentlemen called upon me who, in the course of the conversation, frequently missed the spittoon at five paces; and one (but he was certainly shortsighted) mistook the closed sash for the open window at three. On another occasion, when I dined out, and was sitting with two ladies and some gentlemen round a fire before dinner, one of the company fell short of the fireplace six distinct times. I am disposed to think, however, that this was occasioned by his not aiming at that object; as there was a white marble hearth before the fender, which was more convenient and may have suited his purpose better.

Charles Dickens, fifty-five years old with a horrid comb-over, during a reading tour in the United States in 1867.

THE STRANGEST CIVIL WAR STORY

There's really no way to introduce this other than to say that it ran in *American Medical Weekly* on November 7, 1874, and was picked up by the prestigious British medical journal, *The Lancet*.

L. G. Capers of Vicksburg, Mississippi, relates an incident during the late Civil War, as follows: A matron and her two daughters, aged fifteen and seventeen years, filled with the enthusiasm of patriotism, stood ready to minister to the wounds of their countrymen in their fine residence near the scene of the battle of R—— , May 12, 1863, between a portion of Grant's army and some Confederates. During the fray a gallant and noble young friend of the narrator staggered and fell to the earth; at the same time a piercing cry was heard in the house nearby. Examination of the wounded soldier showed that a bullet had passed through the scrotum and carried away the left testicle. The same bullet had apparently penetrated the left side of the abdomen of the elder young lady, midway between the umbilicus and the anterior superior spinous process of the ilium (between belly button and front hipbone) and had become lost in the abdomen. This daughter suffered an attack of peritonitis, but recovered in two months under the treatment administered.

Marvelous to relate, just two hundred and seventy-eight days after the reception of the minie-ball, she was delivered of a fine boy, weighing eight pounds, to the surprise of herself and the mortification of her parents and friends. She insisted on her virginity and innocence. About three weeks after this remarkable birth, Dr. Capers was called to see the infant, and the grandmother insisted there was something wrong with the child's genitals. Examination showed a rough, swollen, and sensitive scrotum, containing some hard substance. He operated, and extracted a smashed and battered minie-ball. The doctor, after some meditation, theorized in this manner: He concluded that this was the same ball that had carried away the testicle of his young friend, that had penetrated the ovary of the young lady, and, with some spermatozoa upon it, had impregnated her. With this conviction he approached the young man and told him the circumstances; the soldier appeared skeptical at first, but consented to visit the young mother; a friendship ensued which soon ripened into a happy marriage, and the pair had three children, none resembling, in the same degree as the first, the heroic *pater familias*.

What's there to add? Artificial insemination has come a long way in the past century or so.

ACKNOWLEDG- MENTS, SOURCES & PIC- TURE CREDITS

ACKNOWLEDG-
MENTS

My ultimate acknowledgment goes to the man—however mischievous and self-interested—who slapped a Post-it down on the bar at O'Flaherty's off Times Square and started this whole project. Bill Thomas, senior editor at Doubleday, before even greeting me or buying me a drink, handed me the following note: *An Underground Education: All the History You're Not Supposed to Know.*

He lit a fuse I didn't realize that I had been carrying for a decade or so.

My companions for the next two and a half years would be the people (many long dead) who helped me with the actual research: scholars and translators of the arcane who committed his or her opinions to paper. Yes, I have mucked with your work. Please forgive me. My motives were semihonorable, i.e., the entertainment of my fellow man. Don't take it personally: I disagree with most everyone.

More specifically, I want to thank Esther Newberg, Mark Schapiro, J. R. Romanko, Kevin Baker (the fiction writer), my dentist Dr. Gus Kaloudis (a historian in rubber gloves), Dr. Walter Straus (my first friend), Harvard-trained historian Geoffrey Moran (may we meet again at the Kinsey Institute), investigative journalist Gary Taubes (a hairline is not enough), Jack Hitt (we will collaborate someday), Sharon Frost and Margaret Glover at the New York Public Library prints & photograph collection (open prurience is so refreshing). Also, I need to thank the librarians at Columbia University and NYU's Law Library. On the photo front, the Library of Congress is a national treasure for an author on a budget, as is the National Archives. For those with an allowance, I heartily recommend Archive Photo of New York.

My greatest debt, though, is to my family: wife Kris Dahl, who tolerated all the late nights and weekends and my daily morning stupor when there were kids' lunchboxes to be filled; my cerebral nine-year-old daughter, Georgia, who always demanded clear concise explanations on *all* topics; and my omnivorous wrestling son, Ziggy Zacks, who never let the intricacies of the past blot out the giddy present.

Finally, I'd like here to recall two late great teachers who defied conventional wisdom: Nat Glidden, whose seventh grade vocabulary list started with the word "zarf" (a holder for a hot coffee cup); and Professor Orsie Pearl, who wore three watches, with one set to the time in ancient Athens.

SOURCES

ARTS & LITERATURE

Fairy Tales: Basile, Giambattista, *Il racconto dei racconti,* tr. Ruggero Guarini (Milan, 1994); Basile, Giambattista, *The Pentamerone of Giambattista Basile,* tr. Benedetto Croce (London, 1932); Grimm, Jacob and Wilhelm, *Household Stories,* collected by the Brothers Grimm (London, 1882); Mure, Eleanor, *The Story of the Three Bears* (London, 1967); [Southey, Robert] *The Doctor* (London, 1837); Panati, Charles, *Extraordinary Origins of Everyday Things* (New York, 1987); Perrault, Charles, *Contes de Perrault* (Paris, 1967).

Shakespeare: Partridge, Eric, *Shakespeare's Bawdy* (London, 1947); Rubinstein, Frankie, *A Dictionary of Shakespeare's Sexual Puns and their Significance* (London, 1984).

Goya: Karlen, Arno, *Napoleon's Glands and Other Ventures in Biohistory* (Boston, 1984).

Alexander Pope: Pope, Alexander, *The Prose Works of Alexander Pope* (Oxford, 1936).

Thoreau: Burnam, Tom, *The Dictionary of Misinformation* (New York, 1975); Harding, Walter, *Days of Henry Thoreau* (New York, 1966).

Flaubert: Du Camp, Maxime, *Souvenirs litteraires de Maxime Du Camp, 1822–1894* (Paris, 1982); Starkie, Enid, *Flaubert: The Making of the Master* (New York, 1967).

Melville: Henderson, Bill, *Rotten Reviews* (New York, 1986); Hetherington, Hugh, *Melville's Reviewers* (New York, 1961).

Whistler: Bates, Stephen, *If No News, Send Rumors: Anecdotes of American Journalism* (New York, 1989); Gregory, Horace, *The World of James McNeill Whistler* (New York, 1959); Hay, Peter, *The Book of Legal Anecdotes* (London, 1989).

Truman: Bates, Stephen, *If No News, Send Rumors: Anecdotes of American Journalism* (New York, 1989); Tebbel, John & Watts, Sarah, *The Press and the Presidency* (New York, 1985).

Twain: Cary, Henry, *Treasury of Erotic and Facetious Memorabilia;* Twain, Mark, *The Mammoth Cod,* ed. G. Legman (Milwaukee, 1976).

Joyce: Joyce, James, *Selected Letters of James Joyce,* ed. Richard Ellman (New York, 1975).

Coleridge, drugs: Coleridge, Samuel, *Poems* (London, 1993); Latimer, Dean & Goldberg, Jeff, *Flowers in the Blood: The Story of Opium* (New York, 1981); Lefebvre, Molly, *Samuel Taylor Coleridge: A Bondage of Opium* (New York, 1974); Kennedy, Joseph, *Coca Exotica: The Illustrated Story of Cocaine* (Rutherford, N.J., 1985).

Van Meegeren: Franklin, Charles, *They Walked a Crooked Mile* (New York, 1969); Kilbracken, Lord, *Master Forger: The Story of Han Van Meegeren* (London, 1951); Kilbracken, Lord, *Van Meegeren: A Case Study* (London, 1967); Nash, J. Robert, *The Encyclopedia of World Crime* (Wilmette, Ill., 1989); *Time,* July 30, 1945, Sept. 10, 1945, Nov. 24, 1947; *Life,* Nov. 17, 1947.

Misquotes: Boller, Jr., Paul & George, John, *They Never Said It: A Book of Fake Quotes, Misquotes, and Misleading Attributions* (Oxford, 1989); Burnam, Tom, *The Dictionary of Mis-*

information (New York, 1975); Jellison, Charles, *Ethan Allen: Frontier Rebel* (New York, 1969); Ward, Phillip, *Dictionary of Common Fallacies* (New York, 1978).

Newton: Merton, Robert, *On the Shoulders of Giants: A Shandean Postscript* (New York, 1965).

BUSINESS

American Fortunes: Messick, Hank, *Secret File* (New York, 1969); Nash, J. Robert, *The Encyclopedia of World Crime* (Wilmette, Ill., 1989).

Astor & Whitney: Meyers, Gustavus, *History of Great American Fortunes* (New York, 1907) and footnotes in later 1964 edition.

Civil War profiteering: Kaufman, Richard, *The War Profiteers* (Indianapolis, 1970); Meyers, Gustavus, *History of Great American Fortunes* (New York, 1907); Shannon, Fred, *The Organization and Administration of the Union Army, 1861–1865* (Gloucester, Mass., 1928); *Harper's New Monthly Magazine,* July 1864.

Child labor: Abbott, Edith, "A Study of the Early History of Child Labor in America," *American Journal of Sociology, XV* (July 1908) pp. 15–37; Abbott, Grace, *The Child and the State* (New York, 1968); Franklin, Charles, *They Walked a Crooked Mile* (New York, 1969); Trattner, Walter, *Crusade for the Children: A History of the National Child Labor Committee and Child Labor Reform in America* (Chicago, 1970); *Senate Report on the Condition of Women and Child Wage-Earners in the United States* (61st Congress, 2nd session, Doc. #645).

Edison vs. Westinghouse: Conot, Robert, *Streak of Luck* (New York, 1979); Hughes, Thomas, "Harold P. Brown and the Executioner's Current: An Incident in the AC-DC Con-

troversy," in *Business History Review* (1958) pp. 143–165; *North America Review,* Oct., Nov., Dec., 1889; *New York World; New York Times; New York Sun.*

Hearst vs. Pulitzer: New York World; New York Journal; New York Evening Journal (June/July, 1896); Creelman, James, *On the Great Highway: The Wanderings and Adventures of a Special Correspondent* (Boston, 1901); Mott, Frank Luther, *American Journalism: A History of Newspapers in the United States through 260 Years: 1690 to 1950* (New York, 1950); Winkler, John, *William Randolph Hearst: A New Appraisal* (New York, 1955).

Kelloggs: Bruce, Scott & Crawford, Bill, *Cerealizing America: The Unsweetened Story of American Breakfast Cereal* (Boston, 1995); Powell, Horace, *The Original Has This Signature — W. K. Kellogg* (Englewood Cliffs, N.J., 1956).

Morgan vs. Carnegie: Myers, Gustavus, "History of the Great American Fortunes" (New York, 1907).

Singer: Madigan, Carol & Elwood, Ann, *Brainstorms and Thunderbolts: How Creative Genius Works* (New York, 1983).

George M. Cohan: Hay, Peter, *The Book of Business Anecdotes* (New York, 1988).

Piracy: Exquemelin, Alexander, *The Buccaneers of America* (London, 1923); Hibbert, Christopher, *The Roots of Evil* (Boston, 1963); Kaufman, Richard, *The War Profiteers* (Indianapolis, 1970); Maclay, Edgar, *A History of American Privateers* (New York, 1899); Ward, Ralph T., *Pirates in History* (Baltimore, 1974).

Captain Kidd: Dalton, Sir Cornelius, *The Real Captain Kidd: A Vindication* (New York, 1911); Hastings, Patrick, *Famous and Infamous Cases* (New York, 1954); Hibbert, Christopher, *Roots of Evil* (Boston, 1963); Nash, J. Robert, *The Encyclopedia of World Crime* (Wilmette, Ill., 1989).

Vanderbilt: Andrews, Wayne, *The Vanderbilt Legend: The Story of the Vanderbilt Family 1794–1940* (New York, 1941); Lane, Wheaton, *Commodore Vanderbilt: An Epic of the Steam Age* (New York, 1942); Rosengarten, Jr., Frederic, *Freebooters Must Die! The life and death of William Walker, the notorious filibuster of the nineteenth century* (Wayne, Penna., 1976); Scroggs, William, *Filibusters and Financiers: The Story of William Walker and his Associates* (New York, 1916).

Coca-Cola: Allen, Frederick, *Secret Formula: How Brilliant Marketing and Relentless Salesmanship Made Coca-Cola into the Best Known Product in the World* (New York, 1994); Kennedy, Joseph, *Coca Exotica* (Rutherford, N.J., 1985).

British Opium: Latimer, Dean & Goldberg, Jeff, *Flowers in the Blood: The Story of Opium* (New York, 1981).

Cocaine list: Shenkman, Richard & Reiger, Kurt, *One-Night Stands with American History* (New York, 1980); "Nostrums and Quackery," reprints from *Journal of American Medical Association* (Chicago, 1912).

Pocahontas: Mossiker, Frances, *Pocahontas: The Life and Legend* (New York, 1976); Shenkman, Richard, *Legends, Lies and Cherished Myths of American History* (New York, 1988).

Tobacco in U.S.: Goodrum, Charles & Dalrymple, Helen, *Advertising in America: The First 200 Years* (New York, 1990).

Ponzi: Franklin, Charles, *They Walked a Crooked Mile* (New York, 1969); Nash, J. Robert, *The Encyclopedia of World Crime* (Wilmette, Ill., 1989).

Ku Klux Klan: Alexander, Charles, "Kleagles and Cash: The Ku Klux Klan as a Business Organization, 1915–1930," in *Business History Review* (1965, 39:3); Nash, J. Robert, *Encyclopedia of World Crime* (Wilmette, Ill., 1989).

Jews: Baron, Salo, and others, *Economic History of the Jews* (Jerusalem, 1975); Edwards, Jonathan (ed./tr.), *The Jews in Western Europe* (Manchester, England, 1994); Parkes, Reverend James, *The Jew in the Medieval Community* (New York, 1976).

Tulips: Mackay, Charles, *Extraordinary Popular Delusions and the Madness of Crowds* (London, 1841, New York, 1932 reprint); Timbs, John, *Historic Nine Pins: A Book of Curiosities* (London, 1869).

Franklin: Schlessinger, Arthur, *Prelude to Independence* (New York, 1980).

Goodyear: Madigan, Carol & Ellwood, Ann, *Brainstorms and Thunderbolts: How Creative Genius Works* (New York, 1983); O'Reilly, Maurice, *The Goodyear Story* (Elmsford, N.Y., 1983); Panati, Charles, *Extraordinary Origins of Everyday Things* (New York, 1987).

CRIME & PUNISHMENT

Auto-da-fé: Geddes, Michael, *Miscellaneous Tracts* (London, 1730); Scott, George R., *The History of Torture through the Ages* (London, 1941).

Executing women: Naish, Camille, *Death Comes to the Maiden: Sex and Execution 1431–1933* (London, 1991); *National Police Gazette* (April 8, 1899).

London bridge: Mencken, August, *Hang by the Neck* (New York, 1942).

Executing children: Nash, J. Robert, *The Encyclopedia of World Crime* (Wilmette, Ill., 1989); Koestler, Arthur, *Reflections on Hanging* (New York, 1957).

Guillotine, Corday: Arasse, Daniel, *The Guillotine and the Terror* (London, 1989); Burnam,

Tom, *The Dictionary of Misinformation* (New York, 1975); Kershaw, Alistair, *A History of the Guillotine* (London, 1958); Naish, Camille, *Death Comes to the Maiden* (London, 1991); *British Medical Journal* (Dec. 13, 1879); *Bulletin de l'académie de médicin* (Dec. 2, 1879).

Torture: Hibbert, Christopher, *The Roots of Evil* (Boston, 1963); Lea, H. C., *Torture* (Philadelphia, 1973 reprint); Robbins, Rossell, *The Encyclopedia of Witchcraft and Demonology* (New York, 1959); Scott, George R., *The History of Torture through the Ages* (London, 1941); Swain, John, *The Pleasures of the Torture Chamber* (London, 1931).

Medieval ordeal: Hibbert, Christopher, *The Roots of Evil* (Boston, 1963).

Female body research: Gurrieri, Rafaele, "Sensibilità e anomalie fisiche e psichiche nella donna normale e nella prostituta," in *Archivio di psichiatria, scienze penali ed antropologia criminale* (Vol. 13, 1892); Hibbert, Christopher, *The Roots of Evil* (Boston, 1963); Symons, Julian, *A Pictorial History of Crime* (New York, 1966).

Belle Gunness: Burt, Olive, *American Murder Ballads* (New York, 1958); Langlois, Janet, *Belle Gunness* (Bloomington, 1985); Nash, J. Robert, *The Encyclopedia of World Crime* (Wilmette, Ill., 1989).

Maria Barberi: New York World; New York Journal; New York Times (1895, 1896); Nash, J. Robert, *Look for the Woman* (New York, 1981).

Dr. H. H. Holmes: New York Journal; New York World; New York Times; Philadelphia Inquirer; Leslie's Weekly (1895, 1896); Franke, David, *The Torture Doctor* (New York, 1975); Geyer, Frank, *The Holmes-Pitezel Case* (Philadelphia, 1896).

Adam Worth: Adam Worth, alias Little Adam, Theft and Recovery of Gainsborough's Duchess of Devonshire *from the Archives of the Pinkerton's National Detective Agency,* 1903; Horan, James, *The Pinkertons: The Detective Dynasty that Made History* (New York, 1963); Macintyre, Ben, "The Disappearing Duchess," *New York Times* (July 31, 1994); Nash, J. Robert, *The Encyclopedia of World Crime* (Wilmette, Ill., 1989); *New York Times,* Feb. 7, 1902 obituary.

Robert Burns: Burns, Vincent, *The Man Who Broke a Thousand Chains* (Washington, 1968); Nash, J. Robert, *The Encyclopedia of World Crime* (Wilmette, Ill., 1989).

Bonnie Parker: Nash, J. Robert, *The Encyclopedia of World Crime* (Wilmette, Ill., 1989); Phillips, John, *Running with Bonnie and Clyde* (Norman, Okla., 1996).

Bestiality and the law: Evans, E. P., *Criminal Prosecution and Capital Punishment of Animals,* (London, 1987 reprint); Tardieu, Ambroise, *Attentats aux Moeurs* (Paris, 1878).

EVERYDAY LIFE

Toilet training: Cabanes, Augustin, *Moeurs intimes du passé* Vol. I (Paris, 1919); Hitt, Jack, *Off the Road: A Modern-Day Walk Down the Pilgrim's Route into Spain* (New York, 1994); Panati, Charles, *Extraordinary Origins of Everyday Things* (New York, 1987); Wright, Lawrence, *Clean and Decent: The Fascinating History of the Bathroom and Water Closet* (London, 1960).

Graffiti: Witkowski, Gustave, *Seins a l'eglise* (Paris, 1907); Latin teacher, George Coleman, Wethersfield, Conn.

Peter the Great tip: Buvat, Jean, quoted in Cabanes, Augustin, *Moeurs intimes du passé* Vol. I (Paris, 1919).

Ben Franklin: Cabanes, Augustin, *Moeurs intimes du passé* Vol. I (Paris, 1919); Schama,

Simon, *Citizens: A Chronicle of the French Revolution* (New York, 1989).

Underwear: Burnam, Tom, *The Dictionary of Misinformation* (New York, 1975); Ellis, Havelock, *Studies in the Psychology of Sex* (Philadelphia, 1901–1928); Phillips, Janet and Peter, "History from Below: Women's Underwear and the Rise of Women's Sports," in *Journal of Popular Culture* (Fall, 1993); Willet, C. & Cunnington, Phyllis, *The History of Underclothes* (London, 1981).

Breasts and bra: Angier, Natalie, "Put on Your Best Chest—It's Time to Preen," *New York Times*, April 2, 1995; Panati, Charles, *Extraordinary Origins of Everyday Things* (New York, 1987); Phillips, Janet and Peter, "History from Below: Women's Underwear and the Rise of Women's Sports," in *Journal of Popular Culture* (Fall, 1993); Witkowski, Gustave, *Tétoniana: curiosités medicales, litteraires et artistiques sur les seins et l'allaitement* (Paris, 1898).

Howard Hughes: Russell, Jane, *My Path and My Detours: An Autobiography* (New York, 1985).

Breast-feeding and animal nurture: Dewees, Dr. William, *Treatise on the Physical and Medical Treatment of Children* (Philadelphia, 1838); Fildes, Valerie, *Breasts, Bottles and Babies: A History of Infant Feeding* (Edinburgh, 1986); Radbill, Dr. Samuel, "The Role of Animals in Infant Feedings," in *American Folk Medicine: A Symposium* (Berkeley, 1976); Witkowski, Gustave, *Tétoniana: curiosités medicales, litteraires et artistiques sur les seins et l'allaitement* (Paris, 1898).

Corset: Binder, Pearl, *Muffs and Morals* (New York, 1955); Kunzle, David, *Fashion and Fetishism: A Social History of the Corset, Tight-Lacing and Other Forms of Body-Sculpture in the West* (Totowa, N.J., 1982); Mitchell, Margaret, *Gone With the Wind* (New York, 1936); Waldberg, Patrick, *Eros*

in *La Belle Epoque,* tr. Helen Lane (New York, 1969).

Men's legs: Chaucer, Geoffrey, *The Canterbury Tales* (New York, 1928); Laver, John, *The Concise History of Costume and Fashion* (New York, 1969).

Joan of Arc: Fabre, Joseph (tr.), *Procès de réhabilitation de Jeanne d'Arc* (Paris, 1888); Harmand, Adrien, *Jeanne d'Arc: ses costumes, son armure* (Paris, 1929).

Codpiece: Binder, Pearl, *Muffs and Morals* (New York, 1955); Ellis, Havelock, *Studies in the Psychology of Sex* (Philadelphia, 1901–1928); Klonsky, Milton, *Fabulous Ego: Absolute Power in History* (New York, 1974); Rabelais, Francois, *Oeuvres* (Paris, 1929); Rabelais, Francois, *The Works of Rabelais,* ill. Gustave Doré (London, n.d.); Shakespeare, William, *Shakespeare: The Complete Works,* ed. G. B. Harrison (New York, 1968).

Pointy shoes: Binder, Pearl, *Muffs and Morals* (New York, 1955); Laver, James, *The Concise History of Costume and Fashion* (New York, 1969).

Pubic hair: Binder, Pearl, *Muffs and Morals* (New York, 1955); Janson, H. W., *History of Art* (New York, 1973); Sonnini, C. S., *Travels in Upper and Lower Egypt* (London, 1799).

Beards: Binder, Pearl, *Muffs and Morals* (New York, 1955); MacKay, Charles, *Extraordinary Popular Delusions and the Madness of Crowds* (London, 1841).

Men's hair: Binder, Pearl, *Muffs and Morals* (New York, 1955); Felton, Bruce & Fowler, Mark, *Felton & Fowler's Best, Worst & Most Unusual* (New York, 1975); MacKay, Charles, *Extraordinary Popular Delusions and the Madness of Crowds* (London, 1841).

Wigs: Binder, Pearl, *Muffs and Morals* (New York, 1955); Langner, Lawrence, *The Im-*

portance of Wearing Clothes (New York, 1959); Schama, Simon, *Citizens: A Chronicle of the French Revolution* (New York, 1989).

Filthy saints: Donato, Giuseppe & Seefried, Monica, *The Fragrant Past: Perfumes of Cleopatra and Julius Caesar* (Rome, 1989); Ellis, Havelock, *Studies in the Psychology of Sex* (Philadelphia, 1901–1928); Lecky, William, *History of European Morals* (New York, 1910); Panati, Charles, *Extraordinary Origins of Everyday Things* (New York, 1987).

Fart: Cabanes, Augustin, *Moeurs intimes du passé*, Vol. I (Paris, 1919); Panati, Charles, *Extraordinary Origins of Everyday Things* (New York, 1987); Tannahill, Reay, *Food in History* (New York, 1973).

Wives for sale: Menefee, Samuel, *Wives for Sale: An Ethnographic Study of British Popular Divorce* (Oxford, 1988); Phillips, Roderick, *Untying the Knot: A Short History of Divorce* (New York, 1991).

Wife beating: Phillips, Roderick, *Untying the Knot: A Short History of Divorce* (New York, 1991).

Flogging in school: Churchill, Winston, *My Early Life* (London, 1930); Woolf, Virginia, *Roger Fry: A Biography* (New York, 1940) and *The Pearl* (May 1880) all quoted in Gibson, Ian, *The English Vice* (London, 1979).

Curse words: Hughes, Geoffrey, *Swearing* (Oxford, 1991); Grose, Francis, *Classical Dictionary of the Vulgar Tongue*, ed. Eric Partridge (London, 1785, New York, 1963 reprint); Marshall, Mary, *Bozzimacoo: Origins & Meanings of Oaths & Swear Words* (London, 1975); Montagu, Ashley, *The Anatomy of Swearing* (London, 1967).

Castrati: Casanova, Giacomo, *History of My Life* (New York, 1966–1969); Heriot, Angus, *The Castrati in Opera* (London, 1956); Humana, Charles, *The Keeper of the Bed* (London, 1973); Tannahill, Reay, *Sex in History* (New York, 1982).

Bullbaiting: Shakespeare, William, *The Complete Works*, ed. G. B. Harrison, Appendix 5 (New York, 1968); Strutt, Josef, *The Sports and Pastimes of the People of England* (London, 1903).

MEDICINE

Overview: Bettmann, Otto, *A Pictorial History of Medicine* (Springfield, 1956); Bishop, E. J., *An Early History of Surgery* (New York, 1960); Latimer, Dean & Goldberg, Jeff, *Flowers in the Blood* (New York, 1981); Skrabanek, Petr & McCormick, James, *Follies & Fallacies in Medicine* (Buffalo, 1990).

Humors: Bettmann, Otto, *A Pictorial History of Medicine* (Springfield, 1956); Ricci, James, *Development of Gynecological Surgery and Instruments* (Philadelphia, 1949).

Crusader medicine: Munquidh, Usama ibn, "Autobiography" in *Arab Historians of the Crusades*, tr. into Italian by Francesco Gabrielli, tr. into English by E. J. Costello (Los Angeles, 1969).

Heroic medicine and King Charles: Latimer, Dean & Goldberg, Jeff, *Flowers in the Blood: The Story of Opium* (New York, 1981).

Enemas: Breton, Guy, *Curieuses histoires de l'histoire* (Paris, 1968); Cabanes, Gustave, *Molière et ses medicins* (Paris, n.d.); Havard, Henri, *Dictionnaire de l'ameublement* (Paris, 1889); Molière, *Oeuvres complètes de Molière* (Paris, 1946).

Byron: Burnam, Tom, *The Dictionary of Misinformation* (New York, 1975).

President Garfield: Marx, Rudolph, *The Health of the Presidents* (New York, 1960); Shenkman, Richard & Reiger, Kurt, *One-Night Stands with American History* (New York, 1980).

Anatomy: Bishop, W. J., *Early History of Surgery* (New York, 1960).

Burke & Hare: Ball, James, *The Sack-'em-Up Men* (Edinburgh, 1928); Bettmann, Otto, *A Pictorial History of Medicine* (Springfield, 1956); Nash, J. Robert, *The Encyclopedia of World Crime* (Wilmette, Ill., 1989).

President's son: Ball, James, *The Sack-'em-Up Men* (Edinburgh, 1928); Shenkman, Richard & Reiger, Kurt, *One-Night Stands with American History* (New York, 1980).

Mental illness: Hunter, Richard & McAlpine, Ida, *Three Hundred Years of Psychiatry 1535–1860: A History Presented in Selected English Texts* (London, 1963); McCall, Andrew, *The Medieval Underworld* (New York, 1979); Scull, Andrew, "Desperate Remedies: A Gothic Tale of Madness and Modern Medicine" *Psychological Medicine* (1987, pp. 561–577); Valenstein, Elliot, *Great and Desperate Cures: The Rise and Decline of Psychosurgery and Other Radical Treatments for Mental Illness* (New York, 1986).

Tuskegee: Jones, James, *Bad Blood: The Tuskegee Syphilis Experiment* (New York, 1993).

Nose job: Bishop, W. J., *The Early History of Surgery* (New York, 1960).

Barber's pole: Bettmann, Otto, *A Pictorial History of Medicine* (Sringfield, 1956); Bishop, W. J., *The Early History of Surgery* (New York, 1960); Panati, Charles, *Extraordinary Origins of Everyday Things* (New York, 1987).

Vaccine: Bettmann, Otto, *A Pictorial History of Medicine* (Springfield, 1956).

Beaumont's stomach: Beaumont, William, *Observations on the Gastric Juice and the Physiology of Digestion* (1833, 1947 reprint); Bettmann, Otto, *A Pictorial History of Medicine* (Springfield, 1956).

Early gynecology: Barker-Benfield, G. J., *The Horrors of the Half-Known Life: Male Attitudes toward Women and Sexuality in Nineteenth Century America* (New York, 1976); Bettmann, Otto, *A Pictorial History of Medicine* (Springfield, 1956); Ricci, James, *The Development of Gynecological Surgery and Instruments* (Philadelphia, 1949); *Soranus et la médecine antique* (Paris, n.d.); Tannahill, Reay, *Sex in History* (New York, 1982).

Hammurabi: Bishop, W. J., *The Early History of Surgery* (New York, 1960).

Papal eye wash: Hispanus, Petrus (Pope John XXI), *The Treasurie of Medicines* (London, c. 1550).

Dr. Rush: Bettmann, Otto, *A Pictorial History of Medicine* (Springfield, 1956); Hunter, Richard & McAlpine, Ida, *Three Hundred Years of Psychiatry 1535–1860: A History Presented in Selected English Texts* (London, 1963); Vallenstein, Elliot, *Great and Desperate Cures: The Rise and Decline of Psychosurgery and Other Radical Treatments for Mental Illness* (New York, 1986).

Vasectomies: Skrabanek, Petr & McCormick, James, *Follies & Fallacies in Medicine* (Buffalo, 1990).

Spinach: Skrabanek, Petr and McCormick, James, *Follies & Fallacies in Medicine* (Buffalo, 1990).

Dentistry/urine: Fauchard, Pierre, *Le Chirugien dentiste, ou traite des dents* (Paris, 1728, reprint ed.); Lufkin, Arthur, *A History of Dentistry* (Philadelphia, 1948); Panati, Charles, *Extraordinary Origins of Everyday Things* (New York, 1989).

Shit: Cabanes, Augustin, *Moeurs intimes du passé* Vol. I (Paris, 1919).

Human teeth for sale: Guerini, Vincenzo, *A History of Dentistry, from the ancient times to the end of the eighteenth century* (New York, 1969); Lufkin, Arthur, *A History of Dentistry* (Philadelphia, 1948); Young, James, "The Long Struggle Against Quackery in Dentistry," in *Bulletin of the History of Dentistry* (Oct., 1985).

Rotten teeth: Cabanes, Augustin, *Dents et Dentistes* (Paris, 1928); Hurault, Andre, Sieur de Maisse, *Journal of an Embassy from Henry IV to Queen Elizabeth, 1597,* tr. G. B. Garrison and R. A. Jones (London, 1931); Lufkin, Arthur, *A History of Dentistry* (Philadelphia, 1948).

Washington: Lufkin, Arthur, *A History of Dentistry* (Philadelphia, 1948); Dechaume, Michel & Huard, Pierre, *L'Histoire illustrée de l'art dentaire* (Paris, 1977).

RELIGION

Bible: Burke, J. Ashleigh, *The X-RATED Book: Sex and Obscenity in the Bible* (Houston, 1983); *Good News Bible: The Bible in Today's English* (American Bible Society, New York, 1976); *King James Bible.*

Relics: Bentley, James, *Restless Bones: The Story of Relics* (London, 1985).

Bad popes: Chamberlin, E. R., *The Bad Popes* (New York, 1969); Packard, Jerrold, *Peter's Kingdom* (New York, 1985).

Papal conclave: De Rosa, Peter, *Vicars of Christ: The Dark Side of the Papacy* (New York, 1988); Martin, Malachi, *The Decline and Fall of the Roman Church* (New York, 1981); McCall, Andrew, *The Medieval Underworld* (New York, 1979).

Vatican bordellos: Burchard, Johann (ed./tr. Geoffrey Parker), *At the Court of the Borgia* (London, 1963); Cabanes, Augustin, *Les indiscretions de l'histoire,* Vol. I (Paris, 1906); Rodocanachi, Emmanuel, *Courtisanes et bouffons* (Paris, 1894).

Pope's mistress: Burchard, Johann (ed./tr. Geoffrey Parker), *At the Court of the Borgia* (London, 1963); Chamberlin, E. R., *The Bad Popes* (New York, 1969); Durant, Will, *The Story of Civilization: The Renaissance* (New York, 1953); Klonsky, Milton, *The Fabulous Ego* (New York, 1974).

Nepotism: Chamberlin, E. R., *The Bad Popes* (New York, 1969).

Pope's foot: Casanova, Giacomo, *History of My Life,* tr. Willard Trask (New York, 1966–1969); De Rosa, Peter, *Vicars of Christ: The Dark Side of the Papacy* (London, 1988).

Unholy Crusades: Brundage, James, *Richard Lion Heart* (New York, 1974); Connell, Evan, *A Long Desire* (New York, 1979); Delalande, Jean, *Les Extraordinaires croisades d'enfants et des pastoureaux au moyen age* (Paris, 1962); Gillingham, John, *Life & Times of Richard I* (London, 1973); Mackay, Charles, *Extraordinary Popular Delusions and the Madness of Crowds* (London, 1841).

Inquisition: Franklin, Charles, *They Walked a Crooked Mile* (New York, 1969); Hibbert, Charles, *The Roots of Evil* (Boston, 1963); Lea, Henry, *The History of the Inquisition of the Middle Ages* (New York, 1922); Lea, Henry, *Torture* (Philadelphia, 1973 reprint); Robbins, Rossell, *The Encyclopedia of Witchcraft and Demonology* (New York, 1959).

Quakers: Earle, Alice, *Curious Punishments of Bygone Days* (Chicago, 1896); *Fox's Book of Martyrs* (Grand Rapids, 1926).

India: Tannahill, Reay, *Food in History* (New York, 1973); Roberts, Field Marshall, Lord of Kandahar, *Forty-One Years in India* (London, 1898).

Skoptzies: Gould, George & Pyle, Walter, *Anomalies and Curiosities of Medicine* (New York, 1937); Koch, Dr. Walter, *Uber die Russisch-Rumanische Kastratensekte der Skopzen* (Berlin, 1921); Pittard, Eugene, *La Castration chez l'homme . . . recherches sur les adeptes d'une secte d'euniques mystiques, Les Skoptzy* (Paris, 1934).

Flagellants: Cabanes, Augustin, *Moeurs intimes du passé,* Vol. I (Paris, 1909); McCall, Andrew, *The Medieval Underworld* (New York, 1979); Snyder, Louis, *They Saw It Happen: Eyewitness Reports of Great Events* (Harrisburg, 1951).

Noyes's Commune: DeMaria, Richard, *Communal Love at Oneida* (New York, 1978); Noyes, John Humphrey, *Male Continence* (Oneida, N.Y., 1872); Robertson, Constance Noyes, *Oneida Community: An Autobiography, 1851–1876* (Syracuse, 1977); Wilson, Colin & Seaman, Donald, *Scandal! An Encyclopedia* (London, 1986).

Erotic Church art: Bougoux, Christian, *Petite grammaire de l'obscene* (Bordeaux, 1992); Cabanes, Augustin, *Moeurs intimes du passé,* Vol I (Paris, 1909); Hitt, Jack, *Off the Road: A Modern-Day Walk Down the Pilgrim's Route into Spain* (New York, 1994); Weir, Anthony & Jerman, James, *Images of Lust: Sexual Carvings on Medieval Churches* (London, 1986); Witkowski, Gustave, *Seins a l'eglise* (Paris, 1907).

Bugger: Marshall, Mary, *Bozzimacoo: Origins & Meanings of Oaths & Swear Words* (London, 1975).

Penance: adapted from McNeill, John & Gamer, Helena, *Medieval Handbooks of Penance* (New York, 1938).

Mormons: Brodie, Fawn, *No Man Knows My History* (New York, 1945); Embry, Jessie, *Mormon Polygamous Families: Life in the Principle* (Salt Lake City, 1987); Stenhouse, Mrs. T. B. H., *An Englishwoman in Utah: A Life's Experience in Mormonism* (London, 1882); Young, Ann Eliza, *Wife No. 19, or A Life in Bondage . . .* (Salem, 1877).

Voltaire: Voltaire, *Dictionnaire philosophique* (Paris, 1829).

Twain: Twain, Mark, *Letters from the Earth*, ed. Bernard DeVoto, (New York, 1962).

Last Supper: Rudofsky, Bernard, *Now I Lay Me Down to Eat* (New York, 1980).

Rabbits: Tannahill, Reay, *Food in History* (New York, 1973).

Joan of Arc: Gies, Frances, *Joan of Arc: The Legend and the Reality* (New York, 1981).

Christmas: Burchard, Johann (ed./tr. Geoffrey Parker), *At the Court of the Borgia* (London, 1963).

St. Peter's: Lilje, Hans, *Luther and the Reformation* (Philadelphia, 1967); Packard, Jerrold, *Peter's Kingdom: Inside the Papal City* (New York, 1985).

SCIENCE

Inventions: Breton, Guy, *Curieuses histoires de l'histoire* (Paris, 1968); Burnam, Tom, *The Dictionary of Misinformation* (New York, 1975).

Edison: Boorstin, Daniel, *The Americans: The Democratic Experience* (New York, 1973); Conot, Robert, *A Streak of Luck* (New York, 1979); Ramsaye, Terry, *A Million and One Nights* (New York, 1925); Shenkman, Richard & Reiger, Kurt, *One-Night Stands with American History* (New York, 1980).

Muybridge/Naked Baseball: Conot, Robert, *A Streak of Luck* (New York, 1979); Muybridge, Eadweard, *The Human Figure in Motion* (New York, 1955); Ramsaye, Terry, *A Million and One Nights* (New York, 1925).

Newton: Madigan, Carol & Elwood, Ann, *Brainstorms & Thunderbolts: How Creative Genius Works* (New York, 1983).

Newton: Dobbs, Betty Jo Teeter, *The Foundations of Newton's Alchemy* (Cambridge, 1975); Manuel, Frank, *The Religion of Isaac Newton* (Oxford, 1974); Skrabanek, Petr & McCormick, James, *Follies & Fallacies in Medicine* (Buffalo, 1990).

Kepler: Caspar, Max *Kepler,* tr. C. Doris Hellman, (New York, 1993); Skrabanek, Petr & McCormick, James, *Follies & Fallacies in Medicine* (Buffalo, 1990).

Lavoisier: Donovan, Arthur, *Antoine Lavoisier: Science, Administration and Revolution* (Oxford, 1993); Schama, Simon, *Citizens: A Chronicle of the French Revolution* (New York, 1989).

Curie: Langevin, Andre, *Paul Langevin, mon père: l'homme et l'oeuvre* (Paris, 1971); Marbo, Camille, *Souvenirs et rencontres à travers deux siècles* (Paris, 1967); Quinn, Susan, *Marie Curie: A Life* (New York, 1995).

Franklin: Poetica Exotica: Three Delightful, Suppressed Items from the Pens of Three Great American Writers (New York, 1938).

Nobel: Webster, Donovan, *Aftermath: The Landscape of War* (New York, 1996).

Rejected: Skrabanek, Petr & McCormick, James, *Follies & Fallacies in Medicine* (Buffalo, 1990).

Darwin: Brent, Peter, *Charles Darwin: A Man of Enlarged Curiosity* (London, 1981); Burnam, Tom, *The Dictionary of Misinformation* (New York, 1975).

SEX

Penis: Anonymous, *My Secret Life* (various reprint editions); Atkins, John, *Sex in Literature* (New York, 1972); Jordan, Winthrop, *White Over Black: American Attitudes Toward the Negro, 1550–1812* (New York, 1974); Kiefer, Otto, *Sexual Life in Ancient Rome* (London, 1934); Licht, Hans, *Sexual Life in Ancient Greece* (London, 1932); Zacks, Richard, *History Laid Bare* (New York, 1994).

Sexual Accidents: Masters, R. E. L., *Sexual Self-Stimulation* (Los Angeles, 1967); Morand, M., *Memoires de l'academie royale de chirugie* (Paris, 1743); Pouillet, Thesee, *Onanisme chez la femme* (Paris, 1897).

American prostitution: Bullough, Vern and Bullough, Bonnie, *Women and Prostitution: A Social History* (Buffalo, 1987); Evans, Hilary, *Harlots, Whores & Hookers: A History of Prostitution* (New York, 1979); Mackey, Thomas, *Red Lights Out* (New York, 1987); Burnham, John, "Medical Inspection of Prostitutes in America in the Nineteenth Century," in *Bulletin of the History of Medicine,* (May, 1971); Rose, Al, *Storyville, New Orleans: Being an Authentic Illustrated Account of the Notorious Red-Light District* (University of Alabama Press, 1976).

Love manuals: Mirabeau, Comte de (Honoré Gabriel Victor Riqueti), *Erotika Biblion* (Paris, 1783); DeVries, Leonard & Fryer, Peter, *Venus Unmasked, or An Inquiry into the Nature and Origin of the Passion of Love* (London, 1967); Robie, W. F., *The Art of Love* (New York, 1962); *Ormsby's New-York Mail Bag,* September 1863 copy in Clements Library at the University of Michigan; Wile, Douglas, *Art of the Bed Chamber* (Albany, 1992).

Early psychiatry: Ellis, Havelock, *Studies in the Psychology of Sex* (Philadelphia, 1901–1928); Fere, Charles, *L'instinct sexuel* (Paris, 1902); Hirschfeld, Magnus, *Sexual Pathology* (New York, 1932); Krafft-Ebing, Richard von, *Psychopathia Sexualis* (New York, 1947).

Masturbation: Kellogg, Dr. John, *Ladies' Guide in Health and Disease* (Battle Creek, Michigan, 1883); Masters, R. E. L., *Sexual Self-Stimulation* (Los Angeles, 1967); Tissot, M., *L'Onanisme: Dissertation sur les maladies produites par la masturbation* (Avignon, 1792); Zacks, Richard, *History Laid Bare* (New York, 1994).

Wives' orgasms: Jacquart, Danielle & Thomasset, Claude, *Sexuality and Medicine in the Middle Ages* (Princeton, 1988); McLaren, Angus, *A History of Contraception from Antiquity to the Present Day* (Oxford, 1990); Zacks, Richard, *History Laid Bare* (New York, 1994).

Husbands behind wives: Aristophanes, *Lysistrata* (various); Forsberg, Frederich, *Manual of Classical Erotology* (Manchester, 1884); Martial, *Epigrams of Martial* (Cambridge, 1968).

Marital sex: Payer, Pierre, *Sex and the Penitentials* (Toronto, 1984).

Lesbians: Compton, Louis, "The Myth of Lesbian Impunity: Capital Laws from 1270 to 1791" and "A Lesbian Execution in Germany, 1721: The Trial Records," tr. Brigitte Eriksson, both of which appeared in *The Journal of Homosexuality* (Fall/Winter, 1980/81). (It should be noted that the translator, Brigitte Eriksson, denied this author permission to quote directly from her work.); Tardieu, Ambroise, *Attentats aux moeurs* (Paris, 1878); Venette, Nicolas, *Tableau de l'amour conjugale considerée dans létat du marriage* (London, 1779); Weier, Johann, *Witches, Devils and Doctors in the Renaissance* (Binghamton, N.Y., 1991).

Condom: Casanova, Giacomo, *History of My Life*, tr. Willard Trask (New York, 1966–1969); Green, Shirley, *The Curious History of Contraception* (London, 1971); Waitt, Robert, *A Kinsey Report on the Civil War* (unpublished speech, 1963).

Sex slaves: Chesnut, Mary, *A Diary from Dixie* (London, 1905); Day, Beth, *Sexual Life Between Blacks and Whites: The Roots of Racism* (New York, 1972).

Virgin slaves: Klonsky, Milton, *The Fabulous Ego: Absolute Power in History* (New York, 1974).

Harem: Barber, Noel, *Lords of the Golden Horn* (London, 1973); Penzer, N. M., *The Harem* (London, 1930); Rycaut, Paul, *The State of the Ottoman Empire* (London, 1668).

Eunuch: Humana, Charles, *Keeper of the Bed: The Story of the Eunuch* (London, 1973).

Foot binding: Rossi, William, *The Sex Life of the Foot and Shoe* (New York, 1976).

Hermaphrodites: Darmon, Pierre, *Damning the Innocent: A History of the Persecution of the Impotent in Pre-Revolutionary France*, tr. Paul Keegan (New York, 1986); Jones, Jr., Howard & Scott, William, *Genital Abnormalities and Related Endocrine Disorders* (Baltimore, 1971); *Grand Larousse encyclopedique* (Paris, 1960); Paré, Ambroise, *Oeuvres*, Vol. 3 (Paris, 1841).

Masochism: Sacher-Masoch, Aurora von, "Confessions de ma vie" serialized in *Mercure de France* (1907); Sacher-Masoch, Leopold von, *Venus in Furs* (New York, 1947).

Napoleon: Anonymous, *Amours secrettes de Napoleon Buonaparte* (Paris, 1815); Gourgaud, Baron, "St. Helena Journal of General Baron Gourgaud" (London, 1932) quoted in *The Fabulous Ego: Absolute Power in History* by Milton Klonsky (New York, 1974).

Lincoln: A letter formerly in the possession of the Kinsey Institute for Research in Sex, Gender and Reproduction in Bloomington, Indiana.

French photos: Tardieu, Ambroise, *Attentats aux moeurs* (Paris, 1878).

Comstock: Hyde, Montgomery, *A History of Pornography* (New York, 1965); Kendrick, Walter, *The Secret Museum: Pornography in Modern Culture* (New York, 1987); Nash, J. Robert, *The Encyclopedia of World Crime* (Wilmette, Ill., 1989).

Cheesecake: Ramsaye, Terry, *A Million and One Nights* (New York, 1925).

WORLD HISTORY

Democracy: Browning, Robert, "How Democratic Was Ancient Athens," in *The Good Idea: Democracy and Ancient Greece* (New Rochelle, 1995); Cohen, J. M. and M. J., *The Penguin Dictionary of Modern Quotations* (Harmondsworth, 1980).

Power: Dougherty, Steven, *The Bible;* Klonsky, Milton, *The Fabulous Ego* (New York, 1974); Thorndike, Joseph, *The Very Rich: A History of Wealth* (New York, 1976).

Cleopatra: Hughes-Hallet, Lucy, *Cleopatra: Histories, Dreams and Distortions* (New York, 1990); Plutarch, *Lives,* Loeb Classical Library (Cambridge, 1914–1926).

Nero: Suetonius, *The Twelve Caesars* (tr. Robert Graves; ed. Michael Grant) (London, 1989).

Edward II: Hutchison, Harold, *Edward II, The Pliant King* (London, 1971).

Sophia Baffo: Barber, Noel, *Lords of the Golden Horn* (London, 1973); Penzer, N. M., *The Harem* (London, 1936).

Cromwell: Bentley, James, *Restless Bones: The Story of Relics* (London, 1985).

Catherine the Great: Zacks, Richard, *History Laid Bare* (New York, 1994).

Napoleon: Karlen, Arno, *Napoleon's Glands and Other Ventures in Biohistory* (Boston, 1984); Laver, James, *A Concise History of Costume and Fashion* (London, 1969).

Witches: Lacroix, Paul, *History of Prostitution* (New York, 1931); Remy, Nicolas, *Demonolatry* (New York, 1974); Robbins, Rossell, *The Encyclopedia of Witchcraft and Demonology* (New York, 1959); Sprenger, Jacob & Kramer, Heinrich, *Malleus Maleficarum* (London, 1971).

Marie-Antoinette: Naish, Camille, *Death Comes to the Maiden: Sex and Execution 1431–1933* (London, 1991); Schama, Simon, *Citizens: A Chronicle of the French Revolution* (New York, 1989); *Fureurs uterines de Marie-Antoinette, femme de Louis XVI* (1791).

Chevalier D'Eon: Breton, Guy, *Histoires d'amour de l'histoire de France* (Paris, 1955–1965); Bullough, Vern and Bonnie, *Cross-Dressing, Sex and Gender* (Philadelphia, 1993); D'Eon, Chevalier, *Memoirs of the Chevalier D'Eon* (tr. Antonia White) (London, 1970); Kates, Gary, *Monsieur d'Eon Is a Woman* (New York, 1995); Rickman, Thomas, *Life of Thomas Paine* (London, 1819); Shenkman, Richard & Reiger, Kurt, *One-Night Stands with American History* (New York, 1980).

Mata Hari: Breton, Guy, *Curieuses histoires de l'histoire* (Paris, 1968); Keay, Julia, *The Spy Who Never Was: The Life and Loves of Mata Hari* (London, 1987); Wheelwright, Julie, *The Fatal Lover: Mata Hari and the Myth of Women in Espionage* (London, 1992).

Ulrich: Hunt, Morton, *The Natural History of Love* (New York, 1959); Coulton, G. G., *Medieval Panorama* (Cambridge, 1939).

Ilsa Koch: Durand, Pierre, *La chienne de Buchenwald* (Paris, 1982); Nash, J. Robert, *The Encyclopedia of World Crime* (Wilmette, Ill., 1989).

Shrunken heads: Durand, Pierre, *La chienne de Buchenwald* (Paris, 1982).

Hitler: Speer, Albert, *Inside the Third Reich* (New York, 1970); Toland, John, *Adolf Hitler* (New York, 1976).

McCloy: Manchester, William, *The Arms of Krupp, 1587–1968* (Boston, 1964); Bird, Kai, *The Chairman: John J. McCloy, the Making of the American Establishment* (New York, 1992).

AMERICAN HISTORY

Vikings: Connell, Evan, "Vinland, Vinland," in *The White Lantern* (New York, 1979); Horwood, Joan, *Viking Discovery: L'Anse aux Meadows* (St. John's, Newfoundland, 1985).

Columbus: Loewen, James, *Lies My Teacher Told Me* (New York, 1995); Todorov, Tzvetan, *The Conquest of America* (New York, 1982); Williams, Eric, *Documents of West Indian History, Vol. 1, 1492–1655* (Port-of-Spain, Trinidad, 1963).

America: Arciniegas, German, *Amerigo and the New World: The Life & Times of Amerigo Vespucci* (New York, 1978 reprint); Vespucci, Amerigo, *Letters from a New World: Amerigo Vespucci's Discovery of America*, edited by Luciano Formisano, wonderful translation by David Jacobson (New York, 1992).

Cannibalism: Arens, W., *The Man-Eating Myth: Anthropology and Anthropophagy* (New York, 1979); Tannahill, Reay, *Flesh and Blood: The History of the Cannibal Complex* (London, 1975).

Thanksgiving: Loewen, James, *Lies My Teacher Told Me* (New York, 1995); Shenkman, Richard, *Legends, Lies and Cherished Myths of American History* (New York, 1988).

Christmas: Shenkman, Richard & Reiger, Kurt, *One-Night Stands with American History* (New York, 1980).

Witchcraft: Calef, Robert, *More Wonders of the Invisible World* (London, 1701); Mencken, August, *Hang by the Neck* (New York, 1942); Nevins, Winfield, *Witchcraft in Salem Village in 1692* (Salem, 1892); Robbins, Rossell, *The Encyclopedia of Witchcraft and Demonology* (New York, 1959); Rosenthal, Bernard, *Reading the Witch Trials of 1692* (Cambridge, 1993).

Harvard, Yale: Boas, Ralph and Louise, *Cotton Mather: Keeper of the Puritan Conscience* (New York, 1928); Silverman, Kenneth, *The Life and Times of Cotton Mather* (New York, 1984); Wendell, Barrett, *Cotton Mather: The Puritan Priest* (New York, 1963).

Indians: Loewen, James, *Lies My Teacher Told Me* (New York, 1995).

Scalping: Axtell, James & Sturtevant, William, "The Unkindest Cut, or Who Invented Scalping?" *William and Mary Quarterly* (July, 1980, pp. 451–472); Caverly, Robert, *Heroism of Hannah Duston* (Boston, 1875); Eckstorm, Fannie, *New England Quarterly* (IX, pp. 381–382); Shipton, Clifford, *Sibley's Harvard Graduates* (Boston, 1945); Oliver, Peter, *Peter Oliver's Origin & Progress of the American Rebellion: A Tory View*, eds. Douglas Adair and John Schutz (San Marino, California, 1961).

Pirates: Kaufman, Richard, *The War Profiteers* (New York, 1970); Maclay, Edgar, *The History of American Privateers* (New York, 1899); *Harper's New Monthly Magazine* (July, 1864, pp. 596–607).

First President: Wallechinsky, David & Wallace, Irving, *The People's Almanac* (New York, 1975).

Atcheson: Wallechinsky, David & Wallace, Irving, *The People's Almanac #2* (New York, 1978).

Sex scandals, Washington: Shenkman, Richard, *Legends, Lies and Cherished Myths of American History* (New York, 1988).

Jefferson: Dabney, Virginius, *The Jefferson Scandals: A Rebuttal* (New York, 1981).

Cleveland: Sullivan, Michael, *Presidential Passions: The Love Affairs of America's Presidents — from Washington and Jefferson to Kennedy and Johnson* (New York, 1991); Wallace, Irving, and others, *The Intimate Sex Lives of Famous People* (New York, 1981).

Harding: Britton, Nan, *The President's Daughter* (New York, 1927); Russell, Francis, *The Shadow of Blooming Grove: Warren G. Harding in His Times* (New York, 1968); Wallace, Irving, and others, *The Intimate Sex Lives of Famous People* (New York, 1981).

Eleanor Roosevelt: Sullivan, Michael, *Presidential Passions* (New York, 1991); Wallace, Irving, and others, *The Intimate Sex Lives of Famous People* (New York, 1981).

Eisenhower: Miller, Merle, *Plain Speaking: An Oral Biography of Harry S. Truman* (New York, 1973); Sullivan, Michael, *Presidential Passions* (New York, 1991).

Stolen election: Butterfield, Roger, *The American Past: A History of the United States from Concord to Hiroshima, 1775–1945* (New York, 1947); Hoogenboom, Ari, *The Presidency of Rutherford B. Hayes* (Lawrence, Kansas, 1988).

Lincoln and slaves: Franklin, John, *From Slavery to Freedom* (New York, 1967).

Jefferson Davis: Loewen, James, *Lies My Teacher Told Me* (New York, 1995); Shenkman, Richard & Reiger, Kurt, *One-Night Stands with American History* (New York, 1980).

Lincoln assassination: Ownsbey, Betty, *Alias Paine: Lewis Thornton Powell, the Mystery Man of the Lincoln Conspiracy* (Jefferson, N.C., 1993); Roscoe, Theodore, *The Web of Conspiracy: The Complete Story of the Men Who Murdered Abraham Lincoln* (Englewood Cliffs, N.J., 1959); Shively, Charley, *Drumbeats: Walt Whitman's Civil War Boy Lovers* (San Francisco, 1989).

Booth Latin: Evans, Bergen, *Dictionary of Quotations* (New York, 1978).

Lewis Payne: Ownsbey, Betty, *Alias Paine: Lewis Thornton Powell, the Mystery Man of the Lincoln Conspiracy* (Jefferson, N.C., 1993).

Hanging: Ownsbey, Betty, *Alias Paine: Lewis Thornton Powell, the Mystery Man of the Lincoln Conspiracy* (Jefferson, N.C., 1993).

KKK: Hurst, Jack, *Nathan Bedford Forrest: A Biography* (New York, 1993).

Lynching: Loewen, James, *Lies My Teacher Told Me* (New York, 1995); Raper, Arthur, *The Tragedy of Lynching* (Chapel Hill, N.C., 1933 — New York, 1970 reprint).

Jack Johnson: Roberts, Randy, *Papa Jack: Jack Johnson and the Era of White Hopes* (New York, 1983).

Marcus Garvey: DuBois, W. E. B., *The Seventh Son: The Thoughts and Writings of W. E. B. Du Bois,* ed. Julius Lester (New York, 1971); Garvey, Amy Jacques, *Garvey and Garveyism* (New York, 1971); Nash, J. Robert, *The Encyclopedia of World Crime* (Wilmette, Ill., 1989); *The Marcus Garvey and Universal Negro Improvement Association Papers,* ed. Robert Hill (Berkeley, 1987).

Wild West: Burnam, Tom, *The Dictionary of Misinformation* (New York, 1975); Hollon, W. Eugene, *Frontier Violence: Another Look* (New York, 1974); Shenkman, Richard, *Legends, Lies and Cherished Myths of American History* (New York, 1988).

Custer: Hofling, Charles, *Custer and the Little Big Horn* (Detroit, 1981); Utley, Robert, *Custer and the Great Controversy* (Los Angeles, 1962).

Franklin: Untemeyer, Louis (ed.), *A Treasury of Ribaldry* (New York, 1956).

Poe: Pickett, Calder (ed.), *Voices of the Past* (Columbus, 1977).

Zoo: Griffin, Buckley, *Offbeat History* (Cleveland, 1967).

Mrs. Leary's cow: Burnam, Tom, *The Dictionary of Misinformation* (New York, 1975).

Bathtub: Burnam, Tom, *The Dictionary of Misinformation* (New York, 1975).

Shuberts: Berger, Meyer, *The Story of the New York Times* (New York, 1970); Hoyt, Edwin, *Alexander Woollcott: The Man Who Came to Dinner* (New York, 1968).

Karl Marx: Bates, Stephen, *If No News, Send Rumors: Anecdotes of American Journalism* (New York, 1989); Borden, Morton, "Some Notes on Horace Greeley, Charles Dana and Karl Marx," in *Journalism Quarterly* (1957).

Obscenity: Bates, Stephen, *If No News, Send Rumors: Anecdotes of American Journalism* (New York, 1985); Stephens, Mitchell & Frankel, Eliot, "All the Obscenity That's Fit to Print," in *Washington Journalism Review,* April 1981; "Bowdlerizing Butz's Blunder," *Columbia Journalism Review,* Nov.–Dec., 1976.

Henry Ward Beecher: Wallace, Irving, *The Nympho and Other Maniacs* (New York, 1971); Wallace, Irving, and others, *The Intimate Sex Lives of Famous People* (New York, 1981); Wilson, Colin & Seaman, Donald, *Scandal: An Encyclopedia* (London, 1986).

Fatty Arbuckle: Edmonds, Andy, *Frame Up! The Untold Story of Roscoe "Fatty" Arbuckle* (New York, 1991); Yallop, David, *The Day the Laughter Stopped* (New York, 1976).

Charles Dickens: Dickens, Charles, "American Notes," quoted in *Offbeat History* by Griffin Buckley (Cleveland, 1967).

Civil War bullet: Gould, George & Pyle, Walter, *Anomalies and Curiosities of Medicine* (New York, 1937 reprint).

PICTURE CREDITS

Library of Congress, Prints & Photographs Division: pp. 26, 49, 55, 66, 85 (top, bottom), 86, 90, 95, 105, 123 (top), 140, 150 (bottom), 159, 160, 183, 197, 229, 239, 242, 262, 298 (top), 317, 320 (top), 333, 338, 347, 364 (bottom), 365 (top), 366, 369, 371, 372, 374, 377, 378, 385, 387 (top), 391

New York Public Library Picture Collection: pp. 6, 11, 19 (top, bottom), 46, 76, 99, 101, 109, 204, 222, 237, 265, 309, 379, 389

National Library of Medicine, History of Medicine: pp. 82, 177, 184, 186, 193, 201, 202, 288, 298 (bottom)

National Archives: pp. 166, 336, 337 (top, bottom), 376, 380, 381 (top, bottom)

Archive Photos: pp. 20, 29, 130, 146, 212, 256, 315, 332

Dr. Augustin Cabanes: pp. 13, 111, 139, 167

UPI–Corbis/Bettmann: pp. 34, 126, 127, 192

Research Libraries of the New York Public Library: pp. 8, 17

Corbis/Bettmann: pp. 83, 370

New York Academy of Medicine, Rare Book Room: p. 303 (top)

Columbia University Rare Book Room: p. 142

INDEX